Recent efforts to create a European Central Bank (ECB) have stimulated debate on new topics for research into the political economy of the European Community's institutions. These include the exact division of responsibilities of national governments and the ECB – especially concerning exchange rate policy; the need for and design of constraints on national fiscal policies; and the nature of the transition from adjustable parities and national monetary policies to irrevocably fixed parities and a single European monetary policy.

This volume, derived from a joint conference held by the Centre for Economic Policy Research, the Center for German and European Studies at Georgetown University and the International Monetary Fund, in Washington DC, in May 1991, examines these issues and the choices facing policy-makers. It considers the role of a common currency in facilitating transactions and the likely success of the ECB in achieving price stability. It compares the option of strengthening the existing European Monetary System with existing national currencies to the planned creation of a full monetary union. The book draws heavily on the historical experience of the US to identify the problems that may emerge if there is no clear agreement over responsibility for monetary policy, if the ECB does not take responsibility for the stability of the financial system, or if a system of fiscal federalism does not accompany monetary union. The book also considers the implications of EMU for the international monetary system – for the use of the ECU as a reserve currency and for policy coordination among the G-7 countries. The volume thus provides a comprehensive examination of the issues that will be decisive for Europe in its choice of monetary institutions.

Establishing a central bank: issues in Europe and lessons from the US

The Center for German and European Studies

The Center for German and European Studies of Georgetown University, Washington, DC, was founded in 1990 with generous support of the German government. Its purpose is the promotion of scholarship and teaching on domestic and international topics relating to Germany and Europe in general. It offers a two-year degree program leading to the Master of Arts in German and European Studies; students may also be enrolled simultaneously in PhD programs in the departments of Government, History, Economics and German. Financial aid is available on a competitive basis. The Center hosts at least two postdoctoral scholars each year as well as short-term visitors, speakers, and conferences and symposia. The Center's Director is Professor Samuel H Barnes. Professor Gregory Flynn is Director of Programs.

The International Monetary Fund

The IMF is a cooperative intergovernmental monetary and financial institution. The Fund is unique among intergovernmental organizations in its combination of regulatory, consultative and financial functions, which derive from the purposes for which it was established: to facilitate the balanced growth of international trade, promote exchange rate stability, and assist in the establishment of a multilateral system of payments; to provide financial resources to enable its members to correct payments imbalances; and to provide a forum for consultation and collaboration on international monetary problems.

Managing Director
Michel Camdessus
Deputy Managing Director
Richard Erb
Director of Research and Economic Counsellor
Michael Mussa

Establishing a central bank: issues in Europe and lessons from the US

Edited by

MATTHEW B. CANZONERI
VITTORIO GRILLI

and

PAUL R. MASSON

CAMBRIDGE
UNIVERSITY PRESS

CAMBRIDGE UNIVERSITY PRESS
Cambridge, New York, Melbourne, Madrid, Cape Town, Singapore, São Paulo

Cambridge University Press
The Edinburgh Building, Cambridge CB2 8RU, UK

Published in the United States of America by Cambridge University Press, New York

www.cambridge.org
Information on this title: www.cambridge.org/9780521420983

First published 1992
This digitally printed version 2008

A catalogue record for this publication is available from the British Library

Library of Congress Cataloguing in Publication data

Establishing a central bank: issues in Europe and lessons from the US / edited by
Matthew B. Canzoneri, Vittorio Grilli, and Paul R. Masson.
    p. cm.
    Papers presented at the conference: 'Designing a central bank', held 1–2 May, 1991 at
Georgetown University and sponsored by the Centre for Economic Policy Research, the
Center for German and European Studies at Georgetown University, and the International
Monetary Fund.
    Includes index.
    ISBN 0 521 42098 9 (hardback)
1. Banks and banking, Central – European Economic Community countries – Congresses.
2. Banks and banking, Central – United States – Congresses.
3. Fiscal policy – European Economic Community countries – Congresses.
I. Canzoneri, Matthew B.   II. Grilli, Vittorio.
III. Masson, Paul R.   IV. Centre for Economic Policy Research (Great Britain)
V. Georgetown University. Center for German and European Studies.
VI. International Monetary Fund.
HG2980.5.A7E84   1992
332.1′1′094 – dc20   91–46674   CIP

ISBN 978-0-521-42098-3 hardback
ISBN 978-0-521-07069-0 paperback

Contents

xii **Contents**

Figures

Tables

Preface

This book is the outcome of a conference, 'Designing a Central Bank', that was held on May first and second, 1991, at Georgetown University, and sponsored by the Centre for Economic Policy Research, the Center for German and European Studies at Georgetown University, and the International Monetary Fund. The conference was made possible by grants from the Commission of the European Communities under its SPES programme to support the CEPR's research programme on 'Financial and Monetary Integration in Europe', from the Ford and Alfred P. Sloan Foundations as part of their support for CEPR's International Macroeconomics programme, and from the government of the Federal Republic of Germany to the Center for German and European Studies.

The conferences also included a panel discussion on the problems of central bank design for EMU, which served as a progress report on the state of negotiations at the intergovernmental conference, and after-dinner remarks presented by Michel Camdessus, Managing Director of the International Monetary Fund.

We would like to thank Brad Billings of Georgetown University and his staff for organizing the conference, Kate Millward at CEPR for guiding the present volume to press, and John Black of the University of Exeter for his work as Production Editor.

Matthew B. Canzoneri
Vittorio Grilli   November 1991
Paul R. Masson

Conference participants

Alberto Alesina *Harvard University and CEPR*
Samuel Barnes *CGES, Georgetown University*
Bradley Billings *Georgetown University*
Graham Bishop *Salomon Brothers*
Peter Bofinger *Landeszentralbank in Baden-Württemberg, Stuttgart, and CEPR*
Antonio Borges *Banco de Portugal*
William Branson *Princeton University and CEPR*
Guillermo Calvo *IMF*
Michel Camdessus *IMF*
Matthew Canzoneri *Georgetown University*
Alessandra Casella *University of California at Berkeley and CEPR*
David Currie *London Business School and CEPR*
Behzad Diba *Georgetown University*
Barry Eichengreen *University of California at Berkeley and CEPR*
David Folkerts-Landau *IMF*
Peter Garber *Brown University*
Francesco Giavazzi *Università Bocconi and CEPR*
Alberto Giovannini *Columbia University and CEPR*
Morris Goldstein *IMF*
Vittorio Grilli *Birkbeck College, London, and CEPR*
Dale Henderson *Board of Governors of the Federal Reserve System*
Andrew Hughes Hallett *University of Strathclyde and CEPR*
Mervyn King *Bank of England, London School of Economics and CEPR*
Jeroen Kremers *Ministry of Finance, The Netherlands*
Peter Krogh *Georgetown University*
Paul Masson *IMF*
Bennett T McCallum *Carnegie-Mellon University*
John Pattison *Canadian Imperial Bank of Commerce*
Torsten Persson *Institute for International Economic Studies, Stockholm, and CEPR*
Richard Portes *CEPR and Birkbeck College, London*
Massimo Russo *IMF*
Xavier Sala-i-Martín *Yale University*
Luigi Spaventa *Università degli Studi di Roma, 'La Sapienza', and CEPR*
Richard Sweeney *Georgetown University*
Vito Tanzi *IMF*
Eugene White *Rutgers University*
Geoffrey Woglom *Amherst College*

1 Introduction

MATTHEW B. CANZONERI, VITTORIO
GRILLI and PAUL R. MASSON

This book treats a number of themes relevant to the design of new monetary institutions in Europe.

It is important to situate the conference relative to events taking place in Europe. Two years before, in April 1989, the Delors Committee had made public recommendations for economic and monetary union (EMU) in Europe, and in December 1990 the EC member countries had convened two intergovernmental conferences, one on EMU and the other on political union. The intergovernmental conference on EMU was intended to lead to agreement concerning the form and pace of monetary union, including necessary amendments to the Treaty of Rome and the statutes of a central bank that would be created to carry out EC monetary policy.

The Georgetown conference thus was held at the very time that politicians, government officials, and central bankers were wrestling with these issues. Though draft statutes for the European Central Bank had been sent to EC ministers in November 1990, a number of issues remained unresolved. These included the exact division of responsibilities of national governments and the central bank – especially concerning exchange rate policy; the need for constraints on national fiscal policies, and how to design them; and the nature of the transition from a system of adjustable parities and a single European monetary policy. The papers of the conference apply the techniques of economics to the practical questions facing policy-makers, and serve both to inform their choices and to help us to understand how EMU, should it be created, will function. The book considers the role of a common currency in facilitating transactions and the likely success of a European central bank in achieving price stability and it compares the option of strengthening the existing European Monetary System without abandoning national currencies to the planned creation of a full monetary union. The book draws on the experience of other countries, in particular the United States, to identify problems that may emerge, for instance, if there is no clear understanding

1

concerning responsibility for monetary policy, if the European central bank does not manage the payments system, or if a system of fiscal federalism does not accompany monetary union. The book also considers the implications of EMU for the international monetary system – for the use of the ECU as a reserve currency and for Group of Seven (G-7) policy coordination. The volume thus provides a comprehensive examination of issues that will be decisive for Europe in its choice of monetary institutions.

1   The design of a central bank

A folk theorem in the theory of international finance asserts that the EC cannot simultaneously have (1) fixed exchange rates, (2) free capital mobility, and (3) independent national monetary policies. During the transition to EMU, monetary policy will be left in the hands of the national central banks. It remains to be seen whether existing mechanisms for policy coordination will be sufficient to preserve the Exchange Rate Mechanism now that capital controls have been virtually eliminated. And the problem will remain even if EMU is eventually achieved. The draft statutes for the new European Central Bank call for a federation of the existing central banks, modeled after the Bundesbank and the Federal Reserve System. The working relationship between the banks and control of the system as a whole are issues that are currently being debated. **Barry Eichengreen**'s paper draws on early US experience with the Federal Reserve System to warn against leaving the issue of policy coordination unresolved.

Eichengreen provides a concise history of the evolution of decision-making within the Federal Reserve System. In the early years, individual District Banks issued their own notes and controlled their own discount policies. Decision-making reflected regional preferences that were often conflicting. It took two decades for decision-making to be centralized around the Federal Reserve Board and the Federal Open Market Committee. Eichengreen uses a game-theoretic model to describe the behaviour of District Banks before decision-making was centralized. In his model, each bank has targets for its bond portfolio and for national income; decentralized decision-making results in too little stabilization effort. Eichengreen uses the model to analyse five episodes of policy conflict between the District Banks. He concludes that the early history of the Federal Reserve System serves as a cautionary tale for the EC, illustrating the importance of explicit and unambiguous coordination of national central bank policies during the transition to EMU and once EMU is achieved.

Bennett McCallum thought that Eichengreen's discussion of the Federal Reserve System's early operations was both useful and alarming. However, he had some difficulties with Eichengreen's model and was disappointed that Eichengreen's implications for the EC were not more specific. He also noted that the responsibilities of central banks have changed since the founding of the Federal Reserve System and that Eichengreen's account did indeed serve as a cautionary tale for the EC. However, he argued that the faulty design of the Federal Reserve System reflected problems in the US banking structure at the turn of the century and that a poor theoretical framework for policy-making may have played a role in the US experience. He suggested that US history also provides a cautionary tale in the centralization of banking supervision and regulation.

The EMS has been characterized as an asymmetric structure, dominated by the Bundesbank, that has nevertheless performed rather well in recent years in controlling inflation. Current proposals for EMU envisage a more symmetric decision-making process, and two questions naturally arise. Will the new process really reflect the preferences of European citizens? And what kind of monetary policy will result? The paper by **Alberto Alesina** and **Vittorio Grilli** examines the draft statute for the European Central Bank with these two questions in mind.

Alesina and Grilli begin by extending a well known inflation bias model to a median voter setting. In their model, the median voter would choose a central bank governor who is more conservative (or inflation-conscious) than he is himself; in this way, the electorate commits itself to a low inflation policy. Alesina and Grilli note that the central bank governor must not be subject to political pressure or recall if the commitment is to be binding, and they go on to examine the independence of the proposed ECB, as embodied in the draft statutes. Using an index of central bank independence (that is developed in a separate paper), Alesina and Grilli argue that the ECB should be as independent as the Bundesbank.

The second part of Alesina and Grilli's paper focuses on the economic and political diversity that exists in Europe today. Using an extension of their earlier model, Alesina and Grilli argue that a country that is lacking inflation credibility is more likely to gain from EMU, while a country whose output has a high variance and a low correlation with European output is less likely to gain. Economic and political differences are likely to lead to differences in opinion about monetary policy. So, finally, Alesina and Grilli ask whether the voting mechanism described in the draft statutes would lead to a policy that reflects the preferences of European voters. They find a problem that is common to 'district' systems. Using the results of the last general elections in the twelve EC countries, Alesina and Grilli find that the median European voter is currently well to the left of the median of the European Council. They go on to argue that the appointment and voting procedures described in the draft statute of the ECB would result in a monetary policy that could be very different from the preferences of the median European voter.

Peter Bofinger doubted that a low inflation policy could be guaranteed by simply endowing the ECB with the Bundesbank's charter. He thought that the Bundesbank gave price stability because that was what the German people wanted, and he doubted that the median European voter would have the same preferences. **Luigi Spaventa** complimented the paper for its logical rigor, but he contended that the analysis provided no answer for perhaps the most important question of all: what is there in EMU for the Germans?

Much of the public debate on the creation of a European Central Bank, as well its proposed statute, have focused on the price stability objective of this institution. In their chapter, **David Folkerts-Landau** and **Peter Garber** argue that similar attention should be devoted to the other main objective that central banks have traditionally pursued, that is the maintenance of a stable and efficient financial and payment system. They argue that a central bank is not simply a monetary rule; it is also the lender of last resort and the supervisory agency of the financial system. Folkerts-Landau and Garber assert that the importance of these additional objectives depends on the degree of securitization of the financial markets. The higher the degree of securitization, the higher the probability of liquidity crises and thus the more crucial is the existence of a lender of last resort. In highly securitized financial systems a major share of the market transactions is generated by a large number of non-bank intermediaries, several of which are underdiversified, highly leveraged and vulnerable to failure. Folkerts-Landau and Garber contend that the smooth functioning of this type of market rests on the existence of a well functioning payment system, able to support the large turnover in securities needed for liquidity. The larger the number of participants, the more complex the payment system and the greater the likelihood that the system may become gridlocked. In order to prevent liquidity crises, it is necessary for the central bank to monitor the system and inject liquidity in times of emergency. Folkerts-Landau and Garber argue that this systemic risk is much smaller in financial markets with a low degree of securitization, where there are just a small number of large universal banks and payments are cleared internally in these institutions. They conclude that, unless the ECB statue is revised to include basic banking functions, such as lender-of-last-resort, the financial markets in the Community will have to develop into a predominately bank-intermediated system. This will be incompatible with the recent development in some member countries, e.g. the UK and France.

John Pattison, in his discussion, disagrees with the authors' conclusion that the need for a lender-of-last-resort is greater in a highly securitized system. He argues that higher securitization implies that financial intermediaries can dispose quickly of large amount of assets without noticeable variations in their prices. This reduces the need for financial intermediaries to have recourse to central bank liquidity. Pattison suggests that the need for liquidity in the US financial markets is not a consequence of the degree of securitization, but of other institutional factors, like the restrictions on nationwide branch banking.

2 Transition from national central banks to a common central bank

David Currie's chapter sketches the elements of a cost-benefit assessment of EMU against specific alternatives. The current EMS, with infrequent realignments and preponderant influence of the Bundesbank on monetary policies of Exchange Rate Mechansim (ERM) countries, is probably unsustainable without further institutional development, because otherwise pressures for realignment may eventually become too strong to resist. The case for EMU presented in the Delors Report is based on this view. An alternative is simply to continue to strengthen the ERM of the EMS by increasing monetary policy coordination and instituting formal rules concerning the time between realignments and their size (for instance that they be inframarginal, i.e. within existing bands). Another is the UK proposal to introduce a parallel currency, the Hard-ECU, in order to discipline monetary policies of member countries; this might provide an evolutionary alternative to an administered EMU.

Currie argues that there are appreciable risks and uncertainties in moving towards EMU. Though non-German ERM countries would benefit from having a more symmetric system, since they would have a greater say in European monetary policy, these benefits may be lost if the European central bank does not have the inflation discipline of the Bundesbank. Currie questions the commitment to price stability of other EC countries, and stresses the importance of *de facto* independence for the European central bank and its need to establish a reputation for conservative monetary policies. At the very least, a difficult task of institution building is in prospect, and Currie favours building on the successes of the ERM, reinforcing it in the direction of making the Bundesbank more responsive to European-wide considerations, and possibly using a 'hard-basket' version of the existing ECU in which the stronger currencies get increasing weight to enhance monetary policy coordination.

Andrew Hughes Hallett, in his comments, agrees with Currie's general conclusion; in fact, he would go further in criticizing EMU. He argues that both EMU and the Hard-ERM are 'accident prone', requiring greater coordination of both monetary and fiscal policies to make them work. He suggests that the rigidity of EMU is not a good framework for enhanced coordination, which ideally should take a more general and more flexible form.

The theoretical analysis of the costs and benefits of a monetary union has focused on the trade-off between output stability and price stability objectives. It is argued that, even if the ability to stabilize the economy in the face of country-specific shocks will be reduced, a monetary union will provide gains in terms of the credibility of monetary policies. This type of analysis, however, fails to explain why countries that already have independent central banks will have any interest in joining a monetary union. Some other ingredients must be added to the analysis to answer this question, for example the reduction of transaction costs obtained by switching from a twelve-currency to a one-currency system. **Alessandra Casella** proceeds in this direction and shows that in this framework both high and low inflation countries may find it beneficial to join a monetary union. More interestingly, the support for a monetary union is not only a function of inflation performance, but also of the level of development of the economy. Moreover, the stablishment of a monetary union will induce changes in the relative size of domestic and international markets and this, in turn, will generate redistributional effects that will impact on the support for the union. Casella shows that countries characterized by a relatively high level of inflation will find a monetary union more attractive at a low level of economic development, while the opposite is true for low inflation countries. She concludes, therefore, that the international support for a monetary union is likely to be different not only across countries, but also at different points in time, depending on the level of development of the member countries. Today's support for a monetary union could vanish in the future.

Torsten Persson concurs with the basic thrust of Casella's argument, but he questions the robustness of some of her specific conclusions. Using a different setup, Persson also finds that support for a monetary union depends on particular market configuration in the various countries, but not necessarily in the way predicted by Casella's model. Moreover, he argues that the ultilitarian policy-making process assumed by Casella may not be the most plausible to adopt. Persson suggests, as an alternative, a majoritarian policy-making approach and shows that the results would be different in this case.

3   Fiscal policy requirements of a common currency area

The literature on optimal currency areas suggests that the benefits of a common currency have to be weighed against the loss of an important tool for macroeconomic stabilization. Regional imbalances that are caused by inflexibility of nominal prices may be alleviated by a change in exchange rates, accompanied perhaps by a change in regional monetary policy. In a monetary union, this is no longer possible, and, it is asserted, more of the burden for regional adjustment must fall on fiscal policy. Most monetary unions are complemented by a federal fiscal structure that performs this regional stabilization automatically. By comparison, the federal budget of the EC is very small. The paper by **Xavier Sala-i-Martín** and **Jeffrey Sachs** tries to evaluate the importance of the regional stabilizers that are built into the US federal fiscal system.

Sala-i-Martín and Sachs divide the US into nine regions (defined by the US Bureau of the Census) and use regression analysis to estimate the elasticities of federal tax payments and transfers to changes in regional income. They then use the elasticities to assess the importance of the fiscal structure to regional stabilization. They find that 'a one-dollar reduction in a region's per capita personal income triggers a decrease in federal taxes of about 34 cents and an increase in federal transfers of about 6 cents.' So, the one-dollar reduction in regional income only results in a 60 cent decrease in disposable income, with the tax structure providing most of the effect. Sala-i-Martín and Sachs also make some rough estimates for the EC. They calculate that a one-dollar decrease in a European region's income would only decrease its tax payments to the EC by about one half of one cent, a far cry from the 34 cents in the US system.

Both the paper and the comments of **Behzad Diba** and **Alberto Giovannini** questioned the Keynesian analysis behind the worries about macroeconomic stabilization and whether national fiscal authorities or private capital markets would provide the necessary income insurance in any case. Diba noted that the EC has managed rather well in recent years without major exchange rate realignments, but he also noted that if the road to EMU involves constraints on national fiscal policies, the past may be a poor guide to the EC's ability to cope with future regional disturbances. Giovannini noted that national governments in the EC are already providing automatic stabilizers roughly the size of those in the US. But he also noted that the regional approach to fiscal stabilization requires the running of regional fiscal deficits. Like Diba, he worried that constraints on national fiscal policy might prevent some EC governments from continuing these stabilization efforts.

The relationship between monetary institutions and monetary policies has been the subject of intense research, including several chapters of this book, and it is now relatively well understood. Much more uncertain, however, are the channels of transmission between fiscal policies and monetary policies. Much of the current political debate on the future monetary union is focused on the design of measures that will prevent fiscal distress in some member countries from spilling over to the rest of the Community, thus endangering European monetary discipline. According to some, to break the connection between national fiscal conduct and European monetary policies it is sufficient to create an independent European central bank with a statutory prohibition on providing lines of credit to national governments or Community agencies and to accessing primary markets for national public debt. Others believe this measure to be insufficient, doubting the irrevocability of such statutory clauses. Instead, they propose the introduction of fiscal rules that will require member countries to reduce their fiscal imbalance before joining the monetary union, and to maintain their public deficit within present limits as a condition of remaining in the monetary union.

A third point of view is that fiscal rules are unnecessary, since financial markets by themselves impose sufficient discipline on fiscal authorities by changing the cost of borrowing. **Morris Goldstein** and **Geoffrey Woglom**'s chapter analyses the validity of this market-based fiscal discipline by studying the recent experience in the United States. This case is relevant since the US is an important example of a monetary union among states which have a considerable amount of fiscal independence. Importantly, the monetary union has been successful without resorting to federally imposed fiscal rules on member states, just by preventing state governments from having access to central bank financing. It is true, however, that the success of the monetary union may be also due to the fact that state governments have displayed considerable fiscal discipline compared to some European countries. Goldstein and Wolgom investigate if this fiscal discipline can be the result of the constraints imposed by private financial markets. By using a set of survey data on the yields of state general obligation bonds that covers 39 states from 1973 to 1991, they test whether the cost of borrowing has been related to state debts and deficits. Their conclusion is that states with larger stocks of debt and larger fiscal deficits are associated with larger risk premia. Interestingly, however, they also find that states with more stringent, self-imposed, constitutional limits on the amount of borrowing, face a lower cost of borrowing.

Vito Tanzi commented that the existence of larger risk premia on bonds of states with larger debts and deficits does not yet prove the market discipline hypothesis. In fact, for the argument to be complete, it must also be proved that higher interest rates induce governments to reduce their borrowing. The paper, however, does not shed light on this second aspect. Vito Tanzi also noted that fundamental differences exist between the United States and Europe, that make the applicability of this results to the current debate problematic. Possibly the most crucial difference is the level of credibility of the United States union compared to that of a future European union.

4   Global implications of a European central bank

The chapter by **George Alogoskoufis** and **Richard Portes** looks beyond the creation of a European central bank and considers the implications for the international monetary system of the creation of EMU and the replacement of 12 national currencies by the ECU. The international demand for the ECU is likely to be greater than for the national currencies it replaces. It seems likely that EMU will thus hasten the relative decline in the international use of the dollar, but the experience of sterling suggests that reserve currency use changes very slowly. In any case, the quantitative significance for the EC of increased international seigniorage would be limited. Another aspect of EMU is the effect on international monetary policy coordination, currently conducted among the G-7 and in other forums, of having Europe 'speak with one voice' in monetary matters. It may lead to a more symmetric system in which the United States, Japan, and Europe constitute roughly equal poles. Will this stabilize or destabilize the international economy? The authors conclude that EMU is unlikely to undermine the evolution towards greater nominal exchange rate stability among major currencies.

Jeroen Kremers, in his comments, is not troubled by the conclusion of Alogoskoufis and Portes that the international implications – and potential gains to Europe – of EMU are quite modest. He stresses that the advantages of a common, stable currency are mainly *domestic* ones, and are related to those that will result from the creation of a European single market.

Part I The design of a central bank

2 Designing a central bank for Europe: a cautionary tale from the early years of the Federal Reserve System

BARRY EICHENGREEN

1 Introduction

Important questions concerning the structure and operation of a European central bank (ECB) remain to be answered. How much independence should national central banks retain during the transition to a single currency? What voting or mediation rules should be used to resolve conflicts among the national representatives on the ECB's governing council? What role should be played by existing central banks in implementing pan-European policies once the ECB comes into operation?

The Delors Report and the provisional statutes of the ECB, drafted by the governors of European Community central banks in Basel in November 1990, provide clearer answers to some of these questions than others. According to the Delors Report, during the transition to a single central bank ('Stage 2' of the process of monetary unification in the language of Brussels), national central banks will retain full nominal independence in the sense of continuing to issue their own national currencies and to intervene in domestic financial markets, but little real autonomy in that exchange rates will become immutably fixed and hence money supplies and interest rates will be determined by market forces. According to the draft statutes of the ECB, the policies of the new institution will be decided by votes cast by members of the bank's council, consisting of the 12 governors of the existing central banks and 6 executive directors appointed by the European Council. Voting will be by simple majority.[1] Governors and executive directors will be forbidden to accept instructions from national governments or from the European Parliament and Council. Once the ECB comes into operation, national central banks will forsake their remaining autonomy and become mere branch offices of the new institution.

13

Although there exists no precedent for the process of institution-building in which the European Community is currently engaged, the founding and early operation of the Federal Reserve System in the United States provides a suggestive parallel with ongoing developments in Europe. In the early years of the Fed, the individual reserve banks, while issuing bank notes that traded at fixed exchange rates vis-à-vis one another, essentially controlled their own discount policies. As American officials came to appreciate the problems posed by this arrangement, control over policy was gradually transferred to Washington, D.C. The stance of policy came to be determined by the Federal Reserve Board and an Open Market Investment Committee dominated by representatives of the 12 district reserve banks, just as representatives of the 12 European nations are envisaged as sitting on the council of the ECB. Implementation, especially of open market purchases, remained a matter for the individual reserve banks, however. Shifting authority to Washington D.C. did not eliminate regional conflicts in and of itself; neither did it resolve problems of policy implementation so long as individual reserve banks could opt out of System transactions. Only after authority was definitively centralized in the hands of the Board of Governors and the Federal Open Market Committee did the new institution finally come to operate smoothly.

The early history of the Federal Reserve System thus should be read as a cautionary tale.[2] It suggests that Stage 2 of the Delors Plan contains potential sources of instability. It provides an argument for a direct transition from Stage 1 (national monetary autonomy) to Stage 3 (complete centralization of authority).[3] It suggests the need for more thought about the voting and mediation procedures to be used to reconcile and aggregate national interests. It points to the advisability of reducing existing European central banks to mere branch offices of the ECB or of eliminating them entirely.

2   Institutions for decision-making in the early years of the Fed

In the early years of the Federal Reserve System, authority was much more decentralized and disputed than is suggested by many histories of the US central bank.[4] Decentralization created problems not anticipated by the framers of the Federal Reserve Act. In response to those problems, the institutional arrangements initially envisaged were gradually reformed. The first 22 years of the Federal Reserve System's existence (from the Federal Reserve Act of 1913 to the Banking Act of 1935) thus can be characterized as a trial-and-error process leading ultimately to the effective centralization of authority.

2.1 The consequences of the Federal Reserve Act

It seems remarkable, given the extent of decentralization and confusion over the locus of authority, that the newly-created Federal Reserve System succeeded in operating at all. Two factors were responsible for the peculiar state of affairs in which the Federal Reserve Board and the reserve bank Governors found themselves. First, the framers of the 1913 Act, while sensitive to the scope for regional conflict, finessed the issue by creating a federal structure but essentially declining to address the question of how it should operate. Second, the framers inadequately anticipated the problems with which the new institution would be confronted and the instruments with which those problems would be addressed.

The Federal Reserve System was created to provide an 'elastic currency' – that is, one which would be available in the quantities required by the changing needs of commerce and industry. Notes issued by the reserve banks had to be backed with gold to the extent of 40 per cent. The remainder of the collateral could take the form of eligible paper (commercial, agricultural and industrial paper and bankers acceptances), but insofar as eligible paper fell short of 60 per cent, gold had to make up the difference. These regulations applied by federal reserve district. Insofar as a reserve bank possessed gold in excess of that required, it could inject additional notes into circulation.

The framers anticipated that discount policy would be the principal instrument through which elasticity would be lent to American credit markets. When demands for credit rose, for seasonal or other reasons, member banks would discount commercial paper with reserve banks. The volume of discounts provided by the latter could be regulated by adjusting reserve bank discount rates. Discount policy was buttressed by a separate rate charged by each reserve bank for advances on acceptances and government securities.

The Federal Reserve Act was ambiguous about the role of the reserve banks and the Federal Reserve Board in determining the rates charged for discounts and advances. The 1913 Act stated only that 'Every Federal reserve bank shall have the power ... to establish from time to time, *subject to review and determination of the Federal Reserve Board*, rates of discount to be charged by the Federal reserve bank for each class of paper, which shall be fixed with a view of accommodating commerce and business.'[5] A possible interpretation of this passage is that the initiative to alter discount rates lay with the reserve banks but that the Board possessed veto power. Another is that the Board, using its power of 'determination,' might order a change in prevailing discount rates.

As early as January 1915, reserve bank Governors began to complain that the Federal Reserve Board was exceeding its authority in the specificity and scope of its instructions regarding discount policy. They established the Governors Conference as a venue in which to meet and defend their independence.[6] At its second meeting, a number of Governors asserted that the Board had no legal right to impose restrictions on the type of acceptances that could be purchased by reserve banks. Rolla Wells, Governor of the St. Louis Fed, complained that the Board's practice of suggesting discount rates infringed on the prerogatives of the reserve banks. Benjamin Strong, the influential Governor of the Federal Reserve Bank of New York, shared this opinion.[7] Toward the end of 1915 the Governors Conference adopted a resolution criticizing the Federal Reserve Board for its 'exercise of pressure.'[8] The Board's response was to demand that the Governors Conference be discontinued and to insist that the Governors should meet only when called by the Board.[9] Thus, the question of whether the Board or the reserve banks had the final say over discount policy remained far from resolution.

Even more problematic was that the framers of the Federal Reserve Act, having failed to anticipate the importance of open market operations, said even less about the conduct of security transactions than about discount policy. Other than stating that the Federal Reserve Board could issue regulations governing the types of securities the reserve banks might buy and sell, the 1913 Act had made virtually no mention of them. Between 1915 and 1923, the Board made no effort to do significantly more than this.[10]

In particular, the 1913 Act made no provision for coordinating the security sales and purchases of the individual reserve banks. The assumption was that each reserve bank would conduct such purchases and sales independently.[11] Insofar as there existed financial markets outside of New York in which municipal warrants and Treasury securities were traded, there arose the prospect that reserve banks would bid against one another when entering the market. It might seem perplexing that Fed officials worried that competitive open market purchases would have put undue upward pressure on bond prices (downward pressure on interest rates), especially if one assumes that the purpose of open market purchases was to lower interest rates. But in fact, in the early years of the Federal Reserve System, the main purpose of open market purchases was not to lend elasticity to the currency or to otherwise contribute to the conduct of what we would now call monetary policy. Rather, it was simply to enable the reserve banks to accumulate a portfolio of earning assets out of which to pay their expenses. Only after 1922, when the case for open market operations as an instrument for controlling commercial bank reserves had been articulated by W. Randolph Burgess, among others, did the technique begin to come into systematic use.

The approach to the conduct of open market operations agreed by the members of the Governors Conference was to establish maximum and minimum prices at which transactions would take place. In practice, the reserve banks repeatedly violated the agreement when it threatened to prevent them from acquiring the earning assets needed to meet their expenses.[12]

The consequences of these arrangements were highlighted during the business cycle downturn that began in 1920. As a result of the decline in economic activity, the volume of rediscounts fell off, eroding the interest income of the reserve banks. To restore their earnings, they purchased considerable quantities of government securities.[13] The Treasury and the Federal Reserve Board objected that the reserve banks were bidding against one another in the execution of orders and destabilizing the prices of government bonds.

2.2   Formation of the Open Market Investment Committee

In response, in May 1922 there was created on the recommendation of the Governors Conference a committee, comprised of the Governors of the New York, Boston, Philadelphia and Chicago reserve banks, to centralize the execution of orders for purchases and sales of securities.[14] At first, this was just a mechanism to prevent the reserve banks from bidding against one another for earning assets. But in October of the same year the Governors Conference voted to give the committee power to 'make recommendations' to the reserve banks regarding purchases and sales of government securities.[15] Whether their recommendations were binding and whether reserve banks retained the right to conduct open market operations on their individual initiative was left unclear.

These ambiguities were addressed in March 1923, following an extended study of open market operations by the Federal Reserve Board. This study came at the end of protracted dispute between the Board and the reserve banks, led by the New York Fed. Treasury officials objected that reserve bank transactions in government securities were disrupting their debt management operations, and insisted that the Board force the reserve banks to divest their portfolios of government bonds.[16] Adolph Miller, the economist on the Board, presented to his colleagues a proposal that the Board assert its control over the open market policies of the reserve banks. Learning of Miller's plan, the reserve banks rebelled. Governor W. P. G. Harding of the Federal Reserve Bank of Boston denied that the Board possessed more than 'broad supervisory power' and questioned whether it could do more than regulate the type of securities in which the reserve banks could transact.[17] On behalf of the Board, Miller responded that Washington possessed the power to dictate both the volume and composition of the open market transactions of the reserve banks.

A resolution approved by the Board on March 22nd asserted that the Board possessed the authority to 'limit and otherwise determine the securities and investments purchased by Federal Reserve banks.'[18] It added to the committee comprised of 4 reserve bank governors a fifth member, to be appointed by the Federal Reserve Bank of Cleveland, and named the body the Open Market Investment Committee (OMIC). According to the March 22nd resolution, the new committee came 'under the general supervision of the Federal Reserve Board.' This reorganization can be read as an attempt to assert the authority of the Board over the New York Fed in the conduct of open market operations. A separate Federal Reserve System open market investment account, operated by the New York Fed but under the supervision of the OMIC, was established to free the other banks from having to maintain accounts with the New York bank.[19]

The thrust of this resolution was that, while the OMIC would recommend open market purchases and sales to the reserve banks, its recommendations would be subject to approval by the Federal Reserve Board.[20] In practice, the OMIC almost exclusively recommended purchases and sales of bankers acceptances and short-term government securities. Actual purchases and sales were still delegated to the New York Fed and on occasion to other reserve banks.

The critical variables determining the volume of acceptances purchased by the reserve banks were their acceptance rates, which determined the quantity of acceptances offered. In turn, the most important acceptance rate was that of the Federal Reserve Bank of New York, since far and away the largest acceptance market was New York City. In light of this asymmetry among reserve banks, procedures were adopted to redistribute acceptances from New York to other Federal Reserve districts. As acceptances came into the New York Fed, they were allocated to the other reserve banks in proportions set by the OMIC. Open market purchases of government securities, when undertaken by the New York Fed on instructions issued by the OMIC, were then apportioned to the other reserve banks in agreed percentages.

In principle, an OMIC decision to conduct open market purchases not only had to be approved by the Federal Reserve Board but also had to be submitted to the individual reserve banks, which could decline to participate. Similarly, reserve banks had the option of refusing to take their share of the securities accepted by the New York Fed, even though the shares were established by the OMIC. On occasions when this occurred in the 1920s, the New York bank absorbed the residual.[21]

The reserve banks did not concede the Board's right to dictate their open market operations.[22] The 1923 resolutions of the Federal Reserve Board left the reserve banks the right to opt out of open market operations recommended by the OMIC and the Board. More controversial was whether reserve banks were also entitled to conduct open market operations of which the Board did not approve. Some reserve bank officials asserted that this was the case.[23] They threatened to enter the market on their own volition even if the Board disapproved.[24] It appears that they did so on more than one occasion in the 1920s.[25]

These disagreements were aired in meetings of the OMIC and in its dealings with the Board. As early as April 1923 the Board instructed the OMIC to conduct large-scale open market sales, for the purpose of liquidating reserve bank holdings of government securities.[26] The OMIC first voted that maturing Treasury certificates should not be replaced, and then, under Federal Reserve Board and Treasury pressure, agreed to $50 million of sales from reserve bank portfolios. This was not enough for several members of the Board, however, who chastised the head of the OMIC, J. H. Case (chairing the Committee in Strong's absence), for not carrying out the Board's instructions. Case complained that the Board had exceeded its authority by ordering security sales. In his view, the limits on the Board's authority were the same as those which had prevailed prior to the March 1923 resolutions. Ultimately, the OMIC bowed to Washington's pressure, selling a second $50 million of government securities, and thereby reducing its holdings from more than $200 million in April to less than $100 million in July.

2.3 Establishment of the Open Market Policy Conference

By the end of the 1920s, complaints about the growing influence of the Federal Reserve Board and OMIC were widespread in the Southern and Western United States, regions whose reserve banks were not represented on the five-member OMIC. Representatives of these districts argued that the excessive expansion of credit in 1927–29, which supposedly had led to the stock market boom and crash, was the fault of the reserve banks beholden to Wall Street interests that dominated the OMIC. They criticized the latter as a power-hungry, extra-legal body not provided for by the Federal Reserve Act.[27]

Such criticisms were largely responsible for the Federal Reserve Board's decision to dissolve the OMIC in March 1930 and to replace it with a new committee, the Open Market Policy Conference, or OMPC. All 12 reserve banks were represented on the OMPC. The Board endowed it with an executive committee, once again limited to representatives of 5 reserve banks. This time, however, the executive committee was responsible only for executing, not initiating, policy.[28] Substantive policy decisions were to be made instead in regular meetings of the OMPC, with representatives of all 12 reserve banks present. Nothing ensured the leadership or even participation of the Governor of the New York Fed on the executive committee. Thus, the reorganization of the OMIC into the OMPC was seen as an attempt to 'curtail the control exercised by the New York Reserve Bank.'[29]

The establishment of the OMPC significantly clarified lines of authority and control. Once again, however, ambiguities remained. The 1930 resolution was less than clear about who possessed the final say about the conduct of open market operations. It stated that 'The conclusions and/or recommendations of the Open Market Policy Conference, when approved by the Federal Reserve Board, shall be submitted to each Federal Reserve bank for determination as to whether it will participate in any purchases or sales recommended; any Federal Reserve bank dissenting from the proposed policy shall be expected to acquaint the Federal Reserve Board and the chairman of the executive committee for the reasons for its dissent.'[30] Apparently reserve banks could still decline to engage in open market operations recommended by the OMPC.

2.4   The Banking Acts of 1933 and 1935

The Federal Reserve Board at last acquired definitive control over open market operations as part of the Banking Act of 1933. The Open Market Policy Conference was renamed the Federal Open Market Committee (FOMC) and finally given legal standing. In keeping with practice since 1930, it was composed of one representative from each of the 12 reserve banks. At last it was explicitly stated that 'no Federal Reserve bank shall engage in open-market operations under section 14 of this Act except in accordance with regulations adopted by the Federal Reserve Board.' If a reserve bank wished to purchase or sell government securities for its own account, it was now required to first obtain the consent of the Board. Rates of interest and discount on acceptances and bills of exchange had to conform to the regulations of the Board. Final authority over these matters now clearly rested with the Board in Washington, D.C.

The individual reserve banks still retained limited autonomy under the 1933 Act. While prohibited from initiating open market transactions on their own, they had the right to refuse to participate in open market operations recommended by the Board. Moreover, individual reserve banks were still permitted to buy government securities in an emergency as needed to afford relief to banking institutions in their districts.[31]

The 1933 Banking Act contained two revealing provisions. It specified that no officer or other representative of a federal reserve bank was permitted to negotiate with a foreign bank except with the Board's permission. It asserted that the Board was entitled to be represented in all such negotiations and that it had the right to oversee all relations with foreign central banks. This clause was a reaction to a controversy which had arisen in 1927, when Benjamin Strong, the Governor of the Federal Reserve Bank of New York, had initiated negotiations with a group of foreign central bankers and failed to keep the Board apprised.[32] Another provision of the 1933 Act authorized the Federal Reserve Board to fix for each federal reserve district the percentage of member bank loans secured by stock or bond collateral. This clause was an outgrowth of the Board's attempt in 1929 to utilize a policy of 'direct pressure' to ration stock market speculators out of the loan market, a tactic whose implementation was resisted by the New York Fed.[33]

These reforms were consolidated by the Banking Act of 1935.[34] The Federal Reserve Board's name was changed to the Board of Governors of the Federal Reserve System. The composition of the FOMC was changed so that it was now composed of the 7 members of the Board of Governors plus 5 representatives of the reserve banks. The 5 reserve bank appointees were to represent all parts of the country, not just the Northeast and Middle West, as had been the case in the 1920s with the OMIC. Thus, the dominance of Washington, D.C. over the formulation of monetary policy was ensured as much by reducing the influence of the reserve banks of the Northeast and Midwest as by elevating the influence of the Board. Finally, decisions of the FOMC were made binding. Reserve banks were prohibited from engaging in, or (for the first time) declining to engage in, open market operations mandated by the FOMC.

3 Impact on policy

To analyse the impact on policy of the conflicts that arose in the early years of the Federal Reserve System over the control of open market operations and of the different institutional arrangements used to resolve them, I first specify a simple analytical model with which these issues can be addressed. I then use this model to structure my discussions of five critical episodes from the early history of the Fed.

3.1 An analytical model

The model utilized here is an adaptation of that in Eichengreen (1985). I use it in this case to analyse the incentives facing district reserve banks in a national setting, instead of the more familiar problem of the incentives facing national central banks in an international setting. The parallels will be obvious.

Consider the interaction of two reserve banks, referred to as 'New York' and 'Chicago' for reasons that will become evident in Section 3.2.2 below.[35] Each reserve bank minimizes a loss function L. The loss increases as earnings on its bond portfolio deviate from their desired level and as output deviates from its target.

$$L = [(B - \bar{B})^2 + a(Y - \bar{Y})^2] \qquad L^* = [(B^* - \bar{B}^*)^2 + a^*(Y - \bar{Y})^2] \tag{1}$$

Variables with asterisks refer to the Chicago bank, those without them to New York. B (B^*) denotes bonds in the reserve bank's portfolio, $\bar{B}$ the corresponding target number of bonds. Y is nominal income in the economy, $\bar{Y}$ its corresponding target level.[36] a (a^*) is the weight attached to income deviations relative to earnings deviations in the loss function.

$\bar{B}$ can be thought of as the bond portfolio that optimally trades off current interest earnings (which increase with B) against future lender-of-last-resort capacity (which is a decreasing function of B, since additional lending requires open market purchases which are constrained by gold cover restrictions). Similarly, Y can be thought of as indexing not only the current level of income but also the current stability of the banking system.

Y is an increasing function of the (cumulated) open market purchases of the two central banks. The simplest possible specification makes that function linear and additive:

$$Y = B + B^* \tag{2}$$

Expansionary open market operations can raise nominal income by increasing the monetary base (Friedman and Schwartz, 1963) or by countering disintermediation and debt deflation (Bernanke, 1983). In the historical context at hand, I have in mind expansionary open market operations as a means of providing liquidity to a banking system unable to restore its liquidity itself because of asymmetric information about the quality of bank assets and problems of adverse selections.[37]

Each central bank possesses one instrument (open market operations) with which to minimize its loss function.[38] Consider first the simple case in which the two reserve banks are identical in all respects, so that $a^* = a$. Substituting (2) into (1) and minimizing the loss subject to the assumption that the policy of the other reserve bank is given yields the reaction functions for the two banks:

$$\partial L/\partial B = [a/(1 + a)] B^* - [1/(1 + a)]\bar{B} - [a/(1 + a)] \bar{Y} + B = 0 \tag{3a}$$

$$\partial L^*/\partial B^* = [a/(1 + a)] B - [1/(1 + a)] \bar{B} - [a/(1 + a)] \bar{Y} + B^* = 0$$
$$(3b)$$

The reaction functions are depicted in Figure 2.1 B and B^* are lower at the Nash solution N, where the two reaction functions intersect, than at the cooperative solution C, the point where the indifference contours of the two reserve banks are tangent.[39] Each central bank has two objectives: stabilizing the level of output and the banking system, and holding lender-of-last-resort capacity in reserve for the future. Since future lender-of-last-resort capacity depends only on its own bond portfolio, while output economywide depends not only on its own bond portfolio (the larger its bond portfolio, the greater its expansionary open market operations and hence the higher the level of output) but also on the bond portfolio of its counterpart, each reserve bank holds a smaller bond portfolio and engages in fewer expansionary open market operations when it behaves non-cooperatively than when it cooperates. Each reserve bank derives only some of the benefits of open market purchases; the rest accrue as a positive externality to the other bank. At N, it does too little to stabilize output and the banking system currently. Cooperation, were it to be forced on the two central banks by the Board of Governors, is a way of internalizing this externality. Note, however, that starting from the cooperative point C, each reserve bank has the option of reverting to its reaction function so long as it retains the alternative of opting out from cooperative actions mandated by the Board.

What is the effect of introducing asymmetries into the model? Assume for example that $a > a^*$. There are a number of rationales for such an assumption. One can imagine that, compared to Chicago, New York better appreciates the impact of open market operations on macroeconomic stability or attaches a higher weight to economic stability itself. Alternatively, if Y is interpreted as proxying not only for the level of income but also for the stability of the banking system today, Wheelock's (1988) evidence for the 1920s and 1930s that open market purchases, by whatever Federal Reserve bank they were initiated, disproportionately increased the reserves of member banks in the New York district provides a further rationale for the assumption. In this case, open market purchases can be seen as enhancing the stability of the New York Fed's client banks to a greater extent than it enhances the stability of the member banks of the Chicago district, thereby justifying the assumption that $a > a^*$.

This situation is depicted in Figure 2.2. Chicago's reaction function is flatter than New York's. New York is more inclined than Chicago to respond to open market purchases by the other reserve bank with open

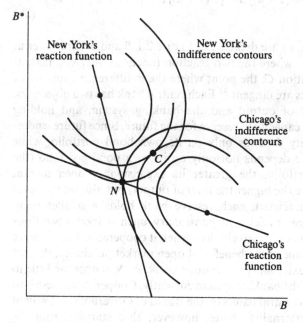

Figure 2.1 New York and Chicago's reaction functions: the symmetric case

market sales of its own, since New York attaches greater weight to the stock of bonds held outside the Federal Reserve System, upon which the level of economic activity depends. By comparison, Chicago is less inclined to respond to New York's open market sales with open market purchases of its own, since member banks in New York benefit more than member banks in Chicago from an increase in the stock of bonds held outside the Federal Reserve System.

Again, current stabilization is underprovided. Both reserve banks hold smaller stocks of earning assets and do less to stabilize output and the banking system at the Nash solution than would be the case if they cooperated.

In summary, the decentralization of control over open market operations for most of the interwar years is likely to have led the stabilization function to be undersupplied. Moreover, reserve banks such as New York whose member banks benefit most from stabilization are likely to have borne a disproportionate share of the burden of supplying it. How important this was for policy can only be determined through the examination of particular historical episodes.

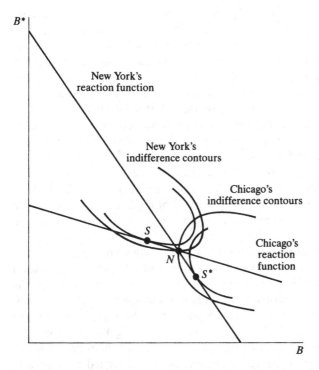

Figure 2.2   New York and Chicago's reaction fuctions: the asymmetric case

3.2   Case studies

Case studies provide a second approach to analysing the impact of differences and conflicts over policy within the Federal Reserve System. They illustrate how the Board's failure to properly impose cooperative behavior on the reserve banks led the stabilization function to be under-supplied. They show how disputes between the Board and the reserve banks led to delays that caused intervention to be provided at inappropriate times, and how differences of opinion between the Board and the reserve banks sometimes led the banks to provide even less of the stabilization function than they would have wished.

3.2.1 The 1927 discount rate reductions

The first episode of controversy occurred in 1927. The economy was in a short-lived recession, popularly attributed to Henry Ford's decision to shut down his assembly lines for six months to shift over from the Model T to the Model A. Great Britain and Germany were experiencing gold outflows, yet hesitated to apply the orthodox medicine, higher interest rates, because economic activity was slowing down. The dilemma led to a famous meeting of Benjamin Strong of the New York Fed, Charles Rist, Deputy Governor of the Bank of France, Hjalmar Schacht, President of the German Reichsbank, and Montagu Norman, Governor of the Bank of England. The four central bankers assembled on Long Island in July 1927 to negotiate a cooperative response. Their solution was a commitment by the Bank of France not to present sterling for conversion at the Bank of England, and a reduction in the Federal Reserve Bank of New York's discount rate designed to repel gold inflows.[40]

These negotiations had been undertaken unilaterally by the Governor of the New York Fed. Strong had kept only one member of the Federal Reserve Board, Daniel Crissinger, apprised of his intentions, and invited only members of the Open Market Investment Committee to attend formal sessions of the summit.[41] Unsurprisingly, Board members and reserve bank officials resented his initiative.[42] Only with reluctance therefore did the OMIC agree on July 27th to discount rate reductions. Several of the reserve banks remained unsupportive, however. In particular, the Chicago Fed, more worried about inflation and speculation than about the weakening economy, refused to go along. On September 6th, the Federal Reserve Board held a special meeting, voting 4 to 3 to force the Chicago Fed to reduce its discount rate.[43] The Chicago bank surrendered.

This decision remains controversial. Adolph Miller argued subsequently that the decision to lower discount rates set the stage for the excessive speculation of the Wall Street boom and ultimately for the crash that inaugurated the Great Depression.[44] I have argued elsewhere that this view is misleading.[45] The 1927 cut in discount rates actually helped to abbreviate the 1927 recession, and there is no evidence that it was in fact responsible for the stock market boom and crash.

In terms of the theoretical model of Section 3.1, this episode can be thought of as an early instance in which the Board compelled the individual reserve banks, principally New York and Chicago, to move from a point like N to one like C. The Board's authority to do so remained disputed, however. Indeed, the controversy provoked by its action inhibited it from taking similar steps in 1928–29.

3.2.2 The Fed's response to the great bull market

A second episode of controversy over authority and control swirled around the restrictive monetary measures taken in response to the 1928–29 stock market boom. The Fed's decision to tighten in order to restrain the rise of the stock market is now regarded as a grave policy error that set the stage for the Great Depression.[46] The impetus to do so came not from the Board, however, but from the Chicago Fed, the same reserve bank that had opposed discount rate reductions in 1927 on the grounds that they encouraged speculation. In January 1928 the directors of the Chicago bank voted to increase its discount rate. This can be thought as an attempt by Chicago to defect from the cooperative solution – that is, to move from C, the equilibrium imposed on the reserve banks by the Federal Reserve Board in September 1927, to a point directly below it on the Chicago bank's reaction function.

This time Chicago's decision was reluctantly accepted by the Federal Reserve Board, which, according to Wicker, wished to avoid repeating the episode of the previous September in which it had embarrassed the Chicago Fed.[47] Only two Board members, Edmund Platt and George James, actually favored the Chicago Fed's proposal to raise the cost of credit. Others worried about seeing 'business penalized for the excesses in the stock market' but yielded on grounds of reserve bank autonomy.[48]

The Chicago Fed's position, that increases in discount and acceptance rates were needed to contain stock market speculation, spread to other parts of the Federal Reserve System in 1928. This is a prediction of the model: once the cooperative solution C cannot be sustained and one reserve bank defects, the other reserve banks will also revert to their reaction functions, raising discount rates and/or reducing open market purchases until the Nash solution at N is reached.

Yet some opposition to higher discount rates remained. Governor Roy Young of the Board continued to oppose rate increases on the grounds that they would injure industry and trade.[49] Young protested when on January 3, 1929 the directors of the New York Fed voted to raise the buying rate on acceptances. He asserted that the action required the prior approval of the Board, a position which George Harrison, the new Governor of the New York Fed, disputed.[50]

This controversy can be understood in terms of two fundamental disagreements within the Federal Reserve System. One concerned the best way to contain speculation on Wall Street without doing damage to business and trade. Members of the Federal Reserve Board, including a reluctant Young, preferred a policy of 'direct pressure' – moral suasion to deter member banks from extending brokers loans and other credits that might be used for speculative purposes. Direct pressure was intended to ration speculators out of financial markets without disrupting the access to credit of legitimate borrowers. The New York Fed preferred discount rate increases, both because it doubted the effectiveness or direct pressure given the fungibility of funds, and because it did not wish to discriminate against its Wall Street clientele.

The second fundamental disagreement concerned reserve bank autonomy.

At the first meetings of the OMIC following Benjamin Strong's death in 1928, the Board submitted to the reserve bank governors a proposal to revise procedures for conducting open market operations. It proposed expanding the size of the OMIC from 5 to 12 members in order to eliminate the dominance of the 5 reserve bank governors from the Northeast and Midwest. No immediate action was taken, however.[51] Two weeks later the Board for the first time vetoed a recommendation forwarded by the OMIC.[52] Both actions were intended to assert the Board's authority over the OMIC, and to signal that henceforth the Board would oversee even the smallest decisions of the latter.

On February 14, 1929, the directors of the New York Fed voted unanimously to increase the discount rate and telephoned the Board to obtain confirmation. When the Board instructed the New York bank to hold off until the Board considered the matter the following day, the directors in New York informed the Board that they would not leave the bank premises until they received a response from Washington, D.C. To assert their dominance, the Board then voted unanimously to veto New York's decision.[53]

This sequence of events repeated itself 10 times over the subsequent 4 months. The directors of the New York Fed voted repeatedly to raise the discount rate; the Board repeatedly vetoed their action. While 'no one questioned the legal right of the Federal Reserve Board to veto our rate increases,' in Harrison's words, continued refusal was 'seriously disturbing to both the officers and directors of the several Federal reserve banks.'[54]

Several of the New York directors threatened resignation on the grounds that their powers had been usurped. The directors were invited to Washington to confer with the Board. Finally in August of 1929 the New York Fed was allowed to raise its discount rate.

In terms of the model, these events are best understood as an attempt by the Board to reassert its authority over the reserve banks in the wake of its loss of influence in 1928. Ironically, that reassertion, while it should have had beneficial consequences in the long run (by facilitating cooperative solutions to the policy game), had adverse consequences in the short run. The conflict delayed the New York Fed's efforts to raise its discount rate to the point that, when the increase finally came, it was no longer timely. But New York's desire to assert its autonomy encouraged it to go through with the increase anyway. By August, when the discount rate increase finally came, industrial production in the United States had already begun to decline. Discount rate increases lent further impetus to the downward spiral of activity.

3.2.3 The Fed's response to the 1929 crash

A third conflict occurred in the aftermath of the October 1929 Wall Street crash. The crash created a liquidity crisis in New York. Brokers who had borrowed from New York banks, pledging stock as collateral, found themselves unable to repay. Almost half of the loans of central reserve city member banks in New York were collateralized by securities; a third were extended directly to stock brokers and dealers in New York City. Immediately following the crash, banks in the interior of the country which had placed money at call in New York repatriated their funds. The New York Fed, seeing its member banks placed at risk, intervened by purchasing $100 million of government securities on the open market.

In terms of the model of Section 3.1, the crash can be thought of as shifting New York's reaction function to the right. This induced open market purchases by the New York Fed (a rise in B) and, given the flatness of their reaction functions, little response by the other reserve banks.

New York's action was undertaken without prior approval by the Federal Reserve Board. Indeed, Harrison authorized this intervention even without consulting all of his own bank's directors.[55] Officials in Washington, DC were torn. The majority of Board members approved in principle of providing additional liquidity to financial markets in distress, but they were alarmed by the precedent represented by New York's unauthorized, unilateral action.[56] Harrison was called on the carpet. He protested that the 1923 agreement between the Board and the reserve banks permitted the latter to purchase securities for their own account. If doing so was ever justified, this was the case in extraordinary circumstances like those of October 1929. Once again the Board disagreed. Open market operations, its members asserted, were at the Board's volition and its volition alone. Governor Young of the Board noted that the Board 'had been given most extraordinarily wide powers [and] that so long as the Board had those powers, they would feel free to exercise them.'[57] Having repeatedly vetoed the New York Fed's attempts to alter its discount rate, the Board threatened to do so again unless the New York bank promised to refrain from engaging in further unauthorized open market purchases. The Board authorized the Governor, should the Board not be immediately available, to act on its behalf in the event of an emergency.

For the moment, the controversy remained unresolved. So long as it persisted, the dispute continued to disrupt the Federal Reserve system's attempt to engineer a concerted response to the economic slump. On October 1st the OMIC had been authorized by the Board to purchase short-term government securities in amounts not to exceed $25 million a week. On November 12th the OMIC, led by Harrison, recommended that the ceiling be raised. The Board vetoed its decision on the grounds that 'the general situation is not sufficiently clarified for the system to formulate and adopt a permanent open market policy at this time.'[58] A bargain was hammered out under which the New York Fed agreed to refrain from further open market purchases for its own account, at least until their legality had been determined, in return for the Board's approval of the OMIC's recommendation. On November 25th the Board confirmed this deal by a narrow margin.[59]

3.2.4 Open market operations in 1932

A fourth conflict concerned the use of open market operations in 1932. Until the Glass-Steagall Act came into effect at the end of February, open market purchases were constrained by the availability of free gold. Glass-Steagall eliminated the constraint and allowed the Fed to inject additional notes into circulation by purchasing government securities.[60]

The Governors of the 12 reserve banks were divided on the efficacy of doing so, however. The majority apparently believed that, in light of the deflation and depressed business conditions that by early 1932 had persisted for almost 2½ years, open market purchases could not hurt and might actually stimulate recovery. A vocal minority, led by the Governors of the Chicago and Boston banks, warned that open market purchases would only provoke another round of inflation and unhealthy stock market speculation.[61] Since money was already plentiful, they argued, open market purchases would serve no useful purpose. It was better, as this view was articulated by James McDougal, Governor of the Chicago Fed, for the Fed to hold its note-issuing capacity in reserve for some future time when it would be of greater value.[62]

Thus, the dispute within the Federal Reserve System is typically portrayed as a disagreement over doctrine.[63] Epstein and Ferguson (1984) suggest, however, that the Chicago and Boston reserve banks had ulterior motives. Member banks in their districts held or were acquiring short-term securities in disproportionate numbers. The earnings of those banks would suffer if open market purchases were initiated and interest rates were reduced. This prompted the Boston and Chicago reserve banks to intervene on their members' behalf by opposing open market purchases.[64]

With the majority of Governors nonetheless supporting open market operations, Harrison attempted to push a purchase program through the OMPC and the Board. On April 12th, 1932, the OMPC approved by a vote of 10 to 1 Harrison's resolution authorizing an additional $500 million of open market purchases to be undertaken as soon as possible. Only Roy Young, now Governor of the Boston Fed, voted no, although McDougal of Chicago warned that this inflationary policy might undermine public confidence.[65] The OMPC purchased $100 million of securities weekly before exhausting its authorization. At that point the OMPC approved an additional $500 million of purchases, despite negative votes by Young and McDougal.[66]

So far there is nothing exceptional about this episode. A difference of opinion existed among the members of the OMPC, and policy was determined by majority vote. The story gets interesting when one observes that the Chicago and Boston reserve banks, and the former in particular, could and did increase the cost to the other reserve banks of carrying out the policy. Chicago and Boston threatened to sit on the sidelines while the other reserve banks purchased securities. Since gold backing restrictions on notes applied individually to each reserve bank, this raised the danger that the cover ratio of the New York Fed or another reserve bank would fall below the legal minimum.[67]

By the end of the June, the gold cover ratio of the New York bank had fallen to 50 per cent, while Chicago's was still 75 per cent.[68] If the New York Fed continued to purchase securities without Chicago's support, its capacity to provide future lender-of-last-resort facilities to banks in its district would be eliminated.[69] In principle, the Board could have forced Chicago to rediscount on behalf of New York, transferring some of its gold there, but officials within the System viewed this step as undesirable on the grounds that it would reveal the depth of division within the Federal Reserve system and therefore demoralize the markets. By June, Harrison himself was questioning the advisability of continuing the program of open market purchases unless Chicago and Boston agreed to participate. As he put it, 'I do not see how this bank [New York] can continue to carry so much more than its share of the load.'[70]

Harrison's efforts to win over officials in Chicago and Boston proved unavailing. Nor did his efforts to get his acquaintances in the Chicago banking and business community to pressure the Chicago Fed bear any fruit. Mounting gold losses compelled the OMPC and the Board to halt open market operations in August.[71] Thus, resistance by a minority of reserve banks, notably Chicago, increased the cost to the others of providing the stabilization function, forcing open market purchases to be abandoned sooner than would have otherwise been the case. In terms of the model of Section 3.1, inadequate cooperation led the stabilization function to be undersupplied.

3.2.5 The 1933 banking crisis

A fifth conflict (the final one considered here) arose out of the banking panic with which Franklin Delano Roosevelt was greeted upon taking office.[72] Panic surfaced first in Michigan in February 1933; by early

March bank runs had spread to virtually every state of the union. The question is why the Fed did not do more to stabilize the banking system. Officials throughout the Federal Reserve System recognized the banking system's need for liquidity. By early March, however, the gold cover ratio System-wide had fallen to 45 per cent. The provision of additional liquidity threatened to violate this most basic provision of the gold standard and, in the prevailing view, to further demoralize financial markets.

Gold losses were borne unevenly by reserve banks, with New York experiencing far and away the greatest pressure. Foreigners, fearing a possible devaluation of the dollar, scrambled to get their money out of the country in order to avoid the capital losses that would result.[73] Since the vast majority of foreign deposits was held by New York banks, gold was drained from the coffers of The New York Fed. In addition, difficulties in Michigan and throughout the interior prompted the liquidation of correspondent balances in New York. In the three weeks ending on March 8th, 1933, New York suffered more than 100 per cent of the gold losses of the Federal Reserve System.[74] On March 4th, when US monetary gold reserves were 44 per cent of the note and deposit liabilities of the Federal Reserve system, the gold backing of the notes of the New York Fed had fallen to the 40 per cent statutory minimum.[75] In terms of the model of Section 3.1 above, this is an example of the situation in which New York was forced to bear a disproportionate share of the stabilization function.

As in 1932, the Chicago Fed was the principal repository of the System's excess gold reserves. At the beginning of March 1933, the Chicago bank's gold reserve was still 65 per cent. In principle, the New York Fed might have obtained additional gold from Chicago. On March 1st, the Chicago Fed lent $105 million to its New York counterpart by purchasing a matching amount of New York's government securities and acceptances under a repurchase agreement. On March 3rd, however, Chicago withdrew its cooperation.[76] Spokesmen for member banks in Chicago were skeptical that the New York banks would be significantly strengthened by the transfer of funds, but they were convinced that their own position would be weakened. They pressured the Chicago Fed to withdraw its support for New York.

On March 4th the Federal Reserve Board considered the situation but declined to compel the Chicago Fed to aid New York.[77] The New York Fed was forced to curtail its lender-of-last-resort activities.[78] the New York Stock Exchange and other exchanges nationwide suspended operations the same day. The bank holiday followed immediately. This can be thought of as the situation at point S^* in the analytical model, where Chicago acts as a Stackelberg leader. Chicago was aware of New

York's commitment to support its member banks and the stock exchange. It could reduce its contribution to stabilizing financial markets in anticipation of New York taking up a part of the slack. Chicago's refusal to provide part of the stabilization function forced New York to shoulder a disproportionate share of the burden. Since the cost to New York of additional lender-of-last-resort activities eventually proved prohibitive, less of the stabilization function was provided than would have been the case had the Board forced the reserve banks to cooperate.

On March 7th the Federal Reserve Board finally compelled Chicago and the other reserve banks to resume interdistrict rediscounting on behalf of the New York Fed. This allowed the latter to resume discounting on behalf of member banks. It became possible to gradually reopen the commercial banks whose operations had been suspended by the bank holiday. The stage was set for reconstruction of the American financial system.

4 Implications for a European Central Bank

While the particulars of this history will not carry over to Europe in the 1990s, some general lessons are certain to apply. In this conclusion I emphasize four implications of the early history of the Federal Reserve System for the design of a European Central Bank.

The first implication is the importance of close coordination among national central banks once monetary unification is achieved. Any attempt to decentralize monetary control at the level of national central banks creates the danger that their stabilization function will be underprovided. Since stabilization has the character of an international public good, no national central bank has the incentive to internalize all of the international spillovers created by its actions. Efficiency requires transnational control.[79] The dangers raised by its absence are acute whether goal of stabilization policy is output or price stability. European policymakers have clearly stated the need to centralize control once a European central bank comes into operation. But the point applies equally well to Stage 2 of the monetary unification process, when exchange rates are immutably fixed but national central banks may retain a considerable degree of autonomy. From this point of view, the current approach to Stage 2 poses considerable dangers.

A second implication is the importance of resolving in advance controversies over the locus of control. If residual uncertainty remains, it is likely that monetary unification will be followed by a period in which national central banks test the limits of their autonomy and take independent action as a way of demonstrating to the newly-established European central bank that some such autonomy remains. This is likely to evoke a strong response by the ECB designed to demonstrate authority. In the early history of the Fed, this process of thrust and parry led to disastrous delays.

A third implication is that, to prevent such controversies from arising, issues of autonomy and control should be addressed explicitly. The same point applies, of course, to the managerial hierarchy of any enterprise, not just to a central bank. But it is in the public sector, where questions of authority and control become politically charged, that the temptation to circumvent them is greatest. Given the politically-charged nature of these issues, the framers of the Federal Reserve Act sought to avoid them. This led to the disputes which disrupted policy for fully two decades. The draft statutes of the European central bank, in their current form, leave open substantial questions of authority and control. The early history of the Fed underscores the need to provide definitive answers before the new institution comes into operation.

The fourth and final implication of this cautionary tale is the importance of endowing any new institution with a model of the central banking function that is coherent and pertinent. In the case of the Fed, this model was missing; hence the centralization of authority in the 1930s was a mixed blessing. On the one hand it permitted the emergence of an institutional structure capable of internalizing the interregional externalities that characterize monetary policy and resolved the disputes over authority and control that had created extended policy deadlocks. On the other hand it enhanced the influence of factions within the Federal Reserve System who least appreciated the role for monetary policy in countering the Great Depression, and undermined the position of others, notably officials of the Federal Reserve Bank of New York, who were most aware of the need for offsetting action. According to the draft statute of the Eurofed, the model of the central banking function is one in which monetary policy should be targeted first and foremost at price stability. Imagine that at some future date the problem is not inflation but, say, bank insolvencies or another potential source of financial instability. Then it is not clear that concentrating the central banking function in a single entity with this charge is the best way of ensuring that policy is adapted to new imperatives.

Nor is it obvious that the adoption of explicit rules and restrictions on operating procedures will be helpful in the long run. In the US case, the failure of the Fed's architects to anticipate the importance of open market operations and the problems created by the free gold constraint graphically illustrate the point. The Great Depression that resulted in part from difficulties thereby created should serve as the ultimate warning to European policymakers.

NOTES

I thank Sonali Vepa and Glenn Yamagata for assistance; the Library of Congress, Columbia University and the Federal Reserve Bank of New York for permission to cite documents in their possession; and Matt Canzoneri and David Wheelock, along with my conference discussants, Bennett McCallum and Eugene White, for helpful comments.

 1 Weighted voting is foreseen for financial matters, such as paying in capital and allocating profits, though the weights remain to be determined. See Committee of Governors (1990), p. 11.
 2 At least two authors (Thygesen, 1989; Miron, 1989) have analysed this tale previously. Neither, however, takes the methodological approaches that I adopt here.
 3 In this paper I do not address the more fundamental question of the advisability of monetary unification. See however Eichengreen (1990). Rather, I assume that it will take place and inquire into the operation of European monetary policy thereafter.
 4 This statement does not apply uniformly, and it certainly is not applicable to all early analyses of Federal Reserve policy. Two excellent accounts of the controversies, upon which I draw heavily, are Clark (1935) and Harris (1933).
 5 Emphasis added.
 6 The Governors Conference, comprised of the 12 reserve bank governors, was an outgrowth of a meeting of reserve bank officials held in Washington on 20–1 October, 1914. It met in December 1914, four times in 1915, four times in 1916 and once in 1917.
 7 US Congress (1971), p. 13; Chandler (1957), p. 70.
 8 The resolution was then forwarded to the Board. US Congress (1971), p. 14; Chandler (1957), p. 73.
 9 US Congress (1971), p. 15. In the event, the Board managed to secure only a suspension of Governors Conference meetings until the end of World War I.
10 Clark (1935), p. 162.
11 Several reserve banks found themselves incapable of doing so owing to the lack of an organized market in the relevant securities within their districts. The only significant market in US government securities in the early decades of the twentieth century was that in New York. Hence at the second meeting of the Governors Conference in January 1915, the other reserve banks appointed the New York Fed as their agent for purchasing securities on the open market. The New York bank not only purchased securities on the instructions of other reserve banks but also resold to them securities already held in its portfolio.
12 Chandler (1957), p. 78.
13 Annual Report of the Federal Reserve Board, 1923, p. 13; Stabilization Hearings on HR. 7895, 1926, p. 863.
14 Stabilization Hearings on HR. 7895, 1926, p. 863.
15 Harrison Papers, Governors Conference, vol. I. 10–12 October 1922, p. 12; Stabilization Hearings on HR. 7895, 1926, pp. 310–11.
16 Chandler (1957), pp. 222–3.
17 Chandler (1957), p. 225.
18 Stabilization Hearings on HR. 7895, 1926, p. 865.
19 Burgess (1936), p. 218.
20 Stabilization Hearings on HR. 7895, 1926, pp. 865–6.

21 Clark (1935), p. 169.
22 Governor Strong, in letters to J. H. Case written in the spring of 1923, complained that the Board had exceeded its authority. Chandler (1957), p. 228.
23 Stabilization Hearings on HR. 7895, 1926, pp. 866–867; Stabilization Hearings on HR. 11806, 1928, p. 403.
24 US Congress (1971), p. 102; Stabilization Hearings on HR. 7895, 1026, p. 866.
25 Chandler (1957), p. 229.
26 The remainder of this paragraph draws in Chandler (1957), pp. 229–32.
27 Kemmerer (1938), pp. 203–4.
28 Friedman and Schwartz (1963), p. 368.
29 Clark (1935), p. 176.
30 Hearings on Banking Systems, 1931, p. 158.
31 Thus, even had the 1933 Banking Act been in effect in 1929, the New York Fed might well have had the option of intervening on behalf of New York banks embarrassed by the liquidation of brokers loans, even without Federal Reserve Board approval. On this 1929 episode, see below, pp. 29–30.
32 For an account of this episode, see below, p. 26.
33 On the 1929 policy of direct pressure, see below, pp. 27–8.
34 A source for this is the testimony of Eccles in Hearings Before the Senate Committee on Banking and Currency, 4 March 1935, 74th Congress, First sessions, pp. 179ff.
35 Obviously, nothing of substance is affected by the convenience of reducing the number of players from 12 to 2.
36 I let Y denote nominal rather than real income or output in order to link it to monetary policy in a particularly simple fashion. Since price and output changes were positively correlated in the critical period considered here, nothing of substance is affected by this assumption.
37 On this 'fire' sale' problem, see Bentson et al. (1986). Stabilizing the banking system would stabilize output through the channels emphasized by both Bernanke and Friedman and Schwartz. Thus, to accept the rest of the analysis it is not necessary to buy into a particular model of the monetary transmission mechanism.
38 It is straightforward to reformulate the model so that the discount rate rather than open market operations is the policy instrument. See Eichengreen (1985) for an example. In applying the model to case studies in Section 3.1 below, I refer to open market purchases and discount rate reductions interchangeably.
39 I have selected a particular point of tangency along the contract curve, that at which the losses of the two banks are equal, on the grounds that they are symmetrical in all respects.
40 The authoritative account of these meetings is Moreau (1954).
41 Wicker (1966), pp. 110–11.
42 Hamlin Diaries (Library of Congress), XIV, pp. 12–13, July 25.
43 Hamlin Diaries, XIV, p. 29.
44 Hearings on Banking Systems, 1931, (Part VII), p. 132 and passim.
45 Eichengreen (1992), chapter 8.
46 For two recent statements of the view, see Field (1984) and Hamilton (1987).
47 Wicker (1966), p. 118. In terms of the model, this can be thought of as an instance where the cooperative solution C is too costly to sustain.
48 Goldenweiser Papers (Library of Congress), memorandum of 28 January 1928.

49 The Governor of the Federal Reserve Board was the 1920s equivalent of what is known today as the Chairman.

50 Harrison cited the fact the New York Fed had for many years changed its buying rate for bills 'without any question or disapproval by the Board'. Young retorted that 'he did not intend any longer to be a rubber stamp.' Harrison Papers, Conversations, vol. 1, memorandum of January 25, 1929, p. 3.

51 Recommendations of the Federal Advisory Council to the Federal Reserve Board, 28 September 1928, printed in *Annual Report of the Federal Reserve Board for 1928*, p. 229.

52 Harrison Papers, Open Market, Vol. 1, Letter from Roy Young to Gates W. McGarrah, Acting Chairman, Open Market Investment Committee, November 27, 1928.

53 Not only was this an attempt to force the hand of the Board, but Harrison noted that the commercial bankers who served as directors of the New York Fed would be placed in an embarrassing position if the Board held its decision overnight and the bankers were then to conduct securities transactions with the inside information that the New York Fed's rate might be raised subsequently. Hamlin Diary, XV, February 14, 1929, pp. 169–70; Harrison, Conversations, Vol. 1, memorandum of February 14, 1929.

54 Harrison Papers, Conversations, Vol. 1, memorandum of April 25, 1929, p. 1.

55 He reached a few of them by telephone at 3:00 in the morning. Stabilization of Commodity Prices, U.S. House Banking and Currency Committee, Subcommittee, hearings (72:1) (April 13, 1932), p. 475.

56 Hamlin Diaries, XVI, pp. 186–89, November 4–9, 1929.

57 Harrison Papers, Conversations, vol. 1, memorandum of November 15, 1929, p. 6.

58 Harrison Papers, Open Market, vol. 1, Letter from R. A. Young to George Harrison, November 13, 1929.

59 Harrison Papers, Miscellaneous, vol. 1, letter, November 25, 1929. For a more detailed account of this episode, see Friedman and Schwartz (1963), pp. 366–67.

60 In arguing that free gold mattered, I follow Wicker (1966) and Epstein and Ferguson (1984) but dissent from Friedman and Schwartz (1963). The free gold problem arose from the fact the Federal Reserve notes had to be collateralized with either gold or eligible (commercial) paper. Treasury securities did not qualify. Insofar as eligible paper fell below 60 per cent of Federal Reserve notes, the remaining share had to be backed with gold. The Fed's free gold fell to less than $400 million in late 1931 and early 1932, limiting the open market purchases that were feasible.

61 Those who had indulged in speculative excesses, in this view, should now be made to pay the price. Additional open market purchases would only reward and encourage the reckless, thereby setting the stage for another round of speculative excesses and leading eventually to another crash and an even more catastrophic slump. On the genesis of the liquidationist view, see DeLong (1990).

62 Harrison Papers, Discussion Notes, Meeting of the Board of Directors, 14 July 1932, pp. 273–4; Friedman and Schwartz (1963), p. 371.

63 See for example Wheelock (1988) for a recent statement of this view.

64 In terms of the analytical model of Section 3.1, this situation can be thought of

as one in which open market purchases have a large (and costly) impact on the first argument of the Chicago Fed's loss function $(B - \bar{B})$.
65 Harrison, Open Market, vol. II, minutes of meeting, April 12, 1932.
66 Harrison, Open Market, vol. II, minutes of meetings, May 17 and June 16, 1932.
67 Harrison, Open Market, vol. II, minutes of meetings, July 14, 1932 reported veiled threats by Boston and, especially, Chicago. Glass-Steagall had only eliminated restrictions on the 60 per cent of the backing that now could be made up of government securities as well as eligible bills, without eliminating the 40 per cent gold cover restriction that remained in place until Roosevelt suspended the gold standard in 1933.
68 Friedman and Schwartz (1963), p. 387.
69 In terms of the analytical model in Section 3.1, this can be thought of as forcing New York to accept a large value of $\bar{B}$, insofar as $\bar{B}$ can proxy not only for interest earnings but also for lender-of-last-resort capacity held in reserve.
70 Harrison, Discussion Notes, vol. II, Meeting of the Board of Directors, June 30, p. 252; Meeting of the Executive Committee, 5 July 1932, p. 257.
71 Harrison, Discussion Notes, Meeting of the Board of Directors, July 7, 1932, p. 265. Eichengreen (1992), chapter 10.
72 The account of the 1933 banking panic presented here draws on Eichengreen (1991), chapter 11.
73 This is the explanation for the 1933 banking crisis emphasized by Wigmore (1987), Temin (1989) and Eichengreen (1991) alike.
74 Wigmore (1987), Table 2.
75 New York was not the only reserve bank forced to limit its purchases of bills because of its low level of reserves. Chandler (1971, p. 219) mentions Philadelphia, Cleveland, Richmond, Atlanta, Kansas City and Dallas as other reserve banks all of which suffered from the same problem.
76 Wigmore (1987), p. 747.
77 James (1938), pp. 1062–3.
78 Wigmore (1987), p. 748.
79 Essentially the same point, in a somewhat different context, is made by Casella and Feinstein (1989). A similar point – that monetary policies have international spillovers that create inefficiencies when they are not taken into account – also applies, of course, in a situation in which nations have independent currencies. See for example the contributions to Buiter and Marston (1985). But one can argue that, so long as nations have independent currencies and retain the option of changing the exchange rate, they are better able to insulate themselves from these spillovers.

REFERENCES

Bentson, G., R. A. Eisenbeis, P. M. Horovitz, E. J. Kane and G. S. Kaufman (1986), *Perspectives on Safe and Sound Banking*, Cambridge, Mass.: MIT Press.
Bernanke, B. (1983), 'Nonmonetary Effects of the Financial Crisis in the Propagation of the Great Depression', *American Economic Review* **73**, 257–76.
Buiter, Willem and Richard Marston, eds. (1985), *International Economic Policy*

Coordination, Cambridge: Cambridge University Press.

Burgess, W. Randolph (1936), *The Reserve Banks and the Money Market*, New York: Harper & Brothers, revised edition.

Casella, Alessandra and Jonathan Feinstein (1989), 'Management of a Common Currency', in Marcello de Cecco and Alberto Giovannini (eds.), *A European Central Bank?*, Cambridge: Cambridge University Press, pp. 131–55.

Chandler, Lester V. (1957), *Benjamin Strong, Central Banker*, Washington, DC: Brookings Institution.

(1971), *American Monetary Policy, 1928–1941*, New York: Harper and Row.

Clark, Lawrence E. (1935), *Central Banking Under the Federal Reserve System*, New York: Macmillan.

Committee of Governors of the Central Banks of the Member States of the European Economic Community (1990), 'Draft Statute of the European System of Central Banks and of the European Central Bank', manuscript, 27 November.

DeLong, J. Bradford (1990), 'Liquidation' Cycles: Old-Fashioned Real Business Cycle Theory and the Great Depression', unpublished manuscript, Harvard University.

Eichengreen, Barry (1985), 'International Policy Coordination in Historical Perspective: A View from the Interwar Years', in Willem Buiter and Richard Marston (eds.), *International Economic Policy Coordination*, Cambridge: Cambridge University Press, pp. 139–78.

(1990), 'Couts et avantages de l'unification monetaire de l'Europe', in Pierre Beregovoy (ed.), *Vers l'union economique et monetaire europeenne*, Paris: Ministere de l'Economie des Finances et du Budget.

(1992), *Golden Fetters: The Gold Standard and the Great Depression, 1919–1939*, New York: Oxford University Press.

Epstein, Gerald and Thomas Ferguson (1984), 'Monetary Policy, Loan Liquidation, and Industrial Conflict: The Federal Reserve and the Open Market Operations of 1932', *Journal of Economic History* **44**, 957–84.

Field, Alexander J. (1984), 'Asset Exchanges and the Transactions Demand for Money, 1919–29', *American Economic Review* **74**, 43–59.

Friedman, Milton and Anna J. Schwartz (1963), *A Monetary History of the United States 1867–1960*, Princeton: Princeton University Press.

Hamilton, James (1987), 'Monetary Factors in the Great Depression', *Journal of Monetary Economics* **13**, 1–25.

Harris, S. E. (1933), *Twenty Years of Federal Reserve Policy*, Cambridge, Mass.: Harvard University Press.

James, F. Cyril (1938), *The Growth of Chicago Banks*, New York: Harper and Brothers.

Kemmerer, Walter (1938), *The ABC of the Federal Reserve System*, Princeton: Princeton University Press (11th edition).

Miron, Jeffrey (1989), 'The Founding of the Fed and the Destabilization of the Post-1914 U.S. Economy', in Marcello de Cecco and Alberto Giovannini (eds.), *A European Central Bank?* Cambridge: Cambridge University Press, pp. 290–327.

Moreau, Emile (1954), *Souvenirs d'un Gouverneur de la Banque de France*, Paris: M. T. Genin.

Temin, Peter (1989), *Lessons from the Great Depression*, Cambridge, Mass.: MIT Press.

Thygesen, Nils (1989), 'Decentralization and Accountability within the Central Bank: Any Lessons from the U.S. Experience for the Potential Organization of a European Central Banking Institution?' in Paul De Grauwe and Theo Peeters (eds.), *The EMU and European Monetary Integration*, London: Macmillan, pp. 91–114.

United States Congress, Committee on Banking and Currency of the House of Representatives, Subcommittee on Domestic Finance (1971), *Federal Reserve Structure and the Development of Monetary Policy, 1915–1935*, 92d Congress, First Session, staff report, Washington, DC: GPO.

Wheelock, David C. (1988), 'Interregional Reserve Flows and the Fed's Reluctance to use Open-Market Operations During the Great Depression', unpublished manuscript, University of Texas at Austin.

Wicker, Elmus (1966), *Federal Reserve Monetary Policy 1917–1933*, New York: Random House.

Wigmore, Barrie (1987), 'Was the Bank Holiday of 1933 Caused by a Run on the Dollar?' *Journal of Economic History* **47**, 839–56.

Discussion

BENNETT T. McCALLUM

Barry Eichengreen's paper provides a useful and authoritative account of operational difficulties generated in the early years of the Federal Reserve system by certain decentralized aspects of that organization's design. In particular, the failure to specify a single decision-making entity with unambiguous control of open market operations led on several occasions to courses of action that appear in retrospect to have been decidedly undesirable. In part the problem stemmed from decentralization *per se* and in part from the absence of clear and well-specified procedures, according to the paper, an absence that left the way open for regional reserve banks and the Washington-dominated Board (in its several manifestations) to take positions designed to gain power vis-à-vis each other, even at the expense of overall system policy objectives.

Eichengreen's historical account impresses me as interesting and of considerable importance. I have no major disagreement with the general outline of his story or his conclusions, but I do have a pair of reservations concerning the paper that are significant enough to warrant discussion.[1] The first of these concerns the 'analytical model' put forth in Section 3.1. In particular, it is unclear to me that this model provides a reliable vehicle for analysis of the type being undertaken. One weakness of the setup is that it is exceedingly static; it involves no explicit consideration of conditions expected to prevail in the future. But the main weakness involves the relationship between the reserve banks' loss function (1) and those of society, i.e., individual members of the economy's population. The expressions in (1) evidently represent objectives of the reserve banks, not society's, for the $(B - \bar{B})^2$ terms would not appear in an objective function designed to reflect the preferences of typical individuals. But then it is unclear what normative meaning can be given to the target levels of nominal income, $\bar{Y}$. The latter could differ from the level that is socially optimal and could do so in either direction. Thus it does not follow that outcomes in which $Y < \bar{Y}$ in the model actually imply policy stances that are too restrictive in terms of individuals' preferences.

My other main reservation can be expressed as a desire for additional help from the paper in understanding just how the early history of the Fed system relates to today's consideration and planning for a European central bank. In his concluding section, Eichengreen mentions four lessons or implications of the historical episodes for the design of a decentralized central bank, but consider what these four lessons are said to be. The first is 'the importance of close coordination among national central banks once monetary unification is achieved. Any attempt to decentralize monetary control ... creates the danger that their stabilization function will be under-provided' (p. 33).[2] Then the second implication 'is the importance of resolving in advance controversies over the focus of the control' (p. 33) and the third is that 'issues of autonomy and control should be addressed explicitly' (p. 34). Finally, the fourth implication 'is the importance of endowing any new institution with a model of the central banking function that is coherent and pertinent' (p. 34). The problem that I see with these lessons is not that they are unwise or incorrect, but rather that they are nonspecific and somewhat platitudinous. The second and third points, in particular, would seem to pertain to *any* central bank, centralized as well as decentralized – and also to any automobile producer, or economic research centre, or organization of almost any kind. Much the same could be said for the fourth lesson, moreover, if the words 'the central banking' were replaced with 'its.'[3] Admittedly the first of the four lessons does pertain specifically to a central banking entity, but even in this case it is unclear just how to develop the connection between the early Fed and the proposed European institution. One major problem is that these are central banks with very different responsibilities. Specifically, one of the most essential duties of the European central bank will be to prevent ongoing inflation – in other words, to provide a nominal anchor for the European price level.

But it was not a responsibility of the Fed's in the 1920s and 1930s to make basic decisions of this type, for the nominal anchor was provided by the gold-standard obligations that the Fed was legally charged to maintain. There are certainly additional duties of importance for central banks in today's regime of fiat money, but this function of controlling the average inflation rate is arguably the primary responsibility. So it is not the case that one can straightforwardly draw conclusions about the European central bank's committee design, its voting rules, or other critical constitutional provisions on the basis of the Fed's early experiences.

In conclusion, I would like to depart somewhat from the specifics of Eichengreen's paper in order to present an argument pertaining generally to the importance of central banking arrangements. In particular, I want to call attention to an argument first outlined in McCallum (1990, pp. 984–5) regarding the relationship between monetary and fiscal authorities. On this subject it is almost certainly true that the most fre-quently-cited publication of the last 15 to 20 years is the Sargent and Wallace (1981) paper entitled 'Some Unpleasant Monetarist Arithmetic.' As most readers will know, that paper included a few technical novelties, but its basic message was the suggestion that an economy's monetary authority cannot prevent inflation, by its own control of base money cre-ation, if an uncooperative fiscal authority adopts a course of action that implies a continuing stream of basic deficits. Formally, the paper empha-sizes that time paths of base money and fiscal (tax & spending) variables are unavoidably related via the government's budget identity, and points out that the relationship makes noninflationary money creation inconsis-tent with ongoing basic deficits.[4] Whether the central bank has control over inflation thus apparently depends upon, in the words of Sargent and Wallace, 'which authority moves first, the monetary authority or the fiscal authority? In other words, who imposes discipline on whom?' (1981, p. 7). Having posed the problem in this way, the Sargent-Wallace paper then goes on to suggest that it might well be the fiscal authority that dominates the outcome. In fact, the paper's analysis proceeds by simply assuming that the fiscal authority dominates, an assumption that is implemented by conducting the analysis with an exogenously given path of basic deficits. In this way the paper seems to suggest that even a determined central bank could be forced by a fiscal authority to create money along a different path than the one desired.

But is this actually possible? It is of course true that fiscal authorities may be able to bring *political* pressure to bear on central banks in ways that are difficult to resist. But the Sargent-Wallace analysis is not devel-oped along political lines; instead it seems to invite the reader to imagine that a politically independent central bank could be dominated in some sort of *technical* sense by a stubborn fiscal authority.

But a bit of thought about the hypothetical experiment indicates that such a conclusion is entirely unwarranted. The point is that an independent central bank is technically able to control its own path of base money creation, but fiscal authorities cannot directly control their own basic deficit magnitudes. For deficits are measures of spending in excess of tax collections; so if a fiscal authority embarks on a tax and spending plan that is inconsistent with the central bank's noninflationary creation of base money, it is the fiscal authority that will have to yield – because it does not have the purchasing power to carry out the planned expenditure. The fiscal authority does not have actual control over the instrument (the deficit) that it is presumed to control in the Sargent-Wallace experiment. Thus a truly determined monetary authority can always have its way, technically speaking, in monetary versus fiscal conflicts. This simple point implies that the design of a central bank's constitution is a matter of utmost importance, just as the existence of this conference volume would suggest.

NOTES

1 At the time of the conference, I had additional objections concerning (i) some econometric evidence pertaining to policy shifts occurring at times of organizational change and (ii) a sixth case study involving post-World War I inflation. Neither of these subsections appears, however, in the present version of the paper.
2 Eichengreen's language seems to associate underprovision of base money (relative to B) with 'underprovision of the stabilization function.' That usage seems unfortunate, since in actual economies an underprovision of stabilization might reflect a situation in which policy is excessively expansive.
3 Thus this lesson pertains to central banking only as a matter of syntax, not as a result of the logic of the discussion.
4 This result pertains to basic deficits, i.e., deficits measured exclusive of interest payments, but not to deficits measured in the conventional interest-inclusive manner (McCallum, 1984).

REFERENCES

McCallum, Bennett T. (1984), 'Are Bond-Financed Deficits Inflationary? A Ricardian Analysis', *Journal of Political Economy* **92**, 123–35.
(1990), 'Inflation: Theory and Evidence', in B. M. Friedman and F. H. Hahn (eds.), *Handbook of Monetary Economics*, Vol. II, Amsterdam: North-Holland Publishing Co.

Sargent, Thomas J., and Neil Wallace (1981), 'Some Unpleasant Monetarist Arithmetic', Federal Reserve Bank of Minneapolis *Quarterly Review* 5, 1–17.

EUGENE N. WHITE

The development of a European federal state by existing national governments represents an extraordinary political achievement. One of the few historical parallels is the formation and evolution of the United States. The operation of the American federal state has been the subject of experiment for over two hundred years, producing a large catalog of mistakes to be avoided. To analyze the dangers hiding in the stepwise formation of a European Central Bank, Barry Eichengreen draws upon the history of the Federal Reserve System – a federal central bank *par excellence* – to provide a cautionary tale for European policy makers. Although the institutional details are different, Eichengreen carefully extracts some key lessons from history to argue that federalized monetary control may be destabilizing. No one who reads the history of the Fed's early years of internecine strife can walk away without some concern for how the European Central Bank's Stage 2 will operate.

In this comment, I would like to suggest three qualifications to the concerns raised by Eichengreen's essay. First, the faulty design of the American federal bank was, in large part, the product of the nations' banking structure at the turn of the century. As Europe's banking structure is not as flawed, the centrifugal forces may not be as great. Secondly, while errors in the design of the Federal Reserve deserve attention, the role of a poor theoretical framework for policy should not be ignored. Lastly, in addition to monetary problems, federalizing the regulation and supervision of banking may create new problems, for which American history also provides a cautionary tale.

While the reasons for adopting a federal structure for a European central bank may be obvious, why the US chose a federal structure and why it had persistent problems is less well known. The Federal Reserve was not designed to accommodate any pre-existing monetary authority of the states. Its origins lie in the reform movement that followed the panic of

1907. The original architects – Senator Nelson Aldrich and his Wall Street advisors – felt that the greatest weakness of the banking system was the absence of a central bank. But, they were astute enough to realize that an institution patterned after European central banks would not be politically acceptable in the US because of the fear of domination by either Washington or New York.

To succeed in Congress, a central bank would have to be acceptable to the majority of banks, which numbered over 20,000 in 1913. No other industry was as well represented in every Congressional district as banking. To make the idea of a central bank palatable to bankers, Aldrich and his advisors proposed multiple reserve banks modelled after the clearing houses. The clearing houses were institutions familiar to all banks, which in addition to clearing and collecting checks had in times of panic helped to modestly expand liquidity. The Federal reserve banks thus seemed to bankers to be only improved private institutions (see West, 1977).

While the Federal Reserve system was ultimately more than an association of clearing houses, it was politically necessary to endow the bankers with considerable control in order to secure passage of the Federal Reserve Act. Consequently, the Board in Washington was appointed by the President, but the officials of the Federal Reserve banks were elected by member banks. The struggle for control persisted for two decades largely because the bankers had no desire to cede their share of control. It is noteworthy that the problem of governance was only eliminated when the banks were themselves crushed by the depression, permitting the passage of legislation to centralize power.

While most discussions of the Fed in the 1930s usually blame poor policy for its mistakes, Eichengreen focuses on structural flaws in governance as the source of the Fed's problems. The dispute over the control of policy between the Board and the Federal reserve banks certainly tarnished the Fed's public image, but it is hard to determine whether the structure of governance or incorrect theory were behind the Fed's mistakes. Although it is difficult to distinguish which of these two factors was more important, the crucial years 1929–33 are instructive.

Here the appropriate counterfactual to ask is what if authority over central banking functions had been wholly delegated to the Board of Governors and the reserve banks had acted as obedient branches. The outcome might have been worse because the Board followed misguided policies, which were only briefly offset by the New York Fed. When the stock market crashed in 1929, the New York Fed stepped in to ensure that liquidity did not dry up in the money markets. However, the bank took this step without the approval of the Board. The Board regarded this move as an act of insubordination with some members disapproving of the action itself. Had the Board been in complete charge, the Fed probably would not have quickly performed its duty as lender of last resort, permitting the crash to have much graver consequences for the economy. Throughout the depression, the New York Fed was more inclined to take what we would regard as the correct policy actions, in contrast to the Board and other Federal reserve banks. Centralization of authority could very well have worsened the Fed's performance.

The cautionary tale provided by Barry Eichengreen is a tale about monetary policy. However, it is important not to lose sight of the other functions of a central bank: the regulation, examination and supervision of banks. According to the current draft of the statues of the European Central Bank, monetary policy in Stage 3 will be completely centralized, but the other functions will be largely left to the national central banks. Each 'branch' will have the power to regulate, examine and supervise its own banks at home and their operations abroad. While monetary policy is clearly the premier task of a central bank, leaving these other functions to the new 'branches' of the European Central bank is not simply giving them an unimportant sop. The history of American banking regulation provides another cautionary tale about the dangers of multiple agencies. The history suggests that without centralized control the central bank 'branch' with the minimal regulatory and supervisory practices will set the standards for the Community.

The unfortunate history of the American regulation of banking can be briefly described. Until the Civil War, states chartered and regulated their own banks. The partial collapse of the banking system during the war led to the creation of a new federal agency of Office of the Comptroller of the Currency, which charters national banks. To crush the state banks, Congress placed a heavy tax on state bank notes, forcing most to close their doors or accept a national charter by 1870. The federal banking regulations were, however, far from minimal and states found it attractive to redesign their banking codes with weaker regulations. Over the next 25 years, the number of state banks grew rapidly; and by 1895 the number of state banks exceeded the number of national banks. Seeing federal preeminence slip away, Congress lowered the minimum capital reserve and other regulations for national banks in the Gold Standard Act of 1900 and the Federal Reserve Act of 1913 (see White, 1983). The competition between federal and state regulators thus relaxed banking regulations.

The creation of the Federal Reserve and later the Federal Deposit Insurance Corporation made matters more complicated. A commercial bank had the 'choice' of three federal regulators. The Comptroller of the Currency was the primary regulator for national banks, the Federal

Reserve for state member banks and the FDIC for non-member state banks. Each agency conducted its own examination and supervision of banks to ensure compliance with federal law and their own guidelines and regulations. Each agency jealously guarded its autonomy and regarded itself as the best. This divided authority posed no serious problems in the heyday of the New Deal banking system when banks activities were narrowly circumscribed. But in the 1960s, when innovation, competition and inflation began to erode the New Deal regime, the absence of any centralized banking regulator was a source of trouble. In this decade, American commercial banks began to seek expanded powers to offer more products and services. As banks were regulated by separate authorities, which possessed considerable autonomy and discretion, new powers were haphazardly granted to banks, creating a very uneven playing field.

Although the three federal agencies regulating commercial banks – the Federal Reserve, the OCC and the FDIC were all supposed to be operating with the same policy objectives, there were substantial differences in their practices. After a long and public dispute over whether to have frequent surprise call reports, President Johnson intervened, ordering the agencies to settle their differences. In 1964, the first Interagency Coordinating Committee was established. Yet this group only discussed issues, and it did not serve to coordinate practices (White, 1991). Each agency developed and maintained its own separate systems for rating bank loans and its own computerized analysis to detect liquidity and solvency problems. This minimal interagency cooperation sank to an all time low in the early 1970s when personal differences between the heads of the three agencies loomed large.

Effective efforts to coordinate these agencies came only when crises arose. After several large bank failures and a widespread weakening of the banking system, the Federal Financial Institutions Examination Council (FFIEC) was created in 1978 to promote uniformity in the supervision of banks. It was charged with producing uniform examination report forms, reporting systems, and common schools for examiners (Golembe and Holland, 1986). But FFIEC ran into each agency's ingrained view of its sovereignty and superiority. Although it increased uniformity, the council remained a collegial body where cooperation effectively required unanimity.

Maintaining different regulations for each class of banks is difficult. The weakest set of regulations tends to dominate the rest because banks can switch regulators by switching their affiliation, which in turn puts pressure on regulators to alter their rules. Attempting to attract jobs and capital, many states also get into the act, by altering banking regulations. In one notable example, South Dakota eliminated usury rates on consumer loans so that Citicorp and others would set up banks to handle their national credit card operations. Maintaining effective examination and supervision is also a problem. One salient example occurred when the United National Bank of Tennessee effectively gave the Comptroller the slip when it switched to a state charter and put itself under the FDIC's authority, only to have a spectacular failure later.

Given that the European central banks will have considerable autonomy and discretion in regulating their 'home' banks, American history should worry European policy makers. If a German bank opens offices in Italy, what will be the response of the Bank of Italy to complaints that German banks have a competitive advantage because of differences in accounting rules, examination practices and other regulations? What will happen if someday, an Italian bank decides to move its domicile from Italy to Germany to take advantage of the different regulations? Even if there is no centralized regulatory and supervisory authority, what sort of organization should be set up to coordinate policy?

In sum, while coordination problems for monetary policy may loom large, they can be eliminated by a more rapid transition to Stage 3 of the European Central Bank plan. Much more consideration needs, however, to be given to the proposed federal structure of banking regulation – or Europe may face some of the perils of American banking.

REFERENCES

Golembe, Carter H. and David S. Holland (1986), *Federal Regulation of Banking, 1986–87*, Washington, DC: Golembe Associates, Inc., pp. 34–37.

West, Robert Craig (1977), *Banking Reform and the Federal Reserve, 1863–1923*, Ithaca: Cornell University Press.

White, Eugene Nelson (1983), *The Regulation and Reform of the American Banking System, 1900–1929*, Princeton: Princeton University Press, Chapter 1.

    (1991), *The Comptroller of the Currency and the Revolution in Banking, 1960–1990*, Washington, DC: Office of the Comptroller of the Currency, Chapter 1.

3 The European Central Bank: reshaping monetary politics in Europe

ALBERTO ALESINA and VITTORIO GRILLI

1 Introduction

One of the most challenging tasks in the process of European integration is the creation of new institutions, such as the European Central Bank (ECB). Important and difficult questions need to be addressed in this process, such as: how independent should the European Central Bank be from political institutions? What voting rules should be adopted by the governing board of the ECB, when deciding about European monetary policy? How do we ensure that the preferences of European citizens will be reflected in the choice of policies of the ECB?

The governors of the twelve central banks of the EEC countries have recently proposed a statute for the ECB which provides some answers to these questions. The purpose of this paper is to address these issues and evaluate the proposed statute from the point of view offered by recent politico-economic models of monetary policy. In particular, we focus upon the trade-off between the objectives of low inflation and output stabilization.[1]

We begin by considering, as a benchmark, the situation in which the political integration of Europe has been completed, so that one can think of a 'European nation' with its legislature and executive. Following Rogoff (1985), we show that the legislature (universally elected in this new 'European nation'), has an incentive to set up an independent Central Bank, and to appoint a governor who is more 'inflation-averse' than the European median voter.

The proposed statute does indeed guarantee a very high level of independence to the ECB. Using the index of independence recently developed by Grilli et al. (1991), we show that the ECB, according to this statute, would be as independent as the Bundesbank currently is from the German government. In fact, the proposed institutional structure of the ECB will be very similar to the current one of the Bundesbank.

We then proceed to consider the more realistic situation in which the political integration of Europe is not complete. Different country members of the union and different groups within each country may have substantially different preferences over the conduct of monetary policy. We analyse how different voting rules for the appointment of the ECB board may lead to different policy outcomes. The proposed statute takes as given the fact that political integration in Europe is not complete. In fact, according to the statute, the executive committee of the ECB, including the President, will be appointed by the European Council, i.e. by the committee of the twelve Prime Ministers, and not by the European Parliament, i.e. a truly 'European' legislative body. Different voting rules, assigning different weights to the member countries, may lead to very different outcomes. We suggest that it is not at all clear that the proposed rules to appoint the board of the ECB and the voting rules within the board, will accurately represent the preferences of the European median voter.

The paper is organized as follows. In Section 2 we consider the choice of a Central Banker in a completely integrated, (politically and economically) Europe; we review Rogoff's (1985) argument which highlights the benefit of an 'independent' and 'conservative' Central Bank. In Section 3 we analyse in detail the proposed institutional structure of the ECB and, in particular, its degree of independence. In Section 4, we consider the situation in which Europe is not completely integrated economically and politically, so that different countries have different preferences over the conduct of monetary policy. In Section 5 we analyse how these different views of the EEC members can be aggregated in various voting schemes; we argue that the preferences of the European median voter may not be well captured by the decision process leading to the formulation of monetary policy, as proposed in the statute. The last section offers concluding comments.

2   The ECB in a politically unified Europe

2.1   Monetary policies in a political union

We first consider the situation in which Europe has achieved political unity so that the European Central Bank can be considered like the national central bank of a country called 'Europe'. Thus, this central bank will pursue goals and implement policies which are truly 'European' in nature. In this section we ignore issues such as the voting rules within the ECB board and the procedures to appoint the latter. We simply assume, for the moment, that in this hypothetical 'European nation', the legislature has appointed a board and a president of the ECB with preferences given below in equation (1). In specifying the economic framework and the Central Bank preferences we follow closely the analysis of Kydland and Prescott (1977), Barro and Gordon (1983) and Rogoff (1985). The preferences of the ECB president and board are given by:

$$\mathcal{L}_E = \tfrac{1}{2}\,\mathscr{E}[\pi_E^2 + b(x_E - \bar{x}_E)^2] \tag{1}$$

where $\mathcal{L}_E$ is the loss function, which depends upon the European inflation rate, π_E, and upon the deviation of European output, x_E, from a given level, $\bar{x}_E$. $\mathscr{E}(.)$ is the expectation operator. Output is determined according to the standard expectational Phillips curve relation:

$$x_E = (\pi_E - \pi_E^e) + \epsilon \tag{2}$$

where π_E^e is the expected rate of European inflation. In (2) we have assumed, without loss of generality, that the 'natural' level of output is zero, and we have set equal to 1 the partial derivative of output with respect to unexpected inflation. ϵ is a random shock with mean zero and variance equal to σ_ϵ^2. It is important to emphasize that the ECB, as well as society, has a target level of output $\bar{x}_E$ which is greater than what would be achieved by the economy without any unexpected inflationary shocks. This wedge between the market-generated, 'natural', level of output (i.e. zero), and the target level $\bar{x}_E$ can be justified by the existence of various distortions in the labour market, such as income taxation or trade unions. These distortions keep the level of employment and output below the level which would be achieved in a non-distorted economy. Thus, the policy-makers have an incentive to circumvent these distortions by generating unexpected inflation which raises the level of economic activity.[2]

The timing of events in this model is as follows: at the beginning of each period, wage contracts are set and, more generally, expectations about inflation are formed. Then, the shock ϵ is realized and observed by the ECB which sets the inflation rate based upon this information.[3] By assumption, wage contracts cannot be contingent on the realization of the shock, nor can they be indexed. Henceforth, to simplify notation, we drop the time subscripts. The time-consistent inflation policy in this set-up is given by:

$$\pi_E = b\bar{x}_E - \frac{b}{1+b}\,\epsilon \tag{3}$$

and the corresponding output level is:

$$x_E = \frac{1}{1+b}\,\epsilon \tag{4}$$

Equation (3) is obtained by substituting (2) into (1), taking the first-order conditions with respect to π_E and then imposing the condition of rationality of expectations.

Equations (3) and (4) highlight the well known time-consistency problem in this model. The term $b\bar{x}_E$ in (3) implies that the average inflation rate is above zero – its target value according to (1) – without any benefits in terms of average or variance of output.

The first-best policy, which would eliminate the inflation bias introduced by the term $b\bar{x}_E$, without reducing the extent of output stabilization, would instead be:

$$\pi'_E = -\frac{b}{1+b}\,\epsilon \tag{3'}$$

This is the inflation rule that the ECB would follow if it could make an irrevocable, and thus credible, commitment. The problem is, of course, that such a policy is time-inconsistent, thus not credible, because of the bank's incentive to generate unexpected inflation in an attempt to increase the average level of output.[4]

The crucial parameter which characterizes this trade-off between average inflation and variance of output is b. The lower this parameter in the Central Banker's objectives, the lower is the average rate of inflation, but the higher is the variance of output, which is given by

$$\sigma_x^2 = \frac{\sigma_\epsilon^2}{(1+b)^2}$$

If $b = 0$ the inflation bias is completely eliminated, but no stabilization is achieved. In this case, in fact, $\sigma_x = \sigma_\epsilon$, i.e. the variance of the shock is completely transmitted to output. A very important question is, then what 'b' should 'society' choose for the Central Bank? It is worthwhile to emphasize that throughout our discussion we disregard as unrealistic the possibility of making the first-best rule, (3'), credible, thus implementable. One important point that our stylized model captures is that the first-best rule may be reasonably complicated, i.e. it may go beyond a simple monetarist rule with a constant rate of money growth. For example, in our model the first-best rule is contingent upon the realization of a random shock; in reality more than one contingency might be relevant. One way of making a rule like (3') credible is to write it into the Central Bank's statute or, perhaps, into the country's constitution. However, it is not realistic to assume that a contingent, reasonably complex monetary rule can be inserted in an unchangeable statute. Obvious problems of supervision and enforcement, particularly if the economic shocks on which the rule is contingent are not easily observable, would make such an institutional arrangement ineffective, if not counterproductive.[5] In what follows we pursue, instead, the idea of choosing an agent with appropriate preferences, to whom the conduct of monetary policy is delegated.

2.2   The optimal ECB in a political union

Suppose now that European citizens vote upon what 'governor' to appoint. By assumption, each possible governor is associated with a different 'b' in his objective function. Thus, the voters in fact vote on what 'b' the Central Bank should have in its objective function. After this parameter (i.e. a governor) is chosen, the Central Bank is independent, that is, the governor can freely implement his desired policy; there is no possibility of recall, or of replacing the governor.[6] The voters differ only with respect to the relative weight which they assign to inflation and stabilization. For example, individual j has preferences given by:

$$\mathcal{L}_E^j = \tfrac{1}{2}\,\mathcal{E}[\pi_E^2 + b^j(x_E - \bar{x}_E)^2] \tag{5}$$

We assume that the voters will choose by majority rule the central banker, i.e. b. The chosen central banker, b is such that there is no other individual, b^i, preferred to b by a majority of voters in a pair-wise comparison. In this set up, majority voting on a pair-wise comparisons results in the selection of the governor most preferred by the voter with the median b in his utility function, i.e. b^m.[7]

Let us determine, therefore, which is the governor most preferred by the median voter. The median voter will prefer the governor who will implement the policy which minimizes his loss. Therefore the governor preferred by the median voter is obtained by solving the following problem:

$$\min_b \tfrac{1}{2}\,\mathcal{E}[\pi_E^2 + b^m(x_E - \bar{x}_E)^2]$$

If a Central Banker of 'type b' is appointed, he follows the policy rule given in (3) which leads to output level given in (4). Thus, using (3) and (4), we obtain:

$$\min_b \tfrac{1}{2}\,\mathcal{E}[(b\bar{x}_E - \frac{b}{1+b}\,\epsilon)^2 + b^m(\frac{1}{1+b}\,\epsilon - \bar{x}_E)^2] \tag{6}$$

The first-order condition implicitly defining the choice of b is given by:

$$b\bar{x}_E^2 - \frac{\sigma_\epsilon^2}{(1+b)^3}(b^m - b) = 0 \tag{7}$$

From this condition we notice that, since at $b = b^m$ the left hand side of (7) is positive, b must be less than b^m. Similarly, since at $b = 0$ the left hand side of (7) is negative, the optimal b must be positive. Therefore, the appointed ECB governor will be more 'conservative' than the median European voter, (i.e. he will value fighting inflation more than the median voter) but not a totally conservative one, i.e. $b > 0$. This argument generalizes to an explicit voting model a point originally made by Rogoff (1985); he showed that society's welfare is maximized if the conduct of monetary policy is delegated to an independent and 'moderately conservative' Central Banker.[8] By taking the total differential of (7) we can also show that:

$$\frac{\partial b}{\partial \sigma_\epsilon^2} = \frac{(b^m - b)}{(1 + b)^3 \left\{ \bar{x}^2 + \sigma_\epsilon^2 \dfrac{[1 + b^m + 2(b^m - b)]}{(1 + b)^4} \right\}} > 0 \qquad (8)$$

since $b^m > b$, and

$$\frac{\partial b}{\partial b^m} = \frac{\sigma_\epsilon^2}{(1 + b)^3 \left\{ \bar{x}^2 + \sigma_\epsilon^2 \dfrac{[1 + b^m + 2(b^m - b)]}{(1 + b)^4} \right\}} > 0 \qquad (9)$$

Thus, the more the median voter is concerned with output (i.e. the higher is b^m) and the more volatile is output (i.e. the higher is σ_ϵ^2) the less conservative is the Central Banker which would be chosen in equilibrium by majority rule.

Finally, it should be stressed that in order to delegate monetary policy to an agent with preferences which are different from those of the majority of the voters, the agent must be independent. Otherwise, the median voter would want to 'recall' the Central Banker when the latter is trying to implement the conservative monetary rule. Therefore, it is important that delegation to the Central Bank is credible. Thus, we now turn to an analysis of the degree of independence of the ECB, according to the proposed statute.

3   The independence of the ECB

Measurement of the degree of autonomy of a Central Bank is far from straightforward, since there does not exist a single indicator that can properly take into account all the different aspects which are relevant in this respect. We have chosen to follow the criteria proposed by Grilli, Masciandaro and Tabellini (1991), where a distinction is introduced between political independence and economic independence of a monetary institution.[9]

3.1   Political independence of the ECB

Political independence is defined as the ability of a Central Bank to choose its economic policy objectives autonomously, without constraints or influence from the government. First, an important element protecting the autonomy of a Central Bank is the guarantee for the governor and for the board of directors of a sufficiently long term of office. Short terms of office could make the directorate of the bank more vulnerable to political opportunistic pressures because of the almost constant uncertainty about their reappointment.[10] In addition, short appointments increase the likelihood that every government (even a short-lived one) appoints a new Central Banker; this would increase the volatility in the conduct of monetary policy (Alesina, 1989). The proposed statute of the ECB sets the term of office for the President at eight years (Art. 11.2), the same as for the Bundesbank. For all the other Central Banks with a specific duration at the President's office, the term is shorter; for example, in the UK it is five years and in Spain it is four years. In Italy, France and Denmark, the governor's mandate does not have an explicit duration. This, however, does not imply a life appointment. On the contrary, as has happened in the past, this could facilitate sudden dismissal of the governor.

Turning now to the board of the ECB, we first notice that the statute of the ECB envisages the creation of two different decision-making bodies: the Council and the Executive Committee, which is a subset of the Council. The Executive Committee is supposed to be elected by the European Council of Prime Ministers for an eight-year term. The other members of the Council are the twelve governors of the EEC national central banks. The duration of their mandate, therefore, will depend on the various national regulations. However, the ECB stature prescribes (Art. 14) a minimum term of five years for all the Council's members. This will require changes in the statutes of the banks of Greece and Spain for which the current term of the governor is four years. The eight-year term of the ECB board is identical to the term of the board of the Bundesbank, and is longer than that of any other European country. For example, in France it is six years, in the UK it is four and in Italy it is three.

A second important factor determining the autonomy of a central bank from political pressures is whether the statute of the bank prescribes an explicit participation of the government in monetary policy decisions. This participation could be in the form of the requirement of a formal approval by the government of monetary policy and/or in the form of the presence of government officials on the central bank board. The proposed statute of the ECB explicitly forbids any representative of the European Council to be part of the ECB's Council (Art. 15.1). The statute only allows the passive presence, i.e. without vote, of a small number of EEC officials at the Board meetings. Moreover, the statute does not require approval of monetary policy either by the EEC institutions, or by national governments. In fact, it explicitly forbids (Art. 7) the members of the ECB's Board to receive any instructions from either community or national political institutions. These regulations are very similar to those of the Bundesbank, and are much stricter than most of the other EEC Central Banks. For example, both in France and in the UK, government representatives are part of the respective Central Bank boards, and monetary policy must be explicitly approved by the government.

In addition, the ability of a Central Bank to pursue its own objectives without political interference is enhanced if these objectives are explicitly stated in the Central Bank statute and thus cannot be easily and arbitrarily changed by the particular government in power. Article 2.1 of the ECB statute states that the main objective of the ECB is price stability. Again, the similarity between the proposed ECB and the Bundesbank is evident. Amongst the EEC countries, only the Central Banks of Denmark and the Netherlands, in addition to the Bundesbank, have the objective of price stability explicitly stated in their statutes. The statement of general price stability objective in the statute of the ECB, although important, is far from a guarantee that the first-best, i.e. the zero average inflation policy given in (3'), becomes enforceable. In our opinion, the statement of price stability as a 'main objective' should be interpreted simply as a measure to protect the ECB board against unavoidable political pressures to pursue short-run expansionary policies, particularly in times of economic distress. It is therefore a way of increasing the independence of the ECB but, by itself, cannot eliminate the time-consistency problem. If credibility problems could be avoided, and first-best policies implemented, by simply writing general objectives into Central Bank statutes, we would not observe so much discussion on monetary institutions and monetary controls.

3.2   Economic independence of the ECB

The second dimension of autonomy of a Central Bank is its economic independence, that is, the ability to use without restrictions monetary policy instruments to pursue monetary policy goals. Specifically, the most important and common constraint to the daily management of monetary policy derives from the Central Bank's obligation to finance public deficits. This constraint is particularly important for countries with high levels of public debt, like Belgium, Ireland and Italy. The similarity between the ECB and the Bundesbank, in this respect also, is quite

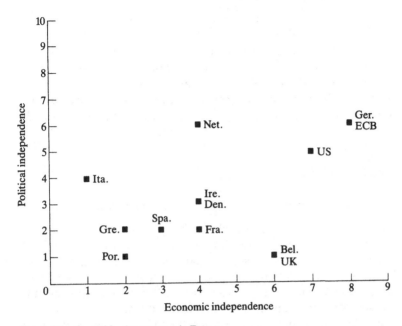

Figure 3.1   Central bank autonomy in Europe

striking. In particular, Article 21.1 forbids the ECB to open lines of credit to community or national public institutions, even on a temporary basis. The same article bans the ECB from participating in the primary market for national government bonds. The ECB is allowed to participate only in secondary markets for government bonds to implement 'open market operations.' This arrangement is very different from the situation in France and Italy, for example, where the Central Banks are allowed to grant credit facilities to their Finance Ministries.

Tables 3A.1 and 3A.2 in the Appendix summarize the political and economic independence of the ECB and compare it to that of the other EEC central banks and the US Federal Reserve. The results of these tables are plotted in Figure 3.1. As already mentioned at the beginning of this section, these indexes must be interpreted with caution. For example, while from the tables the Bundesbank and the Federal Reserve may appear to be highly independent, they are still subject to political inter-ference. As it should be clear from the discussion above, however, the similarities between ECB and the Bundesbank are pervasive. In fact, according to our classification, they practically coincide, and they are far more independent than any other EEC central bank.

In conclusion, if the ECB is created according to this proposed statute, its level of independence will be very high and thus its ability to credibly pursue its objectives should be guaranteed.

Empirical results presented in Bade and Parkin (1982), Alesina (1989), Alesina and Summers (1990) and Grilli, Masciandaro and Tabellini (1991), suggest that independent Central Banks have out-performed more dependent ones. In particular, independent Central Banks appear to have been quite successful in maintaining a low inflation rate without high costs in terms of output stabilization or growth.

4   The ECB without a political union

4.1   Evaluating common monetary policy without a political union

Up to this point we have considered the choice of a common monetary policy in the context of a politically unified Europe. In fact, we have assumed that both the policy decisions and their welfare evaluation were based on a 'European' loss function, given in equation (1). However, in the transition phase before a political union, different countries will still have strong national and political identities and it is therefore likely that the effects of common monetary policies will also be assessed on the basis of national welfare and preferences. In other words, while monetary policy will be set at the European level, thus following (1) and (2), each country will evaluate the consequence of the policy according to its national welfare function, which can be represented by:

$$\mathcal{L}^i = \tfrac{1}{2}\,\mathcal{E}[\pi_E^2 + \beta_i\,(y_i - \bar{y}_i)^2] \tag{10}$$

where

$$y_i = (\pi_E - \pi_E^e) + \mu_i \tag{11}$$

y_i is the output level of country i and μ_i is a country-specific stochastic shock. Notice that, being in a common currency world, we have assumed that inflation is the same in all countries, equal to the European level π_E.[11] Substituting the ECB-time consistent policy given by (3) into (11) and (10) we obtain:

$$\mathcal{L}^i = \tfrac{1}{2}\,\mathcal{E}[(b\bar{x}_E - \frac{b}{1+b}\,\epsilon)^2 + \beta_i\,(\mu_i - \frac{b}{1+b}\,\epsilon - \bar{y}_i)^2] \tag{12}$$

which represents the welfare level achieved by country i when monetary policy is decided at the European level, according to the rule given in (3). We can compare (12) with the loss that would be suffered if, instead, monetary policies were to remain under national control. Following a procedure identical to the one employed to derive (3), we obtain that, in this case, the time-consistent inflation policy for country i is:

$$\pi_i = \beta_i \bar{y}_i - \frac{\beta_i}{1 + \beta_i} \mu_i \tag{13}$$

Output would then be given by:

$$y_i = \frac{1}{1 + \beta_i} \mu_i \tag{14}$$

Therefore, the loss in this scenario is given by:

$$\mathcal{L}_N^i = \tfrac{1}{2} \mathcal{E} \left[\left(\beta_i \bar{y}_i - \frac{\beta_i}{1 + \beta_i} \mu_i \right)^2 + \beta_i \left(\frac{1}{1 + \beta_i} \mu_i - \bar{y}_i \right)^2 \right] \tag{15}$$

Subtracting (15) from (12) we obtain the difference in welfare between a monetary union and a world in which monetary policies are set at the national level:[12]

$$\mathcal{L}^i - \mathcal{L}_N^i = \tfrac{1}{2} \left[\bar{x}^2 (b^2 - \beta_i^2) + (1 + \beta_i) \left\{ \left(\frac{b}{1+b} \right)^2 \sigma_\epsilon^2 - \left(\frac{\beta_i}{1 + \beta_i} \right)^2 \sigma_\mu^2 \right\} \right.$$
$$\left. - 2\beta_i \left\{ \left(\frac{b}{1+b} \right) \sigma_{\epsilon\mu} - \left(\frac{\beta_i}{1 + \beta_i} \right) \sigma_\mu^2 \right\} \right] \tag{16}$$

where σ_μ^2 is the variance of μ_i and $\sigma_{\epsilon\mu}$ the covariance between μ_i and ϵ. Notice that, to economize notation, we dropped the subscript i on σ_μ. For simplicity, we have also assumed $\bar{x}_E = \bar{y}_i \equiv \bar{x}$.

4.2 Country-specific costs of common monetary policies

Equation (16) highlights two distinct components of the difference in welfare under a monetary union instead of deciding monetary policy independently. The first component depends on political divergencies, i.e. differences in preferences as represented by differences between b and β_i. The second component depends on economic dissimilarities as summarized by σ_ϵ, σ_μ and $\sigma_{\epsilon\mu}$.

Consider first the political differences, and to better focus on them let us eliminate the economic differences by assuming $\mu_i = \epsilon$ in all states of the world, so that $\sigma_\mu^2 = \sigma_\epsilon^2 = \sigma_{\epsilon\mu} \equiv \sigma^2$. Then (16) becomes:

$$\mathcal{L}^i - \mathcal{L}_N^i = \tfrac{1}{2} \left[\bar{x}^2 (b^2 - \beta_i^2) + \sigma^2 \left(\frac{b}{1+b} - \frac{\beta_i}{1 + \beta_i} \right) \left(\frac{1 + \beta_i}{1+b} b - \beta_i \right) \right] \tag{17}$$

Equation (17) reveals that participation in a monetary union can improve welfare if the ECB preferences are more conservative than the national preferences, i.e. $b < \beta_i$. This is a restatement of the result of Section 2. A monetary union can be beneficial if it allows countries to 'buy' credibility for anti-inflationary policies. Therefore, the countries that have more to gain from a monetary union, in this respect, are the one with higher inflation biases.

We now turn to the economic differences. Assume, therefore, the absence of political differences, i.e. $\beta_i = b$ (and $\bar{x}_E = \bar{y}_i$ as before). Then, (16) reduces to:

$$\mathcal{L}^i - \mathcal{L}^i_N = \tfrac{1}{2}\left[\frac{b^2}{1+b}\left(\sigma^2_\epsilon + \sigma^2_\mu - 2\rho_i\sigma_\epsilon\sigma_\mu\right)\right] \tag{18}$$

where ρ_i is the correlation coefficient between μ_i and ϵ. Consider first the case in which the two shocks are perfectly positively correlated, i.e. $\rho_i = 1$. Then (18) becomes:

$$\mathcal{L}^i - \mathcal{L}^i_N = \tfrac{1}{2}\left[\frac{b^2}{1+b}\left(\sigma_\epsilon - \sigma_\mu\right)^2\right] \tag{19}$$

Therefore, if there are differences between the variance of national and European output, the welfare of the country will be lower in a monetary union. The intuition is clear; if $\sigma_\epsilon > \sigma_\mu$ then the ECB will be stabilizing too much from the perspective of country i while if $\sigma_\epsilon < \sigma_\mu$ the ECB will not be stabilizing enough.

Consider now the case in which European and national output have the same variability, but are not necessarily perfectly correlated, i.e. $\sigma^2_\mu = \sigma^2_\epsilon = \sigma^2$, but $\rho_i \neq 1$. In this case, (18) reduces to:

$$\mathcal{L}^i - \mathcal{L}^i_N = \tfrac{1}{2}\left[\frac{b^2}{1+b}\,\sigma^2_\epsilon\left(1 - \rho_i\right)\right] \tag{20}$$

Therefore, the smaller is the correlation between μ_i and ϵ the worse off country i is made by its participation in the monetary union. This is because, if ρ_i is low, the ECB will be constantly either over or under stabilizing from the point of view of country i. For example, in the extreme case of perfect negative correlation the ECB would be, contracting when country i experiences a recession, and expanding when country i experiences a boom.

Summarizing, the costs of joining a monetary union depend on the differences in behaviour between national and European output. The larger the differences in output variances and the lower the correlation between domestic and European output, the higher is the potential cost of being part of a monetary union.

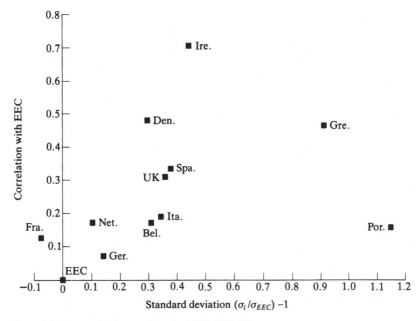

Figure 3.2 Economic distance from the EEC, 1970–89

Following this line of argument, in Figure 3.2 we measure the 'economic distance' from the EEC of the twelve EEC countries according to the standard deviations and the correlation coefficients of the growth rate of their outputs.

Some caution is necessary when inspecting Figure 3.2, since the output series that we observe are the result of national monetary policy which should be excluded from analysis. In fact, output variances and correlations reflect the type and degree of intervention that the national monetary authorities have exerted over the last 20 years.

Figure 3.2 shows that the countries which have more to lose from a monetary union, from a stabilization point of view, are the countries at the periphery of Europe: Greece, Portugal and Ireland, while the least affected will be France, Germany and The Netherlands.

This conclusion, however, does not take into account the 'credibility gains,' discussed above, that can result from a participation in the union, which could compensate for the 'economic distance' from the EEC.[13] In Table 3.1 we report, for each country, our index of 'economic distance' from the EEC, together with the degree of independence of its central bank and its inflation performance during the 1980s. From this table emerges the interesting fact that the countries that have more to lose from

Table 3.1. *Economic distance from the EEC*

	Absolute distance from EEC[a]	Inflation in 1980s %	Central Bank Independence Political + economic
EEC			14
France	0.15	8.40	6
Germany	0.16	3.11	14
Netherlands	0.20	3.35	10
Belgium	0.35	5.58	7
Italy	0.39	12.80	5
UK	0.47	7.71	7
Spain	0.50	11.36	5
Denmark	0.56	7.47	7
Ireland	0.83	10.90	7
Greece	1.02	20.96	4
Portugal	1.16	19.27	3

	Simple correlation coefficient	Rank correlation coefficient
Distance, inflation	0.86	0.69
Distance, independence	−0.66	−0.66
Inflation, independence	−0.82	−9.93

Note: [a] Computed as: $\left[\left(\dfrac{\sigma_i}{\sigma_{EEC}}\right)^2 + (1 - \rho_i)^2\right]^{1/2}$

the stabilization point of view are also the ones that could gain more in terms of credibility of their monetary policies. For example, Portugal, Greece, Ireland and Spain are among the countries with the largest distance from the EEC and, at the same time, the countries with the most dependent central banks and highest inflation. The simple correlation coefficient between distance and inflation is 0.86, and between distance and central bank independence is −0.66. An important question which can be raised regarding this 'credibility gains' explanation of the monetary union is why the countries who do not need credibility, i.e. the 'low β' countries would want to join the union. Even though, according to Table 3.1, the 'low β' are also those more correlated with Europe, thus have less to lose, it is not clear why they would want to engage in this process. The answer has to be that they gain on other grounds, such as the reduction of transaction costs and monetary uncertainty (see Casella, 1991) or the gain from cooperation in monetary policy, which are not explicitly modelled here. More generally, a widely shared view (see Krugman, 1989, for instance) of the process of European economic integration, is that the economic gains are only one part of the story and, perhaps, not the most important. Long-run political gains resulting from the creation of a 'European nation' may be important considerations.

4.3 Appointing the EBC Council without a political union

In the analysis above we have assumed that the characteristic of the ECB (i.e. b) is exogenously given. However, the ECB policy will be decided by a Council that is composed by the national central bank governors. Therefore, each country has the opportunity to participate and affect the policy choice through its central bank governor. Through the choice of the central bank governor, therefore, each country has the opportunity to compensate for its 'economic distance' from the EEC by appointing a governor with appropriate preferences. Given that the ECB Council decisions are taken under majority rule, the policy that will be implemented is the one that is (ex-post) preferred by the 'median' Council member. Therefore, the intensity of preference of each governor does not matter for the policy decision and, thus, a country does not have any strategic incentive to misrepresent its own preferences (in addition to the reasons discussed above). Consequently, the optimal appointment of governor for country i is formally obtained by selecting a governor with a b that minimizes (12). The first-order condition determining this choice is given by:

$$b\bar{x}_E^2 + (1 + \beta_i)\frac{b}{(1 + b)^3}\sigma_\epsilon^2 - \frac{\beta_i}{(1 + b)^2}\sigma_{\epsilon\mu} = 0 \qquad (21)$$

Taking the total differential of (21) it can be shown that:

$$\frac{\partial b}{\partial \sigma_\mu} = \frac{\beta_i \rho_i \sigma_\epsilon}{(1 + b)\{(1 + 3b)\bar{x}^2 + (1 + \beta_i)\sigma_\epsilon^2/(1 + b)^3\}} > 0 \qquad (22)$$

$$\frac{\partial b}{\partial \rho_i} = \frac{\beta_i \sigma_\epsilon \sigma_\mu}{(1 + b)\{(1 + 3b)\bar{x}^2 + (1 + \beta_i)\sigma_\epsilon^2/(1 + b)^3\}} > 0 \qquad (23)$$

Therefore, the smaller the variance of domestic output, and the smaller the correlation between domestic and European output, the more conservative will be the representative chosen for the ECB Council. This is because, if the correlation is low, country i would prefer an ECB which does not stabilize much, since the latter would often stabilize in the wrong direction from the point of view of country i.

We now turn to examine how the objective function of the ECB will be determined, according to the proposed procedures.

5   Voting on European monetary policy

The proposed rules concerning the appointment and voting procedures of the board of the ECB are as follows. The Board is composed of 18 members: the 12 governors of the national central banks plus six members, including the Governor of the ECB, who are appointed by the European Council. These six members also form the Executive Committee of the ECB. The Board votes by majority rule, one person one vote. The Governor's vote has a tie-breaking power. The only exception to the 'one person one vote' rule concerns decisions over the allocation of the seigniorage across countries.

The draft of the statute (at least the version which has been made public), does not specify explicitly the voting rule which has to be adopted by the European Council in choosing the six members which form the Executive Committee of the ECB. Presumably, this voting rule will reflect the relative size of the members of the EEC.[14] The European Council usually deliberates using a qualified majority rule, in which a proposal needs more than 70 per cent of the votes to be approved. The weights are designed so that the four biggest countries alone (Germany, France, United Kingdom and Italy) do not have the required 70 percent majority.

The proposed composition of board clearly reflects that the authors of the statute had two goals in mind. On one hand, they intended to guarantee a 'voice' to every country, even the smallest ones, by including every governor of the national central banks. On the other hand, if the board were composed only by these 12 central bankers, the smaller countries would be overrepresented. The six members, including the Governor, reequilibrate the weights.

An important question can then be asked: how successful will this system of appointments and voting rules be in representing the views of the European voters? The following simple example suggests that such rules may be quite unsuccessful in reflecting the preferences of the European voters. Suppose, for the sake of simplicity, and no loss of generality, that the twelve countries were of equal size. Suppose that in each country there were two parties, 'left' (L) and 'right' (R). In seven countries R has a 51% plurality and holds the position of Prime Minister. In five countries L has a 55% plurality and the Prime Minister. In this case, in a politically unified Europe, L would have a majority. With the proposed rules, instead, the governor and the executive board would be elected by an R majority in the European Council of Prime Ministers. This is of course, a well known problem in the context of election of legislatures with a district system.[15]

In order to emphasize how different outcomes may result from differing voting rules, we have considered, as an example, the results of the last general elections in the twelve EEC countries. We proceeded as follows. In each country we have divided the political parties into five groups: (1) 'extreme left' (EL) which includes communist parties, other minor extremists groups and radical 'green' parties; (2) 'left' (L) which includes socialists and social democratic parties; (3) 'Christian Democrats' (CD) which includes Christian Democratic parties and other centre parties; (4) 'right' (R) which includes conservative parties; and (5) 'extreme right', which includes all the right wing extremist groups.

An important assumption in the discussion which follows, is that parties can be 'aggregated' across nations; that is, for instance, we assume that all the socialist parties in the twelve countries are relatively similar to each other. It should be emphasized that parties aggregate themselves in groups in the European Parliament. In our classification we followed, whenever applicable, this European Parliament grouping.

Clearly, some 'judgment calls' are needed to make our classification, but none of these judgment calls affect the qualitative nature of the issues which we raise. In Table 3A.3 in the Appendix we illustrate our classification for the twelve countries, and we report the percentage of votes and of seats obtained in the last election.

Consider for example the case of Italy, in which the last general elections were held in June 1987. These were the results:

		% Shares	Seats
EL:	Communists, DP, Greens	30.8	138
L:	Socialists, Radical Party,	23.6	143
	Social Democratic Party, Republican Party		
CD:	Christian Democrats,	35.7	237
	Sud Tirol Party		
R:	Liberal Party	2.1	11
ER:	MSI	5.9	35

(Vote shares add to less than 100% due to minor unclassified parties)

We then identify the 'median voter'. In terms of shares, the median is such that on the left of the median we have EL + 82% of L; on the right of the median we have 18% of L + CD + R + ER. We indicate this median in terms of *shares* (m(sh)) with L19, which indicates that the median lies

Table 3.2. *'Median voters' in Europe*

	$m(sh)$[1]	$m(seats)$[2]	PM[3]	Population weights[4]
Belgium	CD 48	CD 35	CD	3.1
Denmark	CD 57	CD 66	R	1.6
France	L 4	L 23	L	17.2
Germany	CD 90	CD 91	CD	18.8
Greece	L 5	R 100	R	3.1
Ireland	R 78	R 89	R	1.1
Italy	L 19	L 20	CD	17.7
Luxembourg	CD 70	CD 69	CD	0.1
Netherlands	CD 66	CD 66	CD	4.5
Portugal	CD 91	CD 84	CD	3.2
Spain	L 20	L 20	L	12.0
UK	CD 15	R 85	R	17.6
EU	CD 80	CD 56[5] CD 33/15[6]		

Notes:
1 $m(sh)$ = median in shares. See text for the definition.
2 $m(seats)$ = median in seats. See text for the definition.
3 PM = political orientation of the current (March 1991) Prime Minister.
4 Population weights = percentage shares of the population of each country in 1988. *Source*: IMF, *IFS*. We do not consider former East Germany since the electoral results considered are pre-German unification.
5 Weighted median.
6 Unweighted median. Since there is an even number of members the median is given by the fourth and fifth CD members, counting from the left.

within the L group with 19 per cent of it on the right of the median. the analogous procedure applied to seats leads to a median in *seats* ($m(seats)$) equal to L20. The fact that the two medians are basically identical underlines the high degree of proportionality of the Italian electoral system.

The first two columns of Table 3.2 report our computations of $m(sh)$ and $m(seats)$ for the twelve countries. These calculations are derived from the information provided in Table 3A.3 in the Appendix. The third column identifies the political orientation of the Prime Minister of the twelve countries. The last column reports the share, in percentage, of the population. As an illustration consider $m(sh)$ of Denmark and The Netherlands. The former is CD57, indicating that 57 percent of CD parties are on the right of the median. This indicates a more right wing median than that of The Netherlands in which 66 percent of CD parties are on the right of the median.

The last line of the Table reports the European median in shares, obtained by computing (using the population weights given in the last column of the Table) the shares of different parties; the third column in this line reports the median for the case of a 'one person one vote' rule in the European Council of the Prime Ministers, and for the case of a vote weighted by the population shares.[16]

The picture emerging from Table 3.2 is quite interesting. The European median in vote shares, m(sh), is significantly on the left of the median of the European council, particularly for the case of unweighted votes. The median in terms of shares is close to the extreme left of the CD group, while the weighted median of the council of Prime Minister is around the middle of the CD group and the unweighted median is on the right of the CD group. In different words, the EL and L combined have about 44 percent of European votes (see Table 3A.3) but less than 30 percent in a weighted vote of the Prime Ministers and 15 percent in an unweighted vote in the European Council.

Let us now consider the Board of the ECB, and let us assume (with a wisp of faith) that the governors of the national Central Banks somehow reflect the preferences of the Prime Minister of their countries. Since this Council votes with a 'one man one vote' rule, the share of the 'left' will be somewhere between the 15 percent unweighted share and the 30 percent weighted share. It would be 15 percent if only national governors were in the Board; 30 percent if all the members of the board were appointed by a weighted vote in the European Council.

The possibility of large discrepancies between medians is even more emphasized by the following hypothetical example. Suppose that an election were held in France and the Socialists fell from the current 49 to say, 43 percent of the vote, leading to a victory of conservative bloc, which gains the Prime Minister position.[17] With everything else unchanged, this would imply that the European Left (EL and L) would now have about 42 percent of the popular vote, less than 12 percent of a weighted vote, and less than 10 percent in an unweighted vote of the European Council, since only Spain would have a 'L' prime minister. With this change in France the last line of Table 3.2 would read: CD 77; CD 18 and CD 15 respectively. This difference is remarkable: in terms of shares only one-fifth of CD would be needed to achieve a left wing majority, in terms of Prime Ministers only a sixth of the CD votes would be needed to achieve a right wing majority.[18] In any way one looks at this situation, it is clear that the almost 50 percent of left voters would be vastly underrepresented in the Board of the ECB.

Two important caveats, however, mitigate the extent of these observations. First, the strong Socialist minorities in countries where the Prime

Minister is non-Socialist, have some influence on policy-making. In one country (Italy) the Socialists are a powerful member of the coalition government and clearly influence the Prime Minister's behaviour in the European Council. More generally, governing parties cannot completely ignore opposition views, particularly if the opposition is strong.

Second, the ideological distance between parties, say Socialists and Conservatives, may be declining, and may be less important than 'national' differences of interests regarding monetary policy. If this is the case, what really matters is the allocation of voting rights between countries, regardless of who is the Prime Minister. However, results by Alesina and Roubini (1990) suggest that partisan differences on economic policies remain significant in several OECD economies.[19]

In summary, this section has highlighted a very simple but important point. The current decision-making rules for the European Community, including the appointment of the executive committee of the ECB, are such that the allocation of 'power' between parties may depart substantially from the relative plurality at the European level of the same parties. This is a feature which is not uncommon in district systems, but the specific nature of the European Council composed in a sense by only 12 'districts,' is more likely to create large discrepancies between the division of 'seats' in the board of the ECB and the shares of popular votes in Europe. In the example which we examined based on current electoral results, the left was disadvantaged. This does not mean, at all, that there is an anti-left bias in the rules. In fact, we would have found the opposite bias, if we had looked at the situation in the late seventies. Thus, it would be incorrect to argue that these voting rules achieve the 'conservative bias' which may be desirable for monetary policies.

This problem occurs, obviously, because the political integration of Europe is far from complete, so that a 'European' government is not formed within a European Parliament with a true legislative function and elected in universal European ballots. Note that we are not necessarily advocating that the truly empowered European Parliament should be elected with a proportional system, in which case the above mentioned discrepancies between medians would disappear by definition. However, even if, say, an English style district system were to be adopted, one certainly would not choose to have 12 districts coinciding with the current twelve country members of the EEC. In other words, there is a tension between a completely unified monetary policy and voting rules over monetary policy which appear dictated by the present European reality of politically independent member states.

6 Conclusions

In a politically unified Europe, the ECB should be an independent 'agent' to whom the European government delegates the conduct of monetary policy. The governor of the ECB should be appointed by the European Parliament and should be chosen such that his preferences are more anti-inflationary than the European median voter. In fact the median voter would vote for a Central Banker more 'conservative' than himself. The appointment process, by virtue of a universally and directly elected European Parliament would ensure that the preferences of European voters would be reflected in the conduct of monetary policy.

We have examined how the ECB as described by the proposed statute will conform to this ideal. We can summarize our argument in three basic points.

First, the proposed statute will guarantee a substantial amount of political independence to the ECB. We concluded that the ECB, according to this statute, will be as independent from national and European political institutions as the Bundesbank. In fact, the proposed statute is in many respects quite similar to that of Bundesbank. Certainly, it is much more similar to the latter than to any other Central Bank in EEC countries.

Second, we emphasized that in a situation in which the EEC is not completely unified economically and politically, different member countries may have substantially different preferences over the conduct of monetary policy. For example, we argued that countries at the periphery of Europe, such as Greece, Ireland and Portugal may have to pay the highest costs of giving up their monetary independence. However, these are also countries which will obtain high benefits in terms of 'credibility' of anti-inflationary policies. In addition, different parties within each country, in general will disagree over the conduct of the European monetary policy.

Third, we argued that the proposed system of appointment of the ECB Board and the voting rules within the Board, may lead to decisions which could be quite far from the preferences of the European median voter. For example, using the last election results in the twelve countries, we showed that the European left would be vastly under-represented in the ECB Board, relative to the proportion of votes received by the left in national elections. These discrepancies, which can be quite substantial, occur because the Board is not appointed by a legislative body elected in European elections. Instead, according to the proposed statute, the monetary policy decisions will be taken using a certain system of weights attributed to the representatives of each country. The reason why the proposed statute of the ECB ignores the European Parliament is, of course, that this body does not have any real legislative power, since a politically united 'European nation' does not exist. However, these voting rules based on a 'non-politically-unified-Europe' may misrepresent the preferences of the European voters.

It has been argued with good reasons (see Krugman, 1989, for instance) that a complete monetary union in Europe is an important intermediate step toward political union. In this paper, on the other hand, we highlighted several reasons why the working of a monetary union will depend crucially on the future political structure the European Community.

Appendix   Common monetary policy with different inflation rates

It is likely that, even if a monetary union is implemented, the rate of inflation will not be equalized across the member countries. Consider, therefore, the case in which inflation in country i is given by:

$$\pi_i = \pi_E + \delta_i \tag{A1}$$

where δ_i is a random shock with mean zero and variance σ_δ^2. In this case, equations (10) and (11) in the text become:

$$\mathcal{L}^{i'} = \tfrac{1}{2}E\left[\pi_i^2 + \beta_i\,(y_i - \bar{y}_i)^2\right] \tag{A2}$$

and

$$y_i = (\pi_i - \pi_i^e) + \mu_i \tag{A3}$$

respectively. Consequently, the expected welfare of country i in the union is now given by:

$$\mathcal{L}^{i'} = \tfrac{1}{2}\mathcal{E}\left[\left(b\bar{x}_E - \frac{b}{1+b}\,\epsilon + \delta_i\right)^2 + \beta_i\left(\mu_i + \delta_i - \frac{b}{1+b}\,\epsilon - \bar{y}_i\right)^2\right] \tag{A4}$$

Subtracting equation (15) from (A4), we obtain:

$$\mathcal{L}^{i'} - \mathcal{L}_N^i = \tfrac{1}{2}\left[\bar{x}^2(b^2 - \beta_i^2) + (1+\beta_i)\left\{\left(\frac{b}{1+b}\right)^2\sigma_\epsilon^2 - \left(\frac{\beta_i}{1+\beta_i}\right)^2\sigma_\mu^2\right\}\right.$$
$$\left. - 2\beta_i\left\{\left(\frac{b}{1+b}\right)\sigma_{\epsilon\mu} - \left(\frac{\beta_i}{1+\beta_i}\right)\sigma_\mu^2\right\} + \beta_i\{\sigma_\delta^2 + 2\rho_{\delta\mu}\sigma_\delta\sigma_\mu\}\right] \tag{A5}$$

$$= [\mathcal{L}^i - \mathcal{L}_N^i] + \beta_i\{\sigma_\delta^2 + 2\rho_{\delta\mu}\sigma_\delta\sigma_\mu\}$$

where $\rho_{\delta\mu}$ is the correlation coefficient between δ_i and μ_i, and we have assumed that δ_i and ϵ are independent. Therefore, unless $\rho_{\delta\mu}$ is sufficiently negative to compensate for σ_δ^2, the results are now less favourable to a monetary union than in the case discussed in the text. The rest of the analysis of Section 4, however, remains unchanged.

Data Appendix

Table 3A.1. *Political independence of central banks*[20]

	Appointments				Relationship with government		Constitution		Index of political independence
	1	2	3	4	5	6	7	8	9
Belgium				*					1
Denmark	*						*	*	3
France	*	*							2
Germany	*	*	*	*			*	*	6
Greece			*					*	2
Ireland	*					*		*	3
Italy	*	*	*		*				4
Netherlands	*	*	*	*			*	*	6
Portugal					*				1
Spain					*	*			2
UK					*				1
US			*	*	*		*	*	5
ECB	*	*	*	*			*	*	6

Notes
1 = Governor not appointed by government.
2 = Governor appointed for > 5 years.
3 = Board not appointed by government.
4 = Board appointed for > 5 years.
5 = No mandatory participation of government representative in the Board.
6 = No government approval of monetary policy is required.
7 = Statutory requirements that central bank pursues monetary stability.
8 = Explicit conflicts between bank and government are possible.
9 = Overall index of political independence, constructed as the number of asterisks in each row.

Comments on the European Central Bank
1 = President appointed by European Council (Art. 11.2).
2 = President appointed for 8 years (Art. 11.2).
3 = Council members: 6 Members of Executive Board: appointed by European Council (Art. 11.3). 12 Governors of National Central Banks: appointed according to their national rules, thus mostly by national governments.
4 = Council members: 6 Members of Executive Board: appointed for 8 years (Art. 11.3). 12 Governors of National Central Banks: appointed for at least 5 years (Art. 14).

Table 3A.1 (cont.)

5 = Council of European Communities representative and/or European Commission representtive may attend meetings of the Council, but they are not part of the Council itself, and thus they cannot vote (Art. 15.1).

6 = Neither the ECB, nor the national central banks, nor the other members of the Council may seek or take any instruction from Community institutions, governments of Member States or any other body (Art. 7).

7 = The primary objective of the System shall be to maintain price stability (Art. 2.1).

8 = Explicit conflicts between bank and government are possible (Art. 2.2 and Art. 7).

Source: Data for the eleven national Central Banks are from Grilli et al. (1991).

Table 3A.2. Economic independence of central banks

	Monetary financing of budget deficit					Monetary instruments			Index of economic independence
	1	2	3	4	5	6	7	8	9
Belgium		*	*	*	*	*		*	6
Denmark	*			*		*	*		4
France			*	*		*	*		4
Germany	*	*	*	*	*	*	*	*	8
Greece				*		*			2
Ireland		*	*	*		*			4
Italy				*					1
Netherlands			*	*	*	*	*		4
Portugal				*		*			2
Spain				*	*			*	3
UK	*	*	*	*		*	*		6
US	*	*	*	*		*	*	*	7
ECB	*	*	*	*	*	*	*	*	8

Notes

1 = Direct credit facility: not automatic.

2 = Direct credit facility: market interest rate.

3 = Direct credit facility: temporary.

4 = Direct credit facility: limited amount.

5 = Central bank does not participate in primary market for public debt.

6 = Discount rate set by central bank.

7 = No portfolio constraints in place since 1980.

8 = No bank loan ceilings in place since 1980.

9 = Overall index of economic independence (being the number of asterisks in columns 1–8).

Comments on the European Central Bank
1 = No Direct credit facility (Art. 21.1).
2 = Purchase of Treasury bonds only on secondary market, thus at market rate (Art. 21.1).
3 = Credit facility never allowed, not even on a temporary basis (Art. 21.1).
4 = Zero amount (Art. 21.1).
5 = Central bank does not participate in primary market for public debt (Art. 21.1).
6 = The Council shall formulate decisions relating to intermediate monetary objectives, key interest rates and supply of reserves (Art. 12.1).
7 = Portfolio constraints are not part of the list of functions the ECB can perform (Art. 18 & Commentary page 10).
8 = The imposition of bank loan ceilings is not part of the list of functions the ECB can perform (Art. 18 & Commentary page 10).
Source: Data for the eleven national Central Banks are from Grilli, Masciandaro and Tabellini (1991).

Table 3A.3. *Electoral data*

	% Shares	Seats
Belgium: Election date 12/87.		
EL: Communist Parties;	0.6	0
L: Socialists (SP and PS);	30.6	72
CD Christian Democrats (CSP and PSC);	35.5	79
R: Party for Freedom and Progress (PVV), Liberal Reformists (PRL);	20.9	48
ER: Flemish Bloc.	1.9	1
Denmark: Election date 5/88.		
EL: Communist Party, Left Socialist Party;	1.4	0
L: Socialist People's Party, Social Democratic Party;	42.9	79
CD Christian Democrats Radical Liberal;	12.3	23
R: Conservative Party, Liberal Party;	31.1	57
ER: Progress Party	10.9	16
France: Election date 6/88.[*]		
EL: Communist Party;	3.4	27
L: Socialist Party and various affiliates;	48.7	276
CD Rally for Republic;		
R: Union for French Democracy; various conservative groups;	46.8[**]	178
ER: National Front	1.1	1

[*] Second Ballot.
[**] In the computations we classified this center/right coalition of parties as R. This is, however, inessential for our results since the median is within L.

Table 3A.3 (*cont.*)

Germany: Election date 1/87.

EL:	Greens;	8.3	42
L:	Social Democrats;	37.0	186
CD:	Christian Democrats (CDU/CSU);	44.3	223
R:	FDP;	9.1	42

Greece: Election date 11/89.

EL:	Communist Parties and various left wing affiliates;	12.5	21
L:	Socialists (PASOK);	40.7	128
CD:			
R:	New Democracy.	46.2	148

Ireland: Election date 6/83.

EL:	Workers' Party;	5.0	7
L:	Labour Party;	9.5	15
CD:	Fine Gael;	27.1	51
R:	Fianna Fail, Progressive Democrats.	56.0	95

Italy: Election date 6/87.

EL:	Communists, DP, Greens;	30.8	198
L:	Socialists, Social Democrats, Republicans; Radicals.	23.6	145
CD:	Christian Democrats, Sud Tirol Party;	35.7	237
R:	Liberals;	2.1	11
ER:	Social Movement.	5.9	35

Luxembourg: Election date 6/89.

EL:	Communist Party; Green Parties.	13.4	4
L:	Socialists;	27.2	18
CD:	Christian Democrats;	31.7	22
R:	Democratic Party (PD).	16.2	11
ER:			

Netherlands: Election date 3/89.

EL:	Left wing group (Groen Links);	4.1	6
L:	Socialists;	34.2	52
CD:	Christian Democrats;	37.6	54
R:	People's Party for Freedom and Progress, Democrat 66.	20.8	31

Portugal: Election date 7/87.

EL:	Communist Party;	12.1	31
L:	Socialist Party Democratic Renewal Party;	27.1	67
CD:	Social Democratic Party;	50.2	148
R:	Democratic Social Culture.	4.4	4

Spain: Election date 6/86.*

EL:	Communists, Bascs;	6.1	13
L:	Socialists;	44.3	184
CD:	Center Parties (PP, CIV, CDS).	40.5	142

*   An election was held in October 1989 followed by disputes about allocations of seats due to alleged irregularities. Since complete results for the 1989 elections were not immediately available in this draft we used the 1986 election results.

** Since the median is within the Socialist Party, it is irrelevant for our analysis how we classify this group of parties in the R or CD categories.

United Kingdom: Election date 6/87.

L:	Labour Party;	30.8	229
CD:	Liberals;	22.6	22
R:	Conservatives.	42.3	375

Note: Vote shares add to less than 100% due to minor unclassified parties.

NOTES

Alesina gratefully acknowledges financial support from the Sloan Foundation. We thank our discussants Peter Bofinger and Luigi Spaventa, Matt Canzoneri, several conference participants, James Alt, Howard Rosenthal, Kenneth Shepsle and participants at the NBER macro and international seminars for helpful comments, and Gerald Cohen and Raiko Mancini for research assistance.
 1 We do not intend to examine all the many macroeconomic issues relevant for the process of European monetary integration. For instance, we do not address the important problem of fiscal convergence. We believe that the simple model focusing on inflation and output stabilization is sufficiently rich to highlight our basic message.
 2 See Persson and Tabellini (1990a) for an in depth discussion of this model and for a survey of the relevant literature.
 3 We could assume, more realistically, that the ECB controls money supply rather than inflation, and add a 'quantity equation' to close the model. This more general specification complicates the algebra without providing any additional insights.
 4 In fact, if the ECB 'announces' the rule (3') and the public believes such an announcement and expects then the ECB has an incentive to deviate from (3') and implement a policy with a positive average inflation rate.
 5 See Canzoneri (1985) for a discussion of monetary rules with asymmetric information over the realization of shocks.
 6 A similar problem in the context of capital taxation is studied in Persson and Tabellini (1990b).
 7 This is because the preferences which have postulated are of the 'intermediate' type as defined by Grandmont (1978). That is, even though two issues are considered (inflation and output stabilization) voters' preferences differ only in one parameter, b. As a result preferences are single-peaked.
 8 Lohmann (1991) has recently extended Rogoff's framework by showing that it is optimal to set a high but finite cost of 'firing' the governor. By choosing a finite cost of 'firing' the governor, society can ensure that in case of 'really bad' realizations of the output shock, the governor will take into account society's preferences for more 'accommodation', for fear of being fired. This argument is not pursued here.
 9 The classification proposed by Grilli *et al* (1990) extends and improves upon earlier work by Bade and Parkin (1982).
10 For an insightful discussion of the effects of the 'reappointment incentive' for governors of central banks, see Alt (1991).

11 In the appendix we analyse the case in which inflation is not equalized across the member countries of the monetary union. The results, however, are not qualitatively different from those discussed above.

12 In pursuing this comparision we are assuming, somewhat unrealistically, that the country shocks (μ_i) are the same under independent policy-making and monetary union.

13 For a discussion of the 'credibility' gains of joining a common currency area see Giavazzi and Giovannini (1989).

14 The weights usually adopted in the European Council are as follows: 10 votes each for Germany, France, Italy and the United Kingdom; 8 votes for Spain; 5 votes for Belgium, Greece, the Netherlands and Portugal; 3 votes for Denmark and Ireland and 2 votes for Luxembourg.

15 For an excellent overview of the issues on the theory of elections of legislatures in a district system see Austen-Smith (1987) and the references cited therein.

16 In computing the 'European median' we ignored, on purpose, the results for the election of the European Parliament. At least until now, this legislative body has been virtually powerless. There is evidence that European voters have used European elections to send 'signals' to their national governments or expressed 'protest votes.' It is very likely that the allocation of seats and shares in the European Parliament could be substantially different if such a body had a legislative authority. Note that the proposed statute of the ECB completely ignores the European Parliament by not granting to this body any role in the appointment or supervision of the board.

17 In what follows, we classify as R the Prime Minister emerging from this hypothetical Socialist loss in France.

18 To be precise, with a 'one person one vote rule' one-sixth of CD (i.e. one vote) would lead to a tie, since there would be 5R, 1CD against 1L, 5CD.

19 These results are consistent with earlier findings by Alt (1985), Paldam (1989a,b) and Alesina (1989).

REFERENCES

Alesina, Alberto (1989): 'Politics and Business Cycles in Industrial Democracies', Economic Policy 4, (8), 55–98.

Alesina, Alberto and Nouriel Roubini (1990). 'Political Cycles in OECD Economies', NBER Working Paper No. 3478.

Alesina, Alberto and Larry Summers (1990): 'Central Bank independence and economic performance: Some comparative evidence', unpublished.

Alt, James (1985): 'Political Parties, World Demand, and Unemployment: Domestic and International Sources of Economic Activity', American Political Science Review 79, 1016–40.

(1991). 'Leaning into the wind or ducking out of the storm', forthcoming in Alberto Alesina and Geoffrey Carliner (Eds), Politics and Economics in the 1980s, University of Chicago Press and NBER.

Austen-Smith David (1987): 'Parties, Districts and the Spatial Theory of Elections', Social Choice and Welfare, 4, 9–23.

Bade, R. and M. Parkin (1982), 'Central Bank Laws and Inflation – A Comparative Analysis,' mimeo, University of Western Ontario.

Barro, Robert and David Gordon (1983). 'Rules, Discretion, and Reputation in a Model of Monetary Policy', *Journal of Monetary Economics* 12, 101–22.

Canzoneri, Matthew (1985): 'Monetary Policy Games and the Role of Private Information', *American Economic Review* 75, 1056–70.

Casella, Alessandra (1991): 'The Impact of Monetary Unification on the Composition of Markets', unpublished.

Giavazzi, Francesco and Alberto Giovannini (1989). *Limiting Exchange Rate Flexibility: The European Monetary System*, M.I.T. Press.

Grandmont, Jean Michel (1978): 'Intermediate Preferences and the Majority Rule' *Econometrica*, 50, 317–30.

Grilli, Vittorio, Donato Masciandaro, and Guido Tabellini (1991): 'Political and Monetary Institutions and Public Finance Policies in the Industrial Democracies', *Economic Policy* 6, (13), forthcoming.

International Monetary Fund. *'International Financial Statistics'*, various issues.

Krugman, Paul (1989): 'Policy Problems of a Monetary Union', unpublished.

Kydland, Finn and Edward Prescott (1977): 'Rules Rather Than Discretion: The Inconsistency of Optimal Plans', *Journal of Political Economy* 85, 473–90.

Lohmann, Suzanne, (1991): 'Optimal Commitment in Monetary Policy: Credibility vs. Flexibility,' *American Economic Review*, forthcoming.

Paldam, Martin (1989a): 'Politics Matter after all: Testing Hibbs' Theory of Partisan Cycles,' Aarhus University Working Paper.

Persson, Torsten and Guido Tabellini (1990a). *Macroeconomic Policy, Credibility and Politics,*' Harwood Academic Publishers.

(1990b): 'Capital Taxation and Representative Democracy', manuscript.

Rogoff, Kenneth (1985): 'The Optimal Degree of Commitment to an Intermediate Monetary Target', *The Quarterly Journal of Economics* 100, 1169–90.

Discussion

PETER BOFINGER

This paper by Alberto Alesina and Vittorio Grilli is an important theoretical contribution to the debate on the establishment of a European Central Bank, which is very much dominated by political considerations. Its main innovations are the application of the time-inconsistency model and of the median-voter model to this issue.

Their approach raises three questions:

– Is it really necessary and in the interest of monetary policy that the division of 'seats' on the board of the ECB coincides with the shares of popular votes in Europe?

– Is the loss function, on which the time-inconsistency literature is based, really the loss function of a rational voter?
– Is it sufficient to copy the model of the Bundesbank Act at the European level if one wants to guarantee price stability in Europe?

The answer to the first question depends crucially on the overall approach to the design of a European Central Bank. In this respect the paper offers two different propositions:

– In Section 3 it presents the widely accepted notion that a central bank has to be designed as a politically independent institution, which is mainly committed to the target of price stability.
– In Section 5 a completely different view is adopted. Here the authors regard a central bank as an institution which should minimize the loss function of the European median voter as far as possible, an assignment which includes not only price stability but also an output target above the natural rate. According to this approach the authors come to the result that – in contrast to the ECB's draft statute – the members of the ECB board should not be appointed by the European Parliament.

It is obvious that the two alternative approaches lead to quite different statutes for the ECB. In this regard it is astonishing that the authors address only the relatively minor point of the appointment process of the ECB Board. If one adopted their idea of a central bank, which has to minimize the loss function of the median voter, in a consistent way, the future ECB would have to be entirely different from its present outline:
– the target of price stability would have to be abandoned as it might be incompatible with the preferences of the median voter,
– the terms of the members of the Board should not be longer than or identical with the terms of the European Parliament – otherwise an even greater under-representation of some parties might occur,
– instead of a federatively structured ECB, which will give national governments of small countries too great an influence on the nomination process of the members of the ECB Council, a strongly centralized system should be adopted.

These examples may suffice. It is evident that the Alesina-Grilli critique, if one takes it seriously, cannot be limited to the nomination procedure alone. It would require an ECB which has not very much in common with the blueprint which the authors accept in Section 3.

This inconsistency leads to an interesting question: how can it be that the outline of the ECB, which was drafted by the European Central Bank Governors in 1990, leads to an institution which does not minimize the loss function of the European median voter? The answer requires a more detailed analysis of the model of Barro and Gordon (1983) that underlies the first main part of the paper. Above all one has to ask whether the voters' loss function is adequately described by this model. As the paper shows, the inflationary bias of central banks depends on the existence of a target value for output which is above the natural rate. Although this loss function is widely accepted in the literature, it cannot be regarded as an adequate representation of the loss function of private individuals. By assumption the natural rate of output is obtained in an optimization process of the individuals reflecting all distortions of the economy. From their perspective a level of output above the natural rate is identical with a real wage rate which is lower than the disutility of their work. Thus, the target output level of a rational voter should always be identical with the natural rate. If one would formulate the social loss function in this way, one could easily recognize that the inflationary bias of monetary policy would vanish. In other words, a central bank which was committed to the target of price stability would always represent the preferences of the European median voter. This is supported by the empirical evidence which shows that countries with low (and predictable) inflation rates experienced higher real growth rates than other countries.

Thus, at least for rational voters, it is possible to solve the contradiction between a politically independent central bank committed to the target of price stability and a central bank which tries to minimize the loss function of the median voter. With such voters both approaches are identical. The design of an ECB would be more or less irrelevant.

In reality, however, most voters, especially outside Germany are familiar neither with the empirical evidence nor with the theoretical literature. Thus, one comes to the not very democratic solution that it is in the interest of the population to shield monetary policy as far as possible from political influences even if this implies that some parties are not adequately represented in the nomination process. The democratic legitimacy of such 'hands-tying' rests on the fact that the statutes of the ECB have to be ratified by the parliaments of all EC member countries. If they accept this approach there is no room left for the Alesina-Grilli critique.

As a final point, one has to ask whether the Bundesbank Act would provide an adequate legal framework for the ECB. As the paper mentions, there are in fact many similarities between the ECB draft statute and the Bundesbank Act. However, one should not overlook that it has also many in common with the predecessor of the Bundesbank, the 'Bank deutscher Länder'. This post-war monetary system of West Germany was established by the Military Governments of the three West Zones in 1948. It was characterized by legally independent Land Central Banks ('Landeszentralbanken') and a central institution, the 'Bank deutscher Länder', which was a common subsidiary of the Land Central Banks. Exactly this legal arrangement is now envisaged for Europe.

A second issue which is not adequately discussed in the present debate concerns the target of price stability, which is mentioned in the Bundesbank Act in a somewhat vague form. The draft statute of the ECB, however, is very precise on this point. The question is whether such a stipulation, which even in its rather unclear form was successful in Germany, will suffice to guarantee price stability in Europe. From a public choice perspective the answer would be negative. Central bankers who maximize their private utility function will only pursue price stability if this improves their public influence and their prestige. In a country like Germany, where their public has a strong preference for price stability, such microeconomic incentives lead to the intended macroeconomic outcome. In Europe, where the public has a much less pronounced preference for price stability, these microeconomic incentives for the members of the ECB Council would be much less stringent. Thus, it may not be sufficient to copy the Bundesbank Act at the European level, if one wants to achieve a low inflation rate in the European Monetary Union. The microeconomic incentives for price stability could be easily enhanced if the members of the ECB Council were given a high, but nominally fixed income over their whole term of office.

REFERENCE

Barro, Robert and David Gordon (1983), 'Rules, Discretion, and Reputation in a Model of Monetary Policy', *Journal of Monetary Economics* **12**, 101–22.

LUIGI SPAVENTA

The project of a European Central Bank (ECB) has great policy relevance, but is hardly a promising subject for theory. A major merit of this paper is that good theory and neat modelling are put to excellent use for discussing the requirements and the implications of the new institution. More than a great deal of literature on the same issue, this paper provides food for thought and, owing to its analytical rigour, allows problems to be set in precise terms: some of these problems, which the paper leaves unsolved, account, as I shall argue, for the difficulties met by a rapid transition to European monetary integration. Let me first summarize briefly the main points made in the paper, and also the more relevant in view of later discussion.

The framework is the time-consistency problem facing monetary authorities which, though disliking inflation, target a level of output greater than the equilibrium rate. The known outcome is higher inflation than in the first-best solution, without any output gain. The higher the value of the parameter expressing the preference for the output target, the higher the inflation rate, but, if the economy is subject to random shocks, the lower the output variance. In the authors' views the ECB will not escape this time-consistency predicament.

In a politically unified Europe, the (directly or indirectly) elected ECB governor would (given a simple structure of preferences) be the one preferred by the European median voter. The latter – it is shown – would choose a 'Rogoff governor': one caring less for output than he does, hence more conservative than he is, and delivering as a result a lower inflation rate. Such a central banker, however, needs independence to fulfil his role and not be subject to pressures to change his policy. The (draft) statute is satisfactory in this respect as it appears to grant the ECB a high degree of independence – at least as high as that of the Bundesbank.

Without political union, a common inflation rate will coexist with different national preferences regarding the trade-off between inflation and output, as well as with the occurrence of country-specific shocks. The paper provides an illuminating analysis of how joining the union and losing monetary independence affects an individual country's welfare. Disregarding country-specific shocks, the union delivers credibility gains or losses, according to whether a country's inflation bias (given by its output parameter) is greater or less than that appearing in the ECB's loss function. Disregarding political differences, economic losses will be greater, the greater the variance of domestic output relative to European output and the smaller its correlation with European output. Considering the situation and the past record of prospective members of the union it turns out 'that the countries that have more to lose from the stabilization point of view' (because of the greater variance and/or the smaller correlation of their output relative to the EC average) 'are also the ones that could gain more in terms of credibility of their monetary policy' (because of their inflation record and of the lack of independence of their central banks).

Let me now state the basic problem arising from, but not solved by, this analysis, if we accept the authors' contention that a credible implementation of the first-best rule on the part of the ECB is an unrealistic possibility to be disregarded. Why should, in this case, a low inflation country (call it Germany) ever agree to join the union?

Consider first the most favourable case, where political unification occurs at the time of full monetary integration. The authors make political unification coincide with the disappearance of differences of national preferences and welfare functions, and hence of differences of national inflation biases in the output-inflation trade-off. This is indeed a very strong assumption: the implied irrelevance of the regional composition of the electorate would be hard to accept even within the existing nation states. If this assumption is relaxed, while still letting the ECB governor be elected by European citizens rather than by national prime ministers, the European median voter will not coincide with, and will probably be less conservative than, the German median voter: in this case the inflation rate set by the ECB will be higher than that which the German central bank would independently set. Even disregarding this possibility, and hence allowing national preferences to converge to German preferences as a result of political unification, it is hard to assume on top, as the authors do,[1] that political union equalizes the distortions existing in labour markets across different countries. It is the existence of such distortions which, in the authors' view, justifies a target level of output higher than the natural level. As long as differences persist, however, 'natural' rates of unemployment will differ across countries (as they differ across regions of more unified national labour markets), so that the wedges between target levels and natural levels are likely to differ. The ECB target level of output is bound to reflect such divergences and is therefore likely to be higher than that of countries with low natural unemployment: the resulting common inflation rate will therefore be higher than that of the latter.

Without a political union, and with the explicit modelling of different national preferences, the problem becomes immediately evident. While a number of high inflation countries would bear economic losses (because of the higher variance of their output), but obtain high credibility gains and hence lower inflation, Germany would stand to lose on all counts. In addition to some (albeit small) economic losses (see Figure 3.2), there would be high credibility losses, as the output parameter, on which the inflation rate depends, is lower for Germany than for Europe. In terms of the rigorous analysis provided by Alesina and Grilli it turns out that the project of monetary union, with a European central bank setting the common monetary policy and the common rate of inflation, is not incentive-compatible when all countries are considered.

The authors consider this problem in passing (pp. 62–3). Their answer is that countries with a lower concern for output, and lower inflation, must be gaining on other grounds: the reduction of transaction costs and monetary uncertainty; or the gain from cooperation of monetary policy; or, more generally (and more vaguely) the 'long-run political gains resulting from the creation of a "European nation"'. There may well be such gains, and I am the last to require that all factors leading to eminently political decisions be susceptible of accurate modelling. Still, I find the authors' answer far less than satisfactory, especially because it conceals the true bone of contention in the long-drawn negotiations on whether, when and how to begin the process towards monetary union. Whatever the other (unmodelled) gains, they would affect all countries; if anything, they would be lower for Germany (as for transaction costs, monetary uncertainty, and especially monetary cooperation, which the leading country of an asymmetric system has no reason to desire). It will then still be the case that Germany bears more losses and obtains less benefits than a number of other countries: it is not surprising that a quick transition to full union is advocated by the latter countries, but resisted by Germany.

The relevant question then becomes whether there is a remedy for this lack of incentive-compatibility.[2] The German solution is to wait for convergence to occur before setting up a European central bank responsible for a common monetary policy. The implicit assumption is that inflation convergence would signal that national inflation biases have also converged to the lowest (German) denominator, as indeed has been the case for the smaller Northern European countries and possibly for France. This may however, take a long time, as the high inflation countries would lose the additional credibility to be obtained from participation to the union. More importantly, the process may be unstable and result in a permanent, two-speed outcome.

The alternative is to minimize German losses by tightening the monetary constitution of the system. Consider the limiting case in which the ECB, while not setting the output coefficient equal to zero (which would increase output variability), were able to make the first-best solution credible: the inflation rate would then depend only on the realized value of a shock and not be affected by the output target. It can be easily shown that in this case: (i) in a politically unified Europe the chosen governor would be as conservative as the median voter and his preferences would be independent of output variability; (ii) in a politically fragmented Europe each country's governor would exactly reflect national preferences; (iii) most importantly, in the latter case, whether a country gains or loses from the union would no longer depend on the difference between its own and the ECB's inflation bias. As a result, and especially as a result of (iii), the major disincentive for Germany to join would be eliminated.

The authors, as recalled above, disregard the possibility of implementing the first-best rule as unrealistic. Their arguments (p. 52) are that it may be complicated, going beyond setting a given rate of money growth, and that to insert a complex and contingent rule in an unchangeable statute would be both unreasonable and ineffective. The explicit statement of the objective of price stability in article 2.1 of the statute helps to protect the ECB against political pressures, but is by itself unable to eliminate the time-consistency problem (p. 56). I fail to consider such objections as conclusive, if for no other reason than because they stem from what is a most useful, but nonetheless hypersimplified model. One may well wonder if central banks tempted to indulge in inflation surprises with a view to a temporary climb along a short-run Phillips curve really belong to the EMS Europe we have known in the past decade. But apart from this, it may be questioned that a credible anti-inflationary commitment must necessarily be enshrined in a 'simple monetarist rule with a constant rate of money growth' to be written in the bank's statute or in a country's constitution (p. 52). Price stability, it has been argued,[3] – does not require unnecessary inflexibility if the medium-term commitment is credible. Perfection is not of this world, but the Bundesbank is deemed to provide the nearest approximation to it: and the Bundesbank has often shown how short-run flexibility can be reconciled with commitment to price stability.[4] In this vein, the strong opposition of the Bundesbank to proposals that the exchange rate policy of the union be left in the hands of finance ministers can be understood, as that would potentially pre-empt the priority of the ECB's anti-inflation commitment.

A major contribution of Alesina and Grilli is thus to highlight a problem to which they provide no solution. Their analysis allows us to understand the true obstacles on the way to monetary union: for some countries the economic benefits are hard to find, while the potential costs can be easily identified. The political desirability of monetary union as a first step towards political integration may be an important but hardly a sufficient incentive. The unanswered question is whether a sufficiently rigorous design can allay the fears which motivate the resistance against an early start or whether we have to wait until a long and uncertain process of convergence is completed.

NOTES

1 By normalizing to zero natural output for all countries and by equalizing for all countries the target levels of output, they also equalize the 'wedge between the market generated, "natural", level of output . . . and the target level'.

2 This question is addressed in Begg et al. (1991).

3 Begg *et al.*, section 2.2
4 Ibid.

REFERENCE

Begg, D., F. Giavazzi, L. Spaventa and G. Wyplosz (1991), 'European Monetary Integration – the Macro Issues', in *Monitoring European Integration: The Making of Monetary Union*, London: Centre for Economic Policy Research.

4 The ECB: a bank or a monetary policy rule?

DAVID FOLKERTS-LANDAU and
PETER M. GARBER

1 Introduction

It is generally agreed that a European central banking institution will be an essential feature of the final stage of the European Economic and Monetary Union (EMU). To this end the EC Committee of Central Bank Governors has recently produced a Draft Statute of the European System of Central Banks and of the European Central Bank.[1] Although differences of views among governments of member states have meant that the Draft Statute remains incomplete in a number of areas, the most fundamental and consequential omission is the lack of a clear mandate for the ECB to undertake traditional banking functions in support of the financial sector.

Central banks have traditionally had two major objectives. First, central banks have sought to maintain a stable and efficient financial and payments system. This has generally required performing certain banking functions for the financial sector, such as providing an ultimate source of liquidity (i.e., a discount window), participating in the payments system, and regulating and supervising key sectors of the financial system. Second, central banks have sought to stabilize the price level and general economic activity by carrying out monetary functions such as open market operations, foreign exchange operations, and the establishment of minimum reserve requirements.

The draft Statute mandates the maintenance of price stability as the explicit primary objective of the ECB,[2] and the necessary monetary functions and operations of the system are defined in accordance with standard practice. The maintenance of a stable financial and payments system, however, is not an explicit objective of the ECB, and only limited banking functions are admitted as one of the system's five tasks. In particular, the system is authorized only 'to participate as necessary in the formulation, coordination and execution of policies relating to prudential supervision and the stability of the financial system,' which falls notably short of being mandated 'to formulate, coordinate, and execute such policies.'[3] There is no obligation for the ECB to initiate support of the banking or payments system. Furthermore, Article 18.2[4] enables the ECB to restrict the scope for, and set the terms of, all open market and credit operations carried out by national central banks to stabilize local financial or payment systems.

The draft Statute thus clearly subscribes to a 'narrow' concept of the System of Central Banks with a single objective – monetary stability – rather than a 'broad' concept with the additional objective of financial-market stability. In this paper we examine the consequences of a 'narrow' central banking system for Community financial markets.

We conclude that in the absence of such banking functions it will be necessary to slow, or even prevent, the ongoing development of Community-wide liquid, securitized financial markets, supported by a large-volume wholesale payments system. Instead, the historically prevalent bank-intermediated financial system will have to be maintained to lower the likelihood of liquidity crises that demand central bank intervention.

In the remainder of this paper, we first examine the relation between securitization and financial crises (Section 2). We then discuss the role payments systems play in securitized financial markets and the involvement of central banks in payments systems (Section 3). In Section 4 we define the central bank's basic choice problem in establishing the extent of its banking functions, and in Section 5 we establish the need for central banks to supervise financial markets. Section 6 concludes the paper.

2   Securitization and liquidity crises

2.1   Securitization[5]

The accelerating securitization of credit claims, ownership claims, and derivative contracts is a fundamental phenomenon in the evolution of financial markets and market institutions. Securitization induces the establishment of new institutions, drives developments in market mechanisms, payments mechanisms, and other institutional arrangements, and above all spurs an increased demand for liquidity. In this section, we shall show that the extent of securitization of credit and ownership claims is a determining factor in defining a central bank's role as lender-of-last-resort. The more securitized are credit, ownership, and derivative contracts, the greater the likelihood of liquidity problems.

As financial systems mature, there has been a general tendency to substitute securitized credit for bank credit, and equity shares for nontradable

Table 4.1. *Domestic and international commercial paper markets,*
1986–90. (Amounts outstanding at end-year, in billions of US dollars[1].)

	Market opening	1986	1987	1988	1989	1990
United States	pre-1960	325.9	373.6	451.6	521.9	557.8
Japan	end-1987	–	13.8	73.8	91.1	117.3
France	end-1985	3.7	7.6	10.4	22.3	31.0
Canada	pre-1960	11.9	14.9	21.0	25.5	26.8
Sweden	1983	3.7	7.8	9.5	15.9	22.3
Australia[2]	mid-1970s	4.1	7.5	7.9	11.1	10.9
United Kingdom	1986	0.8	3.8	5.7	5.7	9.1
Spain[3]	1982	2.5	2.8	3.1	4.2	8.4
Finland	mid-1986	0.4	2.5	4.9	6.9	8.3
Norway	end-1984	0.9	2.1	1.7	2.0	2.6
Netherlands	1986	0.1	0.9	1.0	0.8	2.0
Total		354.0	437.3	590.6	707.4	796.5
ECP	mid-1980s	13.9	33.3	50.6	58.4	70.4
memo-other Euro-notes[4]		15.1	16.9	13.5	11.1	19.1
Grand Total		367.9	470.6	641.2	765.8	866.9

Source: Bank for International Settlements, *International Banking and Financial Market Developments*, August, 1991.
Notes:
1 Converted at end-year exchange rates, except for Australia.
2 End-June of each year converted at end-June exchange rates.
3 Partial coverage.
4 Short-term notes only.

ownership interests.[6] Better known corporations have increasingly obtained credit in the bond market directly. In some countries, most notably in Germany, there has been a significant increase in the number of initial public equity offerings by mid-sized industrial companies. An important form of securitization had been the growth of negotiable high-quality short-term non-bank corporate and bank obligations, i.e., commercial paper and certificates of deposit, (see Table 4.1) and the growth of exchange-traded derivative products such as interest rate futures. Finally, a substantial part of illiquid bank assets had been securitized through the repackaging of bank assets into tradable securities, most notably in the mortgage market.

The extent of securitization is relatively more advanced in some industrial countries, e.g., the United States, the United Kingdom, and France than in others, such as Germany (see Table 4.1 and Figure 4.1). However, an improved ability to circumvent existing restrictions on securitization

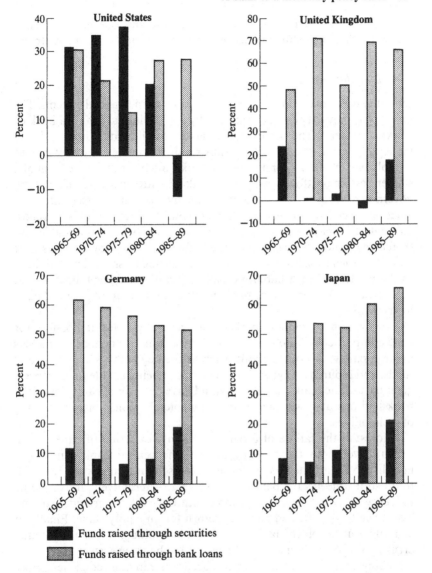

Figure 4.1   Indirect versus securitized funding. (Percent of total business funds raised through securities and bank loans, 1965–89.)
Source: Frankel and Montgomery (1991)

by shifting such activity to less regulated jurisdictions has induced a gradual lifting of existing restrictions on securitization in most countries.[7]

2.2 Liquidity crises

Liquidity crises occur in two basic forms in modern financial systems. The first type of liquidity crisis is triggered by the traditional run on a bank or banking system. The second type relates to illiquidity in securitized money or capital markets. Bank runs result from investor doubts about the solvency of a bank, or a group of banks. Such runs take the form of a sudden shift in portfolios away from bank liabilities in favor of short-term government securities or corporate assets. Events that adversely affect the value of some bank assets may lead to doubts about a bank's solvency, particularly because the larger part of bank assets are nontradable and therefore are not subjected to market-valuation at regular intervals. The bank may then experience difficulty in refinancing its short-term liabilities as the holders of such liabilities make precautionary portfolio shifts. A failure may spill over into the banking system, thus requiring central bank intervention.

Securitization of money markets has generally made it possible for banks, in particular wholesale money centre banks, to finance their assets in large part with bought funds, such as the negotiable CDs, interbank funds, and repurchase agreements. The risk of being unable to refinance a great part of the bank's liabilities would have been significantly less if the bank had operated without relying on wholesale money market funding of its liabilities.

To forestall the failure of a particular bank, or group of banks, from spilling over onto the banking system, the central bank can supply liquidity to the affected banks through its discount facilities and will wish to do so if it deems the banks to be solvent. Alternatively, it can use its influence to induce a selected group of healthy banks to provide liquidity assistance to the affected banks in return for an equity stake. Finally, it can allow an insolvent bank to fail, while avoiding a general banking crisis by supplying liquidity to the rest of the banking system.

Banking crises were a fairly regular occurrence in most countries before the 1940s, leading at times to severe contractions of the money stock with significant negative effects on economic activity.[8] Since then, however, central banks have learned to avoid general bank liquidity crises by providing emergency assistance to the banking system during times of crises. Some typical recent examples of such crises in the UK have been the failure of some large secondary banks in 1973, and the Johnson Matthey Bankers crises in 1984. Both required official support operations. The US Continental Illinois Bank crisis in 1984 also required large scale central bank intervention to prevent contagion to the banking system. Concern about the stability of the banking system led the German Bundesbank in 1983 to request a group of German banks to assist the failing Schroeder, Munchmeyer, Hengst & Co. Bank.[9]

The second type of liquidity crisis – illiquidity in key money or capital markets – occurs as the direct consequence of increased securitization. In securitized money and capital markets, banks are relied upon to supply liquidity to non-bank participants. For example, corporate issuers of money market instruments generally arrange credit lines with banks to assure access to funds on maturity in case problems occur in rolling over the securities. Non-bank financial intermediaries, such as broker/dealers also rely on banks. While they actively supply liquidity to short- and long-term markets as market-makers, dealers also must arrange bank lines of credit to be able to offer this service. Likewise, participants on organized futures and options markets, the heart of the last decade's development in financial engineering, make intensive use of bank lines because of the requirement of nearly instantaneous delivery of cash needed to satisfy margin calls. Credit lines to banks are the only practicable method of assuring such delivery.[10]

A smoothly functioning dealer effectively provides the service of swapping one security for another. The swaps fund the dealer's operation, allowing the dealer to provide liquidity while avoiding the tapping of the dealer's bank line of credit. Nevertheless, only when dealing in very liquid instruments can dealers almost always avoid funding through banks. Dealers maintain credit lines in good funds and securities to finance peak load inventory acquisition or short positions.[11] Low capitalization and high leverage are the essential characteristics of dealers in securities. They therefore tend to be undiversified, highly leveraged, and vulnerable to failure.[12]

The failure of a major money market borrower or dealer may precipitate a liquidity crisis in a money market, such as the commercial paper market. The failure of a borrower can undermine investor confidence and make it difficult for other money market borrowers to roll-over their outstanding obligations, forcing them to draw on their bank lines. The banking system may not be willing to meet this sudden increase for short-term commercial credit because of concern about credit risk.[13] Banks may also be unwilling to continue to finance some dealers because of doubts about their solvency. The banking system may also be unable to generate sufficient funding as the illiquidity or collapse of the CD dealer network may have spread to the CD market because of a lack of invenstor confidence. The ensuing failure among money market borrowers unable to roll-over their obligations, or among dealers unable to fund their positions, will further undermine confidence.

The potential systemic nature of such a situation invites central bank liquidity intervention. An example was the liquidity crisis in the US commercial paper market in 1970, triggered by the Penn Central bankruptcy, as well as the liquidity crisis caused by the October 1987 stock market crash. Both crises required Federal Reserve intervention.[14]

Sudden increases in price volatility in a securitized capital markets are signs of illiquidity that, in turn, can cause precipitous declines in prices and result in bankruptcies among market participants. In capital markets, trading strategies such as stop-loss sales or portfolio insurance rely on market liquidity for their success. For any one small player, the assumption of a liquid market with price continuity is probably reasonable. When all of the selling strategies are triggered simultaneously, however, they have proved to be infeasible. The rest of the market participants may have no knowledge of the existence of such traders because their sell orders lie buried in the future. They will come to the market only if triggered by the proper contingency. When the time comes for these massive sales to occur, the sellers may find no buyers prepared to take the other side of the market at the last reported price, and the price may suddenly collapse. A lack of liquidity in the market may cause a snowballing of sell orders. If the price falls dramatically below its fundamental value due to these liquidity problems, further sales may be triggered. Banks may make margin calls on their loans to security holders and dealers, and cancel lines of credit. This may either bankrupt the holders and dealers or force a sale of their stock, further depressing prices. Hence, working to market, the essence of securitized markets can precipitate bankruptcy from illiquidity among dealers, eliminating dealer networks and inducing a permanent illiquidity and lower prices on securities involved. The spread of insolvencies resulting from price declines and inability to meet margin calls may ultimately affect the banking system as defaults on bank loans mount.

Central bank intervention can prevent liquidity crises caused by large price movements from becoming systemic. The central bank can supply emergency liquidity assistance to the banking system or induce the banking system to supply liquidity to the non-bank market makers. The welfare gain arises from preventing the transformation of liquid into illiquid securities and needless bankruptcies among dealers, and ultimately among banking institutions. If such events are pure liquidity events, then intervention is costless in terms of central bank resources and price level stability.

Alternatively, if the central bank mistakes a fundamental decline of asset prices for a temporary liquidity problem and intervenes, it will either have to (1) weaken the capital of the banking system; (2) countenance price inflation; or (3) absorb some loss itself. By erroneously adding liquidity to a market when the price of the security is higher than its ultimate level, the central bank expands reserves and pressures banks to lend against the securities. If the security price eventually falls as central bank liquidity is withdrawn, market makers will go bankrupt, leaving bad loans on the books of the banks and reducing bank capital. Depositors' confidence in banks will furthermore diminish, and banks will be less able to provide liquidity services in the future. To reduce the damage to the banks of this mistake, the central bank may decide not to contract reserves to their normal level. This leads to a permanent expansion in the money stock and to a rise in the price level.

2.3   Banking markets and liquidity crises

In a financial system without a securitized money market, short-term funding and liquidity management must occur through bank balance sheets, and banks also act as the major brokers and dealers for money. In such a system, there has generally been a small number of large bank players in the market for wholesale funds. Clearing of payments is effectively done internally to banking organizations or among a small group of tightly connected banks.

Few occasions will arise when funds are demanded on a large scale for unexpected settlements. The central bank, therefore, will not often be called upon to provide credit. Alternatively stated, placing most short-term funding on bank balance sheets means that financial markets create few liquid claims, so liquidity problems emerge infrequently.

In addition, a central bank that limits short-term funding to the banking system can make minimum reserve requirements binding and thereby impose a tax on the entire financial system in the form of higher yields and lower prices (liquidity haircuts in the prices) of relatively illiquid securities. Since financial markets would be prohibited from supplying close substitutes to bank products, banks cannot shrink their balance sheets and reserves to a nonbinding level and conduct their liquidity business primarily off their balance sheets.

Thus, financial systems with securitized money and capital markets are more likely to be subjected to liquidity crises than a financial system dominated by the banking market.

2.4   Stifling securitized money markets taxes illiquid issuers

With restricted money markets, large and high quality short-term credits must be carried on bank balance sheets. If a central bank permits large-scale, liquid, and securitized money markets, large institutions that are potential issuers of liquid, short-term securities tend to remove themselves from bank balance sheets, thereby reducing the demand for bank reserves. The price of accessing bank liquidity, therefore, falls for less liquid issuers of securities. A policy of permitting a liquid, securitized money market favors issuers of liquid and illiquid securities by allowing them to access capital more cheaply. If illiquid issues are concentrated among the smaller, riskier firms, the structure of investment by type of firm and type of activity is altered. Alternatively a highly restricted money market will raise the cost of capital to less liquid firms, channeling capital to the larger, lower risk firms.

3   Liquidity and the payments system

The liquidity of financial markets (money, capital, and derivative), as well as the pace of securitization of financial markets, hinges on the ability to settle payments and to move cash.[15] A wholesale payments system capable of processing a large volume of intra-day payment orders is imperative to support the large turnover in securities markets needed for liquidity, the rapidly changing dealer positions financed with repurchase agreements, and margin requirements arising in futures and options markets. In contrast, in a system that lacks such markets, rapidity of payment processing is less crucial since such a large gross turnover and net settlement does not emerge among the numerous entities that are not members of a limited-entry clearing arrangement.

Most wholesale payments systems consist of a central bank that settles payments among a group of clearing banks via their reserve accounts (such as the Fedwire system in the United States) and various private clearinghouse arrangements among subgroups of banks (such as CHIPS for international dollar payments, regional or giro clearing systems in Germany, and netting schemes such as FXNET for foreign exchange transactions).[16] Banks are typically the central participants in wholesale payments systems because of their direct access to 'good funds' (central bank liabilities) for payments, which gives them a comparative advantage in establishing efficient payment arrangements. Good funds constitute the core of any payments system because they are available at full nominal value to make payments under all market conditions (including market crises).

The role of the central bank in a payments system is dictated by the fundamental nature of payments systems: the more effective wholesale payments systems are in supporting securitized money and capital markets, the greater is the credit risk generated within the settlements system, and thus the greater the likelihood of liquidity crises.

In a system of *continuous settlement,* each payment message from one bank to another is accompanied by the good funds specified in the message. As long as the sending bank has sufficient reserves on hand, payments messages are processed without delay. In continuous settlements, receiving banks bear no credit risk from participating in the payment mechanism. This is because the payment must be blocked when the amount of payment exceeds the good funds on hand until more funds are received. If numerous banks face a similar situation, the payments system can become gridlocked. Banks wish to make large payments to each other but cannot send payments because they have not received payments. Thus, a system of continuous settlement on the one hand eliminates credit risk among banks from the day's payments. On the other hand, it does so by reducing the potential speed of transmitting payments. This reduction of liquidity increases the cost of financial activity.

The gridlock problem can be reduced by banks' increasing their reserve holdings. This would involve selling loans to other investors in return for good funds. Bank customers would have to pass-through a higher cost of reserves as the price of increasing processing speed.

To avoid large reserve positions, banks usually engage in *net settlement*.[17] They pay the difference between total payments and total receipts at the end of the day, through a clearinghouse formed for the purpose of executing the net settlement. Good funds held by banks are transferred to the clearinghouse to collateralize partially bank payment orders. Banks can execute delivery of good funds without increasing their total reserves because the individual members of the clearinghouse and their customers believe that net due to positions accumulating during the day are covered by delivery of good funds at settlement.[18]

Credit risk in payment systems arises from the possibility that any of the parties in the chain of intra-day transactions may default on its payment obligations at the time of settlement. If the clearinghouse operates under settlement finality, then the credit risk of the sending bank is distributed over the receiving banks according to the loss-sharing formula adopted by the clearinghouse.[19]

Systemic risk occurs as an outgrowth of settlement risk. The failure of one participant to settle deprives other institutions of expected funds and prevents these institutions from settling in their turn. Thus, although a participant may conduct no business directly with a failed institution, chains of obligation may make it suffer because of the impact that the failed institution has on a participant's ability to settle – that is, the cost of settlement failure reaches beyond the exposure of credited banks to the failing bank.

Settlement at the end of the day is a way for the market to test periodically the liquidity and solvency of the clearing banks. Failure of an institution to settle will either result in an unwinding of all intra-day payments instructions; or under settlement finality, its obligations will be covered by a clearinghouse reserve, or by central bank lending to the clearinghouse or to its members. An unwinding of transactions or failure to fully cover intraday payments made for the delinquent institutions out of clearinghouse reserves will impair the ability of other banks to make payments and hence may produce a systemic liquidity crisis in the absence of central bank intervention.

The failure of an institution to settle can easily be transmitted over the payments system and it could precipitate multiple failures of otherwise healthy financial institutions.[20] As a result, major central banks have played an important role in managing the payments system, including supplying liquidity. For example, the Bank of New York, a major clearing bank in the US payments system, experienced a computer breakdown on November 21, 1985, which led the US Federal Reserve to make an overnight loan of $22.6 billion from the discount window, collateralized by $36 billion in securities. The sheer size of average *daily* payments flows through the domestic and international US dollar wholesale payments system – $1.4 trillion in 1988 – and the difficulties experienced in settling trades and payments following a computer breakdown at the Bank of New York and during the October 1987 equity price downturn have shown that wholesale payments system are a source of systemic risk. In fact, some observers believe 'that the greatest threat to the stability of the financial system as a whole during the October stock market crash was the danger of a major default in one of the clearing and settlement systems.'[21]

A gross or continuous payments system with payment finality and intra-settlement period overdraft facilities, such as the US fedwire system, avoids systemic liquidity crises arising from settlement failures since its payments are final.[22] However, only a central bank has the ability to create a payments system with absolute settlement finality.

In Fedwire payments, the Federal Reserve guarantees unconditionally that a bank payment message sent over Fedwire will be honored as good funds at settlement. If a bank fails to deliver good funds, the Fed supplies the funds without assessing other banks for the deficit in reserves resulting from the failure. Thus, over the course of any day, the Fed insures the market in wholesale payments. Hence, the Fed significantly increases liquidity in the money markets and the efficiency of the payments mechanism. As a result, however, it assumes the risk of making payments for a bank in default. The revenue on reserves deposited with the Fed serves as a compensation for the risk it bears, but it may or may not represent sufficient compensation. There may be more efficient means of charging for this risk-bearing, since in taxing the Fed's net revenues, the Treasury ultimately bears the risk of operating the payment system.

Concerns about the intra-day credit exposure in net-settlement payments systems with payment finality led the Federal Reserve to introduce caps on debit positions with Fedwire and CHIPS, and to propose interest charges on such debit positions. The presence of a cap on the debit position that an individual bank is allowed to run with Fedwire effectively limits the loss that could be incurred by the Federal Reserve as a result of payments instructions sent out over the Fedwire by a failing bank. However, in a situation where investors have lost confidence in a large money centre bank and fail to renew short-term funds, such as maturing certificates of deposit and repurchase agreements, the bank would quickly reach its net debit limit and might then be unable to repay its short-term creditors. As a result, the central bank could be faced with the need to provide funds to the bank through the discount window and hence be subject to the credit risk inherent in the bank asset used as collateral.[23]

In contrast, financial systems with a limited extent of securitization have in practice a small number of large universal banks in the market for wholesale funds. Wholesale payments and securities transactions are cleared internally in these organizations. The risk of nonsettlement is small due to the lack of significant exposure to non-bank financial institutions and an increased ability to work out unexpected problems quickly among the small number of players. Hence, although the clearing banks ultimately clear on the books of the central bank, there is little need for the central bank to provide intra-day credit or stand ready to act as lender-of-last-resort to the clearinghouse to ensure the payments settlement.

3.1 The role of the ECB in the payments system

Although the draft Statute empowers the ECB to issue regulations governing the clearing and payments systems in the Community, it does not mandate the ECB to play an active part in the payments system by providing intra-day credit or to extend lender-of-last-resort guarantees to a clearinghouse.

Current practices regarding clearing and settlement of payments vary widely across member countries. Since mandatory reserves would be held at the ECB, the final settlement of payments among clearing banks would have to occur on the books of the ECB.[24] It will thus be necessary to define clearly the ECB's support for the payments system; whether it will support a gross or continuous settlement system with daylight good funds or it will support a private clearinghouse arrangement by supplying liquidity if the clearinghouse fails to settle.

Such support will be necessary if the ECB wishes to facilitate growth in money market trading volume and development of derivative markets.[25] Failure to support actively the payments surplus in the interest of achieving the efficiency gains from liquid money and capital markets will ensure that the US dollar will continue to act as a vehicle currency for a significant volume of Community financial markets transactions. The dollar clearing facilities currently available, together with strong Federal Reserve (and Treasury) liquidity support, will continue to maintain the US dollar's pre-eminent role in international transactions.

4   The central bank's choice problem

In Section 2, we showed that financial systems with liquid, securitized money and capital markets are more likely to experience liquidity crises than bank-intermediated financial systems. Hence, such financial systems have a greater need for a central bank with a lender-of-last-resort function. In Section 3, we indicated that the greater the extent of securitization, the greater the demands on the wholesale payments system and the greater the need for the central bank to provide daylight credit or to act as a lender-of-last-resort in cases of settlement failure. The elements of a central bank policy role regarding the extent of the central bank's banking functions thus emerges clearly as a *balancing of the cost of lender-of-last-resort operations with the benefits flowing from liquid, securitized financial markets.*

The role and functions of central banks in the major industrial countries emerged during the 19th and early 20th century largely in response to the need to centralize interbank clearing and the holding of reserves. In addition, most central banks also served to monopolize the issue of bank notes and acted as the Government's bank. Central banks supplied liquidity in times of crises (elastic supply of currency) to financial markets and to individual institutions, first in conjunction with their clearinghouse role and then with their note issuance role, by discounting various types of commercial paper.[26][27]

These microeconomic or banking functions were in most instances combined with the monetary function of supporting a metallic standard or fixed parities under the Bretton Woods system, through an appropriate discount policy. With the monetary and economic catastrophes of the 1920s and the 1930s, and the consequent ascendancy of macroeconomics as a separate discipline in economics, the policy objectives of central banks became ever more defined in terms of the macroeconomic goals of economic stabilization, including price level stabilization. The banking role of central banks became intellectually secondary to the monetary role.[28] In practice, however, the new macroeconomic policy operations were only superimposed on, rather than taking the place of, the pre-existing banking operations of the pre-war central banks, which continued to operate fully as banking entities. Although 'operating instruments' such as short-term interest rates were used as levers, whose manipulation might effect the ultimate goals, they simultaneously were used as the central banks' traditional instruments for influencing banking and financial market activity.[29]

Current central banking practices in the major industrial countries tend to support the hypothesis that liquid, securitized financial markets need to be supported by a central bank with broad banking functions – lender-of-last-resort, involvement in the payments system, and the supervision and regulation of the banking system. In particular, central banks in the large industrial countries with highly securitized and liquid financial markets, such as the United States and the United Kingdom, have a clear objective to secure stable banking and financial markets, in addition to their monetary policy objective. The central banks in these countries have repeatedly demonstrated their willingness to act as lender-of-last-resort to the financial system as a whole, as well as to individual institutions,[30] while at the same time imposing a supervisory and regulatory framework to minimize the occurrence of such crises.

On the other hand, central banks in financial systems with predominantly bank-intermediated credit, such as Germany, have not found it necessary to act as lender-of-last-resort. Consistent with the tradition of its early predecessor the 19th century Reichsbank, the German Bundesbank lacks a mandate to act as a lender-of-last-resort, and has only limited supervisory and regulatory responsibilities.[31]

The welfare loss of liquidity crises can be partly offset by a central bank acting as lender-of-last-resort to the financial system or to individual institutions. However, in any credit operation that it undertakes in the lender-of-last-resort role, a central bank will incur the credit risk and potential losses, associated with the claims it acquires when expanding its liabilities to supply liquidity. Such losses will occur when the market value of the collateral is less than the amount of the loan or advance to the banks concerned.[32] As a remuneration for such credit risk, the central bank receives income from holding the reserve balances of the banking system.

While the monetary effects of the liquidity operations can be sterilized, the central bank's losses on acquired bank assets fall ultimately to the taxpayers. In effect, the taxpayer has assumed the credit risk inherent in bank assets that serve as collateral for central bank lending. Such losses will have to be balanced against the benefits derived from liquid, securitized financial markets with an efficient payments system. Furthermore, the moral hazard generated by the presence of a lender-of-last-resort will have to be mitigated by supervision and prudential regulation of the financial system by the central bank.

4.1   Policy choice

To reduce the expected cost to the public sector arising from the central bank's lending operations undertaken to stabilize financial markets, the central bank can restrict the extent to which financial markets are securitized, it can eliminate payments system risk by requiring continuous settlement with payment finality, and it can impose supervisory and prudential requirements on the banking system. These restrictions will reduce the likelihood of liquidity crises and may reduce the loss to the central bank if a crisis occurs. Such policies, however, tend to restrict the activities of banking firms, limit the range of available instruments, increase the cost of operating the payments system, and generally reduce liquidity in financial markets, all of which will increase the total cost of the financial transactions supporting a given volume of real activities.[33] In the extreme, the central bank can restrict the financial system to operate largely through bank intermediation.

In practice, central banks have, for historical reasons or otherwise, chosen different positions along the credit risk – financial market efficiency trade-off ranging from the highly liquid securitized capital markets in the United States to the predominately bank-intermediated financial system in Germany. The draft Statute for the ECB would seem to leave very little room for the ECB actively to stabilize Community financial markets. Implicitly therefore, the Statute foresees a bank-intermediated financial system without any significant further securitization of finance.

It will then not only be necessary to restrict the further development of liquid, securitized financial markets and large volume wholesale payments systems in the Community financial system, but it will also be necessary to scale-back such developments in the UK and French financial markets.

An important reason why banking functions, in particular lender-of-last-resort operations, cannot be undertaken by national central banks is that such operations may have monetary effects and may be costly in terms of central bank resources. It will be more difficult for national central banks to resist calls to come to the assistance of a local banking system than for a multi-national ECB. Thus, even if the monetary effects of a liquidity operation by a national central bank could be undone by the ECB, it is nevertheless advisable to control banking operations from the centre. Nor could the ECB rely on its ability to avoid a systemic crisis by financing a group of European banks to form a 'lifeboat' to assist a bank or a group of banks in need of liquidity. The diversity of banks across member countries and the lack of cohesion among these banks rules out such operations.

It has been argued that an announced commitment of a central bank to serve as a lender-of-last-resort in a liquidity crisis leads to moral hazard. Knowing the contingencies under which the central bank will support asset prices, market participants will take positions that make liquidity problems and therefore central bank interventions more likely. Rather, the argument goes, the central bank should make no announcement of its responsibility to provide liquidity to financial markets. Implicitly, it would be well known that it would serve as lender-of-last-resort, however. If market participants think that a lack of explicit commitment reduces the set of contingencies in which the central bank will support asset prices, they will be less likely to take positions in which intervention is required. These are exactly the arguments that we have made throughout the paper about how financial markets develop in the presence of central bank liquidity support. It does not follow, however, that implicit liquidity support is superior to explicitly announced support – implicit support is simply an alternative name for a policy of fostering illiquid financial markets. Of course, lack of an explicit liquidity announcement need not reduce the set of contingencies in which market participants believe that the central bank will intervene. The public may in fact believe that the central bank intends to intervene more than it would under an explicit announcement, and market participants may assume positions that make a liquidity crisis even more likely.

5 Supervision and regulation of banking systems

In addition to restricting the extent of securitization of financial interme-diation, central banks can reduce the credit risk incurred during liquidity operations through an appropriate regulatory and supervisory regime on financial systems (not exclusively on banking systems). The regime would be designed to limit the expected losses on bank assets acquired during a liquidity operation to a desired level. In particular, regulations can be designed so that disturbances from the activities of banks other than those relating to payments and liquidity do not spill over into the payments system and become systemic.[34] Such regulations include risk-related capital requirements, separation of investment banking activity from payments activity, position limits, and frequent assessment of the solvency of the bank through examination of its balance sheet. The more restrictive the regulatory and supervisory regimes, however, the greater the total cost of financial transactions, specifically the cost of making payments.

The draft Statute does not envisage an active role for the ECB in the prudential supervision of financial institutions,[35] which is consistent with the limited banking functions mandated in the draft Statute for the ECB. As long as the ECB does not intend to supply liquidity as a lender-of-last-resort to stabilize Community financial markets, it will not be necessary to restrict the amount of credit risk it might assume under such operations through supervisory and regulatory policies.[36]

If, however, the ECB does assume a lender-of-last-resort role, then it will also have to assume a supervisory and regulatory role at the centre of the Community financial system, rather than leave such activities to the national central banks or other agencies. This is because the assignment of responsibility for the supervision of the banking system should avoid inter-agency conflict of interest. Such conflict would arise if the central bank puts its resources at stake, while another agency is responsible for establishing the solvency of central bank debtors. For example, the supervision of the banking system, i.e., the assessment of the market value of banking assets, could be subject to intense political pressure leading to a delay in corrective measures. An independent central bank with its own resources at stake is more likely to assess the solvency of potential borrowers sufficiently accurately to protect its own resources. Thus, as long as there is any potential for central bank lending to credit institutions, the central bank should be responsible for supervising the banking system.

A second argument in favor of centralizing the responsibility for bank supervision in the central bank relates to the central bank's first-hand involvement in liquidity support operations. To reduce credit risk to a minimum and in order to establish the modalities of its intervention (e.g., open market operations versus discount window) the ECB will have to establish quickly whether it is facing a pure liquidity crisis or an insolvency crisis. The initial problem will most likely have become apparent at the time payments are settled, and hence speed is of the essence if a systemic payments crisis is to be avoided. The expertise and information necessary to conduct a successful liquidity operation at minimal credit risk requires the intimate involvement of the central bank with the banking system. During the October 1987 stock market crash, for example, the successful intervention by the Federal Reserve required a knowledge of dealer obligations to the banking system, of the potential magnitude of margin calls, and of the position of the money centre banks. It is unlikely that such expertise can be developed and retained outside the ECB.

6 Conclusions

The draft Statute for a System of European Central Banks, the centre-piece of EMU, defines a 'narrow' ECB – a central bank shirking basic banking functions such as lender-of-last-resort to financial markets and the payments system, and supervision and regulation of banking markets. In this paper, we have demonstrated that this choice will also determine the future structure of the Community financial system. In particular, an ECB eschewing any substantive banking function will have to guide the development of Community financial markets in the direction of a predo-minately bank-intermediated financial system, avoiding any significant degree of liquid, securitized markets, including markets for short-term corporate obligations, bank liabilities, repurchase agreements, derivative instruments, and equity products.

Alternatively, if Community financial markets are to develop further towards liquid, securitized financial markets with a high-volume wholesale payments system, then it will be essential for the ECB to assume a well-defined lender-of-last-resort function, as well as supervisory and regulatory responsibilities.

A policy choice in favor of a bank-intermediated Community financial system, which would inevitably result in a higher cost of financial trans-actions supporting a given volume of real transactions, would imply that a significant portion of intra-Community financial transactions would continue to use the dollar-based financial system.

NOTES

The views expressed are the authors' alone and do not necessarily represent the views of the International Monetary Fund.

1 Sent to the EC Ministers on November 19, 1990, and amended on April 11, 1991. The proposed European System of Central Banks ('System') is to consist of a central institution, the European Central Bank (ECB), and of partici-pating central banks of the Member States of the Community ('national central banks').

2 *'Article 2 – Objectives*
  2.1 The primary objective of the system shall be to maintain price stability.
  2.2 Without prejudice to the objective of price stability, the system shall support the general economic policy of the Community.'

3 See Article 3. Further references to the banking functions of the System are equally restrictive. In particular, Article 18.1 enables the System to 'conduct credit operations with credit institutions and other market participants' but only to achieve the limited monetary objectives of the System. Article 22 enables the System to 'provide facilities ... and issue regulations to ensure efficient and sound clearing and payments systems', but it does not enable the system to extend credit or liquidity support to the payments system. Article 25.1 enables the ECB only to 'offer advice and to be consulted in the interpretation and implementation of Community legislation relating to the prudential supervision of credit and of the financial institutions'. Article 25.2 offers the possibility of designating the ECB as a competent supervisory authority but such a transferal of competence must be specified by further Community legislation.

4 'Article 18.2. The ECB shall establish general principles for open market and credit operations carried out by itself or the national central banks, including the announcement of conditions under which they stand ready to enter into such transactions'.

5 The term 'securitization' has frequently been used in the financial press to describe the creation of high-quality negotiable, liquid securities by setting aside illiquid claims, such as mortgage obligations, consumer receivables, etc. to fund such securities. We employ the term here to describe a broader phenomenon, namely, the creation of any credit, ownership, or derivative claims that are publicly tradable, either in an organized market or over-the-counter, and whose prices are, therefore, determined at frequent intervals in an open market. Thus, commercial paper and negotiable certificates of deposit are securitized instruments, while the interbank market in central bank liabilities, such as the US Federal Funds market, is not securitized. The most important quantitative example of securitization involves disintermediation from the banking system.

6 To the extent that it existed, the historical comparative advantage of banking institutions in assessing credit risk, in monitoring borrower behaviour, and in dealing with nonperforming debtors is being eroded by, inter alia, advances in information technology, innovations in credit-worthiness signalling mechanisms, and improvements in the legal system. Furthermore, financial intermediaries, acting as agents rather than as principals, such as investment banks, have been increasingly innovative in designing techniques and instruments to bring borrowers and non-bank lenders together. The growth of institutional investors, such as pension funds and insurance companies, has also created growing demand for securitized debt and equity. Finally, a growing stock of outstanding tradable financial instruments increases the scope for financial institutions to make a market in these instruments, thus increasing liquidity and reducing transaction costs.

7 Folkerts-Landau and Mathieson (1988).

8 The ability to create currency through the open market purchase of securities or direct lending against eligible collateral has allowed central banks to supply liquidity in times of crisis and thereby guarantee the exchange rate between

bank deposits and currency. In fact, during the period from 1793 to 1933 the United States experienced at least 17 banking crises, while none have occurred since 1933, the beginning of active Federal Reserve intervention. Thus, the systemic financial instability in banking and payment systems was eliminated through the introduction of the central bank clearinghouse where banks would hold their clearing balances and that stood ready to assist banks to convert bank deposit liabilities into currency by taking bank assets as collateral (Schwartz, 1988).

9 During the secondary banking crises in 1973 in the UK the Bank of England organized a 'lifeboat,' a group of primary clearing banks that provided liquidity to the affected banks. The failure of several of the secondary banks is estimated to have resulted in significant losses ($234 million) for the Bank of England, as well as for the lifeboat ($117 million). The Bank of England also arranged a lifeboat for Johnson Matthey Bankers to prevent the failure of the bank from having systemic consequences. The final cost of the operation is yet to be determined.

The Federal Reserve Bank of Chicago advance $3.5 billion to Continental Illinois Bank during a run on the bank, and the FDIC extended full coverage to all depositors (see US Treasury, 1991).

10 The payment of fees for the use of such credit lines serves as compensation to banks for maintaining reserves and for satisfying regulatory capital requirements and other restrictions necessary to access their lines of credit to a central bank. Such payments are reflected in the market yields of money market instruments. Securities whose dealers or issuers rarely expect to draw on bank lines of credit to provide liquidity are most liquid, and this is expressed in relatively low market yields. Securities whose dealers expect frequently to use bank lines are relatively less liquid, and the higher probability of having to incur the costs of using the reserves of the banking system manifests itself in a relatively higher yield, or equivalently in the haircut in price, for such securities (Garber and Weisbrod, 1990).

A liquid, securitized money market provides perfect substitutes for both bank liabilities and assets. It, therefore, allows a banking system to shrink or to expand its balance sheet so that reserve requirements are nonbinding – that is, banks hold the amount of reserves that they want to minimize the total costs of effecting end-of-day net settlement of all the payments generated from inside and outside the banking system, including from the money markets.

11 For a discussion of the impact of available dealer liquid resources on securities market spreads, see Grossman and Miller (1988).

12 For US dealers in securities, the SEC requires 'net capital' of 6⅔ percent of liabilities where net capital is defined as net worth plus subordinated debt and adjusted for a haircut reflecting the volatility of securities positions.

13 For example, during a recent period in August 1991 securities dealers in the US securities market were forced to draw on their lines of credit with the money centre banks after the rate on repurchase agreements – their traditional source of funding inventories – had unexpectedly risen to levels that could have impaired the solvency of some of the dealers. The sudden increased demand for funds sent banks into the Fed Funds market, which drove the Fed Funds rate to above 30 percent and induced the Federal Reserve to lend in excess of $3 billion through the discount window in order to preserve orderly markets.

14 The Federal Reserve actively supplied liquidity to the banking system through the discount window, and it encouraged the banking system to maintain and extend credit lines to dealers and other market makers so as to avoid a chain of bankruptcies.

15 By cash, we mean 'good funds' – that is, central bank deposits that can shift rapidly through a system of settlement.

16 See Folkerts-Landau (1991).

17 The Swiss payments system is an important exception, in that it is a gross settlement system without intra-day credit extension.

18 In settling net positions, the clearinghouse makes a claim that in the event that one member is in bankruptcy, it has the right to offset payments due from that member with payments due to that member. The clearinghouse makes prior claims over all other creditors to the bankrupt member's liabilities to the clearinghouse to the extent that they are offset by that member's claims on the clearinghouse. Much of the security the clearinghouse adds to the payments mechanism is derived from liability rules. Reserve requirements protect the payments mechanism in a similar fashion. They are assets of the several member banks, but the clearinghouse has prior claim to them in the event of bankruptcy.

19 The US Federal Reserve is an example of a clearinghouse that bears the risk of settlement failure. Reserves of individual banks serve as a guarantee to the Fed of the delivery of good funds against end-of-day net due to positions, but the Fed is covered against a bank's nonsettlement only by that bank's reserve deposits. CHIPS now also operates as a collateralized clearing corporation with settlement finality for payments generated in the Eurodollar and foreign exchange markets.

20 Some of these concerns have been discussed in recent conferences and symposia. For example, the Group of Thirty Symposium on Clearance and Settlement Issues in the Global Securities Markets in London in March 1988; and the International Symposium on Banking and Payment Services, sponsored by the Board of Governors of the Federal Reserve System, June 7–9, 1989; and the Williamsburg Payments System Symposium of the Federal Reserve Bank of Richmond, May 20, 1988.

21 Greenspan (1989)

22 The US Fedwire system is the Federal Reserve's nationwide wire system for transferring funds and US Government securities among foreign and domestic depository institutions operating in the United States. Fedwire is the world's largest wholesale payments settlement mechanism, with an average daily value of transactions of $700 billion (excluding CHIPS net settlement) in 1989. Fedwire payments are made by debiting and crediting reserve accounts maintained by depository institutions at their Federal Reserve banks. The Fedwire payment is finally and irrevocably paid when a reserve bank sends a payment message to a receiving depository institution. The Federal Reserve Bank will execute the payments instruction even if it leads to a debit balance. If the sending bank failed while in overdraft, the risk would be borne by the Federal Reserve Bank. Such an overdraft must, however, be settled by the end of the day, hence the term 'daylight overdraft.'

23 A large proportion of the assets of money centre or clearing banks is financed by short-term funds – certificates of deposit, repurchase agreements, interbank loans – and it is possible that a loss of such funding could make it necessary for

the bank to discount assets other than the eligible government securities. In this case the central bank would be exposed to the private credit risk inherent in such assets.

24 In the Federal Reserve system, each district Federal Reserve Bank has a formal identity, and member banks formally maintain deposit accounts with their district Federal Reserve Bank. Funds move instantly from one member to another, however, even though they have accounts with different district Federal Reserve Banks. There is no central Federal Reserve Bank like an ECB, however, where the district Feds keep funds for interdistrict settlement. Settlement across district Feds occurs through a manipulation under the direction of the Open Market Committee, which reallocates Treasury securities on the balance sheets of the district Federal Reserve Banks.

25 The only Community-wide payments system currently operating is the ECU Clearing and Settlement System. The 45 participating clearing banks, located in 10 EC countries, use SWIFT as netting center, and settle final clearing balances in sight deposits accounts they maintain at the BIS. Such accounts are not allowed to show a debit balance. Clearing banks with a debit position have to obtain ECU funds from creditor banks through bilateral operations. If a clearing bank has insufficient funds in its ECU account to cover its end-of-day settlement obligations, then all intra-day payments instructions will be unwound and those pertaining to the debtor bank will be eliminated. The new clearing balances will be established and added to the clearing for the following day. In securitized financial systems, with high-volume wholesale payments flows among clearing banks, such as unwinding is very likely to cause illiquidity in several other participating institutions (Humphrey, 1984). For this reason, the CHIPS system adopted settlement finality with explicit loss-sharing arrangements in 1990.

26 The German Reichsbank, founded in 1875, was the only major exception; although it supplied liquidity to the financial system during crises by purchasing prime bills on the open market, it did not act as a lender-of-last-resort to individual banks. The risk that a bank failure might lead to generalized illiquidities in the banking system was perceived to be negligible, and the Reichsbank stood aside in a number of bankruptcies among the largest banks. As a result, it also was able to avoid any role in supervising or regulating commercial banks. It appears that the structure of bank liquidity of German commercial banks made such an aloof position vis-à-vis individual banks possible. In particular, the ratio of cash to banks' sight deposits was relatively high and the ratio of bank capital to bank deposits was also comparatively high and, therefore, the risk of contagion among banks was relatively smaller. Thus, individual bank failures were unlikely to spill-over, and generalized liquidity shortages could be met with open-market purchases of bills and supervision and regulation of banks could be performed by a separate agency. In short, liquidity problems were unlikely because all markets, including banking markets, were kept notably illiquid. See National Monetary Commission (1910a), and Goodhart (1988).

27 See Goodhart (1988); Bagehot (1922); Willis (1923); Smith (1936); Sprague (1910); National Monetary Commission (1910a, b, c, d, e, f).

28 This change is especially noticeable in the evolution of post-World War II textbooks on money and banking. These became essentially second-rate macroeconomics texts, reflecting the view of central banking prevalent in

macroeconomics, in which the role of central banks was economic stabilization and the role of banks was purely a mechanistic balance sheet activity of producing deposits that formed a key part of the controllable money supply.

29 The rapid collapse of the main schools of thought in macroeconomics, and the fracturing of macroeconomics itself as a coherent discipline, in the 1980s has engendered an understanding that a central bank cannot play an activist role in stabilizing real economic activity, leaving the attainment of price stability as the main macroeconomic goal. The only consideration of central banking policy as a banking rather than as a monetary policy in the recent academic macroeconomics literature is Sargent and Wallace's (1982) paper on the real bills doctrine vs. price level stability. Sargent and Wallace show that a policy based on a real bills doctrine is welfare maximizing when capital markets are constrained. The result is tainted, however, by its being reached in the context of an overlapping generations model of money demand.

30 The experience of the US Federal Reserve System is the most relevant as a model for the new European system of central banks and the ECB. The Fed's view were clearly formulated by Chairman Volcker in 1983: 'A basic continuing responsibility of any central bank – and the principal reason for the founding of the Federal Reserve – is to assure stable and smoothly-functioning financial and payments systems. These are prerequisites for, and complementary to, the central bank's responsibility for conducting monetary policy as it is more narrowly conceived.

To these ends, the Congress has over the last 70 years authorized the Federal Reserve (a) to be a major participant in the nation's payments mechanism, (b) to lend at the discount window as the ultimate source of liquidity for the economy, and (c) to regulate and supervise key sectors of the financial markets, both domestic and international. These functions are in addition to, and largely predate, the more purely "monetary" functions of engaging in open market and foreign exchange operations and setting reserve requirements; historically, in fact, the "monetary" functions were largely grafted on to the "supervisory" functions, not the reverse' (Federal Reserve System, 1984).

31 The Bundesbank's experience undoubtedly served to form views about the role of the ECB. For example, Dr. H. Tietmayer, member of the Board of the Bundesbank, made the case for a narrow ECB. '... if too many tasks were to be assigned to the European Central Bank this could complicate the conduct of monetary policy. The ECBS should be free, therefore, from responsibilities other than those for monetary policy. In particular, banking supervision should not be assigned to the ECBS, but should be left with national authorities, if only to prevent the ECBS from being forced into a "lender of last resort" function that would not be compatible with its task of safeguarding the currency ...' (Deutsche Bundesbank, 1991).

32 For example, in a wholesale payments system with daylight credit and settlement finality, such as Fedwire, it may be possible for a bank to send a sufficient volume of payments messages to exceed the value of its assets.

33 For example, the absence of extensive derivative markets raises the cost of hedging operations. It is a general proposition that any restrictions on the number and type of instruments that make financial markets less complete lead to inefficient resource allocation.

34 Garber and Weisbrod (1990) have established elsewhere that banks have a comparative advantage in supplying liquidity, hence it is efficient to restrict

those activities of banks that do not relate to the payment system or supplying liquidity.
35 Article 25.2 holds out the possibility of designating the ECB as a complete supervisory authority but such a transfer of competence would have to be specified by Community legislation.
36 Germany is the only major industrial country with a central bank that does not have a substantial supervisory function.

REFERENCES

Bagehot, W. (1922), *Lombard Street*, London: Kegan, Paul & Co.
Deutsche Bundesbank (1991), Auszuge aus Presseartikeln, 11 November.
Federal Reserve System (1984), 'The Federal Reserve Position on Restructuring of Financial Regulation Responsibilities,' *Federal Reserve Bulletin*.
Folkerts-Landau, D. (1991), 'Systemic Financial Risk in Payment Systems', IMF Occasional Paper No. 77.
Folkerts-Landau, D. and Donald J. Mathieson (1988), 'Innovation, Institutional Change, and Regulatory Response in International Financial Markets', in William S. Haraf and Rose Marie Kushmeider (eds.), *Restructuring Banking and Financial Services in America*, Washington, DC: American Enterprise Institute for Public Policy Research, pp. 392–423.
Frankel, Allen B., and John D. Montgomery (1991), 'Financial Structure: An International Perspective', *Brookings Papers on Economic Activity* 1, 257–309.
Garber, P. M., and Steven R. Weisbrod (1990), 'Banks in the Market for Liquidity', NBER Working Paper No. 3381.
Goodhart, Charles Albert Eric (1988), *The Evolution of Central Banks*, Cambridge, MA: MIT Press.
Greenspan, A. (1989), 'International Payment System Developments', speech before the International Symposium on Banking and Payment Services, Washington: Federal Reserve Press Release.
Grossman, S., and M. Miller (1988), 'Liquidity and Market Structure', *The Journal of Finance* 43, 617–34.
Humphrey, David B. (1984), *The US Payments System: Cost, Pricing, Competition and Risk*. Monograph Series in Finance and Economics, Salomon Brothers Center for the Study of Financial Institutions.
National Monetary Commission (1910a), *The Reichsbank and Renewal of its Charter*, Vol. X, Washington, DC: Government Printing Office.
(1910b), *Articles on German Banking and German Banking Laws*, Vol. XI, Washington, DC: Government Printing Office.
(1910c), *The German Inquiry of 1908* (Stenographic Reports), Vol. XII, Part 1 and Vol. XIII, Part 2, Washington, DC: Government Printing Office.
(1910d), *The Great German Banks*, Vol. XIV, Washington, DC: Government Printing Office.
(1910e), *Banking in France and the French Bourse*, Vol. XV, Washington, DC: Government Printing Office.
(1910f), *Banking in Italy, Russia, Austro-Hungary and Japan*, vol. XVIII, Washington, DC: Government Printing Office.
Sargent, T., and N. Wallace (1982), 'The Real Bills Doctrine vs. The Quantity Theory: A Reconsideration,' *Journal of Political Economy* 90, 1212–36.

Schwartz, Anna J. (1988), 'Financial Stability and the Federal Safety Net', in William S. Haraf and Rose Marie Kushmeider (eds.), *Restructing Banking and Financial Services in America*, Washington, DC: American Enterprise Institute for Public Policy Research, pp. 34–63.

Smith, Vera (1936), *The Rationale of Central Banking*, London: P. S. King & Son Ltd.

Sprague, O. M. W. (1910), *History of Crises Under the National Banking System*, National Monetary Commission, 61st Congress, 2nd Session, Senate Doc. No. 538, Washington, DC: Government Printing Office

U.S. Department of the Treasury (1991), *Modernizing the Financial System*, Washington, DC: February.

Willis, Henry Parker (1923), *The Federal Reserve System*, New York: The Ronald Press.

Discussion

JOHN C. PATTISON

1   Introduction

The issue addressed in the paper by Folkerts-Landau and Garber is whether the 'Draft Statute of the European Central Banks and the European Central Bank' erred in limiting the European Central Bank ('ECB') to a monetary role rather than including responsibility for financial stability. One could rephrase this by saying, should the ECB be a Federal Reserve system or a Bundesbank? Clearly the authors have decided that Europe needs an ECB modelled on Federal Reserve lines.

I am going to respond by looking at three major building blocks on which their conclusion rests. These are of broad interest to commercial bankers and central bankers, bank regulators and ultimately those in the political system who give direction to the framework of bank operations and regulation.

These three foundations are: first, the assumption that central banks should have a broad mandate to deal with what are bank solvency, supervisory and regulatory matters; second, that the extent of securitization, rather than simply bank creditworthiness, increases the need for a central bank to be a lender of last resort; and third, that well functioning payments systems require central banks to take private sector credit risk.

Before proceeding it should be fully appreciated that these are very important economic and financial issues. They are rendered even more significant by the difficulties experienced by bank and non-bank financial intermediaries in many countries and by the opaqueness of many of the financial regulatory, supervisory and payment processes to both the public and to academics who have not generally delved into the back-offices of the financial system. This paper makes a particularly worthwhile contribution to these issues in their application to the ECB.

2   Central banks as supervisors

The authors illustrate how central banking evolved from banking institutions to having responsibility for macroeconomic policy superimposed on them. Today many central banks, particularly the US Federal Reserve System and the Bank of England have banking and financial objectives in addition to those of monetary policy. However, no two central banks are the same and the assumption that certain institutional designs provide an argument for the newly proposed European model is insufficient.

The authors are correct in that the differences in scope among central banks are largely explained by differences in the structure of national financial markets. Whereas they identify the most important factor as the relative sizes of securities versus banking markets, I would argue that the most important factor is the probability of a major failure leading to systemic risk. This probably is a function of a much larger number of variables such as the size distribution of banks with direct access to the clearing system. The US experience with a large number of banks and a large number of other financial institutions is rare. Moreover, without nationwide branch banking in the US to provide liquidity to banks, there is a greater onus on the Federal Reserve System to provide liquidity and lender of last resort facilities. As this illustrates there are also a number of policy and political variables which make generalization difficult.

Another point worth greater discussion is the distinction which the authors make between insolvency risk and liquidity risk.[1] I would argue that all central banks are sensitive to liquidity crises such as those stemming from the Penn Central problem or the 1987 stock market crash. Central banks can take liquidity out of the system as quickly as it is injected, thereby not subordinating their goals of monetary control to supervisory type issues. However, in most countries central banks deal with a small number of clearing banks who then make their own credit judgements concerning smaller financial institutions at those difficult moments. In the United States with the large number of banks, credit risk confronts the Federal Reserve directly. To a lesser extent this is also true of the Bank of England. In the latter case, the risk stems from the large number of foreign banks and a number of relatively small merchant banks and accepting houses.

Another factor which deserves comment is that even those central banks which seem to eschew a broad mandate, usually go some way down the road. Even the Bundesbank has a significant regulatory function which involves the supervision of 'approved persons', and the use of the system-wide integration of lending data on individual institutions to assess bank risk. These supervisory functions together with moral suasion and their market clout suffice to reduce or eliminate systemic risk that in other countries might necessitate the provision of liquidity to troubled institutions.

The authors provide a very convincing argument for a broad central bank role in their discussion of the impact of credit risk in payments systems such as Fedwire. As they conclusively illustrate, the more efficient the payments system in a complex financial market, the greater the credit risk internalized within the settlements system. Payments systems that are not irrevocable and final, run the risk that unwinding transactions could cause failures in parties unrelated to those in default.

In the European context, the authors note that the netting of ECU transactions using SWIFT is problematic since all payment instructions for the day will be unwound if a counterparty has insufficient funds at the end-of-day settlement.

In some countries the need for a broader mandate for central banks has been reduced by large banks clearing for small ones, particularly for foreign banks. This shifts the locus for the decision as to whether one is facing a liquidity or an insolvency problem to the large clearing banks from the central bank. Inevitably this leads to a structure where a decision has been made implicitly in the design of the financial system that some institutions are 'too big to fail'.

The authors state that the assignment of responsibility for bank supervision should avoid conflicts of interest among agencies. However, conflicts will occur between the monetary and supervisory functions in a single institution. It could be argued that better decisions will be reached if each agency focuses on its particular goal rather than an individual agency trading them off. This would be because of the specialization of each and the better use of a larger number of better targeted instruments.

3   Securitization and the role of the central bank

I disagree with the authors, who assert that the extent of securitization is positively correlated with the need for the central bank to act as a lender of last resort. I speak to this point as someone who has run the domestic funding and treasury operations of a large bank. The extent of securitization does increase the probability of individual failures to settle. In aggregation large banks will find that offsetting transactions reduce the significance of this problem. Since most countries have a small number of large banks through which most transactions pass in the clearings this is mainly a problem for the smaller institutions. Even with a 25 percent fall in the Dow Jones Index in October 1987 and greater falls in places such as Sydney and Hong Kong, the remarkable outcome was that the system was not at all imperilled by the danger of the failure of large institutions because their creditworthiness was immediately and sharply reduced by the market fall. The larger problems were that credit judgements had often assumed too little asset coverage for collateral for non-financial customers. In my experience the collateral which banks take for lending to financial institutions such as brokers/dealers and investment banks is government securities and acceptances at major banks, not commercial debt obligations. The latter are usually sold to a large number of end buyers.

Even more favourably, securitization has meant that banks have many types of liquid, short-term securities which can be purchased or sold at little change in price according to day-to-day liquidity needs. In addition, there are many thousands of corporate and government institutions, if not tens of thousands, which place money in the money market every day. Both these factors reduce the probability that major banks will need recourse to central bank liquidity as financial markets are securitized.

4 Payments systems and systemic risk

One of the implicit distinctions in the above discussion is that the risks were clearing risks or credit risks attendant upon the behaviour of an individual bank. One factor which should be clarified is that clearing risks are stochastic processes. Banks must adjust their reserve positions with the central bank according to their expectations as to the magnitudes of expected gains and losses through the clearing system. In my experience this can be easily managed in a large bank as you are dealing with a zero-sum game with a small number of participants, one of whom is the central bank. Even so, every once in a while it is possible to be spectacularly wrong in either direction as, for example, oil companies make large payments, other large unanticipated commercial transactions are made, governments shift funds and so forth. However, although these can impact reserve positions they don't affect solvency as funds are on hand; they may simply be invested in short-term securities awaiting settlement on a different date. In support of the authors' thesis, the central banks know enough about the cash positions of all major clearing participants as well as their short-term liquid asset and liability positions to separate liquidity from solvency questions. I should add that this applies in almost all countries with the possible exception of the US system with its large number of banks.

The authors are convincing on two related points. One is the potential threat of systemic problems in the design of the payments system. Second is how this risk is borne, and in particular, on efficient and inefficient ways to run a payments system.

I would conclude that central banking and bank supervisory systems would not have to overlap except for the vital need to control the incidence of credit risk and to stop it cascading through the payments system. Once again, the practical implications depend upon the number of banks in the system and their riskiness. To reiterate an earlier point, the 'too big to fail' concept is not so much a credit judgement as it is designed to keep the payments system from gridlock or worse.

Even so there is nothing that stops a central bank contracting credit advice from bank supervisors the same way that Moody's or Standard & Poor's reports are used by the private sector. However, the authors would contend that the ECB has no mandate to play a role in the payments system on a European wide basis. The risk inherent in settling ECU is an example of a gap that needs to be closed to facilitate the financial integration of Europe. There is no doubt that such matters are important institutional questions for the future of integrated European financial markets.

5   Further implications

I would like to suggest five points for further thought.

First, it is probably not a coincidence that the Draft Statute for the ECB did not lead to a mandate to stabilize European financial markets. Notwithstanding the current macroeconomic issues facing Germany, as Europe becomes more of a DM zone I would expect the private sector to make its own choices in favour of DM assets and liabilities. Why should the Bundesbank propose or support a Draft Statute which could efficiently lead to a parallel central banking regime and a competitive currency to the DM? Moreover, I believe that the long run will show European financial markets developing around a DM base because the marketplace prefers a real currency to a composite one such as the ECU.

Second, there is a large literature on the economic and bureaucratic decision-making processes of central banks. I am a sufficient believer in the rationality of central banks, irrespective of how much one may like the outcome, to suggest that there is a self-interested rationale behind the Draft Statute.

Third, the authors discussed conflicts of interest and moral hazard with one notable exception. This is the conflict between securities regulators, who have responsibility for banks as issuers of securities and for the full, plain and true disclosure of material facts concerning them, and the central bank or banking supervisor who may not want this information disclosed for systemic reasons.

Fourth, the authors are careful to differentiate between a temporay liquidity problem and an underlying reduction in asset prices and credit worthiness. However, while this distinction can sometimes be made quite easily, in some circumstances the central bank could be put in the invidious position of encouraging a credit expansion for the wrong reasons at the wrong time.

Fifth, it seems that the main issue in this paper is but one of a large number of complex issues involving the regulation of financial institutions in Europe, such as deposit insurance for branches using the single license, harmonization of regulation and so forth. These need to be treated in an interdependent fashion rather than as stand-alone issues.

In conclusion, the authors have provided a good and thoughtful paper with implications enough to keep central bankers, commercial banks and governments working for some time to come. While I may disagree about the institutional architecture, I agree with the authors that the issues in their paper require successful treatment by an appropriate agency.

NOTE

1 Another distinction which needs to be kept clear is that between being a provider of liquidity and being a lender of last resort.

RICHARD J. SWEENEY

David Folkerts-Landau and Peter Garber have given us a stimulating and well written paper on a major issue in designing a European central bank. There are many parts of the paper I like a great deal; it would be easy to use my allotted space to praise their paper and to summarize the parts I particularly liked. The discussant's role, however, is to focus on areas of disagreement. The main disagreement is that the authors of this very well written paper do not make their case as clearly as possible. As I read the paper, sometimes between the lines, the authors make a case for an ECB that is involved with the payments system (supervising it or running it, and also insuring it) and with regulating banks. Two conventional justifications for such involvement and regulation are market failure and the danger that expectations, perhaps destabilizing, might cause avoidable damage. The authors do not really argue these justifications as strongly or as clearly as they might. I want to highlight where these issues arise in their analysis.

Their paper considers three types of crises: runs on banks; a stock market crash; and pressure on the payments mechanism. It is useful to consider each in turn.

Bank Runs Bank runs are a classic fear about financial and monetary systems. The fear seems to have (at least) three bases. First, runs might lead to bank failures and thus substantially reduce the money stock, causing deflation and a recession or even depression. Developed country monetary authorities can now offset any money stock effects caused by bank runs even if the authorities allow banks to fail, perhaps in some numbers. There is no need on this score for the central bank to regulate banks or carry out other central bank functions that F-L and G identify.

Second, healthy banks may be forced to 'close their doors.' This provides a justification for a lender of last resort that will discount economically sound assets of the banks. This discounting provides liquidity in the sense that banks do not have to sell their assets on short notice in a jittery market and take prices that are less than could be obtained if sold over a longer time. Liquidity in this sense is inversely related to the amount of time expected or required to sell an asset at its fair market value; one problem with reading the paper is that it is often unclear exactly what the authors have in mind by the term liquidity.

It is not clear that central bank discounting does much on the score of liquidity. The sorts of assets that the central bank (at least the Fed) will discount are those that can be sold very quickly on the open market. Discounting mainly offers a subsidized higher price (by applying a below-market discount rate) than the banks could obtain on the open market. In some few cases the market for such highly liquid assets may not function or the payments system may break down; in such cases central bank discounting replaces the market. This point really has to do with the payments system discussed below. It is not clear how bad 'closing doors' may be. If the bank's assets really are valuable, then over the time required to convert them at reasonable, obtainable prices, depositors and other bank creditors will get back all of their funds plus accrued interest. The cost is doing without the use of the funds for a few days or weeks or conceivably months; even in this case, there should be credit available elsewhere for the bank's creditors to smooth these problems. The securitization that the authors stress helps with the problem by making the asset side of the bank's balance sheet easier to assess, an aspect the authors seem to overlook.[1]

It is puzzling that the F-L and G Paper, an excellent one, omits discussion of two key issues about banks closing their doors. They do not mention federal deposit insurance or the idea that some banks are 'too big to fail.' From recent US economic history the reason there have been no bank runs on federally insured institutions is because of the insurance, not because of the Fed acting a lender of last resort. It would be very useful to know how deposit insurance, absolute up to some large amount of deposits, fits into the authors' scheme. On the one hand, it is not clear that lender-of-last-resort functions particularly improve the market under the circumstances of the past decade in the US. On the other hand, it is clear that deposit insurance is not something lightly to be undertaken; I have some sympathy for the view that deposit insurance is likely to cause major problems for a financial system and the taxpayers who ultimately guarantee it. These problems arise because of bad incentives for bank decision makers; the effects of these bad incentives can be ameliorated by regulation, but this is rather redundant compared to not having bad incentives in the first place. Similarly, the notion that banks are too large to fail adds to the stability of a banking system but at the cost of encouraging bad resource allocation. On this score, it would be good if F-L and G could spell out more institutional details on EC country banks (the paper is in general very good and informative on institutions and their roles). For example, though the authors tell us that the Bundesbank does not regulate German banks, I wonder if the major German banks are too big to fail? And are they somehow regulated in ways that act to reduce the guarantor's risk? So far then, the only activities of central banks that are not done pretty well by financial markets are open-ended deposit insurance and guarantees that some banks are too big to fail, activities that are at the least questionable.

Third, bank failures may be contagious in the form of altering expectations that have real effects on the economy. There is a long history of believing that the credit system is unstable: it is, for example, a thread throughout the work of John Hicks. Other economists view bankruptcy of financial institutions as no different in effect from that of a comparable sized manufacturing firm (Alchian and Allen, 1972). For example, if creditors come to doubt the solvency of a bank, they may run on it. If the bank fails in the sense of closing its doors, creditors of other banks may have their Bayesian beliefs shifted by the failure and start their own runs. One of the goals of founding the Fed was to create an elastic currency supply. The Fed was to provide currency to banks to meet these runs, in return for safe bank assets that were discounted. This arrangement made a good deal of sense: If the demand for base money rises, the only ways of satisfying it are to increase the stock of base money or to let price deflation increase the real stock, a process easily understood from Patinkin (1965). If the Fed were to allow deflation to work its way out, there might be great instability. As one bank fails, there are runs on other banks. Depositors may rationally realize that the process will cause deflation. Further, they may understand that this deflation will cause defaults on banks' assets and hence more bank failures. The system then has an inherent instability, one based on expectations that are rational; this is similar in spirit to Irving Fisher's debt deflation process. The Fed's actions to increase base money see to it that the outcome will not be deflation and hence short circuit the run by destroying its rational basis. Notice, however, that this stabilization is mainly a result of the Fed attempting to prevent deflation, not through it acting as a lender of last resort, even less it acting to save banks that are 'too big to fail.'

In today's world, the elastic supply of currency is not nearly the issue it was. When people flee bank money, they do not turn to base money but rather to high quality debt. There was, for example, a noticable 'flight to quality' in the form of federal government debt at the time of the October 1987 stock market crisis. In such a case, it is not clear what role the central bank should play beyond expanding base money to satisfy whatever vestigial increase in base-money demand might arise.

One might go further and argue that expectations have strong bandwagon effects (and I have some sympathy for this view[2] or that the system is subject to bubbles and that runs on one or a few banks can have destabilizing effects on the whole system. Appropriate central bank action depends on the expectational problem involved. The authors, so admirably clear on so many points, are not clear on what expectations mechanisms they have in mind. Another way of thinking about the expectations issue is to note that in general the case for government action involves some type of market failure. The authors have not spelled out a particular type of market failure; pointing to bad things that might happen to private markets is not the same thing as pointing out market failure. My guess is that the case they have in mind relies on expectations. I am quite willing to entertain this view, since I have evidence that speculative markets driven by expectations often appear to be systematically inefficient to some extent. But we really need to be told the expectations mechanism and how this leads to market failure. We must also consider government failure: in the US federal deposit insurance and the doctrine that some banks are too big to fail have led to substantial social costs.

Stock-Market Crashes F-L and G provide a lucid discussion of how progressive securitization creates vast financial market interdependencies; this is reminiscent of detailed input-output tables for the US economy. The authors' discussion shows that securitization has a symbiotic relationship to liquidity. On the one hand, economic agents buy and sell securities because they believe that they will be able easily and quickly to realize the fair market value of the assets in a short time – the essence of liquidity. On the other hand, the greater the degree of securitization, the more liquid markets become. Securitized assets may not normally be very liquid; for example, many corporate bonds trade relatively infrequently in thin markets (Warga and Welch, 1990; Eberhart and Sweeney, 1991). For this reason it is difficult in the US to mark-to-market the value of financial firms' assets even if the assets are securitized. In less securitized economies where banks are the major intermediaries, it is even harder to assess accurately the value of the banks' assets; on this margin such banks are more liable to runs than if there were greater asset-side securitization.

The dense input-output network of financial relations is put under great stress when the stock market crashes as in October 1987 (or more mildly in October 1989). One agent's ability to make the transactions s/he desires and to carry out his/her economic function is contingent on a vast array of other agents making their desired transactions. Serious failures of this dense network are exactly liquidity crises: agents are unable to realize quickly the fair market values of their assets. The probability of this dense network failing in a serious way is not clear. Neither is it clear what a central bank should do to help. The authors discuss the central bank supplying liquidity and urging banks to supply liquidity. By the central bank supplying liquidity, I presume they mean open market operations that increase the stock of base money, as apparently happened in October 1987. The central bank may also reduce the discount rate or allow banks to borrow more than otherwise at the discount window, or reduce the grade of asset accepted for discounting. It is not clear that any of these is wise as long as the central bank is supplying an adequate amount of base money; given this is so, the other actions would seem to be propping up banks that might be insolvent. It is not clear that propping up insolvent banks is preferable to keeping them running but transferring ownership to creditors. Further, it is not clear how such actions would affect non-bank agents who are experiencing liquidity problems. For example, a leveraged dealer/broker who is caught short and looks like a bad credit risk is not much helped by the Fed injecting base money or by banks having easier access to the discount window. Further, it is not clear how Fed exhortations to banks to provide liquidity are going to help: do such exhortations mean banks should go against their better judgment, or merely that they should calm down and make loans that really are sensible?

The market survived the crash of 1987. During this crash, a number of brokerage houses and dealers went under. Further, at times the market was effectively closed for individual stocks and at other times the futures and cash markets were out of touch with each other because of poor execution. Both of these phenomena showed that the market was less liquid than some sanguine agents thought; there may well be agents who found the markets even more liquid than they would have thought in the circumstances. We do not know whether agents now view the market as more or less liquid than they believed before. It is interesting to note that the circuit breakers desired by the SEC and the NYSE and now in place are designed in effect to limit liquidity and force agents to accumulate and sift information while held temporarily in an illiquid state. The point of raising circuit breakers is not to endorse them – I do not – but to point out that some observers find the costs of temporary illiquidity small enough to make it worthwhile to impose it.

Breakdowns of the network of financial transactions are illiquidity that leads to further illiquidity. To the extent that agents are surprised by the extent of these breakdowns, the agents are less willing later to take open positions. To the extent that illiquidity is an issue, circuit breakers are surely costly, though there may be offsetting gains in giving the market time for reflection.

When there are market breakdowns, they are costly to those who cannot carry out desired transactions. For example, if I am sure the market is going down further, I may want to sell out my positions, presumably to someone on the other side of the market who has differing views. When we cannot make the transaction and the fall in the market that I anticipated occurs, I lose in an opportunity sense and the partner on the other side of the transaction gains by the same amount; overall, this breakdown simply results in a distribution effect. Of course, if I am at all frequently caught in such distribution effects, I will cut back on my market activity and thereby make the market less liquid; this may be the real cost of market breakdowns. It is hard to see what central bank policy can reasonably do about such breakdowns.

Suppose an agent goes bankrupt because of inability to make transactions in a market that is suddenly illiquid. This is, recall, a distribution effect. Of course the value of remaining assets will have to be sorted out and distributed to claimants. My impression is that the settlements after the October 1987 crash were relatively smoothly handled and taken in stride.

The authors do not say it, but I have the impression that they think a crash might snowball, with illiquidity leading to insolvency, to more illiquidity, more insolvencies and a mighty crash in the end. This might happen. The easiest way for this to happen might be through expectations that become more and more gloomy, pushing down market values of many assets in a downward spiral. This possibility has to be spelled out though, particularly the expectations mechanism, for us to evaluate its plausibility and likelihood and to evaluate where there is much a central bank can do beyond changing the stock of base money appropriately. A snowball effect might constitute a case for government doing something to prevent or ameliorate the problem. Another way to invoke the government is to argue that liquidity is an externality provided by the thickness of markets and number of participants, and hence the government might intervene to increase liquidity. It is not clear how the central bank is to do this for non-banks, in general or during crashes.

Clearing Systems The third type of crisis is a breakdown in the clearing systems that banks and other major players use, whether for foreign exchange transactions or federal funds or similar financial transactions. The authors paint a picture of the likelihood of gridlock under a system where a bank must have reserves at the clearing house at every second to cover a claim that is made against the bank. Reasonably, the clearing mechanism may allow for day-end settlement. With this system, if a bank cannot cover its claims, either the clearinghouse must make good out of its reserves, the member banks must be forced to bear the costs by some formula, or the day's transactions must be unwound. Unwinding the transactions is not a good idea – it magnifies the uncertainty beyond the net amount involved (in effect it forces individual banks to face some risks that the system as a whole can diversify). In the long run, if the clearing-house bears the risk, it must charge system users enough to cover costs; whether this is better than allocating any costs *ex post* to members depends on the formulas used in either. It is clear that either system can be made to work.

If the clearinghouse bears the risk, there is always the possibility that it may become insolvent. The authors argue that only a government agency with access to the Treasury can guarantee that the payments system will not run into this problem. I would say, only a government agency that can print money, that is, only the central bank or the part of government that controls the central bank, can make this a credible guarantee. We have much evidence that state governments cannot make credible guarantees;

for example, the nineteenth century saw state defaults on bonds, and the Depression saw city defaults.

Do we want the central bank to guarantee the clearinghouse? This is a cost and benefits issue. What are the costs of reducing to zero the probability of clearinghouse failure? Surely the authors are correct that government guarantees will lead to government regulation. This regulation has a well known set of costs from the industrial organization literature. The benefits are the avoidance of a clearinghouse default. Suppose an unguaranteed clearinghouse could not cover the loss. We are not told how bad this would be. One might be able to construct an externality case that the economy would be wounded in a major way by an unravelling of many transactions networks. On the other hand, it is not clear that this is an externality any more than a major setback is in any industry that figures in the input-output table.

Further, it is not clear that clearinghouse insolvency would lead to any social costs. One scenario is that the major members of the clearinghouse would quickly and with little friction pay in more capital to make the clearinghouse solvent once again. There are, after all, likely a few members that are large enough to act quickly together and are exposed enough to make free-riding an unimportant problem. Other scenarios are possible, but it would seem that it is up to the authors to show why there will be social costs.

Again, one might argue that the visible failure of the clearinghouse, even if new capital is supplied within hours, might so shake expectations that an undesirable evolution is set off. But this is a case for the authors to make.

In sum, this stimulating paper still has a ways to go to make its case. The basic micro route for justifying intervention or regulation is market failure. The authors have not made this case. Nor have they used one of the basic macro routes, that expectations would be destabilizing in the absence of central bank action. This is not to say that the case cannot be made; but the paper does not make it.

NOTES

1 Even on the liabilities side, I think the authors sometimes confuse the effect of securitization. At one point they argue that a system that relies on banks for intermediation rather than on securitization will give banks fewer problems since creditors cannot take away their deposits or other forms of credit to banks on the short notice that wholesale money center banks are subject to in the US. This seems to confuse the maturity of assets with securitization. It is quite possible that banks have many sight liabilities even if banks are the main form of intermediation. The real problem here is a mismatch of assets and liabilities

in terms of maturity and liquidity, and this mismatching can happen under any degree of securitization.

2 Sweeney (1986) and Surajaras and Sweeney (1991) present evidence that technical trading rules make risk-adjusted profits in foreign exchange markets; one possible explanation for these profits is the existence of bandwagons.

REFERENCES

Alchian, A. A. and W. R. Allen (1972), *University Economics*, 3rd ed., Belmont, CA: Wadsworth Press.

Eberhart, A. and R. J. Sweeney (1991), 'Bond Prices as Unbiased Forecasts of Bankruptcy Settlements.' Washington, DC: Georgetown University, School of Business Administration, Working Paper.

Patinkin, D. (1965), *Money, Interest and Prices*. New York, NY: Harper and Row.

Surajaras, P. and R. J. Sweeney (1991), *Profit-Making Speculation in Foreign-Exchange Markets*. Boulder, CO: Westview Press (forthcoming).

Sweeney, R. J. (1986), 'Beating the Foreign Exchange Market,' *Journal of Finance* **41**, 163–82.

Warga, A. and I. Welch (1990), 'Bondholder Losses in Leveraged Buyouts.' Columbia University, Graduate School of Business, Working Paper.

Part II Transition from national central banks to a European Central Bank

5 Hard-ERM, hard ECU and European Monetary Union

DAVID CURRIE

1 Introduction

The vision of Monetary Union in Europe is of long standing. The Werner Report of 1970 advocated the attainment of Monetary Union by 1980, but was buried beneath a soaring oil price and the collapse of Bretton Woods and the move to generalised floating in the early 1970s. The European Community, with some key exceptions, returned to an adjustable peg exchange rate system in 1979 with the launch of the Exchange Rate Mechanism (ERM for short). Helmut Schmidt and Valery Giscard d'Estaing embarked on the ERM against majority technical advice from economists at the time, but despite that the ERM must be judged an appreciable success: much more durable than its critics expected, and much more successful in establishing a credible and stable framework for anti-inflationary policy. Even the British have finally been won round.

In the early years of the ERM, parity realignments were frequent and sometimes large, on occasions requiring the temporary closure of foreign exchange markets while bargaining over the realignment went on. These frequent realignments were necessary because of the diversity of inflation rates between the participating countries. But the gradual convergence of inflation rates, itself a product of the ERM, led over time to smaller and less frequent realignments. This is illustrated in Figure 5.1, which shows realignments of the participating countries against the Deutsche Mark, which over this period did not devalue against any currency. As Figure 5.1 shows, with the exception of Italy, there has been no realignment within the ERM for well over four years. (The Figure depicts the logarithm of the non-German exchange rates, relative to the DM, measured such that the absolute change reflects the proportional change in the exchange rate). Moreover, the Italian devaluation of January 1990 is the

127

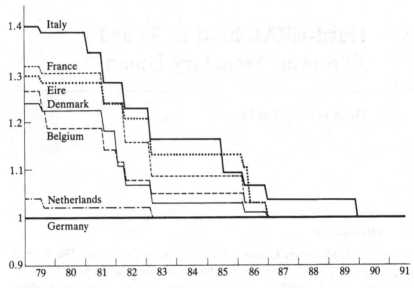

Figure 5.1   Realignments against the DM, 1979–91

exception that proves the rule: the band of variation for the Lira was narrowed at the bottom end of its former broad band, leaving the floor unchanged and requiring a lowering of the central parity and ceiling. This represented a strengthening, not a weakening, of commitment to the ERM by the Banca d'Italia. Thus the evolution of the ERM over the past decade can be represented as an evolution from a soft to a hard form, as European policymakers found the ERM a comfortable framework for conducting anti-inflationary macroeconomic policy.[1] The absence of any realignment over the past year or so, with the double shocks of German union and the Gulf War, is testimony to the durability of the ERM.

The success and durability of the ERM has been an important force in putting EMU back on the agenda. The Heads of State agreed in 1988 to set up a committee to examine possible approaches to EMU, and the Delors Committee reported in 1989 (Committee for the Study of Economic and Monetary Union, 1989). Since then, the agenda has advanced rapidly, with the establishment of an Inter-Governmental Conference on EMU and European central bankers developing their ideas for monetary coordination ahead of EMU. The pace of change has been so rapid that EMU has even forced issues of political union onto the agenda, with Chancellor Kohl explicitly linking the two issues. The present impetus may not be sustained, particularly with German attention diverted to its Eastern domestic problems. Therefore the British Government may well succeed in its aim of slowing the process appreciably, particularly with a tone of moderation, not stridency, that makes it easier for Germany to embrace the UK's position. But the direction of change is likely to be sustained, driven forward by the essential political change in Europe in the 1980s: the switch by France under Mitterrand from a Gaullist to a Communautaire position within Europe.

The creation of the ERM in 1979 did, by contrast, represent a regime change, creating a formal structure of cooperation between the participating central banks, and restricting each country's freedom to alter its exchange rate outside narrow limits by the requirement to secure the agreement of the other member states. By contrast, the evolution of the ERM from its loose, soft form in the early 1980s to its hard form of the past four years or so has taken place without much institutional adaptation. The Basle-Nyborg Agreement of 1987 did increase the availability of the 'very short-term financing facility', which reduced the vulnerability of the ERM system to speculative attack by increasing the funds available to central banks for intervention: it was probably helpful in strengthening the credibility of the ERM in important respects. But there has been little institutional adaptation to reduce the incentive for participating countries to alter their central parities within the system, and realignments represent a real possibility: only last year Karl Otto Pöhl was urging a devaluation on the French, for example, and there are continued calls for a devaluation of sterling. For these reasons, I would characterise the shift from the Soft- to Hard-ERM as a process switch, not a regime change.[2] Because of this, the Hard-ERM cannot be relied upon as a durable system without further institutional development. However, it is not hard to envisage the form that such institutional development might take: it would be straightforward to embody the current near-absence of exchange rate realignments by allowing realignments only after an elapse of years (say, three or four) and insisting that they be intra-marginal (so that the new band overlaps with the old). This would allow central parities to change only very slowly, and would institutionalise the current Hard-ERM arrangement.

This approach of buttressing the advantages of the current Hard-ERM arrangement is not in favour in Europe. Instead the debate focuses on moving forward to monetary union. One possible reason for this is political: the view that moving towards monetary union offers the best means of strengthening the political cohesion of the European Community. But there are also two principal economic reasons: that EMU is a preferable regime, yielding higher net welfare benefits; and that the current Hard-ERM arrangement is not stable. The second argument concerning the stability of the Hard-ERM can be divided further into two parts: that the Hard-ERM is not incentive-compatible for the individual countries participating in it; and that it may be unstable in the dynamic sense, for example, because of the phenomenon of currency substitution.

I wish to discuss the relative benefits of the EMU and Hard-ERM in some detail, together with the issue of incentive-compatibility, which applies as much to EMU as to the Hard-ERM. I deal briefly now with the issue of currency substitution. It is clear that exchange rate stability over prolonged periods will make agents in different countries increasingly indifferent in the choice of currency denomination of money holdings. Thus money demand functions may demonstrate increasing instability. If the monetary authorities choose to attempt to target monetary aggregates, then instability may well result. Currency substitution between DM and non-DM deposits may make the formulation of monetary policy in Germany more difficult, and thus may generate swings in German inflation. Fixed parities will generalise these swings throughout the Community (see Hughes Hallett and Vines, 1991).

My own view is that these worries are exaggerated. Monetary authorities, including the Bundesbank, have increasingly adopted pragmatic methods of monetary control, allowing interest rates to be guided by growth of nominal income in the medium to long term and a variety of indicators in the short term. Financial innovation, which also has also induced instability in monetary aggregates, is likely to increase its impact with harmonisation of financial services regulation after 1992. This will make the pragmatic setting of monetary policy all the more needed. In these circumstances, currency substitution will add somewhat to the problem of interpreting monetary conditions and setting interest rates, but should not induce undue instability.[3] Were the problem more serious than this, it would already have shown up between the stable currencies of the Community, most noticeably between the Dutch Guilder and the DM. Moreover, the switch to a single currency in Europe will throw up exactly the same problems of interpretation of monetary aggregates, at least over an extended transitional period. For these reasons, I do not consider currency substitution to be a serious concern for the current Hard-ERM arrangement.

In analysing the performance of alternative monetary arrangements in Europe, economics has most to offer in analysing the steady-state, systemic properties of the alternative regimes. It is a general characteristic of the methodology of economics that it allows us to say much more about steady states, in which of course I include stochastic steady states, than about the dynamics of transition from one stochastic steady state to another. I do not think that we need to be too apologetic about this, particularly when examining the design of particular regimes. The calculus of discounting may lead us to give weight to the short run at the expense of the long run. But it would be unwise to choose a regime on the basis of its transitional ease rather than its long-run systemic properties. A necessary, but not necessarily sufficient, condition for a desirable regime is that its long-run steady-state and stochastic properties should be satisfactory.

2   The benefits of EMU

In considering the benefits of moving to EMU, the most tangible benefit is that of a single currency in Europe. The resource benefits from eliminating intra-European currency transactions is not large in itself: estimated by the Commission to be in the range $\frac{1}{4}-\frac{1}{2}\%$ of Community GDP.[4] Larger output gains are seen as accruing from the elimination of currency risk, estimated perhaps generously by the Commission at around 2% of Community GDP. Allowing for induced investment and adjustment to a higher capital stock resulting from these efficiency gains applies a multiplier to these gains; and assuming constant returns to capital taken alone, as in the new endogenous growth literature, gives permanent gains to growth. These calculations are pretty soft, and perhaps should not be taken too seriously, but it is clear that the potential benefits could be significant.

What then are the disadvantages? The traditional approach to the issue of monetary union is provided by the literature on optimal currency areas. This suggests that the benefits of eliminating currency exchanges in a monetary union will be larger the greater the degree of intra-union trade; while the costs of abandoning exchange rate flexibility will be smaller the higher the degree of labour mobility, the higher the degree of nominal wage and price flexibility, the more diversified the industrial structures of the constituent economies, and the larger the proportion of common, rather than country-specific, shocks. Applied to Europe, this analysis yields a fairly mixed answer. Labour mobility is clearly rather low in Europe, and much lower than in the United States. But Europe qualifies rather better on the other criteria. An important reason for the progressive abandonment of the nominal exchange rate instrument in Europe in the 1980s is the view that it is an ineffective means of obtaining adjustments in relative competitiveness except in the rather short run: nominal exchange rate changes tend to lead rather quickly to higher inflation, so that over a two to four-year horizon gains in competitiveness are eroded through higher prices and wages. My reading of the optimal currency literature is that it provides a compelling case neither for, nor against, monetary union.

3   The benefits of reputation

However, the answers provided by the optimal currency area literature are limited in one rather crucial respect: they neglect the importance of policy disturbances in choosing between alternative regimes. A change of regime may well involve a change in the institutional structure of policy-making (for example, a move from many monetary authorities to a single one), as well as in the incentive structure facing policy-makers (for example, in the incentives to engage in inflationary policies). These changes can be expected to alter policy, and thereby alter the inefficiencies and shocks to the economy that arise from policy. There is substantial evidence to suggest that policy is an important source of disturbance to the economy, so this neglect matters.

It is for these reasons that the non-German monetary authorities have increasingly sought to 'tie their hands', in the phrase of Giavazzi and Pagano (1988), by fixing their exchange rate against the Deutsche Mark. Against this background, the key question is not the desirability of retaining the exchange rate instrument: that has been largely given up. Rather, it is whether EMU will provide a better or worse framework for delivering low and stable inflation. The Commission takes a predictably positive view of this matter. Using simulations on the IMF's international model, MULTIMOD, they see the evolution of the ERM through to EMU as a steady reduction of inflation and output variability. The document suggests also that EMU will deliver low, as well as stable, inflation, but this need not be so.

One can think of this issue quite straightforwardly in a Barro type world where the only real impact of monetary policy is via monetary surprises. Figure 5.2 shows the familiar one-period trade-off between inflation and output that arises in such a world. A government with reputation will be perceived to resist the temptation to inflate to secure short-term output gains, and so equilibrium will be at a low inflation outcome at the origin O. However, without reputation, the private sector will expect the government to inflate to move to position A. Because this is anticipated, equilibrium will be at a high rate of inflation at point B, where the government has no incentive to spring a monetary surprise.

Although the diagram makes this point in a very simple framework with no nominal inertia that can give rise to short-run Keynesian effects, it is important to stress that the point is valid in a much more general class of models. My colleagues and I have investigated the effect of reputation in a wide class of analytical and empirical models, (see, for example, Currie *et al.*, 1989) and this finding is quite robust. It is not specific to the

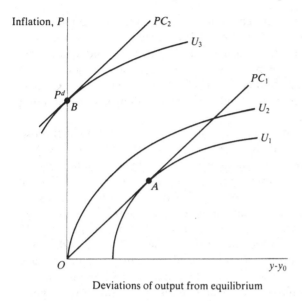

Figure 5.2   Short-run inflation-output trade-off in a Barro world

particular assumptions of the Barro world, which is nonetheless the most convenient framework for exposition.

With flexible exchange rates, Germany enjoys low inflation at the origin O by virtue of the Bundesbank's reputation, while other less fortunate European economies experience high inflation. Within the ERM, the commitment to fix the exchange rate against the Deutsche Mark allows the monetary authorities of these other countries to borrow the reputation of the Bundesbank and enjoy low inflation. What allows them to secure reputation in fixing their exchange rate when they are unable to do so in pursuit of purely domestic objectives is the institutional framework of the ERM: the external commitment to other countries gives the exchange rate objective a credibility that internal objectives alone lack.

4   Will the European Central Bank be independent?

What then is the impact of EMU and the creation of a single European Central Bank? The answer to that question depends rather critically on the structure of decision-making within the new European Central Bank. The proposed structure is one where European monetary policy is set by a committee comprising the governors of the national central banks, supplemented by a few wise experts. With this arrangement, it is clearly possible that the policy preferences of the inflation-prone economies will dominate those of Germany and other low inflation countries. In principle, it is conceivable that such an arrangement would deliver not best-practice monetary policy but worst-practice, condemning Europe to high inflation at point B. In practice, it is likely that the weight of German objections to such an outcome would deliver something better; but it may well not deliver best monetary practice.

The possibilities are illustrated in Figure 5.3. The left hand panel shows inflation rates, for Germany on the horizontal axis, the rest of ERM on the vertical axis. A well-functioning EMU will deliver low inflation, and will therefore be at the origin (taken to be desired inflation). That is marked EMU^B. A badly designed EMU may deliver the worst case of high inflation without reputation: that is denoted as EMU^W. Or there may be an intermediate case in the middle, EMU^{AV}. For comparison, the Hard-ERM and floating are included: in this stylised world, ERM delivers low inflation on the back of the Bundesbank's reputation, and therefore coincides with EMU^B, while floating delivers low inflation for Germany and high inflation for everyone else. The Soft-EMS regime, which gives partial credibility gains to high inflation countries, will lie between the floating and Hard-ERM cases. Taking account of the resource and welfare gains of eliminating residual exchange rate risk and from moving to a single currency, the left hand panel translates into the right hand welfare map: this plots welfare *losses*, so that the aim is to be as close as possible to the origin. Clearly the desirability of EMU relative to Hard-ERM depends crucially on the design of EMU. Progress towards EMU may move us towards low inflation, as the Commission argues; but it may not.

It is clear from this diagram why Germany gains in economic terms from EMU only if the independence of the European Central Bank is assured. The diagram also suggests that the same is true of the other ERM countries. However, our discussion so far has neglected the stabilization issue, and once this is taken into account other ERM countries may prefer EMU even without a strong commitment to price stability. This is because of the asymmetrical character of the ERM, based on German leadership in monetary policy. This means that European monetary policy is set on the basis of essentially German domestic considerations. Consider, for example, a supply shock that impacts asymmetrically between countries, pushing up inflation in Germany but not elsewhere. Under current arrangements, this will lead to a tightening of German monetary policy, and this will have to be followed elsewhere in Europe, despite being inappropriate outside Germany. The result is a loss of welfare for the other ERM countries relative to that of Germany. The

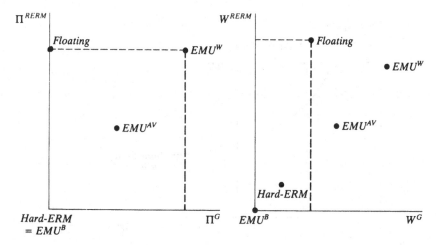

Figure 5.3   Bargaining over ERM versus EMU in a Barro world

benefit that Germany obtains from the Hard-ERM relative to the Soft-ERM or floating derives from this stabilization role: in the face of asymmetrical shocks, the poorer coordination between ERM members under the Soft-ERM imposes a higher cost on Germany, relative to the Hard-ERM case where monetary policy is coordinated largely on German terms. The current shock in Europe resulting from German reunification is an excellent illustration of this point. Under EMU, the sharing of responsibility means that monetary policy will be more directed to European-wide considerations, so that the welfare losses will be more evenly shared. Thus in terms of the right-hand panel, the Hard-ERM point, will tend to move up vertically relative to the others, and may therefore perform worse from the perspective of non-German participants than an indifferent EMU or even the Soft-ERM.

It does not follow from this that the other ERM countries should prefer an indifferent EMU or the Soft-ERM to the Hard-ERM. For there is the alternative that the Bundesbank might soften its position, and pay attention to broader European-wide macroeconomic developments in setting German monetary policy. This is illustrated in Figure 5.4. This plots an indifferent EMU and floating as before. However, the Hard-ERM now becomes a locus of welfare points. This locus plots what happens to welfare as the Bundesbank varies the weight that it puts on non-German policy concerns. With full weight given to German concerns ($a = 1$ at the left hand end of the locus), the welfare loss is low in Germany and high elsewhere: as more weight is given to non-German concerns, welfare losses elsewhere fall, while they rise for Germany. As illustrated, there are

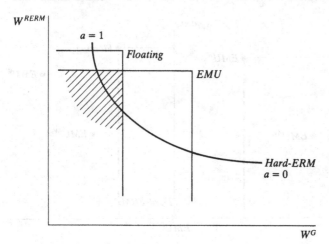

Figure 5.4   Bargaining over ERM versus EMU

a range of values of a for which the Hard-ERM is superior to EMU. The hatched zone shows the region in which the Hard-ERM is also superior to floating. As illustrated, the Hard-ERM is incentive-compatible only if the Bundesbank is willing to take some account of European-wide developments in the setting of German monetary policy. Figure 5.4 is hypothetical, but Currie *et al.* (1990) examine this issue formally in a simulation model, with a variety of aggregate supply and demand shocks. The results support the general conclusion: that is, if EMU leads to a loss of reputation in monetary policy, a Hard-ERM arrangement may well be superior; but that the Hard-ERM is unlikely to be incentive-compatible unless the Bundesbank pays regard to European-wide, rather than simply German, macroeconomic developments.

What benefits does Germany derive from the Hard-ERM arrangement relative to either floating or Soft-ERM on the one hand or EMU on the other? In terms of anti-inflation performance, Germany enjoys low inflation under either Hard-ERM or floating. EMU has the major political disadvantage that the ECB may be softer on inflation than the Bundesbank. From the German perspective, the Hard-ERM offers better stabilization of asymmetric shocks, avoiding the coordination problems that arise under either floating or a Soft-ERM. It is an empirical question whether these benefits are large enough for Germany to be willing to consider European-wide stabilization sufficiently to make the Hard-ERM incentive-compatible from the perspective of the other member countries. Thus it is possible that the hatched zone in Figure 5.4 is empty. However Currie *et al.* (1989) find that it is not, and that there is a range over which a Hard-ERM outperforms both EMU and a Soft-ERM or floating.

This case against EMU and in favour of the current Hard-ERM arrangement rests on the possible lack of credibility of a European Central Bank, and this argument is well-recognised. It is usually met by the counter-argument that the need for an independent central bank is generally accepted. The European Commission's document (*European Economy*, 1990) on the benefits of EMU devotes five pages to an analysis of this issue, setting out the conditions for a stable and credible monetary regime. Referring to the proposed European System of Central Banks that will become the European Central Bank or Eurofed, the Delors Report states that 'the System would be committed to the objective of price stability'. This is much more specific than the Bundesbank Act which requires the Bundesbank 'to regulate the amount of money in circulation and credit supplied to the economy, ... with the aim of safeguarding the currency', which leaves open the theoretical ambiguity of whether it is internal purchasing power or the external value against other currencies which is to be stabilised. (See Bofinger, 1990. As an aside, this, of course, means that the Bundesbank is able within its statutes to give some weight to broader European considerations in the interests of preserving the Hard-ERM and exchange rate stability. Whether it wishes to do so, is another question.)

Despite this, there are grounds for doubt. The draft statutes follow the commitment to price stability that I have just quoted by adding 'subject to the foregoing, the System should support the general economic policy set at the Community level by the competent bodies'. This would leave ample scope for acrimonious debate between national finance ministers and the European Central Bank as to whether or not the general economic policy of the Community was consistent with price stability, and should therefore be supported by the Central Bank. It is encouraging that the guidelines for the European Central Bank have been drafted to be more Teutonic than the Bundesbank, and give it considerable independence. But it is significant that an issue within the Intergovernmental Conference is whether or not responsibility for the external exchange rate of the Community should lie with the finance ministers, ECOFIN, or with the European Central Bank, and there are signs that ECOFIN might win out. If fiscal policy is left to be determined by national governments and the extra-European exchange rate is determined by finance ministers, then monetary policy is pinned down. National governments jointly can then determine monetary policy in the medium to longer run, and no careful drafting of statutes for an independent central bank will avoid that. There is, of course, some scope for finance ministers to exert influence over short-run exchange rate policy. But if there is any doubt over the European Central Bank's responsibility in the longer run, its independence will be weakened.

Perhaps more fundamentally, one may question whether it is the statutes and constitution of the Bundesbank that have delivered low inflation, or whether it does not owe rather more to the inflation-aversion of the German people, scarred by the experience of hyperinflation. It is often argued that the credibility of the Bundesbank owes much to the punishment that it would face were it to renege. That punishment in turn depends on the preferences of the society. Of course, German aversion to inflation may have been softened by many years of low inflation, and some other countries, notably France, have themselves developed a commitment to low inflation as a consequence of the experience of the 1970s and early 1980s. Nonetheless, it is clear that, outside a small core of member states, there is a greater tolerance of inflation. If this is so, a European Central Bank will inevitably face less censure from a European public less averse to inflation, and that in turn may mean less credibility. To avoid this requires a constitutional set-up that ensures that the low-inflation vote wins out, but that is a hard trick to pull off.

5   The coordination of fiscal policy

Let me now bring fiscal policy into the discussion. The Delors Report argued two key points about fiscal policy in EMU: first, that the European Central Bank should not finance budget deficits by monetary expansion; and second, that binding fiscal rules would be required to limit the freedom of national governments in fiscal policy. The first of these is generally accepted, but of course it may easily be undermined by the issue of where responsibility for exchange rate policy lies: if finance ministers determine exchange rate policy and national fiscal policy, the European Central Bank will be forced, in effect, to monetise national budget deficits. The second point was widely attacked on a variety of grounds, and has since been softened to the need for 'a system of coordination and self-imposed constraints', but the form that this might take is still open.

To consider the consequences of fiscal coordination in this context, consider the standard Hamada diagram depicted in Figure 5.5 (see Hamada, 1985). On the axes are the fiscal/monetary mix of the two countries: country two on the vertical axis, with a move up representing a looser fiscal/tighter money mix; country one on the horizontal axis. The objective function of country 1 defines a set of indifference curves, connecting points of equal welfare, as perceived by country 1. In the absence of spillovers, these indifference curves would be vertical lines,

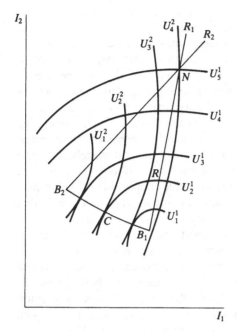

Figure 5.5   Hamada diagram

with the welfare level defined uniquely by the instrument setting I_1. But with spillovers, the instrument setting I_2 influences the welfare of country 1. As a consequence, the indifference curves become curved around the bliss point B_1 (or point of highest welfare) of country 1. Similar indifference curves map out points of equal welfare around the bliss point, B_2, of country 2.

Efficient policies are those for which the indifference curves of the two countries are tangential. These are represented by the contract curve joining B_1, and B_2. These policies are Pareto-efficient, in the sense that one country's welfare can rise only if the other country's welfare falls.

Uncoordinated decision-making need not lead to policies on the efficient contract curve. This may be seen from Figure 5.5 as follows. In the absence of coordination, country 1 will treat country 2's policy as given when deciding upon its own policy. For any I_2 setting, it will therefore choose I_1 to maximize its welfare. Thus it chooses I_1 to give the point of tangency between the indifference curve and the horizontal line corresponding to I_2. Varying I_2 then traces out the reaction function, R_1, of country 1, connecting the horizontal points on its indifference curves. The reaction function, R_2, of country 2 can be defined similarly, depicting the optimal choise of I_2 for given I_1. R_2 connects the points where the indifference curves of country 2 are vertical.

The outcome of uncoordinated decision-making is the Nash point, N, given by the intersection of the two reaction functions. At this Nash outcome, both countries are doing the best they can, given the policies of the other country. But the outcome is inefficient. The Nash point is Pareto-inferior to at least a subset of coordinated policies lying on the contract curve. As depicted, each country would like to be able to engage in expansionary fiscal policy relative to the other: hence the positions of the bliss points, B_1 and B_2. This may arise in a variety of models: it may be for Keynesian reasons to obtain a demand boost without undue interest rate consequences, that may have undesirable supply-side effects; it may also be because this secures a real exchange rate appreciation, facilitating output growth without inflation; it may also occur because an expansionary fiscal policy allows governments to reconcile distributional demands placed on it. Some of these advantages may be short-run in character, but fiscal policy may readily succumb to these pressures. Given this set-up, the uncoordinated outcome will be at the Nash point, N, where the two reaction functions, R_1 and R_2, intersect. Non-coordination leads to an outcome with a lax fiscal/monetary mix and unduly high interest rates. This conclusion is familiar for a world of flexible exchange rates, either floating or the Soft-ERM. And it has applicability to the 1980s, most obviously for the US and Reaganomics, but also to many countries in Europe which saw rising public debt to GDP ratios.

Will EMU contain these pressures? Here there are two starkly contrasted possibilities.[5] If countries can enjoy a fiscal expansion without a rise in the real interest rate that they face, then fixed expansion within EMU may well be attractive: keep demand high, real interest rates low, and inflation controlled by the fixed peg to the DM. In this case tendencies to fiscal expansion will be intensified. By contrast, if risk premia on individual national debt emerge, when governments borrow unduly, then EMU will dampen the tendency to over-expansionary fiscal policy.

The original Delors Report was sceptical about the ability of market-determined risk premia to coordinate fiscal policy in this way, and I think it was right. First, there is the empirical point that this mechanism could have operated under the Soft-ERM, yet there is rather poor evidence for substantial risk premia linked to national over-borrowing. Second, there is the point that expansionary fiscal policies are not necessarily synonymous with debt problems and default, so that risk premia need not emerge, at least on a scale required to moderate borrowing. And finally there will be considerable pressures on a European Central Bank, independent or otherwise, to accommodate fiscal policy, of course in support of (and I quote) 'the general economic policy set at the Community level by the competent bodies.' We see those pressures at work in the case of the US Fed in response to the Savings and Loans fiasco. National default would pose major problems for the Community, and markets might well suppose that the European Central Bank would help out. Moreover, the ECB will be unusual in facing twelve (or more) distinct Treasuries, with possibly no substantial central federal debt. This means that the ECB could undertake this bailing out without altering the stance of its overall monetary policy, by buying-in debt of countries in the course of its open market operations where debt problems are pressing and selling in those countries where they are not. These problems have not arisen in Germany, but I suspect that owes more to the debt-aversion and inflation-aversion of the German public than any specific market mechanism via risk premia.

I therefore conclude that fiscal coordination will be necessary for a well-functioning EMU. But it does not follow that coordination alone will be sufficient. This is because of the problem of credibility of the fiscal authorities. Just because finance ministers get together to coordinate, they will not magically acquire reputation in policy: look for a counter-example to the Community's agricultural ministers. Coordination of fiscal policy without reputation need not help, as Rogoff (1985) has shown for monetary policy. Our preliminary results suggest that it does help, but not much. And the consequences of lack of reputation can be seen in Figure 5.6.

Consider the independent conduct of monetary and fiscal policy, with both set of authorities sharing the same objective function. (This is the set-up relevant to an independent central bank, so that monetary policy is set independently of fiscal policy.) If both have reputation, then their preferences are as shown in the lower left part of the diagram centred around B^R. In this case the monetary authorities set monetary policy on the vertical axis to reach B^R, and the fiscal authorities do likewise with fiscal policy on the horizontal axis.

If both lack reputation, then again the preference maps of the two authorities coincide, but it is as though they are centred around a point to the north-east at B^{NR}: both monetary and fiscal authorities think that a surprise expansion can give rise to a better outcome so that they set policy to achieve B^{NR}. The private sector anticipates this, so the benefits are largely illusory: the distance of B^{NR} from B^R gives some measure of the welfare costs of lack of reputation.

The different positions of the two bliss points, B^R and B^{NR}, in Figure 5.6 reflect the consequences of absence of the reputation in a Barro-type world. A government without reputation considers that it can gain a

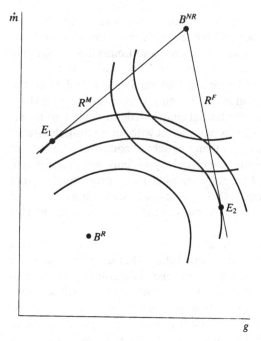

Figure 5.6   The implications of lack of credibility

short-run output advantage by springing an expansionary surprise on the private sector, and therefore chooses to run a more expansionary monetary and fiscal policy. But because the private sector can anticipate this, the expected and therefore actual inflation rate is higher in the absence of reputation. In more general dynamic models, the analysis of the absence of reputation is more complex dynamically, but the same qualitative features arise: the non-reputational outcome is to the north-east of the reputational one, in terms of the axes of Figure 5.6.

Now consider the mixed case where one authority has reputation and the other does not: the most relevant case is where the monetary authorities have reputation, while the fiscal authorities do not. The policy outcome is then determined as a game between the two authorities, with the fiscal authorities as a follower, and the monetary authorities as a leader.[6] The preference map of the monetary authorities is that in the south-west corner centred on B^R; that of the fiscal authorities is in the north-east corner, centred on B^{NR}. The reaction function of the fiscal authorities is R^F, and equilibrium is at E_2, which clearly represents an inefficient outcome. In the short run, the independent European Central Bank may offset the expansion of the fiscal authorities by a more contractionary monetary policy, though the net result may well be a rise in inflation. In the long run it is likely that E_2 will lie somewhat to the north-east of B^R, as shown in Figure 5.6. This means that there is likely to be higher inflation as a consequence of the fiscal authorities' lack of reputation.

What should be done about this? There are, of course, clever debt games that can in principle be played to lock the fiscal authorities into a position where they do not wish to borrow excessively. But one doubts the practicality of these as effective disciplines. Current discussions within the IGC centre on devising simple rules for the conduct of fiscal policy. One suggestion is that medium-term fiscal plans for each member state should be discussed publicly by finance ministers as a form of coordination. This may help, but one doubts whether it would dispose of the problem. I could spend much longer discussing the form of possible simple fiscal rules: my colleagues and I have done much work to devise simple rules that mimic the policy under reputation, and that can be done. But it is not at all simple to devise rules that are sufficiently transparent and intuitive to be incorporated into a draft minute for agreement by Finance Ministers. One simple indicator under consideration – the level of borrowing as a proportion of GDP – does not work well: it varies enormously across member states and is not related in any way to debt sustainability, or to the thrust of fiscal policy. Equally unhelpful is the use of the basic balance as an indicator. Any guidelines for fiscal policy will have to cope with considerable differences in initial positions. Perhaps that is why the Germans, supported by others, are pressing for much more convergence before moving beyond Stage 1 or the strengthened Hard-ERM.

6   Transitional arrangements

If the transition to EMU is to be protracted, the process of transition requires careful management. Otherwise there is a real danger, as Giovannini (1991) argues, that the transition will prove unstable, and the Hard-ERM will revert to floating.

A striking feature of the Delors Report is the lack of substance that it gives to the transitional, Stage 2 of the process towards EMU. It was this gap that the British proposals for an evolutionary approach to EMU were intended to fill. First came a proposal for competing currencies, launched at a meeting of finance ministers in Antibes in September 1989. This was quickly modified to a proposal for competing currencies within the framework of the ERM (H. M. Treasury, 1989), a proposal better understood as competition between monetary policies, rather than currencies (Currie, 1989b). The basic idea was that the removal of barriers to the use of currencies would allow the holders of money to choose freely between alternative currencies: the resulting competition between monetary authorities would impose an anti-inflationary discipline on the individual central banks. Arguably this is close to how the Hard-ERM currently operates (Currie, 1989a). EMU could arise from such competition if one currency becomes predominant: if this were the outcome, then EMU would have occurred as a result of individual consumer choice, and not imposed. Not surprisingly, this vision of EMU resulting from spontaneous choices by individuals was seen by other member states as a formula for putting off EMU indefinitely, an objective that was known to be welcome to the UK government on political grounds.

This British evolutionary approach was then developed further in June 1990 by the proposal for a Hard-Ecu (H. M. Treasury, 1990). The current Ecu is a weighted average of the 12 community currencies. As such, though the weights have changed occasionally, the Ecu has reflected average performance, devaluing against the DM, and appreciating against the lira. The proposal is to create a new Hard-Ecu that at realignments never devalues against any of the Community currencies.

There are two ways of doing that:

(1) Change the weights of the Ecu on realignment, increasing the weight of the hard currencies and reducing that of the weak ones. This we may term the 'Hard-basket'.
(2) Make the Ecu an independent currency managed by a new institution – this is the British Hard-Ecu. The new institution, called the European Monetary Fund (EMF), would ensure through its open market operations that the Hard-Ecu never devalues.

There are, I think two main reasons why the British favoured of these possibilities the Hard-Ecu rather than the hard-basket. First, the scheme was originally branded as 'competing currencies', and the hard-basket does not fit the competing currency bill. Second, the British government has still not accepted the final goal of the EMU. If parity realignments continue, and the DM continues its track record as a non-depreciating currency, then the DM weight will rise over time, and the hard-basket tends asymptotically to the DM.

The British proposal is then that the Hard-Ecu becomes a common currency, free to be used throughout the Community. Whether it becomes a single currency, displacing existing Community currencies, is a matter of consumer choice – this may or may not occur. If it does, EMU will emerge from an evolutionary, decentralised market process rather than through centralised decision-making in Brussels.

Now interest rates on the Hard-Ecu will have to bear a certain relation with interest rates on the individual Community currencies. There is a view that this means that the European Monetary Fund will have no freedom of manoeuvre. That is incorrect. What is crucial is whether the new institution is a price-taker or can influence interest rates, and that depends on its market power.

Initially one might think that this market power would be quite small. The Hard-Ecu would not appear much more attractive than the DM, and the Bundesbank would very much have the market clout. To be a transitional arrangement, the new institution would have to increase its market influence over time.

The British scheme has a proposal that ensures this. The repurchase provision says that if the new institution raises interest rates on the Hard-ECU and acquires community currencies, the national central banks would have an obligation to repurchase their currencies with hard currencies. To do so, they may well have to borrow Hard-Ecus from the new institution at the higher rate of interest. This provides a powerful mechanism for the new institution to fix interest rates.

On the British proposal, this repurchase arrangement would come into force in Stage 2. Once it does, we have an effective European Central Bank. But in the meantime, we have the basis for an unfortunate power struggle between the European Central Bank and the Bundesbank, which could well follow the messy path of the early years of the Federal Reserve System that Eichengreen (this volume) describes.

It therefore seems more sensible to use a hard-basket, rather than the Hard-Ecu, as the transitional device towards a single currency. Stage 2 then becomes a process in which cooperation between the Community central banks increases, and the structures for cooperation become more formalised and centralised, resulting eventually in an ECB.

A hard-basket could well play an increased role instead of the DM as a reserve currency for the European banking system. As this role increases, so the backing from national currencies could become one-for-one, so that they are fully backed, as for Scottish banknotes. At that point, monetary coordination would be complete. The move to a single currency and the elimination of national currencies could then be a matter of political and administrative convenience.

7   Conclusions

The upshot of my analysis is that there are appreciable risks and uncertainties in moving towards EMU. EMU could work out well; but it could work out rather badly. Given the poor track record of the Community in other fields – agriculture, trade, the Uruguay round, foreign affairs – it would not be surprising if governments wish to move slowly. There is an interesting analogy to be drawn here with Ken Binmore's (1989) analysis of the process of moving towards a social contract; he shows that this involves a series of small, discrete steps, involving the building of trust and credibility between the partners to the social contract.

Those who see the Hard-ERM as unstable will see this gradual approach as non-viable – we either rush forward, or go back to a looser arrangement (Giovannini, 1991). I do not agree. However, to ensure that the Community does not go backwards, there would be advantage in underpinning the Hard-ERM by greater institutional constraints, limiting the frequency and size of any future realignments and possibly moving to tighter bands.

A longer-drawn-out transition to EMU means that substance needs to be given to Stage 2 of the Delors process. It should not be regarded as a stage to skip over, but rather it needs to be designed carefully to avoid the inflationary possibilities of a poorly designed EMU. The British Hard-Ecu scheme is inappropriate: it leaves open appreciable scope for muddle and conflict in Stage 2. An increased role for the Ecu, possibly making it a hard-basket, and strengthening the framework for monetary cooperation in Europe is the right way forward.

NOTES

The support of the Economic and Social Research Council (grant no. W116251003) and the Leverhulme Trust is gratefully acknowledged.
1 This may be for the reputational advantages of 'tying one's hands' noted by Giavazzi and Pagano (1988).
2 Here I use the term 'regime change' to describe shifts in process accompanied by supporting changes in institutions, describing as process switches the case where shifts in the policy processes are unaccompanied by institutional change. For further discussion, see Currie (1992).
3 See Canzoneri and Diba (1991) for the argument that, under plausible assumptions about monetary policy, higher currency substitution may indeed reduce instability.
4 See *European Economy* (1990).
5 For a fuller discussion of the issue, see Bovenberg *et al.* (1991).
6 The sense in which the monetary authorities act as leaders is a little special. Having reputation, they are able to set monetary policy credibly over time, so that the problem of time-inconsistency does not arise. The fiscal authorities lack credibility, and therefore are tempted to adopt an over-expansionary policy in the short run, despite the longer-run problems that this may generate. However, fiscal policy is set period by period against the background of a credible pre-determined medium-term path for monetary policy. In this sense, the fiscal authorities act as followers. For further details, see Currie and Levine (1991).

REFERENCES

Binmore, Kenneth (1989), 'Social Contract I: Harsanyi and Rawls', *Economic Journal* **99**, Supplement, 84–102.

Bofinger, Peter (1990), 'Unresolved Issues on the Road to Economic and Monetary Union in Europe', CEPR Discussion Paper No. 405.

Bovenberg, A. Lans, Jeroen J. M. Kremers and Paul R. Masson (1991), 'Economic and Monetary Union in Europe and Constraints on National Budgetary Policies', *IMF Staff Papers* **38**, 374–98.

Canzoneri, Matthew B. and Behzad T. Diba (1991), 'Currency Substitution and Exchange Rate Volatility in the European Community', mimeo, Georgetown University.

Committee for the Study of Economic and Monetary Union (1989), *Report on Economic and Monetary Union in the European Community*, European Community.

Currie, David (1989a), 'European Monetary Union or Competing Currencies: Which Way for Monetary Integration in Europe?' *Economic Outlook* **14**, 18–24.

(1989b), 'Competition in Policies, not Currencies', *Financial Times*, 15 November.

(1992), 'European Monetary Union: Institutional Structure and Economic Performance', *Economic Journal* (forthcoming).

Currie, David and Paul Levine (1991), 'The International Coordination of Macroeconomic Policy: A Survey', in D. Greenaway, M. Bleaney and I. Stewart, (eds.) *Economics in Perspective*, London: Routledge.

Currie, David, Paul Levine and Joseph Pearlman (1989), 'European Monetary Union or Hard-EMS?', *European Economic Review*, forthcoming.

Eichengreen, Barry (1992), 'Designing a Central Bank for Europe: A Cautionary Tale from the Early Years of the Federal Reserve System', this volume.

European Economy (1990), 'One Market, One Money', **44**, 1–351.

Giavazzi, Francesco and Marco Pagano (1988), 'The Advantages of Tying One's Hands', *European Economic Review* **32**, 1055–82.

Giovannini, Alberto (1991), 'Is Economic and Monetary Union Falling Apart?', *International Economic Outlook* **1**, 36–41.

Hamada, Koichi (1985), *The Political Economy of International Monetary Interdependence*, Cambridge, MA: MIT Press.

H. M. Treasury (1989), *An Evolutionary Approach to Economic and Monetary Union*, HMSO.

(1990), 'Economic and Monetary Union', *Treasury Bulletin*, 14–16.

Hughes Hallett, Andrew and David Vines (1991), 'Adjustment Difficulties within a European Monetary Union: Can They be Reduced?', CEPR Discussion Paper No. 517.

Rogoff, Kenneth (1985), 'Can International Monetary Policy Cooperation be Counterproductive?', *Journal of International Economics* **18**, 199–217.

Discussion

DALE W. HENDERSON

My comment is divided into two sections. Section 1 is a summary and critique of the comparison of three monetary policy regimes, Floating, Hard-ERM, and EMU, contained in Currie's Sections 2–4. Section 2 is a discussion of commitment technologies.

1   Floating, Hard-ERM, and EMU

Using a simple two-region model of Germany and the rest of the ERM (RERM), Currie compares three alternative policy regimes: Floating, Hard-ERM, and EMU.[1] He assumes that different 'commitment technologies' are available under the various regimes. The result he emphasizes most is that a Modified Hard-ERM may be superior to EMU for both Germany and the RERM under his assumptions about commitment technologies.[2]

An inflation bias world   In order to make the logic of his argument clear, Currie begins by analysing a world in which policy-makers face only inflation bias problems. The inflation bias problem faced by a policy-maker in a closed economy is shown in Currie's Figure 5.2. Suppose that the policy-maker's loss (L) rises with squared deviations of output (y) from a desired rate (y^*) above the natural rate (y_o) and with squared deviations of actual inflation (p) from zero:

$$L = (1/2)[a(y - y^*)^2 + p^2] = (1/2)\{a[(y - y_o) - (y^* - y_o)]^2 + p^2\} \tag{1}$$

U_1, U_2, and U_3 in Currie's Figure 5.2 are iso-loss contours representing successively higher levels of loss. The marginal rate of substitution between inflation and the deviation of output from its natural rate is given by the slope of the iso-loss contours:

$$\frac{dp}{d(y - y_o)} = - \left[\frac{\frac{\partial L}{\partial (y - y_o)}}{\frac{\partial L}{\partial p}} \right]_{L=L} = - \frac{a[(y - y_o) - (y^* - y_o)]}{p} \tag{2}$$

Suppose also that the deviation of output from the natural rate depends positively on the difference between actual and expected inflation:

$$y - y_o = (1/\beta)(p - p^e) \tag{3}$$

which can be arranged as

$$p = p^e + \beta(y - y_o) \tag{4}$$

PC_1 and PC_2 in Figure 5.2 represent this relationship for $p^e = 0$ and p_e equal to its positive equilibrium value, respectively. If the policy-maker cannot commit to deliver zero inflation, the economy will suffer from an inflation bias. That is, equilibrium inflation will be positive even though output is always at its natural rate. The policy-maker minimizes his loss by setting his marginal rate of substitution between inflation and the deviation of output from its natural rate equal to the trade-off between inflation and the deviation of output from its natural rate:

$$-\frac{a[(1/\beta)(p - p^e) - (y^* - y_o)]}{p} = \beta \tag{5}$$

where $y - y_o$ has been eliminated from the marginal rate of substitution using equation (3). In a rational expectations equilibrium the rate of inflation must be positive. Suppose $p^e = 0$ as at point A in Figure 5.2. The policy-maker would have an incentive to choose a positive p because the marginal rate of substitution (slope of U_2) would approach infinity if he chose $p = p_e = 0$, and the trade-off (slope of PC_1) is only β. Only when p^e takes on a high enough positive value does the marginal rate of substitution equal the trade-off when the policymaker chooses $p = p^e$ as at point B in Figure 5.2 where $y - y_o = 0$. Of course, if the policy-maker can commit to deliver zero inflation, the economy will not suffer from an inflation bias. The inflation bias problem faced by the policy-maker in an open economy is the same in most respects.

Currie considers three regimes. First he considers what he calls the Floating regime. Under this regime each policy-maker chooses the value of his own monetary instrument in order to minimize his own loss given the value of the other policy-maker's monetary instrument, and the exchange rate takes on whatever value is implied by the values of the monetary instruments. Under the commitment technology for the Floating regime, the German policy-maker can commit to choose the value of its monetary instrument that yields zero inflation, but the RERM policy-maker cannot. Thus, under Floating the German inflation rate is zero and the RERM has the positive inflation rate implied by the theory of inflation bias.

Next he considers what he calls the Hard-ERM. Under this regime the German policy-maker chooses his monetary instrument to minimize his own loss given that the RERM policy-maker pegs the DM exchange rate, and the RERM policy-maker chooses his monetary instrument to peg the DM exchange rate. Under the commitment technology for the

Hard-ERM, the German policy-maker can commit to choose the value of his monetary instrument that yields zero inflation just as he can under Floating, and although the RERM policy-maker cannot commit to choose the value of his monetary instrument that yields zero inflation, he can commit to choose his monetary instrument to peg the DM exchange rate. Thus, under the Hard-ERM the inflation rate in both Germany and the RERM is zero. The German policy-maker chooses the value of his monetary instrument that yields zero inflation for Germany. In order to peg the DM exchange rate the RERM policy-maker must choose the value of his instrument that yields zero inflation for the RERM.

Finally he considers what he calls the EMU. Under this regime a single European policy-maker minimizes a joint loss function in which the German and RERM loss functions receive equal weight. There may be two currencies or one. If there are two, the single policy-maker chooses the values of the monetary instruments in Germany and the RERM subject to the constraint that the DM exchange rate remains fixed. If there is one, the single policy-maker chooses the value of the monetary instrument for that currency. Under the commitment technology for EMU, the European policy-maker cannot commit to follow the monetary policy that yields zero inflation. Thus, under EMU both Germany and the RERM have the positive inflation rate implied by the theory of inflation bias.

Currie's analysis of an inflation bias world leads to an unambiguous conclusion. Germany is indifferent between Floating and the Hard-ERM, and the RERM prefers the Hard-ERM to Floating and EMU. Therefore, when the interests of both countries are taken into account the Hard-ERM is the preferred regime.[3] Currie extends his analysis in order to establish that the Hard-ERM might be superior to other regimes in more complex settings. He allows for the benefits of moving to one currency under EMU and considers what happens when policy-makers face stabilization problems as well as inflation bias problems.

Currency transactions costs and currency risk Currie recognizes that a comparison of alternative regimes should take account of differences in currency transactions costs and currency risk under the three regimes. He assumes that moving from Floating to Hard-ERM would yield benefits from reduced currency risk, so even Germany would prefer Hard-ERM to Floating.[4] He acknowledges that moving from Hard-ERM to one currency under EMU would yield benefits from reduced transactions costs and currency risk.[5] However, he goes on to argue that both Germany and the RERM may continue to prefer the Hard-ERM to EMU even when these benefits are taken into account because inflation performance may be sufficiently better.

Stabilization problems Currie also recognizes that a comparison of alternative regimes should take account of the stabilization problems faced by policy-makers as a result of disturbances to their economies. In Section 4 he allows for stabilization problems in the Hard-ERM and EMU regimes. It should not be surprising that the Hard-ERM regime may be less attractive for the RERM than the EMU regime when certain stabilization problems are present. Under the Hard-ERM the German policy-maker sets European monetary policy on the basis of German concerns. The interesting shocks to consider are goods demand and supply shocks.[6] For shocks that affect Germany and the RERM in equal but opposite ways (asymmetric shocks) and shocks that affect Germany alone (idiosyncratic German shocks), the change in European monetary policy that makes Germany better off is likely to make the RERM worse off. Only for shocks that affect Germany and the RERM in exactly the same way (symmetric shocks) is it obvious that the interests of Germany and the RERM coincide. Under EMU the European policy-maker sets European monetary policy in a cooperative way. Therefore, for asymmetric and idiosyncratic shocks, Germany is likely to be worse off and the RERM is likely to be better off under EMU than under ERM.

Currie goes on to suggest what I will call a Modified Hard-ERM regime. Under this regime the German policy-maker chooses his monetary instrument to minimize a weighted sum of the German and RERM loss functions where the weight on the German loss function can vary from zero to one and the two weights always sum to one. Currie makes the claim that there are parameter sets for which a Modified Hard-ERM with a weight on the German loss function of about 0.5 is superior to EMU on stabilization grounds alone for a wide variety of shocks. His claim is backed up by the simulation experiments in CLP (forthcoming). It is easy to see why the Modified Hard-ERM might be the same as EMU for both Germany and the RERM on stabilization grounds. It is less easy to see why it can be better. However, CLP show that it can be. No clear explanation of this result is provided by either Currie or CLP. The explanation must be that the German policy-maker's ability to commit himself enables him to achieve better stabilization performance as well as better average inflation performance, but it would be nice to know more.

The result that Currie emphasizes most is that a Modified Hard-ERM regime may be superior to EMU for both Germany and the RERM under his assumptions about commitment technology. The Modified-ERM will yield better average inflation performance for both regions and, provided that Germany gives enough weight to the loss function of the RERM, a stabilization performance that is roughly comparable. The combination of average inflation performance and stabilization performance may be sufficiently better under the Modified Hard-ERM to outweigh the benefits from reduced transactions costs and currency risk under EMU.

Currie's result for the comparison of a Modified Hard-ERM and EMU, is interesting and should be taken seriously. However, a healthy dose of skepticism is in order. The evidence in CLP (forthcoming) that stabilization performance might be comparable under the two regimes comes from a small simulation model with made up coefficients. Even in this model for some shocks it is possible for the German policy-maker to achieve stabilization performance under the Modified Hard-ERM that is roughly comparable to the stabilization performance under EMU only if he puts a weight on RERM loss that is equal to or greater than the weight he puts on his own loss, and it is not clear whether a German policy-maker would be willing or able to behave in this way. In addition, Currie may well be underrating the ability of the European policy-maker to commit himself under EMU.

Currie does not discuss stabilization problems in the Floating regime in Section 4. However, in CLP (forthcoming) it is shown that Floating may be preferred to both the Hard-ERM and EMU by both the German policy-maker and the RERM policy-maker for some shocks because stabilization performance may be sufficiently better. As an example of a shock for which the stabilization outcomes for both Germany and the RERM are best under Floating, CLP present a transient aggregate supply shock in Germany. It is not too surprising that Floating yields a better stabilization outcome than EMU for both Germany and the RERM. Having the European policy-maker act so as to keep the DM exchange rate fixed is worse for both policy-makers than having them keep their monetary policy independence even though they engage in non-cooperative behaviour. It is also not too surprising that Floating yields a better stabilization outcome than Hard-ERM for the RERM.[7] However, it is surprising that Floating yields a better outcome than Hard-ERM for Germany. Having the RERM act so as to keep the DM exchange rate fixed is apparently worse for Germany than having the RERM keep its monetary policy independence and engage in non-cooperative behaviour.[8]

At the conference there was general acknowledgement that floating exchange rates dominate fixed exchange rates on stabilization grounds for some asymmetric and idiosyncratic shocks. However, it was also clear that it was the view of many if not most of the participants that the members of the ERM should continue to keep their exchange rates fixed and that they should eventually adopt a single currency. This view did not seem to be based on firm evidence about what kinds of shocks are most frequent in European countries. Indeed many were willing to concede that the evidence is mixed. Rather the view seemed to be based on the judgment that any possible stabilization benefits of floating exchange rates are more than outweighed by other economic benefits and political benefits of fixed exchange rates and the eventual adoption of a single currency.

2   Commitment technologies

In many games, when it is assumed that players engage in myopic non-cooperative behaviour, the equilibrium payoffs for all players are very low. One way of modifying games so that the players can achieve better equilibrium payoffs is to assume a commitment technology under which some kind of commitment is possible. As stated before, Currie explores two such commitment technologies in his Floating and Hard-ERM regimes.

Many economists, including myself, have resisted exploring commitment technologies like those assumed under Currie's Floating and Hard-ERM regimes because the specification of the commitment technologies is not complete. Under each of these commitment technologies, policy-makers have an incentive to renege on their commitments unless they face harsh enough punishments for doing so. The harsh punishments that Currie's policy-makers will incur if they renege on their commitments are not spelled out in detail. Therefore, it is not clear why the policy-makers should honour their commitments. What is clear is that there is no supranational authority that can impose harsh punishments on policy-makers who break their commitments.

Currie has some discussion of why policy-makers might honour their commitments under the Floating and Hard-ERM regimes. Under Floating and Hard-ERM regimes, the German policy-maker can commit to deliver the value of his monetary instrument that will yield zero inflation. Currie argues that the German policy-maker might keep to this commitment to avoid punishment by the German people, who are particularly sensitive to inflation as a result of having experienced hyperinflation. However, he does not say what the punishment would be. Under Currie's Hard-ERM regime, the RERM policy-maker cannot commit to deliver the value of his monetary instrument that will yield zero inflation but can commit to deliver the value of his monetary instrument that will cause the DM exchange rate to remain fixed. He argues that while the RERM policy-maker might not keep to a commitment to deliver the value of his monetary instrument that will yield zero inflation to avoid punishment by the RERM people, he might keep to a commitment to deliver the value of his monetary instrument that will cause the DM exchange rate to remain fixed in order to avoid the political costs of breaking an international agreement. However, he does not say what these political costs would be.

Even though the specification of commitment technologies like those assumed by Currie is not complete, it seems worthwhile to use them. They are one way, if not the only currently available way, of modeling important aspects of some policy regimes that we want to understand better. Of course, it is important to try to improve the specification of commitment technologies and to look for alternative modeling strategies.

If we are prepared to assume commitment technologies under which some kinds of commitment are possible, we can use cooperative game theory to analyse alternative regimes. For example, Klein (1991) uses cooperative game theory to analyse a fixed exchange rate regime in a two-country world that is subject to both money demand and output demand shocks. He finds that for many assumptions about the variances of the shocks there are allocations of adjustment duties between the two policy-makers that are cooperative equilibria.

NOTES

1 These three regimes are also considered in Currie (forthcoming) and Currie, Levine, and Pearlman (forthcoming), hereafter CLP (forthcoming). Currie (forthcoming) provides diagrammatic representations of the regimes. CLP (forthcoming) refer to the Floating and Hard-ERM regimes as the Non-EMS and Hard-EMS regimes and consider a fourth regime which they refer to as Optimal Policy.

2 Currie's derivation of the results in this paper is based on the more formal derivation in CLP (forthcoming).

3 Currie takes one minor shortcut. According to his Figure 5.3, the RERM is indifferent between Floating and EMU, and the text says nothing different. In fact, as is recognized in CLP (forthcoming) the RERM prefers Floating to EMU for the reason first recognized by Rogoff (1985). Under EMU, monetary expansion in the RERM leads to an increase in the RERM CPI only because it leads to an increase in the price of RERM output. The European policy-maker varies the German money supply in order to keep the DM exchange rate fixed. Under Floating, monetary expansion in the RERM leads to a larger increase in the RERM CPI. The RERM CPI rises not only because the price of RERM output increases but also because the RERM currency depreciates against the DM. Since monetary expansion is more inflationary under Floating there is less incentive undertake it. Private agents know this, so under Floating the inflation rate can be lower in the rational expectations equilibrium.

4 In the right hand panel of his Figure 5.3, regimes are ranked taking into account not only loss from inflation but also loss from currency transactions and currency risk. According to this panel Hard-ERM is superior to Floating for Germany. Since German inflation loss is the same under the two regimes, Currie must be assuming that loss from currency risk is lower under Hard-ERM.

5 He cites the Commission estimates of possible benefits from the elimination of intra-European currency transactions and currency risk (1/4 to 1/2% and 2% of Community GDP, respectively) and records some skepticism regarding these estimates but concludes that 'potential gains could be significant.'

6 The German policy-maker can and will offset the effects of any money demand shock in Germany without having any effect on the RERM. The RERM policy-maker must offset the effects of any money demand shock in the RERM as a matter of course in order to keep the DM exchange rate pegged.

7 It is also not too surprising that the Modified Hard-ERM can dominate Floating for the RERM if Germany gives a low enough weight to its own objectives. Apparently, in this case it pays for the RERM to give up the monetary policy independence it has under floating in order to avoid the inefficiency associated with non-cooperative behaviour.

8 The CLP result that Floating is better than the Hard-ERM for Germany in the case of a supply shock in Germany is all the more surprising given a result from Canzoneri and Henderson (1991), hereafter CH. CH consider a shift up in demand for the United States (US) good matched by a shift down in the demand for the rest of the world (ROW) good. For this disturbance floating with non-cooperative behaviour is definitely better for both the US and the ROW than fixing the real exchange rate by making equal and opposite changes in the two money supplies if the policy-makers put a heavy enough weight on employment. However, floating with non-cooperative behaviour is unambiguously worse for the US than a regime that CH call fixed-exchange-rate leadership. Under this regime the US policy-maker chooses his monetary instrument to minimize his own loss, but the ROW policy-maker chooses his monetary instrument so as to keep the real exchange rate fixed. It seems that we need more analysis of regimes in which one policy-maker acts to keep the nominal or real exchange rate fixed.

REFERENCES

Canzoneri, Matthew B. and Dale W. Henderson (1991), *Monetary Policy in Interdependent Economies: A Game-Theoretic Approach*, Cambridge, MA: The MIT Press.

Currie, David (forthcoming), 'European Monetary Union: Institutional Structure and Economic Performance,' *Economic Journal*.

Currie, David, Paul Levine, and Joseph Pearlman (forthcoming), 'European Monetary Union or Hard-EMS?,' *European Economic Review*.

Klein, Martin (1991), 'Bargaining for the Choice of Monetary Instruments in a Simple Stochastic Macro Model,' CEPR Discussion Paper No. 553.

ANDREW J. HUGHES HALLETT

For what is intended to be one of the most far reaching changes in economic organisation this century, there has been extraordinarily little formal analysis of the costs and benefits of monetary union. There have, of course, been many accounts of what the policy-makers intend should happen. But issues of this importance cannot be settled by expectations and intentions (especially if they come from interested parties) unless supported by sufficient analytic evidence. David Currie's paper is therefore a valuable review of his own assessment of monetary policy under EMU and whether it is likely to be an improvement over alternative regimes. In fact he finds EMU is likely to be inferior to other arrangements unless certain additional conditions on increasing the effectiveness of policies within the union can also be met. As that seems improbable in practice, and anyway implies that it is the design of monetary policy rather than monetary union which lies at the heart of better economic performance, I would like to pick out four implications of Currie's analysis.

Explicit coordination and ERM both dominate the more rigid EMU regime.

The most striking result is that optimal cooperative policies and the Soft-ERM regime appear preferable to EMU. Even the Hard-ERM regime is preferable to EMU. These results are shown in Figures 5.3 and 5.4, but are seen more clearly in Figures 5 and 6 of Currie *et al.* (1990) on which the discussion of pp. 134–8 actually depends. Those results are obtained from a conventional Barro-Gordon model of two inter-dependent economies which are symmetric except in their demand and supply responses to exchange rate movements (the latter innovation to create a 'centre' and a 'periphery' country).[1] It is a pity that the model, preferences, and associated figures are not reproduced, since it is hard to interpret or explain the results without them. Nevertheless the results are:-
(i) Full coordination dominates all other regimes for all values of a (the bargaining power of Germany within ERM/EMU), although it contains adjustable, but not necessarily frequently adjusted, exchange rates. (ii) The Soft-ERM regime effectively dominates EMU, although neither is a full reputation solution. (iii) Soft-ERM also dominates Hard-ERM for $0.4 \le a \le 1$, which includes the crucial case of $a = 1$ where German reputation and policy effectively drives the whole system.[2]

These conclusions are consistent with other results (e.g. Hughes Hallett and Vines, 1991, or Masson and Melitz, 1991, with no extra fiscal flexibility), but not with those in *European Economy* (1990) for the reasons which are given in point 2 below. Notice that the 'optimal', 'EMU' and 'Hard-ERM' schemes are all cooperative; the latter two having restrictions on the exchange rate variable, and the former two having fixed values of $a = \frac{1}{2}$ (but why? Currie *et al.*, 1990, p. 11, shows that they are also loci of welfare points). Soft-ERM is a non-cooperative Stackelberg regime where only the leader has reputation. EMU has the extra restriction of no reputation even for Germany. Now if the reputation effects are fairly small (and they seem to be small because the distance of the EMU outcomes, with no reputation at all, from Hard-ERM, with full reputation, is smaller than the distance of the other solutions from Hard-ERM), and if hard is quite hard, then the EMU line (when a is allowed to vary in Figure 4) will converge on the Hard-ERM line as $a \rightarrow 1$. But if $a \rightarrow 0$ the lines will diverge since the German objective function places a penalty 25 times higher on inflation than losses of output compared to other countries (see Currie *et al.*, 1990). Consequently the overall penalty on inflation falls as a falls in both the EMU and Hard-ERM regimes – but it rises on the exchange rate (defined by inflation differentials) term in the ERM case. That means the penalty on inflation falls more slowly in the ERM case than it does in the EMU case. Hence inflation worsens as $a \rightarrow 0$ in both schemes, but it worsens faster under EMU. We therefore get Figure 5A.1 as a general result. In other words, the ERM scheme does indeed dominate EMU for any given a value, because EMU's rigidity is a significant restriction which more than offsets any policy coordination gains which may be implied.

Exchange rate stability does not ensure price stability. Hence the crucial issues are the design of monetary policy and the operation of the central bank, not monetary policy per se.

Like any major change, EMU implies costs as well as benefits. The EC Commission's preferred estimate of those benefits is about 1.5% of GNP, which is very similar to the consensus estimate of the potential gains from policy coordination at the G7 level (Currie *et al.*, 1989). In the policy coordination debate such gains were generally regarded as rather small, being roughly the same size as the range between typical 1-year-ahead growth forecasts made for the OECD countries. It would not take much in the way of costs to overturn the benefits of EMU. It is therefore important to focus, as Currie does, on those costs and on just how much coordination EMU would in fact induce.

A significant degree of price and exchange rate stability has been achieved under the EMS arrangements of the 1980s, as member countries have sought lower inflation and German financial credibility. It is argued

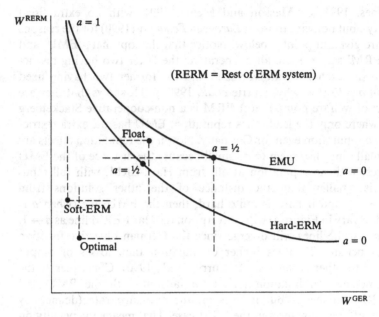

Figure 5A.1 Cooperation versus bargains in an EMU/ERM framework

that a tighter ERM, or EMU itself, would therefore be a better framework delivering price stability in the future, although it is important to
note that non-member countries actually did just as well, if not better,
with similar reductions in inflation and smaller losses in output during the
1980s.

Does this mean that EMU, or a Hard-ERM, can be expected to eliminate not only inflation differentials but also inflation itself? And have we
found a way of overcoming the conventional trade-off between price
stability and higher output? The Commission clearly thinks so, basing
their arguments on a series of simulations of their own construction
performed on the IMF's MULTIMOD system. Currie's results (as do the
results of many other analysts) imply quite the opposite because, although
the underlying objectives give 'overwhelming priority to controlling
inflation', the floating and EMS regimes dominate most, if not all, of the
EMU and Hard-ERM outcomes. That may happen because compromise
within EMU effectively neutralises the Bundesbank's reputation as the
EMS's lynch-pin, and leads to average rather than best-practice policies.
But it is more likely to happen because exchange rate stability cannot
guarantee price stability without some price anchor. That would require
even tougher monetary controls and greater independence than the

Bundesbank currently supplies (even tougher because the natural convexity of preferences would otherwise lead the central bank to adopt 'poor-practice' monetary policies; see the next paragraph). The new central bank's statutes cannot supply such an anchor. Its independence is intended to be similar to the Bundesbank. But with fiscal policy (and perhaps the ECU exchange rate) under the control of national governments, and a statutory requirement to respect national growth objectives without any obvious mechanism for resolving conflicts between the resulting price and output targets, a new central bank facing 12 self-interested governments is unlikely to be able to exercise the same, let alone stronger, monetary control. An example illustrates the point. Suppose countries A and B are of equal size and structure, but that A suffers a 10% inflation shock (as in the German reunification programme, for instance). Under floating, A's prices rise 10%, B's stay constant and the European price index rises 5%. But under EMU and the same monetary control rules, inflation is spread: prices rise 5% in both A and B. Hence the European price index still rises 5% and nothing has been gained. This happens because under floating, with some attention to the output targets, A's inflation is ultimately accommodated by depreciation against B and the rest of the world. On the other hand, under the EMU regime A's inflation is only partially accommodated (vs. just the rest of the world now) but, because it cannot be localised, twice as many goods suffer the smaller price rises. So the impact on the price index is the same, and removing inflation differentials via EMU does not remove inflation. To do that requires a policy change. That was the point of my work with Vines, and Currie's analysis yields exactly the same conclusion.

Now suppose country B is four times larger than A. Under floating, A's 10% price rise leaves B's prices unaffected and the European price index 2% higher. Under EMU, inflation is equalised so prices rise 2% everywhere. Again there is no gain, except that if people worry more about inflation the higher it gets (i.e. they have convex preferences, and the past year's experience in the UK strongly suggests that they do: 2% inflation hardly matters at all, 10% matters a good deal more than 5 times as much) then the small country will like its gain under EMU more than the large country dislikes its loss. But, by the same token, convexity means that, whereas an individual country will try very hard to rid itself of 10% inflation, the EMU authorities would try much less than proportionately as hard to remove 2% or 5%. Hence we must expect a European central bank to be *less* effective in controlling inflation than an equally constituted Bundesbank. The only way out of this bind, and to give the new central bank the same power to reduce inflation as currently enjoyed by an EMS led by the Bundesbank, is to move to tougher monetary control rules. Simply to change the exchange rate regime will not do.

Hence, I think we are correct to concentrate first on the design of monetary policy and the new central bank – and only then on EMU itself, except that the latter will not bring any extra benefits if monetary policy has been correctly designed in the first place. Confirmation of this proposition comes from investigating why the Commission did not reach the same conclusion. In *European Economy* (1990), EMU is defined as the combination of exchange rate fixity *and* a tougher monetary control rule, so that you cannot tell if the gains are coming from EMU itself or from the change in policy regime. It is easy to show that removing the new control rule (so that the central bank follows the same type of monetary rule under both floating and EMU) makes EMU inferior to floating, while removing the EMU assumption when the stronger monetary control rules are in place scarcely affects the outcomes (Hughes Hallett and Vines, 1991). Evidently what matters is monetary policy, rather than a particular exchange rate regime; and it may well be that institutional changes in the form of a new central bank would be the best outward and visible sign of this new spiritual grace in policy-making.

The Hard-ERM/EMU regimes are accident-prone; greater (fiscal) coordination will be needed to provide policy effectiveness as well as stability in the face of shocks and policy errors.

Other work in this area stresses the importance of fiscal flexibility to compensate for the constraints which a single monetary policy within EMU imposes.[3] Naturally enough, if we deprive countries of one policy instrument they will have to use their remaining (fiscal) instruments more intensively to solve their domestic problems and to smooth the fluctuations which remain in national outputs or prices after the single monetary policy has been used to control the European averages. That has to be done by adjusting each fiscal policy relative to the common monetary policy in such a way as to improve the outcomes for one country without damaging them for another. That inevitably requires a more active coordination of the policy instruments which lie outside the EMU framework as currently defined, and implies that *policy mix* becomes the instrument at the national level.

This explains why it is useful to analyse the underlying policy interactions in the form of the Hamada diagram in Figure 5.5. Currie gets the usual result that non-cooperative policies outside the ERM/EMU framework lead to poorer outcomes because policy makers fail to internalise some of the costs. As drawn, countries prefer fiscal expansions for themselves and end up with unduly lax fiscal policies and overtight money to compensate (a response typical of the US in the 1980s). But if countries

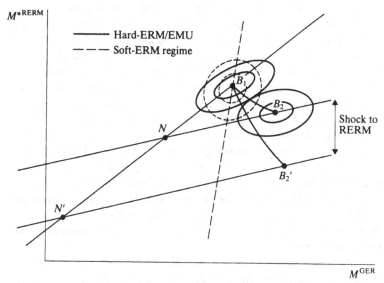

Figure 5A.2   The EMU/ERM regimes are not robust

prefer fiscal discipline at home, the picture reverses (B_1 and B_2 inter-change) as in Figure 5A.2 and they end up with unduly restrictive fiscal policies but less monetary contraction. That is the usual European situ-ation. In either case the outcomes are improved with explicit coordi-nation, not only between countries but also between fiscal and monetary interventions.

But Figure 5A.2 implies much more than this. It is easy to show that, as countries move from floating through a loose EMS regime to a Hard-ERM and finally to EMU, currencies become more and more substitutable. That implies increasingly parallel optimal reaction func-tions because under a Hard-ERM or EMU regime it no longer matters which currency is used to finance fiscal expenditures or to restrict the aggregate money supply.[4] With a virtually fixed link between currencies, the overall impact of fiscal expenditures or money supply changes on any country will be more or less the same whether they are carried out in German Marks or Italian Lire. Narrowing the angle between reactions functions like this implies two things:

(a) The inefficiencies (welfare losses) of a lack of fiscal coordination become more and more marked as the ERM regime is tightened towards EMU. As was clear in Figure 5A.1, it is the coordination of policies, not EMU or ERM *per se*, which matters for delivering a better performance; and

(b) since the reaction functions are linear in exogenous variables/shocks, asymmetric shocks (or asymmetric reactions to given shocks) will move the relative position of the reaction functions and cause exaggerated displacements of the non-cooperative solution (see Figure 5A.2).

Hence if comparative advantage and specialisation serve to maintain or increase the incidence of asymmetric shocks and responses in the union (and the evidence is that they do; see de Grauwe and Vanherverbeke, 1991), then a Hard-ERM or EMU will undermine the stability of the system by making it more accident prone. That lack of robustness is very clear in the empirical regime rankings reported in Minford and Rastogi (1990), for example. The coordinated solutions, however, lie along a shorter and less disturbed line. Thus on their own ERM/EMU regimes are unstable and inefficient; but they become robust and yield gains when supported by coordinated fiscal and supply-side policies.

The real aim should be closer cooperation between policy-makers rather than a common currency.

If greater coordination is a necessary condition for progress to EMU to be successful, it also highlights the chief difficulty with the EMU idea. EMU is a rigid system in which all countries have to behave as if they were identical in structure, preferences and shocks. Hence the calls for 'convergence'. Yet it is clear that countries are not all identical, and it is well known that you get the best out of coordination when you exploit the comparative (policy) advantages of each participant fully. Indeed the gains only flow when you do that, for exactly the same reason that you would never choose to write a book with someone who was identical to yourself in preference to someone whose talents were complementary. So while EMU may capture some of the gains of better coordination, it cannot capture all of them. It is at best a partial coordination device. As we have seen here, a less rigid policy regime would better exploit any comparative advantages in structure or preferences, and therefore yield a better, more coordinated performance. The crucial question is, how much better? On that we have no direct evidence, but one might guess it would be quite a lot better since other studies have shown exchange rate targeting to be a poor substitute for explicit coordination even when it improves on the historical policy choices (Hughes Hallett, 1991).

NOTES

1 The ERM regimes are called EMS regimes in Currie *et al.* (1990).
2 There is some confusion here since Currie's Section 4 claims that Hard-ERM outperforms Soft-ERM, whereas the results being quoted (Currie *et al.* 1990, p. 37) show it to be the other way round when Soft-ERM is their non-EMS

solution. Identifying Soft-ERM with non-EMS appears to be correct since Currie *et al.* (p. 9–11) specify non-EMS to be a German-led Stackelberg regime with floating and EMS reputation for the Bundesbank. An independent float is not consistent with Stackelberg leadership since it necessarily implies that the followers tie themselves to German discipline (within certain limits). Rather than lie between floating and Hard-EMS, such a regime should have better coordination properties in an asymmetric world because it is less rigid (see point 4 below). Hard-EMS has the same form, plus extra penalties on the exchange rate terms and cooperation, with $a \simeq 1$ (hence tighter bands, and outcomes worse for REMS but no better for Germany). An independent float would also imply worse results for an REMS which cannot even borrow a reputation. This is the only interpretation which fits both Figures 5.3 and 5.4 and Currie *et al.* (1990), although no formal definitions of Soft-ERM and floating have been given and nothing in Figure 5A.1 actually turns on identifying soft-ERM with the German-led 'non-EMS' solution.

3   e.g. Masson and Melitz (1991), Begg (1990), Hughes Hallett and Vines (1991).

4   Figure 5A.2 describes policy responses constrained by economic behaviour, inclusive of the exchange rate regime, so that progressively tightening the ERM bands (until EMU is reached) leads to increasingly parallel reactions. If, in addition, EMU also produces convergent preferences (B_1 and B_2 merge) the reaction functions coincide, conforming that two identical countries would always want to react the same way.

REFERENCES

Begg, D. K. H. (1990), 'Alternative Exchange Rate regimes', paper presented at the CEPR International Macro Workshop, Perugia, July, 1990.

Currie, D. A., G. H. Holtham and A. J. Hughes Hallett (1989), 'The Theory and Practice of International Policy coordination: Does Coordination Pay?' in R. Bryant, D. Currie, J. Frenkel, P. Masson and R. Portes (eds), *Macroeconomic Policies in an Interdependent World*, Washington DC: IMF.

Currie, D. A., P. Levine and J. Pearlman (1990), 'European Monetary Union or Hard-EMS?', London Business School Discussion Paper 05–90, forthcoming in *European Economic Review*.

De Grauwe, P. and W. Vanherverbeke (1991), 'Is Europe an Optimal Currency Area? Evidence from regional data', CEPR Discussion Paper No. 555.

The European Economy (1990), 'One Market, One Money', Occasional Paper No. 44, EC Official Publications, Luxembourg, (October).

Hughes Hallett, A. J. (1991), 'Target Zones and International Policy Coordination: The Contrast Between the Necessary and Sufficient Conditions for Success', *European Economic Review* **35**, (November).

Hughes Hallett, A. J. and D. Vines (1991), 'Adjustment Difficulties within a European Monetary Union: Can they be reduced?', CEPR Discussion Paper No. 517, and in J. Driffill and M. Beber (eds), *A Currency for Europe*, London: Lothian Foundation Press.

Masson, P. and J. Melitz (1991), 'Fiscal Policy Interdependence in a European Monetary Union', *Open Economies Review* **2**, 113–36.

Minford, A. P. L. and A. Rastogi (1990), 'The Price of EMU' in K. O. Pöhl *et al.* (eds), *Britain and EMU*, London: Centre for Economic Performance, London School of Economics.

6 Voting on the adoption of a common currency

ALESSANDRA CASELLA

1 Introduction

The debate over the adoption of a common currency in the European Community has focussed on savings of transaction costs as one of the leading advantages of a monetary union. As international transactions continue to expand, and as they become more complex, the small losses involved in exchanging currencies may grow to sizable fractions of total values, and the savings realized through a common monetary standard may therefore be nonnegligible. The EC has estimated direct, 'mechanical' savings to be of the order of 0.5 per cent of Community-wide GDP (*European Economy*, 1990), with unequal distribution across countries. The belief that transaction costs are one of the main motivations for a common currency is shared by policy-makers and financial journalists (see for example the editorials of *The Economist* in the last two years), by academics (Canzoneri and Rogers, 1990), and, I believe, by public opinion in general.

But if transaction costs are important, they must play a role in determining the composition and the size of the different markets. A common currency would then imply not only lump-sum savings, but a change in the partition of traders between domestic and international activities. This is the view studied in the paper.

Since a monetary union requires a common monetary policy and a common inflation rate, if inflation is distortionary there is a second channel through which monetary unification may affect the formation of markets. The final effect will be a combination of the two forces.

I explore these issues with a simple model where heterogeneous agents belonging to two separate countries sort themselves among markets. For simplicity, I assume that the two countries have identical structure, but that one provides a more stable currency, which is used in all international transactions.

The change in market borders caused by the adoption of a common currency triggers distributional effects, as individuals move between markets, and gain or lose trading partners. The result is disagreement among the citizens of each country over the desirability of the regime. In the model, a referendum is held in each country, asking all citizens to choose between a national money and the creation of the currency union. The results of the referendum generally differ in the two countries, since their initial conditions as high and low inflation economies are different. Still more interesting, the results change with an exogenous development parameter that influences the size and the productivity of markets, suggesting that the adoption of a common currency may be desirable only at particular stages in the evolution of trade.

In particular, the majority of voters in the high inflation country favors monetary unification at lower stages of development, when productivity is low, and transaction costs stemming from the use of the foreign currency in international trade are high relatively to income. In the low inflation country, on the contrary, the creation of a common currency wins the referendum at higher levels of development, when international markets are wide. Providing the international reserve currency then imposes a serious constraint on independent monetary policy. The conclusion is that monetary unification wins a majority of favorable votes in both countries only at intermediate values of the development parameter.

Two aspects of this result deserve to be stressed. First of all, the analysis identifies one reason why the more stable country may eventually favor a common currency. In the current European debate, the German desire to proceed with monetary unification – especially before the reunification of Western and Eastern Germany – is rarely addressed, and most standard formal models are ill-equipped to explain it. Still, the Bundesbank has often expressed concern at the rising international role of the Deutschemark, possibly fearing the lack of flexibility that accompanies the management of an international reserve currency. Several authors believe that such lack of flexibility has been a source of weakness in the past for the dollar and for sterling (see for example Caves, 1968, and Solomon, 1977).

Second, the model ties the choice of monetary regime to the development of markets. By stressing that the attitude towards a common currency changes over time, the model allows us to face explicitly the question of the appropriate moment for the reform. This aspect is again remarkably absent from most discussions of the topic.

The paper proceeds as follows. The next section presents the model. Section 3 characterizes the equilibrium, and Section 4 discusses the results. Section 5 concludes.

2   The model

To study how the size of markets, and therefore individual and aggregate income, responds to the monetary regime, we need a model where monetary policy and transaction costs affect individual decisions on trade.

The framework presented in this paper is borrowed, with few modifications, from Casella and Feinstein (1990b). A continuum of traders is uniformly distributed along a line extending from − 1 to 1, and is divided into two halves, representing two identical countries. Each trader's position represents his endowment. Country 1 is formed by agents from − 1 to 0, and country 2 by agents from 0 to 1, so that on average the distance between the endowments of traders belonging to the same country is less than the distance between them and foreign endowments. There is no migration.

In each country, some traders belong to a purely domestic market, while the others enter the international market. Once a trader has decided which market to join, he is randomly matched to a partner among those who have selected the same market.

The central assumption of the model is that the return from a transaction, divided equally between the two partners, depends on the two endowments and on an index of monetary discipline. Ignoring taxes, for the moment:

$$y_{ij} = f(x_i, x_j, d)$$

where y_{ij} is each agent's share of the joint return, x_i and x_j are the endowments of agents i and j, and d is the index of monetary discipline, negatively correlated to inflation π:

$$d = d(\pi), \quad d' < 0, \quad d(0) = \bar{d}, \quad d(\bar{\pi}) = 0$$

(the prime sign indicates the first derivative). I assume that inflation is bounded between zero and an upper limit $\bar{\pi}$, so that d reaches the upper bound $\bar{d}$ when inflation equals zero, and zero when inflation equals $\bar{\pi}$.

The assumption that inflation reduces real returns from trade should be seen as a 'reduced form' relationship. In its simpler version, it may represent a delay in converting nominal returns from trade into real assets; in this case, inflation would reduce real returns proportionally. Alternatively, it may arise from more complex links between inflation and markets, summarizing the idea that inflation not only affects the returns from a given set of economic exchanges, but modifies the relative gain from different transactions. The effect of inflation on relative prices, and therefore on real activity, is a recurrent and important point in the literature. It has been extensively documented, and explained with mechanisms ranging from menu costs (Sheshinski and Weiss, 1977) to information imperfections (Lucas, 1973) to thin markets (Casella and Feinstein, 1990a). This is the approach I follow in this paper, and specifically I assume:

$$y_{ij} = 1 + |x_i - x_j|(\beta d - |x_i - x_j|) \tag{1}$$

where 1 is just a scale term, β an exogenous parameter and $|x_i - x_j|$ the distance between the two endowments.[1]

Equation (1) is depicted in Figure 6.1, and has two characteristic features. First, each trader x_i has an ideal partner at distance $\beta d/2$, with the return from trade declining symmetrically as the realized distance falls short of or exceeds the ideal one. Second, the return from all matches is higher the higher is βd.

If inflation were not a concern and βd were very large, the gains from cooperation would increase monotonically the more dissimilar (distant) the two partners were (over the limited support we have assumed). This is a standard assumption on gains from trade: as partners engage in a joint venture, the more diversified are their specific talents and expertise the higher is their potential return. However, the scope for cooperation with a very distant partner is limited by inflation: while inflation reduces the profit from all exchanges, it affects most the transactions between agents with very different endowments, and therefore reduces the distance between ideal partners.

A model where inflation makes the gathering and processing of information more difficult, à la Lucas, can readily provide the background for equation (1). If inflation reduces the ability to monitor the activity of one's partner – to understand the effective market demand for, his good, to read his balance sheets – it is reasonable to believe that this will be more damaging the more distant, and therefore unfamiliar is his type. Thus even if potential gains increase with distance, inflation reduces sharply the return from trading with faraway partners, and effectively constrains the ideal difference between traders' endowments. In this formulation, money is modelled as unit of account, indeed as language, more than as means of payment or story of value. The focus is on the role of the currency used for invoicing.

The parameter β represents the extent to which monetary discipline is essential for trade. Since at higher β the same return can be obtained with a lower d, i.e. with higher inflation, it is appropriate to interpret β as the ability of the economy to prevent distortions brought by inflation. Thus β represents the level of financial development; it will be interpreted more generally as a development parameter. In all cases, however, I will assume that a monetary unit of account is established in both countries.

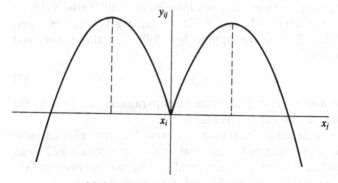

(a) Output as a function of x_i's partner

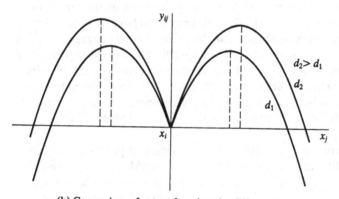

(b) Comparison of output functions for different d

Figure 6.1   The production technology

When traders belonging to the same country are matched, they are assumed to use their national currency; when international traders meet, however, they will conduct their transaction in the more stable of the two currencies at their disposal. The trader who has to exchange between currencies faces transaction costs. Therefore, agent i from country 1, matched with agent j from country 2, will have an after-tax return of:

$$y_{ij} = 1 + |x_i - x_j| \, (\beta \max(d_1, d_2) - |x_i - x_j|) - t_1 - c \qquad (1')$$

where c is positive if $d_2 > d_1$, but equals 0 otherwise (and correspondingly for the trader from country 2). If the two countries share a common currency, this currency is used in all trades, and no transaction costs are incurred.

Inflation is created by a government financing its deficit through money creation. Therefore, for given government expenditure, the index of monetary stability d must be increasing in taxes. If t are per capita lump-sum taxes, I assume:

$$d = F(t) \quad F' > 0, F'' < 0$$

where a double prime indicates the second derivative. The decreasing returns are required for an equilibrium with finite d. Again, this equation is a reduced form stating that the lower is inflation the more difficult becomes reducing its impact on markets even further. For simplicity, F will take the form:[2]

$$d = t^a \quad a = 0.5 \tag{2}$$

This specification will give rise to linear solutions. Nothing substantive will depend on the specific value of a, as long as the parameter is smaller than 1.

In each country taxes are collected from all citizens. If we wanted to stress seigniorage revenues collected from foreigners by the country providing the reserve currency, we could modify equation (2). We could correct the specification so that a given level of d could be obtained with lower direct taxes the larger the circulation of the currency. In general I will ignore this much debated aspect in the present paper. However, when relevant, I will discuss its influence on the results.

Government expenditure is exogenous, and its financing, the trade-off between inflation and direct taxes, is decided so as to maximize the average expected income of all citizens. With national currencies, the policy choice is made separately in the two countries. When the two countries share a common currency, on the other hand, policy decisions must be coordinated and d, the index of monetary stability, must be the same everywhere. Since the two countries are identical, with a common currency it will be assumed that the level of government expenditure is also identical, and the optimal policy will determine d and t so as to maximize the average expected income over the citizens of both countries.

The timing of the model is as follows: first, traders learn their type, then they decide which market to join, finally inflation and taxes are determined. The goal is to characterize a perfect foresight Nash equilibrium, where at d^* – the equilibrium value of d – the composition of markets is optimal, and no trader wants to deviate to a different trading pool. It is then possible to compare the equilibrium under national currencies to the equilibrium with a single money, and to hold a referendum asking the inhabitants of the model to choose between the two regimes. The purpose of the model is to study how the agents' vote differs at different values of the development parameter β.

3   Solution

Consider the problem from the point of view of agent i. Once he enters a market, he is matched randomly with a partner, and his return depends on the distance between the two of them, and on inflation. For a given expected level of inflation, he will therefore join the market where the expected distance between him and a random partner maximizes his expected return. This choice determines the division in trading pools and thus the trade-off between inflation and taxes in the two countries, and finally the inflation rate which in equilibrium was correctly anticipated by all traders.

The properties of this model are discussed in detail in Casella and Feinstein (1990b). The central idea is that, for any given market, each trader's expected distance from a random partner depends on his position on the line. This generates heterogeneous tastes over policy decisions, or, for given policy, different returns from joining a specific market. Exogenous changes that affect market size and composition, for example the establishment of a common currency, are accompanied by distributional effects that are directly correlated to the agents' position on the line. In addition, the impact of a change in regime depends on the value of the parameter β, suggesting the possibility that a reform that would be defeated by popular vote at a certain stage of development may be favored at a different stage.

In this section, I characterize the equilibria in the two monetary regimes when the two countries are divided into three markets; two domestic markets, one in each country, and in international one. With the functional form assumed in equation (1), each market must be formed by a single segment of adjacent traders (see the proof in Casella and Feinstein, 1990b), and therefore the partition of all traders into the three markets must be as depicted in Figure 6.2; the international traders are located on either side of the border between the two countries, while the two domestic markets are formed by agents near the external edges of the two countries. Notice that the average distance between traders in the international market need not be larger than the average distance between domestic traders. From this point of view, the approach differs from traditional international trade analysis based on comparative advantage (à la Heckscher-Ohlin). It is closer to Ricardian models of heterogeneous technologies, or to imperfect competition models of international intraindustry trade (as in Helpman and Krugman, 1985).

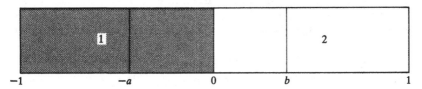

Figure 6.2   The partition into three markets

Consider first the case in which there are two separate national currencies, and two separate monetary policies. Let us call $-a$ the border agent
between the domestic and the international market in country 1, and b the
similar border agent in country 2. Thus the two domestic markets go from
-1 to $-a$ (in country 1) and from b to 1 (in country 2), and the
international market from $-a$ to b. We want to determine a and b, d_1 and
d_2, and verify that this configuration is indeed an equilibrium.

The first observation is that a symmetric equilibrium with international
trade, where $d_1 = d_2$, cannot exist as long as transaction costs are fixed
and finite: each country would have an incentive to lower its inflation just
ϵ below the other country's level, ensuring the use of its currency in all
international exchanges, and saving the transaction costs.[3] Therefore I
will assume that country 2 issues the reserve currency, implying $d_2^* > d_1^*$.

Consider $x_i = b$, the trader at the border between the international and
the domestic market in country 2. His identity is defined by the condition
that he must be indifferent between joining either market. If $d_2 > d_1$, he
uses currency 2 in all trades without facing transaction costs. Therefore
from his point of view there is no inherent difference in the functioning of
the two markets, and he is indifferent between them only if the expected
distance from a random partner is the same in both markets: the two
markets must have the same size. It follows that:

$$b = (1 - a)/2 \tag{3}$$

The equivalent condition defining the border trader between the domestic and the international market in country 1 is less simple, since a
citizen of country 1 uses different currencies when trading with domestic
or with foreign partners. Consider agent x_i in country 1. If he belongs to
the domestic market, he always uses currency 1, and never pays transaction costs. His expected income is:

$$Ey^D = 1 + 1/(1 - a)[\beta d_1(\int_{-1}^{x_i} (x_i - x_j)dx_j + \int_{x_i}^{-a} (x_j - x_i)dx_j)$$
$$- \int_{-1}^{-a} (x_i - x_j)^2 dx_j] - t_1$$

If he belongs to the international market, whenever he is matched with a trader from country 2 he gains access to currency 2, but faces transaction costs. His expected return is:[4]

$$Ey^I = 1 + 1/(a+b)[\beta d_1(\int_{-a}^{x_i}(x_i - x_j)dx_j + \int_{x_i}^{0}(x_j - x_i)dx_j)$$

$$+ \beta d_2(\int_{0}^{b}(x_j - x_i)dx_j) - \int_{-a}^{b}(x_i - x_j)^2 dx_j - bc] - t_1$$

The marginal trader $x_i = -a$ must be indifferent between joining the domestic or the international market. The value of a is then implicitly determined by the condition:

$$Ey^I|_{x_i = -a} = Ey^D|_{x_i = -a} \qquad \text{where} \ -a\epsilon[+1, 0]$$

or, solving the integrals explicitly, and using equation (3):

$$3\beta d_2(1 + 2a - 3a^2) + 6\beta d_1(3a^2 - 1) + 3(1 + a^3)$$
$$- 7a(1 + a) = 12(1 - a)c \qquad (4)$$

The optimal level of inflation, or equivalently the variable d, is determined in each country so as to maximize the average expected return of the country's citizens.

In country 1, average expected income EY, is:

$$EY_I = \int_{-I}^{-a} Ey^D dx_i + \int_{-a}^{0} Ey^I dx_i$$

and d_1^* is the value of d_1 that maximizes it. Solving explicitly, we find:

$$d_1^* = \frac{\beta}{6}[(1-a)^2 + \frac{2a^3}{1+a}] \qquad (5)$$

Exactly the same logic can be applied to country 2. Recalling that traders from country 2 use currency 2 in all transactions, we can derive the expected income in the international and in the domestic market. Integrating with respect to x_i, we obtain expected average income, and a standard maximization with respect to d_2 yields the optimal level of d_2:

$$d_2^* = \frac{\beta}{6}[\frac{2}{1+a} - \frac{3(1-a)(2-a)}{4}] \qquad (6)$$

For given parameter values, equations (3), (4), (5) and (6) form a system of four equations in four unknowns, and can be solved simultaneously to find the equilibrium values of a, b, d_1 and d_2.

We must verify that this solution is indeed an equilibrium, and therefore that no trader would want to change market at the realized values of the endogenous variables. The temptation to deviate is zero for the border traders, since this is the condition defining them. In addition, equilibrium requires that such temptation reach a maximum exactly at the borders. Consider x_i belonging to the domestic market in country 1. The temptation to deviate to the international market, T_i, is:[5]

$$T_i(x_i) = Ey_i^I - Ey_i^D$$

where the expected income in the two markets must be calculated taking into account that x_i belongs to the interval $[-1, -a)$. solving the integrals explicitly, we find that T_i is everywhere concave in x_i, and therefore reaches its maximum at $x_i = -a$ if and only if its first derivative with respect to x_i is nonnegative at $x_i = -a$. This corresponds to the requirement:

$$\beta d_1 + \beta/(a + b)(d_2 b + d_1 a) \leq 1 + b \tag{7}$$

In country 2, identical reasoning leads to the condition:

$$2\beta d_2 \leq 1 + b \tag{8}$$

Finally, the equations above have been derived for the case:

$$d_2^* > d_1^* \tag{9}$$

We must verify that this inequality is realized.

Summarizing, if the two countries have national currencies and independent policies, there exists an equilibrium where the traders of each country are divided into two groups, one engaged in domestic transactions and the other joining the international market. The borders between markets, $-a$ and b, and the variables d_1^* and d_2^* are determined by equations (3), (4), (5) and (6), and the equilibrium conditions (7), (8) and (9) must be verified.

In this model, a country is defined as a subset of agents who share a common policy, specifically the sources of financing of the government budget. With a common currency and a common policy, therefore, the role of the border between the two countries disappears: international trade is not identified by any characteristic feature that distinguishes it from domestic exchange. In other words, if the world is divided into three markets, but there is a common currency, the only possible equilibrium has the three markets being of identical size, since only in that case would the marginal traders be indifferent between them.

With a common currency, therefore, the international market is formed by agents belonging to the interval $[-1/3, 1/3]$, while the two domestic markets go from -1 to $-1/3$, and from $1/3$ to 1.[6] The three markets are mirror images of each other. If x_i belongs to the international market, his expected income Ey_i^I equals:

$$Ey_i^I = 1 + (\beta/6)d(1 + 9x_i)^2 - x_i^2 - 1/27 - t \tag{10}$$

where d and t are equal across both countries. Since the three markets are identical, the expected income of a domestic trader in country 1 is easily derived from equation (10) by scaling x_i down by 2/3 (i.e. by substituting x_i with $x_i - 2/3$), and similarly for a trader in the domestic market of country 2. Average expected income is the same in each market, and indeed in each country and in the world, and is given by:

$$EY = 1 + (2/9)\beta d - 2/27 - t \tag{11}$$

The optimal value of d is then:

$$d^* = \beta/9 \tag{12}$$

Finally, equilibrium requires that the temptation to deviate be highest at the borders between markets. This corresponds to the condition:

$$\beta d^* \le 2/3$$

or, substituting (12):

$$\beta^2 \le 6 \tag{13}$$

The equilibrium with three separate markets exists only when β is not too high. At higher values of β, the size of the markets becomes too small, traders want to be matched with partners at larger distances, and the three markets unite in a single trading pool. This is immediately clear in the case of a common currency, but the same mechanism dictates conditions (7) and (8) when there are two national currencies.[7]

Of course, it is possible to study the switch to a common currency when there is a unique market. However, this begs the question of the impact of the monetary regime on market formation, and is not pursued in this paper.

4   Results

In this section, I present and discuss the impact on market formation, expected income and monetary discipline of the three exogenous factors present in the model: the level of transaction costs, the value of the development parameter β, and the monetary regime. When studying equilibria with national currencies, I will make use of numerical simulations, since no simple analytical solution can be derived.

Consider first the role of transaction costs. By assumption, these costs are present only when the two countries have different currencies, and affect the return from international transactions for those traders whose national currency is weaker. Intuitively, we expect that higher transaction costs, ceteris paribus, must reduce the size of the international market in country 1, while increasing the participation in this market by citizens of country 2 (Recall that b, the border between the two markets in country 2, equals $(1 - a)/2$). The total size of the international market is:

$$a + b = (1 + a)/2$$

and therefore it falls at higher transaction costs.

The impact on monetary stability is also straightforward. In country 1, the larger domestic market requires higher monetary discipline, and d_1 should rise at higher transaction costs. In country 2, d_2 is chosen so as to facilitate trade in two markets, each of which has size $(1 + a)/2$. Since the optimal degree of monetary discipline is an increasing function of market size, d_2 falls as higher transaction costs reduce the value of a. These intuitions were confirmed by numerical analyses. Figure 6.3 depicts the results.

Transaction costs have effects both on average expected income and on its distribution, in both countries. In country 1, average expected income should fall as costs rise, both because of the direct impact of the costs, and because foreign trade is reduced. The reduction in income is not uniform: it affects most those agents still involved in international trade, whereas domestic traders near the border between the two markets actually benefit from the increased number of potential partners. In country 2, higher transaction costs raise average expected income as they reduce the need for monetary discipline. This conclusion would be different at higher values of β, when the marginal return of d is higher, but the values of β required for such reversal are not compatible with an equilibrium with three separate markets.[8] Again, the impact on expected income is not uniform: traders switching from domestic to international transactions benefit most, while domestic traders who now find themselves near the border of the market are hurt by the loss of potential trading partners. Figure 6.4 compares market structure and expected returns for all agents, in the two cases $c = 0.01$ (the dashed line) and $c = 0.05$ (the solid line), with β set equal to 1.

Two observations are in order. First, transaction costs are here discussed as an exogenous parameter, determining markets' composition. If they are affected by regulations or capital controls, then we can think of them as an endogenous policy instrument, and the results on distribution suggest that, as long as foreign trade involves a minority of the population, capital controls could theoretically win a popular referendum.

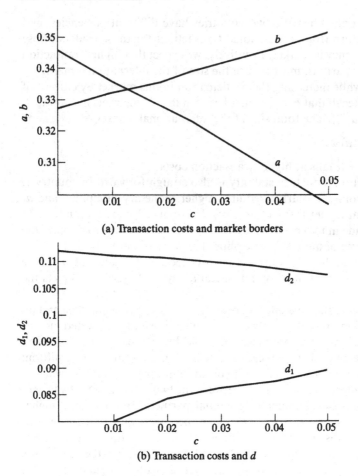

(a) Transaction costs and market borders

(b) Transaction costs and d

Figure 6.3   The role of transaction costs ($\beta = 1$)

Then we would be able to say not only what their effects should be on markets and inflation, but also when they are most likely to be approved. It turns out that in the model discussed so far capital controls, in the form of higher transaction costs, are never approved by a majority of the citizens of country 1. However, part of the result stems from ignoring the tax benefits that capital controls may bestow on the rest of the country.

For example, and this is the second observation, if we consider explicitly the increase in seigniorage revenues stemming from increased use of the national currency, capital controls may be more popular. From the point of view of country 2, the extra seigniorage increases the attractiveness of

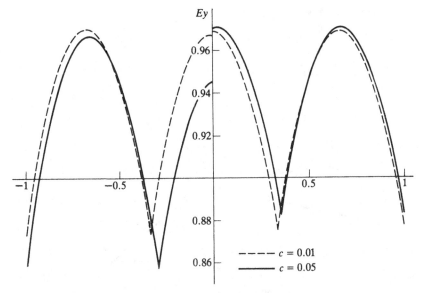

Figure 6.4 Expected individual income and transaction costs ($\beta = 1$)

foreign traders in the international market, and shifts preferences against high transaction costs abroad.

The second exogenous parameter playing an important role in the model is β. Higher values of β increase the return from larger markets, for given d, and at the same time raise the equilibrium value of d: higher development is accompanied by larger markets, and by lower inflation. If the two countries share a common currency, the three markets must be identical, for any β, and thus the composition and the size of the markets are invariant to changes in the parameter. The positive effect of higher β on the variable d and on expected income is then immediately clear from equations (10), (11) and (12). Notice that the impact of β on expected income is largest for those traders near the border between markets, since these are the traders faced with the highest expected distance from a random partner.

If the two countries have two national currencies, changes in β affect the borders between markets. In country 1, higher β and higher returns decrease the importance of the fixed transaction costs, and more traders join the international market. In country 2, some traders close to the border shift from foreign trade to domestic transactions, to compensate for the inflow of agents from country 1 in the international market. The net effect is that the international market and the domestic market in country 2 expand, while the domestic market in country 1 contracts. (Figure 6.5(a)).[9]

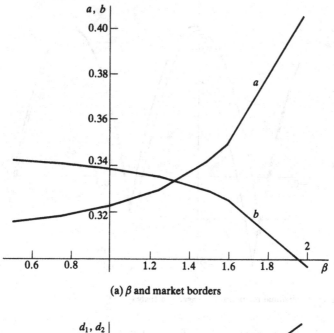

(a) β and market borders

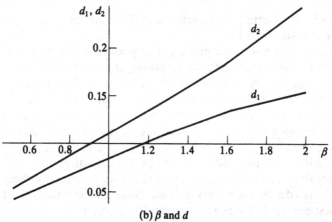

(b) β and d

Figure 6.5   The role of β ($c = 0.025$)

The change in borders also implies that while both d_1 and d_2 rise with β, the increase is smaller in country 1: the use of currency 2 has expanded and the importance of currency 1's stability has decreased. (Figure 6.5(b)).[10]

Finally, at higher β average expected income is higher in both countries. International traders from country 1 are the group benefiting the most, as

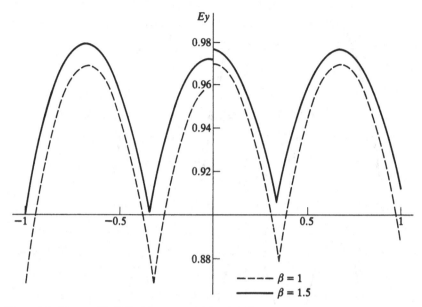

Figure 6.6   Expected individual income and β ($c = 0.025$)

the loss due to the transaction costs is now minor, and the possibility of free-riding on the stability of currency 2 is very valuable. Figure 6.6 depicts expected income for all agents as a function of their location in the two cases $\beta = 1$ (the dashed line) and $\beta = 1.5$ (the solid line), for $c = 0.025$.

We are now ready to address the central question of the paper: what is the outcome of a referendum proposing a choice between national currencies and a common money? From the point of view of the citizens of country 1, a common currency has three separate effects: it means zero transaction costs when trading with foreigners; it eliminates the possibility of free-riding on the stability of the foreign currency, and it affects the borders between markets. We know from the analysis above that a reduction in transaction costs, with the accompanying market changes, is advantageous to country 1, but so is free-riding on currency 2. The tradeoff between the two forces depends on the value of the parameter β: at low β transaction costs are high relatively to income, while the value of gaining access to currency 2 is limited, since the international market tends to be smaller and the difference in the stability of the two currencies less pronounced. At high β, the relative strength of the two effects is reversed. Therefore we expect country 1 to be more in favor of a common currency at low β, and change its position later.

The impact of the common currency on country 2 is more subtle, since it

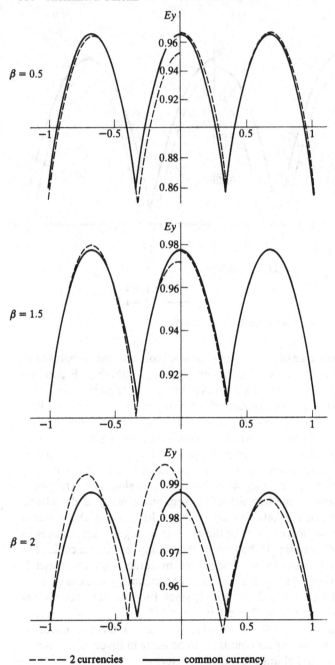

----- 2 currencies   —— common currency

Figure 6.7   Expected individual income and monetary regime

depends only on the influence of the monetary regime on market formation. At low β, national currencies involving transaction costs for citizens of country 1 reduce the size of the international market. This is advantageous for country 2, since it limits the degree of monetary discipline that it must supply. At high β, however, the transaction costs play a small role, and larger numbers of traders from country 1 join the international market. Providing a currency sufficiently stable to sustain the increased volume of international transactions becomes more and more costly. We expect the preference for a common currency to dominate in country 2 when β becomes large enough.

These conclusions are confirmed by numerical analysis, and are shown in Figure 6.7. The expected return for all traders is depicted in the two cases of national currencies (the dashed line) and a common currency (the solid line) for the three different values $\beta = 0.5$, $\beta = 1.5$ and $\beta = 2$ (all for $c = 0.025$). In Figure 6.7, the intermediate value of β is the only one at which a common currency is preferred by a majority of the traders in both countries. More generally, this outcome is consistent with a set of intermediate β values.[11]

As always in this model the distributional effects are important, and emerge clearly in Figure 6.7. The traders most often in disagreement with the majority view are in both countries the domestic traders near the border between the international and the domestic markets. These are the only traders hurt by an expansion of the international market, since such expansion implies for them a loss in potential trading partners. For some parameter values, the result of the referendum can be different from that obtained by comparing average expected income in the two regimes. For example, for $\beta = 1.6$ and $c = 0.025$, a common currency would have only 43% of the votes in country 1, even though it leads to a slightly higher average expected income. However, this is the exception. The popular vote and the aggregate measure are generally in agreement.

Finally, notice that the results of the paper are sensitive to the decision to ignore international seigniorage revenues. If these revenues are important, they move the preferences of the country providing the reserve currency against the common currency, and the preferences of the less stable country in favor of the common currency. However, they do not alter the conclusion that the adoption of a common currency could only occur at intermediate levels of β.

5 Conclusions

Two countries deciding to adopt a common currency must share the same monetary policy and face the same inflation rate. They save on the transaction costs present in international trade when traders have different monetary standards.

In this paper, I have studied the impact of these two factors on the composition of markets. If inflation generates distortions, and if only a fraction of the citizens of a country engages in international trade, then the establishment of a common currency must modify the borders between domestic and international markets. This triggers distributional effects, possibly different in the two countries, and creates disagreement among citizens over the desirability of the currency union.

With the help of a very simple model where the formation of markets is endogenous, I have looked at the result of a referendum asking the citizens of the two countries to choose between national currencies and monetary union. The outcome of the referendum is typically different in the two economies, and changes at different levels of development, suggesting that a common currency will be favored by a majority of traders in both countries only at a particular stage.

In particular, I have assumed that the two countries have identical structures, but that one issues a more stable currency employed in international trade. The high inflation country has to balance the tradeoff between free-riding on the monetary discipline of the foreigners, in the international market, and paying transaction costs. The importance of transaction costs declines at higher productivity, even with growing international exchanges, and therefore preferences move against a common currency at higher stages of development. The low inflation country, on its part, must evaluate the costs of providing monetary stability to all traders in the international market. This becomes increasingly costly as markets expand, and preferences here move towards a common currency at higher levels of development. Only at an intermediate stage may the citizens of the two countries agree on monetary unification.

The analysis highlights two points that deserve more discussion. First, the low inflation country may suffer from the lack of flexibility inherent in being the provider of the international reserve currency. It may then welcome the establishment of a common currency as a more balanced way of sharing responsibility. Second, the desirability of a monetary union may be a function of the intensity of exchanges, and more generally of the development of markets. Thus the prospects for a common European currency may be more favorable now than they have been in the past, and possibly more favorable than they would be in the future.

NOTES

I thank the editors of this volume, Jim Levinsohn, Maurice Obstfeld, Torsten Persson and the participants at the conference for comments and advice. The paper was written at the Hoover Institution, whose hospitality and financial support I acknowledge with gratitude.

1 Notice, however, that the analysis could be conducted under the weaker assumption that inflation reduces real returns proportionally. If a common currency implies a change in inflation rates, it will still affect the formation of markets.

2 The decreasing returns in equation (2) can be encountered either when direct taxes are converted into lower inflation, or at the successive stage when inflation is translated into the 'discipline index' d. As the most straightforward example of the latter case, consider a steady state where at the end of each period each citizen holds one unit of real domestic currency. If G is total government expenditure, T total tax revenues, μ the rate of money creation and M/P the stock of real balances in the economy, then the government's budget constraint is:

$$G = T + \mu M/P$$

or, in per capita terms, using the fact that $\mu = \pi$:

$$g = t + \pi$$

Then d is given by

$$d = (g - \pi)^{a} = t^{a}$$

where it is assumed that inflation tax revenues cannot exceed government expenditure.

3 However this policy is not approved by a majority of the citizens, as long as less than half of them are involved in foreign trade. A symmetrical equilibrium exists if the transaction costs are paid by all traders matched with a foreigner, regardless of the currency used in the trade.

4 Notice that an undesirable effect of the random matching is that a trader may well be matched with a partner from the same country, even in the international market.

5 The condition ensuring that no trader wants to deviate to the market closer to his is sufficient to prevent deviations to the third and more distant market.

6 Recall that markets must be formed by unique segments of adjacent traders.

7 An equilibrium with two markets, whose border may or may not coincide with the boundary between the two countries, is also possible as long as $\beta^2 \leq 6$. With $a = 0.5$, the constraint on β necessary to prevent deviation to a neighbouring market is identical independently of the number of markets. When $\beta^2 > 6$, a single market is the unique equilibrium. For a detailed discussion of the transition to larger markets, see Casella and Feinstein (1990b).

8 In this model all equilibria are such that, for given β, the partition with the highest sustainable number of markets always yields the highest average return. In other words, given β, the smaller are the equilibrium markets, and the smaller is d, the higher is expected income. The point is discussed at length in Casella and Feinstein (1990b).

9 Among the citizens of country 2, this mass of traders in the international

market declines as β rises. However, this is an artifact of the assumption that everybody must trade. I conjecture that the result would be different if I had allowed agents with negative expected return from trade to abstain from joining any market.

10 This result deserves more thought. The idea that relatively more unstable currencies are used less as markets expand and trade becomes more international seems at least intuitively appealing. However, in the EC at least, inflation rates have been converging in the last decade.

11 Notice that there are admissible parameter values such that no β exists for which the monetary union wins a majority in both countries.

REFERENCES

Canzoneri, M. and C. Rogers (1990), 'Is the European Community an Optimal Currency Area?', *American Economic Review* **80**, 419–33.

Casella, A. and J. Feinstein (1990a), 'Economic Exchange in Hyperinflation', *Journal of Political Economy* **98**, 1–27.

(1990b), 'Public Goods in Trade: On the Formation of Markets and Political Jurisdictions', NBER Working Paper No. 3554, December.

Caves, R. (1968), *Britain's Economic Prospects*, Brookings Institution, Washington, DC.

Commission of the European Communities (1990), 'One Market, One Money'. *European Economy* **44**, 251–68.

Helpman, E. and P. Krugman (1985), *Market Structure and Foreign Trade*, Cambridge, Ma: MIT Press.

Lucas, R. E. (1973), 'Some International Evidence on Output-Inflation Tradeoffs', *American Economic Review* **63**, 326–34.

Sheshinski, E. and Y. Weiss (1977), 'Inflation and Costs of Price Adjustment', *Review of Economic Studies* **44**, 287–303.

Solomon, R. (1977), *International Monetary System, 1945–76*, New York: Harper and Row.

Discussion

TORSTEN PERSSON

In the debate about monetary unification in Europe, two major economic arguments have been launched by those that favor adopting a common currency. One argument has to do with cementing the credibility gains for low-inflation monetary policy already achieved by the EMS; the other has to do with saving on transactions costs. Academic economists have devoted more attention to the former than to the latter argument. At the same time it is unclear how broad the support is for complete monetary integration – both among policy-makers and among the public – in different countries.

In this light, Alessandra Casella's paper is an interesting and original addition to the theoretical discussion about monetary union. The motivation for the paper runs roughly as follows: if the savings of transaction costs are important enough to constitute a major argument in favor of a common currency, we should expect them to affect economic behaviour; in particular, they should change the economic interaction between agents in different countries. The implied reformation of markets is likely to have asymmetric effects on different agents in a given country. There will thus be distributional effects, the nature of which will shape the degree of political support for monetary unification.

I find this logic and the general approach of the paper convincing. When it comes to the particular approach to modelling the interaction between market formation, policy-making and politics, I am perhaps a little less convinced. The random matching model employed in the analysis is attractive from a theoretical point of view, but it also complicates the analysis a great deal and requires many simplifying assumptions. These assumptions notwithstanding, it is hard to derive analytical results and it becomes necessary to rely on numerical simulations. In the end the reader is left wondering about the robustness of specific results.

What I would like to do in this comment is to suggest an alternative simpler model, which I believe captures the gist of Casella's basic argument, but still lends itself to relatively simple analysis. I will use the model to discuss the issues she takes up in the paper, particularly whether a majority of the public would support adopting a common currency and what characteristics of the economy make such an outcome more likely. I will also use it to discuss some additional issues.

1   An alternative model

There are two countries, each populated by a continuum of individuals. Agent i in a given country has preferences over her private consumption equal to private income y^i and over government consumption g according to

$$u^i = y^i + \tilde{V}(g)$$

where $\tilde{V}(g)$ is a concave function. Private income net of transactions costs depends on whether the agent transacts with foreign citizens in the 'international market' or with domestic citizens in the 'domestic market', such that

$y^i = (1 + \omega) - a(1 - c^i)Min[D(\pi),D(\pi^*)]/\beta$ if i trades in the international market

$y^i = 1 - (1 - c^i)D(\pi)/\beta$ if i trades in the domestic market

These expressions are the counterpart of equation (1') in Casella's paper. The first term on the right-hand side of each expression is the gross income from transacting in that market: ω thus represents a premium on international transactions. The second term is the cost of transacting in the market. Following Casella, β is a positive parameter measuring the importance of transactions costs in general. In the domestic market, where everyone uses domestic currency, the transactions costs get higher at an increasing rate if domestic inflation π goes up. That is, $D(\pi)$ is an increasing convex function. Transaction costs are continuously distributed in the population according to the idiosyncratic parameter c^i. This parameter has a distribution function $F(c^i)$ with bounded support within the unit interval.

In the international market everyone uses foreign (domestic) currency if the foreign currency is more (less) stable than domestic currency, π^* is lower (higher) than π. The transactions costs in the international market are higher, *ceteris paribus*, even if domestic currency is used (due to $\pi \leq \pi^*$). They are higher still if foreign currency is used (due to $\pi > \pi^*$). That is

$$a = \frac{a^h \text{ if } \pi > \pi^*}{a^l \text{ if } \pi \leq \pi^*}, \quad a^h > a^l > 1$$

Finally, if there is only one common currency, this currency is of course used in all transactions in both countries.

2   Market formation

The single economic decision agent i makes in the model is to maximize her private income by choosing in which market to transact. It is easy to see that only agents with relatively high c^i – that is, with relatively low idiosyncratic transaction costs – will take advantage of the higher return in the international market. But the way agents sort themselves into markets differ somewhat in the low-inflation country and in the high-inflation country.

Consider first the low-inflation country, whose currency is used in international transactions. It is easy to show that the lower bound on c^i, above which agents will sort themselves into the international market can be written as a function of the model's parameters: $C(a^l, \beta, \omega, \pi)$. Anything that decreases the relative net income in the international market makes fewer agents choose to transact in the international market. Thus, C is higher if a^l or π is higher, or if β or ω is lower.

In the high-inflation country there is a similar lower bound: $C^*(a^h, \beta, \omega, \pi, \pi^*)$. Sorting depends on a^h, β and ω in the same way as in the low-inflation country, but since now foreign currency is used in international transactions, it is now a higher π^* which decreases the proportion of domestic agents in the international market, while a *lower* π has the same effect (as long as $\pi > \pi^*$).

With a common currency, sorting in both countries takes place as in the low-inflation country.

3   Policy preferences

Let us next study agents' policy preferences over inflation. Clearly inflation has a cost in the model, since it tends to decrease private income by increasing transactions costs. To introduce a trade-off, I follow Casella and make government spending an increasing function of inflation $g = G(\pi)$. The utility of government consumption can then be written as an increasing and concave function of π: $V(\pi) \equiv \tilde{V}(G(\pi))$. With this assumption, agents' preferences over inflation will be single-peaked, with the preferred inflation rate at the point where the marginal cost of lower private income equals the marginal benefit of higher government consumption.

Since the marginal cost of inflation varies systematically across agents depending on their idiosyncratic transaction costs, their preferred inflation rates, π^i, differ too. Figure 6A.1(a) plots π^i against c^i in the low-inflation country. The figure illustrates how agents with higher c^i and thus lower marginal transaction costs generally prefer a higher π. But the relation between π^i and c^i has a discontinuity at C, because the marginal agent in the international market has higher marginal transactions costs than the marginal agent in the domestic market.

Figure 6A.1(b) plots the analogous relation in the high-inflation country. The qualitative difference relative to the low-inflation case is that π^i is constant above C^*. This is because agents in the international market now use foreign currency when transacting, so that the marginal transaction cost is decided by π^* rather than by π.

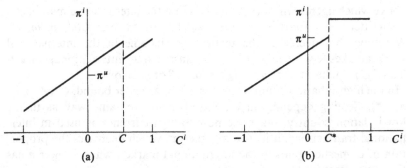

Figure 6A.1   Policy preferences when the majority transacts in the domestic market

4   Utilitarian policy-making

Suppose first we model the policy-making process as in Casella's paper: that is, equilibrium policy – both in the absence and presence of monetary union – is set by a utilitarian planner. The outcome will generally depend, not only on parameters but on functional forms. The following preliminary discussion is based on the assumption that the functions $V(\cdot)$ and $D(\cdot)$ are quadratic and the distribution of c^i is symmetric around its mean of 0 in both countries.

We can then infer from parameter values which of the two countries will have the higher inflation rate in the absence of monetary union. Whichever the initial policy configuration, however, the common inflation rate with a common currency will be a weighted average of the two pre-union rates.

Let us then pose the central question in Casella's paper, namely how a proposal of monetary union would fare in a referendum and how the outcome depends on parameter values. There are a few different cases to consider. Suppose first that the parameter values are such that a majority of the population belongs to the domestic market. (As previously discussed, this will happen when ω or β is high, or when a is low.) Figure 6A.1 (a and b) illustrates the policy preferences in the low-inflation and high-inflation countries, respectively, when C and C^* are both positive – recall that the average and median citizen has $c^i = 0$. It also illustrates the equilibrium pre-union inflation rates with a utilitarian planner, labeled π^u in the figure. The utilitarian inflation rate is below the rate preferred by the average and median citizen in the low-inflation country, but above the rate preferred by the median in the high-inflation country. In both cases, the reason is the discontinuity in policy preferences plus the fact that the planner gives weight to the policy preferences of the minority in the international market in his policy decision.

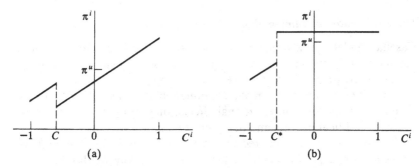

Figure 6A.2 Policy preferences when the majority transacts in the international market

Because individual policy preferences are single-peaked, we know that the median voter will be decisive in a referendum on a common currency. As the figure is drawn, the citizen with $c^i = 0$ is the pivotal voter in both countries (the following argument will hold even if this is not the case). Since the median in the low-inflation country wants a higher inflation rate and the median in the high-inflation country wants a lower inflation rate, moving to a common currency brings the equilibrium rate in the right direction for both of them. Consequently, both the pivotal voters will both vote yes in a referendum, provided that the two countries are not so different that the inflation rate moves too much.

Consider instead a parameter constellation illustrated in Figure 6A.2 (a and b), such that a majority of the population in both countries transacts in the international market. Reversing the previous argument, the pre-union equilibrium inflation rate is now too high for the pivotal citizen in the low-inflation country. From her viewpoint, the planner pays too little attention to transactions costs when weighing in the minority preferences of the citizens in the domestic market. And the inflation rate is too low for the pivotal citizen in the high-inflation country. She is free-riding on the foreign currency, so from her viewpoint the planner pays too much attention to the concerns over domestic inflation of the minority in the domestic market. A proposal of a common currency will now, of course, be voted down in both countries.

At a general level, these preliminary results – and obvious extensions to cases where the pivotal voter is in different markets in the two countries – confirm Casella's conclusion that universal support for a common currency can be expected only for some market constellations. At a specific level, the results are somewhat different, suggesting that her detailed results may not be all that robust. In particular, the present analysis identifies the proportions of citizens who are dependent on international and domestic transactions as determinants of the support for a crucial common currency.

5   Majoritarian policy-making

Casella models policy-making, before and after the adoption of a common currency, as choices by a utilitarian social planner. But this is not necessarily a plausible positive model of the policy process. A similar logic as the one advanced in the introduction suggests that if there are potentially important distributional effects, they will get reflected in the domestic political process and in equilibrium policy.

Of course, much of the recent work on the political economy of macroeconomic policy has modeled monetary policy in this vein and has tried to characterize the resulting political distortions. In that light it is interesting to reverse the assumptions in Casella's paper and in the previous section. To do so, assume instead that equilibrium policy, both before and after the adoption of a common currency, reflects majoritarian preferences. And instead pose the normative question how the move to a common currency would affect welfare, once we evaluate the outcome for each country by a social welfare function defined over the utility of its citizens.

For the purposes of this discussion, let us assume that equilibrium policies are determined by majority vote and take the social welfare function to coincide with the objective of a utilitarian social planner. In this case, we get conclusions exactly opposite to those we got under utilitarian policy-making. Suppose that a majority in both countries transact in the domestic market. Then we may just reverse the argument in connection with Figure 6A.1: from the viewpoint of our hypothetical utilitarian social planners, the median voter in the low-inflation country sets too high an inflation rate, while the median voter in the high-inflation country sets too low an inflation rate. Moving to a common currency with a common inflation rate in between the two pre-union rates, thus makes the outcome worse in both countries. But if the majority of the population belongs to the international market, as in Figure 6A.2, a common intermediate inflation rate diminishes the political distortion and increases the utilitarian objective in each country.

The upshot of the preliminary analysis in this section and the previous section is thus that there seems to be an interesting duality between the positive and the normative results: a commitment to adopting a common currency may be particularly valuable precisely in the situation when the move to a common currency is unlikely to gather universal majority support.

6   Concluding comments

Alessandra Casella's analysis of transactions costs and market formation has raised a number of new issues in connection with monetary union and policy-making in Europe. In this comment, I have discussed some of these issues in the context of a model, which is theoretically less appealing than the one in Casella's paper but which permits analytical solutions. One can think of several extensions of the analysis. In this comment, I have briefly dealt with a normative issue: under what circumstances is monetary union desirable given that the equilibrium policy reflects majoritarian rather than utilitarian preferences? It is easy to think of other extensions. For example, Casella mentions the possibility of incorporating the cross-country distribution of the revenues from seigniorage collection in the analysis. I hope that her stimulating paper will stimulate further work on the adoption of a common currency.

Part III Fiscal policy requirements of a common currency area

7 Fiscal federalism and optimum currency areas: evidence for Europe from the United States

XAVIER SALA-I-MARTÍN and JEFFREY SACHS

1 Introduction

1.1 Some background

The issue of the appropriate exchange rate (ER) system for Europe is now hotly debated. Yet the question of whether Europe should have a single currency is not new. It goes back to the very first debates surrounding European economic integration of the late 1940s and the 1950s.[1] From the very beginning people have asked what, in our opinion, is a central question: why do ER problems seem not to exist within some subsets of countries or within a country with a diversity of regions (as, for instance, the United States), while they do exist in the world as a whole? Put differently, why has the 'irrevocably fixed' ER system within the US functioned well, while the Gold Standard and the Bretton Woods systems collapsed? Economists have phrased this question in the following way: what constitutes an optimum (or at least reasonably good) currency area?[2]

Different schools have answered this question differently. Classical economists argued that the key variable to exchange rate regimes is transactions costs. Because these transactions costs represent social losses, they should be minimized and the way to do it is to have a single worldwide currency. Thus the entire world is an optimum currency area. J. S. Mill puts it in a very illustrative way:

> '... So much of barbarism, however, still remains in the transactions of most civilized nations, that almost all independent countries choose to assert their nationality by having, to their own inconvenience and that of their neighbors, a peculiar currency of their own.'[3]

Of course, in order to explain the existence of different currencies Mill had to claim a kind of 'barbarism', a view that is not shared by many of his 20th century followers. The New Classical economists claim that one has to weigh the costs of having heterogeneous currencies against the benefits of each country being able to achieve its own optimal rate of money growth. Because they view the process of money supply as essentially a tax on existing money holdings, they see no reason why money growth (or inflation) should not be viewed within the problem of optimal taxation for each country. Hence, they explain the existence of different currencies according to structural differences across countries that lead to different optimal tax rates. For instance, it has been argued that the private technology for evading income taxes in Italy is superior to that in Germany so the optimal inflation tax in Italy may be larger than in Germany. Thus the two countries should enjoy different currencies. See for instance Canzoneri and Rogers (1990).

Another view, associated with Monetarist and Keynesian economists puts the money supply process (and therefore the exchange rate regime) in the context of stabilization policies. Mundell (1961) argued that only regions within which there is relatively high labour mobility should have a unique currency.[4] His (now canonical) example is the following: suppose we have two regions (A and B), each producing one good (a and b respectively) and populated by households who consume a little bit of both goods so that there is interregional trade. Suppose that, starting from a full employment equilibrium position, there is a permanent shift of preferences from good a to good b (ie, at initial relative prices, everybody prefers relatively more of good b and less a). If the relative price between the two goods (the real ER) does not change, there will be a trade imbalance (a deficit for A and a surplus for B). Equilibrium can be restored at the initial relative price by changing the supplied quantities of both a and b. This can be achieved by moving people from region A to region B.

Yet another way to restore equilibrium is by changing the relative price and maintaining the initial quantities. In turn, this can be done through two different channels: the first one involves changing the nominal exchange rate and leaving the nominal prices in the two regions unchanged. This possibility is not present, however, when both regions have the same currency. The second way of moving the real ER is to change the nominal price levels. In the case we are considering, the price level in A has to go down relative to that in B. If prices and wages adjust immediately, the real ER jumps to the new equilibrium level and that is the end of the story. But the economists who support these stories believe that price levels are 'sticky' (possibly due to small menu costs). In this case, the new equilibrium real ER will slowly be reached, but only after a period of 'over-employment' in B and deflation and unemployment in A.[5]

The longer it takes the nominal prices to adjust, the more severe will be the recession in A. Hence, according to this view, if labour is not highly mobile, A and B should have flexible ER so the monetary authorities can stabilize the two regions' output through independent monetary policies.[6] Thus, as mentioned earlier, this view holds that only regions within which there is high labour mobility should have flexible exchange rate systems.

Should Europe have a unique currency? The Keynesian answer, according to what we just have seen, depends importantly on whether the EEC is strongly affected by the type of 'real' shocks we just described or rather by 'monetary shocks' like changes in the demand for money.[7] If we conclude that real shocks are important, then we have to analyze factor mobility among regions (or sectors). The 1992 liberalization will abolish all major constraints on labour mobility, so in principle there seems to be good reason to substitute all individual currencies by a single one. But there are barriers other (and perhaps more important) than legal ones. Europeans have very different cultures and languages, as well as important and well known imperfections in housing markets that stifle mobility even within countries, not to mention between countries. These barriers will still exist after 1992. Hence, under this Keynesian view, if Europe decides to have a common currency, interregional shocks will generate unemployment in some regions and inflation in others. The very survival of the monetary union (and, with it, the political and other forms of unification) could be threatened.[8]

But let us imagine that, for whatever reason, Europeans go ahead and fix their exchange rates forever by creating a unique European currency. What can be done to minimize the possibility of collapse? This can be answered by analysing the regions of the United States. One could think of the US as a collection of regions or states linked by a system, of irrevocably fixed exchange rates. And one can argue that this system has worked reasonably well over the last couple of hundred years. The question is, what did it take?

The first thing to understand is that, even though one might be tempted to think that there are no major interregional shocks requiring large changes in the real exchange rate across regions of the US, this is simply not true. What is true is that, because there are no current account data, policy-makers and journalists do not associate these situations with open economy problems that require large real exchange rate movements. The second point is that, contrary to most people's beliefs, labour mobility across the United States is fairly limited. In a related study Barro and Sala-i-Martín (1991a) found that, ceteris paribus, an increase in a state's per capita personal income by 1% raises net immigration only by enough to raise the state's population growth rate by 0.026% per annum. This slow adjustment through net migration means that population densities do not adjust rapidly to differences in per capita income adjusted for amenities.

1.2   Fiscal federalism and exchange rates

It has been argued that one of the reasons why the US exchange rate system has held up reasonably well is the existence of a 'Federal Fiscal Authority' which insures states against regional shocks.[9] In addition to the mechanisms already mentioned (devaluation, labour movements or recession), there is another way of maintaining a fixed parity without major real imbalances: having a redistribution of income from 'adversely shocked' to 'favorably shocked' regions.[10] After a permanent taste shock like the one proposed by Mundell, we can be closer to full employment without changing the nominal ER or the nominal prices if we tax region B sufficiently and give the proceeds to region A (or reduce tax in A). This will, under some reasonable assumptions about relative demands increase demand for good 'a' and reduce demand for 'b' at the initial relative prices. The tax and transfer policy will mitigate (although not completely eliminate) the initial regional imbalance.

We should note at this point that this interregional public insurance scheme does not even need to be 'conscious': a proportional income tax together with acyclical expenditures and transfers (e.g. unemployment benefits) will automatically work as a tax/transfer system that helps to defend fixed ER parities. Even better, if (as we will see it is the case in the United States) the income tax is progressive and the transfer system is countercyclical, the fraction of the shocks insured by the fiscal system will be even larger.

In addition to this automatic insurance scheme, the federal government may want to have other tools available in order to be able to stabilize large non-stationary shocks such as the S&L crises in the United States or the German unification shock in Europe.

There is set of questions that immediately comes to mind:

(i)   Couldn't the regional governments stabilize output by running countercyclical deficits?

Regional governments (e.g. states within the United States) could try to stabilize regional income by themselves, running budget deficits during regional recessions and surpluses during booms, but such a policy is likely to be much less effective than a federal arrangement. The problem with regional fiscal policy is that budget deficits have to be repaid by higher taxes or lower spending by the same region at some point in the future.

Short-term gains in stabilization may be lost in the future, or even worse, short-run stabilization could be frustrated by Ricardian equivalence if the future taxes are incorporated into consumers' budget constraints. This Ricardian equivalence does not, however, frustrate stabilization when the fiscal policy is carried out by a federal authority, because in that case, the federal arrangement explicitly redistributes the intertemporal tax and spending patterns across regions according to the shocks hitting the regional economies. Lower taxes paid by a region in recession are *not* matched in present value terms by higher future taxes paid by the same region, but rather by higher taxes paid by all regions in the federal area.

Another reason why state and regional governments cannot really smooth income with countercyclical deficits is that, to the extent that factors of production are mobile, they may tend to remain in the state while taxes are low and leave when taxes increase. In other words, when regional governments run large deficits, firms and workers expect future tax increases. Of course that means that they will both tend to leave the region at the time of the tax increases, which will reduce the regional government tax base. Because state governments may fear this reaction, they will choose not to run large state deficits, which substantially reduces the potential role for income-smoothing regional deficits. Recent history shows that regional governments (both in the United States and in Europe) may already be in financial trouble, so further deficits seem like infeasible strategies at this point (see the paper by Goldstein and Woglom in this volume for evidence on this issue).

(ii)   Isn't this insurance scheme infeasible in Europe because the richer countries are already complaining about more redistributional policies to help the South?

No. This paper does not ask whether the federal fiscal system actually promotes long-run income equality.[11] One may want to argue that a federal government is needed to reduce long-run income inequalities through taxes and transfers. But this is not the purpose of the present study and our findings have nothing to do with whether the federal government has other programs to reduce the long-run dispersion of per capita income. In other words, in the federal insurance scheme, the rich countries would not have to pay more than the poor countries.

As an example, let us imagine two countries: R (rich) and P (poor) who decide to create a federal union. Imagine that the rich country has an income of 1,000 Ecus and the poor has an income of 500 Ecus. Suppose that they decide to pay an income tax of 10% to the central government. The government will from then on give a transfer of 100 Ecus a year to R and a transfer of 50 Ecus to P. Note that in the first year there are no net transfers so this program is not designed to redistribute income from Rich to Poor.

Let us imagine that during the following year R suffers an adverse shock that reduces its income by 100 Ecus while P sees its income increased by 100 Ecus. The taxes paid to the Federal Government would still be 10% of income so R would pay 90 Ecus and P 60 Ecus. The transfers received from the central government would still be 100 and 50 Ecus respectively. In effect, therefore, there would be a transfer from P to R by the amount of 10 Ecus. In other words, the insurance scheme we are proposing redistributes income from the country that suffers a favorable shock to the country that suffers an adverse shock, regardless of whether they happen to be Rich or Poor! In particular, it is independent of any other programs the federal governments may want to implement in order to reduce income inequality in the long run.

(iii)   Couldn't private insurance markets do the same job?

In principle it is true that an auto worker in Detroit can write a contract with an economics professor in Massachusetts that insures each other's wage against interregional shocks. The problem with this argument is that, due to the practical difficulties in monitoring the wages from people living thousands of miles away, these type of contracts are subject to moral hazard and adverse selection problems that will in practice prevent them from existing.[12] It is shown in Sala-i-Martín (1990) that state GDP and GNP behave very similarly over the periods for which both data are available (which includes the sample considered in the empirical section of this paper). If these contracts were important, the behaviour of GDP and GNP would be very different.

The main goal of this paper is to find out empirically how important is this insurance role of the Federal Fiscal system across the United States' regions. The rest of the paper is organized as follows. In Section 2 we highlight the empirical method used. In Section 3 we describe the data. In Section 4 we report the main empirical results. In Section 5 we quantify the importance of the empirical findings. The last section concludes.

2   Basic method

Our goal is to find by how many cents the disposable income of region i falls when there is a one-dollar adverse shock to that region's income, and when the region belongs to a federal fiscal union. That is we want to see

$$\Delta YD = \Delta Y + \Delta TR - \Delta TX \tag{1}$$

where disposable income – YD – is defined as the sum of GDP – Y – plus transfers from a federal government – TR –, minus taxes paid to the federal government – TX –, with all of the variables to be thought of as discounted present values (note that ΔY in (1) involves only current output however):

Suppose that the tax and transfer system works so that each 1 percent increase in Y produces a β_{TX} percent increase in taxes to the federal government, and a β_{TR} percent increase in transfers from the federal government. In other words,

$$\beta_{TX} = \frac{\Delta TX/TX}{\Delta Y/Y} \text{ and } \beta_{TR} = \frac{\Delta TR/TR}{\Delta Y/Y} \tag{2}$$

Then, combining (1) and (2) we have that

$$\Delta YD = \Delta Y^* \lambda \tag{3}$$

where $\lambda = (1 - \beta_{TX} TX/Y + \beta_{TR} TR/Y)$. Procyclical taxes ($\beta_{TX} > 0$) and countercyclical transfers ($\beta_{TR} > 0$) stablilize disposable income in the face of external shocks.

Our empirical strategy will be to estimate the two key elasticities β_{TX} and β_{TR} using United States' state or regional data. The US is a good laboratory because it consists of several economically distinct regions, linked together by a federal government and using an 'irrevocably fixed ER system'. We will divide the United States into nine census regions and try to estimate their federal tax and transfers elasticities (ie their β_{TX} and β_{TR} coefficients). We choose the nine census regions for two convenient reasons. First, the size of the individual regions is then similar to the average size of a member of the European Community. Second, the division we choose is made by the Bureau of the Census to define census region. Thus, we cannot be accused of constructing the regions so as to fit the data better. One could argue that an even more natural unit is the 'state' because states have independent fiscal units (state governments). This is true, but since the ultimate goal of this paper is to apply the results to the European community, the US map with fifty states would look too different from the European one.[13] The regions (as defined by the Bureau of the Census) are described in Table 7.1. To calculate the coefficients β_{TX} and β_{TR}, we will think about the following empirical implementation (which builds on Sala-i-Martín, 1990, Chapter 4):

$$ln(TAX_i) \qquad = a_{TX} + \beta_{TX} ln(INCOME_i) + \gamma_{TX} TIME + v_i \tag{4}$$

$$ln(TRANSFER_i) = a_{TR} + \beta_{TR} ln(INCOME_i) + \gamma_{TR} TIME + \epsilon_i \tag{5}$$

where TAX refers to real tax revenue per capita, $INCOME$ is real income per capita and $TRANSFER$ is real value of transfers per capita. The

TIME variable reflects upward/downward trends in relative taxes that are not explained by the relative variations in income. These long-term movements are not cyclically correlated with relative income

The straight implementation of these two equations involves at least three problems. First, we may encounter simultaneity biases. Since higher taxes may depress regional economic activity, simple least squares estimates of equation (4) will have a downward bias. If we think of taxes as being lump-sum, an increase in federal taxes will reduce disposable income and, therefore, aggregate expenditure and output. We should mention here that this is true even if Ricardian Equivalence in the Barro (1974) sense holds. The reason is that people in region A may think that the higher tax rates they are paying now may be used to finance lower taxes in some other regions either now or in the future. Hence, their current human wealth falls with tax increases. Of course we could think of this as being the 'space dimension version' of Blanchard (1985): in his model, people think they can shift taxes to future yet unborn generations which they do not really care about. Here agents think they can shift taxes to people of other regions which they do not really care about either. The discount rates that Blanchard interprets as probability of death can be interpreted here as the 'probability of my taxes being paid by the people of some other state'. If, more realistically, taxes are distortionary rather than lump-sum, there will be additional negative effects on income of a rise in taxes, such as the disincentive to labour supply and investment.

The same type of arguments apply to transfers. Suppose that a decline in activity leads to a rise in transfers, through countercyclical spending programs such as unemployment insurance. If we try to estimate this negative relationship between economic activity and transfers, the estimated coefficient on economic activity will tend to be biased towards zero, since higher lump-sum federal transfers will ceteris paribus tend to increase disposable income and consumption and therefore increase activity in the region. We will try to solve this simultaneity problem by instrumental variables estimation.

The second problem we may encounter is that of endogenous US budget deficits. One can argue that when the overall US suffers a recession, the Federal Government runs a deficit (maybe because optimal tax rates are smooth). If tax rates remain constant and transfers increase or remain constant, the federal government absorbs some of the initial shock. Barro (1979) finds that a one-dollar shock to US income generates an increase in the federal deficit of about 1.8 dollars. In order to make sure that we are not picking up these federal deficit effects, we want to see how the federal taxes and transfers for a specific region change when the regions' income changes by 1% relative to the rest of the nation. That is, we will estimate changes in regional taxes and transfers holding the overall US GNP, taxes and transfers constant. The two modified equations will therefore be the following:

$$ln(RELATIVE\ TAX_i) = a_{TX} + \beta_{TX}\ ln(RELATIVE\ INCOME_i)$$
$$+ \gamma_{TX}TIME + v_i \tag{4'}$$

$$ln(REL.\quad TRANSFER_i) = a_{TR} + \beta_{TR}\ ln(RELAT.\quad INCOME_i)$$
$$+ \gamma_{TR}TIME + \epsilon_i \tag{5'}$$

where relative X refers to the ratio of state i's X to the overall US value of X (where X is either tax revenue, transfers or personal income). Since the relevant variables are not in relative terms, the coefficients β_{TX} and β_{TR} tell us by what percentage the region's taxes and transfers change (relative to the rest of the country federal taxes and transfers) when its income changes by 1% holding constant the changes in US aggregate income.

The third empirical problem we have to deal with involves the error terms. Even though we will start by estimating (4') and (5') with standard ordinary least squares, there is no a priori reason to assume that the error terms are homoscedastic or that they are uncorrelated across regions. Therefore we will estimate the systems of equations allowing for correlation across equations and also allowing for the regional shocks to have different variances in different regions.

3 Data

The data we use are available by state. We aggregate them according to the Bureau of the Census regional definitions which are reported in Table 7.1. The personal income data are net of transfers of taxes and are taken from the Survey of Current Business (SCB). To calculate income per capita we use the population data reported by the SCB.

The lack of a regional or state consumer price index forces us to deflate regional variable by the overall US CPI. This could potentially be a problem if there were large regional relative price movements. Of course, we know that the relative prices will not change in response to nominal or monetary shocks. We tend to think, however, that the response to real shocks (such as productivity changes or consumer preferences shifts) involve changes in relative prices. Internal migration could also have effects on relative prices mostly through changes in the prices of non-tradeables (the most important item of which is probably housing). Given that the data, to the best of our knowledge, do not exist, the best we can do for now is to use aggregate US price data (consumer price index) and hope that these errors are not very large. Sala-i-Martín (1990, Chapter 3) uses city price data for over 30 SMAS to show that these errors are

Table 7.1   *US census regions*

---

(1)   New England (NENG): Connecticut, Maine, Massachusetts, New
      Hampshire, Rhode Island and Vermont.
(2)   Middle Atlantic (MATL): New Jersey, New York and Pennsylvania.
(3)   South Atlantic (SATL): Delaware, Florida, Georgia, Maryland, North
      Carolina, South Carolina, Virginia and West Virginia.
(4)   East North Central (ENC): Illinois, Indiana, Michigan, Ohio and
      Wisconsin.
(5)   East South Central (ESC): Alabama, Kentucky, Mississippi and Tennessee.
(6)   West North Central (WNC): Iowa, Kansas, Minnesota, Missouri,
      Nebraska, North Dakota and South Dakota.
(7)   West South Central (WSC): Arkansas, Louisiana, Oklahoma and Texas.
(8)   Mountains (MTN): Arizona, Colorado, Idaho, Montana, Nevada, New
      Mexico, Utah and Wyoming.
(9)   Pacific (PAC): Alaska, California, Hawaii, Oregon and Washington.

---

probably very small since the largest inflation differential between any
two cities is almost 9% over the last 60 years (which corresponds to an
annual inflation differential of about 0.14%).

Thus, regional nominal income per capita is deflated by US CPI to
create real income per capita. The relative real income per capita data is
the ratio of a region's real income per capita to the overall US real income
per capita.

The tax variable includes personal tax and non-tax payments to the
Federal government as reported by the SCB (which includes individual
and fiduciary income taxes, estate and gift taxes and nontax payments)
plus contributions to social insurance. Of course these are not all the taxes
collected by the Federal Government: in particular we are missing corporate taxes (which, including Federal Reserve Banks, amounted about
10% of total federal receipts in 1986) and indirect taxes and customs
duties (which amounted about 6% of total federal receipts in 1986). The
reason why we are omitting these tax receipts is that the data are not
available at a state level (The Tax Foundation in Washington started
collecting these kind of data in 1981 so we could not find state-disaggre-
gated federal tax receipts before that date). Since we are missing only 17%
of the total, we think that our estimates would not change much if the
missing taxes were included.[14]

We deflate the tax data by the US CPI and we divide by population to
calculate real federal tax payments per capita. Again we divide the
regional variable by the US variable to get relative real federal tax
payments per capita.

Total nominal transfers from the federal government to the state (or region) is the sum of direct transfers to individuals (as reported by the SCB) plus federal transfers to state and local governments. The direct transfer payments to individuals include social security and other retirement plans, income maintenance payments (food stamps, supplementary secondary income for the aged, the disabled and others), veteran benefits payments and payments to nonprofit institutions. Notice that unemployment benefits are not directly included here since unemployment programs are not run by the federal but, rather, by the state governments (although they are indirectly included there to the extent that the federal government increases its transfers to the state government when a state suffers high unemployment). The reason we include transfers to state and local governments is that federal help to region A after a negative shock may involve direct transfers to state and local governments which then either decrease taxes or increase transfers to the private sector (as is the case with unemployment benefits).

A more comprehensive measure of 'federal fiscal help' would include government purchases and project awards. We do not include them in our study for two reasons. First, we did not find time series data on federal purchases by state long enough to match our sample. The Tax Foundation has collected these data since 1981, but the data do not exist before then. Second, these data correspond to 'contracts' not to actual expenditure: the final site of the supercollider will be Texas but this does not mean that all the money will be spent there. Scientists from Massachusetts, workers from Seattle and financial lizards from New York could very well benefit from the money awarded to Texas. Hence, for our purposes, these data are not that useful after all.

There are also other kinds of important transfer payments that are not included in our study up to this point. The federal government transfers involved in shutting down the failed savings and loan institutions would not be picked up the categories of transfer payments we are using, and yet the transfers involved are very large. As an illustration, as of mid-1988, there were 127 FSLIC-insured thrift institutions in Texas with a negative net worth (according to so-called GAAP accounting rules). These institutions had a combined negative net worth of about $151 billion, or about 60 percent of the state's GNP! If Texas were an independent country, these bank failures would produce an extreme financial crisis that would cripple the Texas economy, a large decline in net wealth, and perhaps a significant external debt crisis, to the extent that deposits in the failed institutions were from outside of Texas. Instead, the crisis will produce, at much lower cost, an enormous transfer of income to Texas from the rest of the United States.

We will deflate the transfer data with the US CPI and we will divide by population to calculate real federal transfer receipts per capita. Again we will divide the regional variable by the US variable to get relative real federal transfer receipts per capita.

4   Estimation

4.1   Instruments regressions

As mentioned earlier, the systems (4') and (5') are subject to simultaneity bias problems. To solve this potential problem we will try to find instruments. Candidates for instruments are aggregate variables that may affect different regions in different ways due to the different production structures, etc.

Our list of proposed instruments includes the real price of oil (*ROILP*), US aggregate GNP growth (*DGNP*), and the real value of the US $ (*DOLLAR*). Since regions differ markedly in their natural endowments and product specialization, one may expect that changes in the relative price of oil will affect regions differently. The aggregate growth variable is included on the grounds that different regions will have industrial mixes with different sensitivities to economy-wide business cycle conditions (e.g. services are less cyclical than heavy industry). The real value of the dollar vis-à-vis a basket of foreign currencies is included because different regions have a different mix of tradeables versus nontradeables, and thus will be differentially affected by the extent to which the dollar fluctuates in value versus foreign currencies. There is no good reason to think that these aggregate shocks affect relative taxes and transfers through any channel other than relative income changes. So, in principle, they should be good instruments so long as they are correlated with initial income.

In Table 7.2 we show how well these proposed instruments correlate with relative income. We see that the regressions are highly successful for 8 out of the 9 regions. The exception is the Pacific region (PAC) with an adjusted $\bar{R}^2$ coefficient of about 0.35. The other regions' $\bar{R}^2$ range from 0.65 in WNC to 0.92 in ENC. We can reject the hypothesis that all coefficients are zero for all regions at a 1% significance level (5% for PAC).

Some of the partial correlations in Table 7.2 are interesting. We observe that relative income for NENG is significantly positively correlated with the real value of the dollar (*DOLLAR*) and negatively correlated with the real price of oil (*ROILP*), which reflects the negative wealth effect mentioned above. We also see that when the US grows faster, New England's relative income goes down. The Middle Atlantic region is very similar to

Table 7.2   *Instrumental regressions*

| | | | RHS VARIABLES | | | | |
REGIONS	C	TIME	DGNP	ROILP	DOLLAR	$\bar{R}^2$	F-stat
NENG	−0.225	0.020	−0.435	−0.002	0.00099	0.90	42.5
	(−4.19)	(10.5)	(−2.42)	(−2.97)	(5.49)		
MATL	−0.078	0.009	−0.373	−0.001	0.0007	0.84	24.14
	(−2.33)	(7.28)	(−3.34)	(−3.36)	(5.85)		
SATL	−0.140	0.006	−0.071	−0.0008	0.0003	0.65	9.01
	(−3.68)	(4.53)	(−0.60)	(−2.17)	(2.26)		
ENC	0.262	−0.012	0.322	−0.0008	−0.0007	0.93	54.22
	(8.91)	(−11.9)	(3.29)	(−2.42)	(−7.22)		
ESC	−0.13	−0.007	0.273	0.00007	−0.0006	0.82	20.38
	(−5.70)	(−7.67)	(3.43)	(0.26)	(−7.21)		
WNC	0.118	−0.006	0.058	0.000001	−0.0006	0.66	9.21
	(2.88)	(−4.17)	(−0.96)	(−0.34)	(−3.83)		
WSC	−0.219	0.0003	0.228	0.0047	0.00002	0.79	17.15
	(−2.72)	(−0.12)	(−0.84)	(5.58)	(−0.08)		
MTN	−0.027	−0.005	0.150	0.0017	−0.0002	0.79	17.32
	(−0.87)	(−4.62)	(1.47)	(5.30)	(−1.89)		
PAC	0.134	−0.001	−0.020	0.0005	−0.00012	0.37	3.35
	(4.07)	(−0.85)	(−0.18)	(1.50)	(−1.15)		

Note: The dependent variable is per capita real income of each region relative to the US total. The variable *TIME* is a time dummy. *DGNP* is the growth rate of overall US GNP. *ROILP* is the oil price in real terms. *DOLLAR* is the real value of the US dollar (weighted average). The numbers in parenthesis are *t*-statistics. See Table 7.1 for regional definitions. Sample period 1970 to 1988.

NENG. It does very well when the dollar is strong and relatively poorly when oil prices rise. MATL also does poorly when the US as a whole grows faster. The long-run trend in its relative income is positive.

   South Atlantic's relative income is also positively correlated with the *DOLLAR* and negatively correlated with *ROILP* and *DGNP*. This later variable, however, is not significant. The long-run trend is positive. East North Central is a very interesting region. Its relative income is very negatively correlated with the *DOLLAR* and the *ROILP*. This region is a major producer of industrial goods (cars) and it is hurt by foreign imports when the dollar is strong. It is also hurt by higher oil prices (as oil is a complementary good for cars). Different from all the above regions, ENC does relatively well when the US as a whole grows faster. The long-run trend is negative.

East South Central's relative income seems not to be affected by the real oil price (its coefficient is negative but insignificant). This region is hurt in relative terms by a strong dollar and by weak US growth. Its long-run trend is significantly negative. West North Central presents a negative trend and significant relative correlation with the dollar. Its income barely moves when the US GNP growth or the oil price change. West South Central income is very strongly and positively correlated with the real oil price. Given that the states in this region are major producers of oil, this is not surprising. Even though none of the other instruments is significant the remarkable fit ($\bar{R}^2$ of 0.79) shows that this region's relative income is largely determined by oil prices.

The Mountain region is also very positively correlated with oil (some of its states – such as Wyoming – are also major oil producers). The negative correlation between its relative income and the real value of the *DOLLAR* is significant at the 8% level. Finally, the Pacific region is really disappointing. The adjusted R^2 is really low and none of the variables is significant. We have tried eliminating the smaller states (in particular Alaska and Hawaii) but the problem does not seem to come from any of them, but rather, from California. If instead of relative income we regress relative taxes on relative unemployment rates, the coefficients for PAC are very similar to the other regions. This leads us to think that there could be some problem with the Californian income data. In the absence of further work, we should look at the Pacific results with some skepticism.

4.2   Relative taxes equations

We can now proceed to estimate the relative tax and transfers equations (4′) and (5′). The results for the tax equations are displayed in Table 7.3. Each regression has been estimated by three different methods. Columns one and two refer to simple OLS estimates. The first column shows the β_{TX} coefficient and its standard error (the constant and time trend which have been included in the regression are not reported separately[15]). The second column reports the adjusted R^2 and standard error of the regression. Hence, the OLS estimate of β_{TX} for New England is 1.275 (s.e. = 0.0539), the $\bar{R}^2$ is 0.98 and the standard error of the regression is 0.009.

Note that the coefficients for the relative income variable – β_{TX} – reported in Table 7.3 fluctuate around 1.35.[16] The largest OLS estimate corresponds to the South Atlantic (SATL) region – $\beta_{TX} = 1.738$ (s.e. = 0.146) – and the smallest is the Rocky Mountains with $\beta_{TX} = 1.254$ (s.e. = 0.1566). Similar numbers apply for the IV and SUR estimates.

Table 7.3   *Relative taxes versus relative income*

REGION	OLS		IV		SUR	
	β_{TX} (s.e.)	$\bar{R}^2$ [s.e.]	β_{TX} (s.e.)	$\bar{R}^2$ [s.e.]	β_{TX} (s.e.)	$\bar{R}^2$ [s.e.]
NENG	1.275	(0.98)	1.280	(0.98)	1.233	(0.98)
	(0.0539)	[0.0090]	(0.0580)	[0.0089]	(0.0358)	[0.0091]
MATL	1.391	(0.95)	1.434	(0.95)	1.324	(0.95)
	(0.0845)	[0.0094]	(0.0908)	[0.0095]	(0.0563)	[0.0096]
SATL	1.738	(0.89)	1.693	(0.89)	1.688	(0.89)
	(0.1462)	[0.0099]	(0.1834)	[0.0100]	(0.1022)	[0.0100]
ENC	1.370	(0.97)	1.403	(0.97)	1.501	(0.96)
	(0.0938)	[0.0078]	(0.1030)	[0.0078]	(0.0730)	[0.0083]
ESC	1.379	(0.78)	1.336	(0.78)	1.355	(0.78)
	(0.1907)	[0.0141]	(0.2057)	[0.0141]	(0.1328)	[0.0141]
WNC	1.591	(0.62)	1.694	(0.62)	1.658	(0.62)
	(0.2948)	[0.0255]	(0.3443)	[0.0226]	(0.2033)	[0.0225]
WSC	1.323	(0.98)	1.375	(0.98)	1.292	(0.98)
	(0.0537)	[0.0108]	(0.0623)	[0.0111]	(0.0414)	[0.0109]
MTN	1.254	(0.80)	1.260	(0.80)	1.174	(0.80)
	(0.1566)	[0.0134]	(0.1718)	[0.0134]	(0.1046)	[0.0135]
PAC	0.535	(0.37)	0.261	(0.34)	0.6152	(0.36)
	(0.3315)	[0.0166]	(0.5220)	[0.0169]	(0.1920)	[0.0166]
RESTRICTED (1)	1.333	—	1.361	—	1.335	—
	(0.0277)		(0.0321)		(0.0233)	
P-VALUE	0.05		0.08		0.187	
RESTRICTED (2)	1.275	—	1.360	—	1.335	—
	(0.0492)		(0.0318)		(.0233)	
P-VALUE	0.05		0.08		0.05	

Notes: The left hand side of these regressions are the logs of real relative taxes described in the text. The equations have been estimated with a time trend and a constant, not shown separately. The OLS estimates are reported in columns one and two. Each group of four numbers corresponds to the β_{TX} coefficient and its standard error, the adjusted R^2 and the standard error of regression. The restricted (1) systems have been estimated with individual constants and time trends. The p-value corresponds to the test of equality of coefficients across regions. The likelihood ratio statistic follows a chi-square distribution with 8 degrees of freedom. The restricted (2) corrects for heteroscedasticity and allows each region to have its own variance of the error term. The middle two columns reproduce the OLS estimates using instruments reported in Table 7.2. The last two columns refer to seemingly unrelated regressions where the errors are allowed to be correlated across equations. The sample period is 1970–88.

The coefficients reported in columns 3 and 4 refer to the Instrumental Variables regressions. As we argued previously, the reason for using this method is the possible existence of simultaneity bias since higher relative tax rates may reduce relative regional income. Notice that the estimates of β_{TX} are very similar to ones reported for OLS regressions.

Finally in columns 5 and 6 we allow for the regional shocks to relative taxes v_i to be correlated across regions. In order to allow for that we estimate all the regions at the same time in a seemingly unrelated regression estimation system (SUR). Again the estimates are not very different from the OLS ones, suggesting that the correlation of error terms across equations may not be that important.

We are now interested in testing the hypothesis of similar β_{TX} coefficients across regions. If, as we have conjectured, the elasticity coefficient β_{TX} reflects mostly the progressivity of the federal tax system, we should expect these coefficients to be constant across regions. In the last six rows of Table 7.3 we report the β_{TX} coefficients when all regions are constrained to be equal. The constrained OLS coefficient is 1.333 (s.e. = 0.0277). The test for equality of β_{TX} coefficients across regions can barely be rejected at the 5% level (p-value = 0.044). The restricted IV coefficient is 1.361 (s.e. = 0.0321) and the test for equality across regions cannot be rejected at the 5% level (p-value = 0.076). The constrained SUR coefficient is 1.335 (s.e. = 0.0233) and the test for equality across regions cannot be rejected at the 5% level (p-value = 0.177).

The last three rows of Table 7.3 report the restricted β_{TX} coefficients when we estimate the system of regions correcting for heteroscedasticity. The weighting method employed gives more weight to the regions whose standard error of the regression (which is reported in Table 7.3) is smaller. Note that constrained weighted OLS coefficient is 1.275 (s.e. = 0.0492) and p-value 0.05, the constrained weighted IV β_{TX} coefficient is 1.360 (s.e. = 0.0318), and the constrained weighted SUR coefficient is 1.335 (s.e. = 0.0233). We also estimated unconstrained weighted systems which allows us to test the hypothesis of equality of the β_{TX} coefficients across regions. We find that we cannot reject the hypothesis of regional equality at the 5% level in any of the three cases.

In summary, the estimated β_{TX} coefficients fluctuate around 1.35 and we cannot reject the hypothesis that they are equal across regions. This implies that, holding constant the aggregate US variables and adjusting for whatever factors affect the long-run movements in regional taxes, a 1 percent increase in a region's income increases its federal tax payments by 1.35 percent (statistically significantly larger than one). Since there is no 'intentional' reduction in tax rates when a region suffers an adverse shock, these findings just reflect the progressive nature of the US tax system.

Table 7.4   *Average real income, taxes, transfers and disposable income*
($)

REGIONS	AVG. Y	AVG. TX	AVG. TR	AVG. YD
NENG	10,960	2,914	1,917	9,963
MATL	10,879	2,936	2,140	10,056
SATL	9,580	2,389	1,746	8,937
ENC	10,282	2,712	1,680	9,250
ESC	7,602	1,880	1,680	7,398
WNC	9,790	2,446	1,707	9,051
WSC	9,162	2,412	1,523	8,273
MTN	9,470	2,330	1,652	8,792
PAC	11,336	2,839	2,026	10,523
US	10,094	2,607	1,811	9,138

Note: The sources of the data are explained in Section 3 in the text. The tax variable has been adjusted for the missing corporate taxes and indirect taxes and custom duties which, as discussed in the text, represent about 20% of federal taxes over the sample period considered.

A simple numerical example will further clarify what the numbers found mean. Consider an economy with an average tax rate of 20% (the average tax rate for our US regions can be calculated to be around 20% from Table 7.4). Suppose further that the average marginal tax rate is about 30%.[17] The β_{TX} coefficient for this economy (which the ratio of marginal to average tax rates) would be exactly 1.5. If the average marginal tax rate were 27%, the β_{TX} coefficient would be 1.35. Hence, our estimates are exactly in the ball park.

4.3   Relative transfers equations

The picture for transfers (Table 7.5) is a bit different. We expected to observe a negative coefficient reflecting the fact that, holding constant US aggregate variables, an increase in regional income would reduce the transfers received from the federal government. The OLS estimates show that, out of nine regions, six are significantly negative, one significantly positive (MATL) and two are not statistically significantly different from zero (one positive point estimate corresponding to ESC, and one negative, corresponding to WSC). The restricted OLS estimate is -0.181 (s.e. $= 0.0409$), but the equality of β_{TR} coefficients across regions can be rejected at the 5% level (p-value $= 0.000$). The instrumental variables

Table 7.5   *Relative transfers versus relative income*

REGION	OLS		IV		SUR	
	β_{TR} (s.e.)	$\bar{R}^2$ [s.e.]	β_{TR} (s.e.)	$\bar{R}^2$ [s.e.]	β_{TR} (s.e.)	$\bar{R}^2$ [s.e.]
NENG	−0.230 (0.54)		−0.212 (0.54)		−0.262 (0.53)	
	(0.0818) [0.0136]		(0.0883) [0.0136]		(0.0629) [0.0137]	
MATL	0.246 (0.37)		0.269 (0.37)		0.222 (0.37)	
	(0.1259) [0.0140]		(0.1343) [0.140]		(0.0649) [0.0140]	
SATL	−0.999 (0.88)		−1.299 (0.84)		−1.019 (0.88)	
	(0.1401) [0.0095]		(0.2001) [0.0108]		(0.0912) [0.0095]	
ENC	−0.368 (0.93)		−0.355 (0.93)		−0.313 (0.93)	
	(0.1392) [0.0116]		(0.1523) [0.0116]		(0.0664) [0.0116]	
ESC	0.126 (0.68)		0.197 (0.68)		0.053 (0.68)	
	(0.1723) [0.0127]		(0.1866) [0.0128]		(0.1129) [0.0128]	
WNC	−0.585 (0.90)		−0.600 (0.90)		−0.529 (0.90)	
	(0.0702) [0.0054]		(0.0817) [0.0054]		(0.0474) [0.0055]	
WSC	−0.018 (0.45)		0.007 (0.44)		−0.041 (0.44)	
	(0.1026) [0.0206]		(0.1157) [0.0207]		(0.0806) [0.0207]	
MTN	−0.708 (0.94)		−0.778 (0.94)		−0.618 (0.93)	
	(0.1426) [0.0122]		(0.1576) [0.0123]		(0.0860) [0.0123]	
PAC	−0.591 (0.38)		−1.418 (0.88)		−0.595 (0.91)	
	(0.3808) [0.0190]		(0.6725) [0.218]		(0.0918) [0.0190]	
RESTRIC-TED (1)	−0.181 —		−0.171 —		0.192 —	
	(0.0409)		(0.0458)		(0.0217)	
P-VALUE	0.00		0.00		0.00	
RESTRIC-TED (2)	−0.327 —		−0.306 —		−0.266 —	
	(0.0424)		(0.0472)		(0.0211)	
P-VALUE	0.00		0.00		0.10	

Notes: The dependent variable is the log of the real relative transfers from the federal government. See also Notes to Table 7.3.

estimates reported in columns three and four are very similar to the OLS ones (which reflects the fact that we are estimating the relative income regressions in Table 7.2 with high precision). The restricted estimate is −0.171 (s.e. = 0.0458) and can be rejected to be equal across regions at the 5% level (p-value = 0.000).

The results corresponding to the SUR system are reported in columns 5 and 6 of Table 7.5. The restricted SUR estimate is a bit higher than the OLS one although not significantly so (β_{TR} = −0.192, s.e. = 0.0217).

The results for the weighted restricted systems are reported in the last three rows of Table 7.5. The weighted OLS estimate is -0.327 (s.e. $= 0.0424$). This point estimate is just a weighted average of the OLS estimates above, where the weights are the standard errors of the OLS equations. Notice that, because the regions with positive OLS β_{TR} estimate have relatively high standard errors, the restricted weighted OLS estimate is higher than the unweighted one (where all regions receive the same weight).

Something similar happens with the IV regressions. Because the regions that had positive IV estimates had high standard errors, the weighted estimate is much higher than the unweighted one.

Finally, the results for the weighted SUR system are surprising. When we estimated the unconstrained weighted system (not reported in the Table)[18] we found that ALL the point estimates were negative and significant! The constrained estimate is -0.226 (s.e. $= 0.021$) and equality across regions cannot be rejected at the 5% level (p-value $= 0.1$). The better estimates of β_{TR} when we use a weighted SUR system are probably due to the cross-equation interaction of error terms being relatively important for the transfers equations.

Summarizing, the relative transfer coefficients $-\beta_{TR}$ – for a system of nine US regions display some instability if they are estimated giving equal weight to all regions. If we correct for heteroscedasticity, however, the coefficients are much more stable. The restricted unweighted numbers fluctuate around -0.20 while the restricted weighted β's move around -0.30. The apparent instability of the β_{TR} coefficients is not surprising since, unlike taxes, the federal transfer system in the US is not really set as an automatic reaction to personal income.

5   Calculating the federal impact on disposable income

The β coefficients estimated in Section 4 tell us by what percentage the relative taxes and transfers of region i increase when there is a one percent increase in that region's relative income. Looking back to equation (1), we want to ask now, how many cents the federal government actually absorbs when there is a one-dollar shock to the relative per capita income of a region. To do so we can evaluate the estimated elasticities at the average income, tax and transfers. When average income in region i increases by one dollar, the average tax payment increase by $\lambda_{TX} = \beta_{TXi}*TX_i/Y_i$ and the average transfer falls by $\lambda_{TR} = \beta_{TR}*TR_i/Y_i$, where TX_i/Y_i is the average tax rate and TR_i/Y_i is the average transfer for that region. The final disposable income for region i increases by $\lambda = 1 - \lambda_{TX} + \lambda_{TR}$ cents after a one-dollar shock to that region's income.

Table 7.6   *Changes in taxes and transfers due to a 1-dollar shock to income*

Method	λ_{TX} cents	λ_{TR} cents	$\lambda = 100 - \lambda T_X + \lambda_{TR}$ cents
OLS	34	-3	62
	(35, 33)	$(-5, -2)$	(59, 65)
IV	35	-3	62
	(36, 34)	$(-5, -1)$	(58, 60)
SUR	34	-3	62
	(36, 33)	$(-4, -3)$	(60, 64)
WOLS	33	-6	61
	(35, 30)	$(-7, -4)$	(57, 61 65)
WIV	35	-6	59
	(37, 33)	$(-7, -3)$	(56, 63)
WSUR	34	-5	61
	(36, 33)	$(-6, -4)$	(59, 63)

Individual regions' estimates of λ (OLS)

NENG	34	-4	62
MALT	38	5	67
SATL	43	-23	38
ENC	36	-6	58
ESC	34	4	69
WNC	40	-10	50
WSC	35	-0	65
MTN	31	-14	55
PAC	13	-25	62
AVERAGE	34	-8	58

Notes: λ_{TX} measures the fall in federal taxes that follows a one-dollar reduction in a region's total income ($\lambda_{TX} = \beta_{TX}*TX/Y$). Thus, 34 means that when a region's income falls by one dollar, the tax payments from that region to the federal government go down by 34 cents. λ_{TR} measures the increase in transfers from the Federal Government that follows a one-dollar increase in a state's income per capita ($\lambda_{TR} = \beta_{TR}*TR/Y$). Thus -6 means that when a region's income per capita falls by one dollar, transfers from the federal government to that region increase by 6 cents.

The first few rows display the λ's associated with the restricted β's from Tables 7.3 and 7.5. OLS, IV, and SUR correspond to the restristed OLS, IV and SUR systems. WOLS, WIV and WSUR correspond to the restricted weighted OLS, IV and SUR systems. In parenthesis the λ's associated with two standard deviations from the corresponding point estimate for β.

The last few rows display the regional λ's corresponding to the unrestricted unweighted IV systems. The average is the unweighted average of all the λ's above.

In Table 7.6 we use the estimated β coefficients from Tables 7.3 and 7.5 to calculate the corresponding λ's. The first few columns use the restricted estimates. The rows labeled OLS, IV, and SUR display the λ's corresponding to the restricted OLS, IV and SUR estimates of Tables 7.3 and 7.5. The rows labeled WOLS, WIV and WSUR report the λ's corresponding to the restricted weighted OLS, IV, and SUR estimates of Tables 7.3 and 7.5. The numbers in parenthesis refer to the λ's that correspond to two standard deviations away from the point estimates of β. For instance, the restricted OLS numbers suggest that when a typical region in the US suffers a one-dollar adverse shock to its personal income, its average federal tax payments reduce by something between 33 and 35 cents (with a point estimate of 34 cents) and its transfers increase by somewhere between 2 and 5 cents (with a point estimate of 3 cents) so that the disposable income falls by something between 59 and 65 cents (with a point estimate of 62 cents).

Notice that the results for λ_{TX} are very stable across Table 7.6 and move between 34 and 37 cents to the dollar. This stability is due to the stability of the β_{TX} coefficients in Table 7.3. The results for λ_{TR} when we use the weighted estimates are a bit larger than the ones we get by using the unweighted ones: the unweighted λ_{TR} are in the neighborhood of -0.03 while the weighted ones fluctuate around -0.06. Correspondingly the unweighted overall λ's move around 0.62 for the unweighted estimates and around 0.60 for the weighted ones.

The second half of Table 7.6 shows the λ estimates for each of the nine regions. Notice that the estimated λ_{TX}'s are extremely stable (except for the Pacific region). This again is due to our earlier finding that the β_{TX} coefficients are very stable across regions. The average tax response to a dollar shock is 34 cents. The estimated λ_{TR} fluctuate a lot more across regions, and therefore, so do the overall λ's. The average transfer response to a dollar regional shock is 8 cents. The corresponding average total response to a dollar regional shock is 58 cents. Notice that these results are not very far from the ones we got using the restricted estimates.

Taken as a whole, Table 7.6 suggests that when the average region suffers a one-dollar adverse shock to its personal income, its federal tax payments are reduced by something between 33 and 37 cents, the transfers received from the federal government increase by somewhere between one and eight cents so the final disposable income falls by only 56 to 65 cents. Hence, the fraction of the initial shock that is absorbed by the federal fiscal system is between one-third and one-half. Most of the action comes from the tax side which probably reflects the progressive nature of the US federal tax system.

6   Final remarks

We have argued that the US can be viewed as a set of regions tied by an 'irrevocably fixed ER' and that this ER arrangement seems to work effectively. One of the reasons for this reasonably efficient system, could be that the federal fiscal system absorbs a substantial fraction of interregional shocks. This reduces the need for nominal exchange rate realignments.

The existence of this federal fiscal system does not mean that there are no interregional adjustments to be made but, rather, that they are made without devaluations (or major pressures on the one-to-one fixed parities) and without extraordinary recessions.

We tried to estimate empirically the effects of such a federal fiscal system and we found that a one-dollar reduction in a regions' per capita income triggered a decrease in federal taxes in the neighbourhood of 34 cents and an increase in transfers of about 6 cents. The final reduction in disposable per capita income was, therefore, of only 60 cents. That is, between one-third and one-half of the original one-dollar shock is absorbed by the Federal Government.

The much larger reaction of taxes than transfers to these regional imbalances reflects that the main mechanism at work is the progressive federal income tax system which in turn reflects that the stabilization process is automatic rather than discretionary. Our estimates do not include the large one-time transfers that occur when there are large one-time disasters (such as the S&L crises and the huge transfers from the US to the few states involved). Hence, we are underestimating the role of the federal government as a partial insurer against regional shocks.

Some economists may want to argue that this regional insurance scheme provided by the federal government is one of the key reasons why the system of fixed exchange rates within the United States has survived without major problems. And this is a lesson to be learned by the proponents of a unified European currency: the creation of a unified currency without a federal insurance scheme could very well lead the project to an eventual failure.

On the other hand, it could be (rightly) argued that Europe already has a federal system of the type proposed here, insofar as there are European Community taxes. Some simple calculations based on rough estimates show that this is close to negligible: the average VAT tax rate (as a ratio of GDP) for members of the EEC is of the order of 0.5%. Let us assume that the average and marginal tax rates are roughly similar (that is let us assume that tax rate is always constant). This would yield β_{TX} equal to one. The corresponding λ_{TX} would then be about 0.005. That is, if a European region or country suffers a one dollar adverse shock, its tax payments to the European Community will be reduced by half a cent. This contrasts with the 34 cents we found for the United States. Thus, European fiscal federalism has a long way to go.

NOTES

We would like to thank Robert Barro, Willem Buiter, Barça Campió, Behzad Diba, Alberto Giovaninni, and participants at the CEPR/CGES/IMF conference 'Establishing a Central Bank for Europe' at Georgetown University for helpful comments on this and/or on an earlier version that circulated with the title 'Federal Fiscal Policy and Optimum Currency Areas: Lessons for Europe from the United States'.

1 See Hartland (1949), Lerner (1951), Meade (1957).
2 The phrase 'optimum currency area' was coined by Mundell in his classic (1961) paper.
3 John Stuart Mill (1894, p. 176).
4 Although they did not use the phrase 'optimum currency area' the concept of a unique currency for regions with high labour mobility had already been outlined by both Lerner (1951) and Meade (1957). See also Tower and Willett (1976).
5 From a Keynesian perspective, therefore, the question of the appropriate exchange rate regime cannot really be separated from the debate on the importance and causes of nominal rigidities. Of course the existence of nominal rigidities is at the very heart of the current macroeconomic debate. See Blanchard (1990) for a survey.
6 Other criteria mentioned in the literature are 'the degree of openness' (if the marginal propensity to import is very high, a small decrease in income in A and a small increase in B will restore equilibrium); the size of transaction costs (a unique currency reduces transaction and accounting costs); and the extent of financial market integration (high capital mobility would facilitate borrowing and lending; of course that would not help with a permanent shift in preferences but it would certainly be very important if the perturbations were temporary). We will not discuss them because we think that (at least in 1992) Europe will satisfy the two requirements.
  Finally, some economists (Kenen, 1969), argue that open economies should have fixed ER only if they have a variety of exports. If an economy exports only one good, then a single shock may require a major real adjustment.
7 The debate over fixed versus flexible ER does not stop at the analysis of 'what kind of shocks are you more likely to suffer?' Some of the current debate stresses the 'disciplinary' effects of having fixed ER (Giavazzi and Pagano, 1988, Giavazzi and Giovannini, 1989, and Canzoneri and Henderson, 1988). These researchers use a Barro-Gordon (1983) type of model to stress that the existence of fixed ER increases the anti-inflationary reputation of a single government and, therefore, reduces the real costs of a deflationary policy. For a criticism see Obstfeld (1988).
8 The way this problem has been handled up to now in the EMS has been through devaluations. There were 11 episodes of realignment in the first 10 years of the EMS (Giavazzi and Giovannini, 1989).
9 Kenen (1969) was the first to use this kind of argument.

218   Xavier Sala-i-Martín and Jeffrey Sachs

10 Hartland (1949) analysed the implicit interregional transfers within the US. She looked at the treasury fund movements from industralized to agricultural regions in response to the government policy of supporting farm prices in the 1930s. She concluded that 'the most important determinant in the maintenance of regional balance of payments equilibria in this country has been the mobility of productive factors, especially that of capital'. The argument is that the role of the government was not to carry out the actual transfers but to facilitiate private capital movements. See also the Reply by Fels (1950) and Hartland (1950).
11 The issue of convergence across US states and European regions is studied in Sala-i-Martín (1990), Barro and Sala-i-Martín (1991a and b). Sala-i-Martín (1990) also studies the role of the US Federal Government in promoting regional convergence.
12 See Eichengreen (1991) for a discussion of this topic.
13 An even better division would be one based on the 12 Federal Reserve Districts. The tax and transfers coefficients we estimate here, however, are not sensitive to the choice of region. Mulligan and Sala-i-Martín (1991) use 12 Federal Reserve regions in a paper that studies the interplay between money and output in a system of irrevocably fixed exchange rates.
14 The missing proportion is a little larger for the beginning of the sample: about 25%. The income tax receipts have remained more of less constant over the sample.
15 All the systems allow for each region to have its own constant and time trend.
16 The Pacific region is once again an exception with $\beta_{TX} = 0.535$ (s.e. $= 0.3315$). Its large standard error, however, implies (as we will see in a second) that its OLS estimate is not significantly different from the rest since we cannot reject the hypothesis of equality of β_{TX} across regions.
17 The average marginal tax rate in the United States has fluctuated over the sample. It was 27% in 1970 and progressively increased until it reached a maximum of 38% in 1981. The Reagan tax cuts brought it back down to 34% by 1985. See Barro (1990) for a discussion of these numbers.
18 The results were as follows: NENG $= -0.329$ (s.e. $= 0.052$), SATL $= -0.202$ (s.e. $= 0.034$), MATL $= -0.404$ (s.e. $= 0.041$), ENC $= -0.117$ (s.e. $= 0.032$), ESC $= -0.770$ (s.e. $= 0.063$), WNC $= -0.480$ (s.e. $= 0.030$), WSC $= -0.225$ (s.e. $= 0.037$), MTN $= -0.210$ (s.e. $= 0.056$), PAC $= -0.378$ (s.e. $= 0.036$)

REFERENCES

Barro, R. J. (1974), 'Are Government Bonds Net Wealth?', *Journal of Political Economy* **82**, 1095–1117.
(1979), 'On the determination of the public debt', *Journal of Political Economy* **87**, 940–71.
(1990), *Macroeconomics*, 3rd edition. Wiley.
Barro, R. J. and R. Gordon (1983), 'Rules, Discretion and Reputation in a Model of Monetary Policy', *Journal of Monetary Economics* **12**, 101–21.
Barro, R. J. and X. Sala-i-Martín (1991a) 'Convergence across States and Regions', *Brookings Papers on Economic Activity*.
(1991b), 'Convergence', *Journal of Political Economy* forthcoming.

Blanchard, O. J., (1985) 'Debt, Deficits, and Finite Horizons', *Journal of Political Economy* **93**, 223–47.

Canzoneri, M. and D. Henderson (1988), 'Is Sovereign Policy Bad?', Carnegie-Rochester Conference Series on Public Policy, No. 28.

Canzoneri, M. B. and C. A. Rogers (1990), 'Is the European Community an Optimum Currency Area? Optimal Taxation versus the Cost of Multiple Currencies', *American Economic Review* **80**, 419–33.

Eichengreen, B. (1991), 'Is Europe an Optimum Currency Area?', NBER Working Paper No. 3579, January.

Fels, R. (1950), 'Interregional Payments: A Comment' (on Hartland, 1949), *Quarterly Journal of Economics* **64**.

Giavazzi, F. and A. Giovannini (1989) *Limiting Exchange Rate Flexibility: The European Monetary System*, MIT Press.

Giavazzi, F. and M. Pagano (1988) 'The advantage of typing one's hands: EMS Discipline and Central Bank Credibility', *European Economic Review*, **32**, 1055–75.

Goldstein, M. and G. Woglom (1992) 'Market-Based Fiscal Discipline in Monetary Unions: Evidence from the US Municipal Bond Market', this volume.

Hartland, P. (1949), 'Interregional Payments compared with International Payments', *Quarterly Journal of Economics* **63**.

(1950), 'Reply (to Fels)', *Quarterly Journal of Economics* **64**.

Kenen, P. (1969), 'The Theory of Optimum Currency Areas: an Eclectic View, in R. Mundell and A. Swoboda (eds.) *Monetary Problems of the International Economy*, Univ. of Chicago Press.

Lerner, A. (1951), *Economics of Employment*, McGraw Hill, NY.

Meade, J. E. (1957), 'The Balance-of-Payments Problems of a European Free-Trade Area', *Economic Journal* **67**, 379–96.

Mill, J. S. (1894), *Principles of Political Economy*, New York.

Mulligan, C. B. and X. Sala-i-Martín (1991) 'Money and income across the States of the United States', manuscript in progress.

Mundell, R. (1961), 'A Theory of Optimum Currency Areas', *American Economic Review* **51**, 657–65.

Obstfeld, M. (1986), 'Capital Controls, the Dual Exchange Rate and Devaluation', *Journal of International Economics* **20**, 1–20.

(1988) 'The Advantage of Tying One's hands: Comment on Giavazzi and Pagano', *European Economic Review* **32**, 1077–82.

Sala-i-Martín, X. (1990), 'On Growth and States', Unpublished PhD Dissertation, Harvard University.

Tower, E. and T. Willett (1976), 'The Theory of Optimum Currency Areas and Exchange-Rate Flexibility', Special Papers in International Economics, Princeton University.

Discussion

BEHZAD T. DIBA

This paper's main text presents some empirical evidence on how federal taxes and transfers serve as a regional insurance scheme in the United States. The authors also argue that the lack of a comparable federal fiscal system in the European Community significantly hinders the EC's prospects as an optimum currency area. They conclude that major fiscal changes in the direction of federalism may be an essential prerequisite for an eventual European Monetary Union.

I find the paper's empirical analysis of US data very interesting. It seems worth emphasizing that Sala-i-Martín and Sachs deliberately abstract from any intertemporal smoothing effects of the overall (Federal State and Local) fiscal system in the US in estimating the interregional smoothing effects of Federal taxes and transfers.

The US fiscal system may affect intertemporal consumption or disposable income both through its effects of the deadweight loss from taxation (as in Neoclassical models) and through the functioning of progressive taxes and entitlement programs as automatic stabilizers (as in Keynesian models). These intertemporal effects, however, should not directly depend on which level of government collects the taxes and undertakes the expenditures.

Sala-i-Martín and Sachs appropriately abstract from the intertemporal effects of the US fiscal system in face of national disturbances; their empirical analysis focuses on the ratios of regional-to-national taxes, transfers, and incomes. Thus, their finding that Federal taxes and transfers attenuate the effect of regional income shocks by about forty percent correctly measures the magnitude of the interregional insurance provided by fiscal federalism *per se*.

Turning to implications of their analysis for the EC, Sala-i-Martín and Sachs draw on two basic premises. The first premise is that government provision of interregional insurance is desirable because financial markets are incomplete and comparable private insurance schemes are not likely to emerge in the absence of government intervention. The second premise is that cultural or linguistic barriers to labour mobility within the EC, in conjunction with regional disturbances, hinder the development of an optimum currency area *because* national price levels are not flexible.

One may, of course, argue about the validity or importance of these premises on several grounds. Moreover, even accepting the two premises (as I am willing to do) would not seem to establish the authors' main argument. The main argument, I think, postulates that the two premises *interact* significantly. That is, the paper seems to claim that the absence of fiscal federalism is a major obstacle to EMU, and that the presence of price rigidities and a common currency would significantly strengthen the case for government provision of regional insurance.

In articulating their argument, Sala-i-Martín and Sachs emphasize the effects of *permanent* changes in preferences for goods produced in different countries. They suggest that, with sticky prices and a common currency, such changes would lead to unemployment in some regions and overemployment in others, and that a federal fiscal system would have the advantage of reducing these regional imbalances. The possibility of permanent shocks may seem relevant because lending and borrowing on EC-wide financial markets may cope with transitory regional shocks (more on this below) but cannot offset permanent shocks.

This emphasis on permanent shocks, however, seems misplaced. In the long run, I presume, the real exchange rate does not depend on the nominal exchange-rate regime or on the empirical significance of short-run price rigidities. Thus, abstracting from transitory shocks (and the transition to new long-run equilibria), the case for or against fiscal federalism in the EC seems independent of the case for or against EMU.

From the long-run perspective, of course, assessing the desirability of government provision of regional insurance in the EC would involve complicated microeconomic considerations (equity, efficiency, market failure, etc.). These considerations, however, pertain to government provision of insurance in general and are conceptually distinct from the macroeconomic issues addressed in the paper. These macroeconomic issues necessarily involve consideration of transitory shocks or of transitions to new long-run equilibria.

Assessing the desirability of a regional insurance scheme during the transition (while price levels adjust) to new long-run equilibria is also complicated. On one hand, such a scheme would make the transition less painful. On the other hand, by the same token, the scheme would probably slow down the requisite quantity and factor-supply responses to permanent shocks.

At any rate, once we focus on transitory shocks or transitions to new long-run equilibria, national fiscal policies within the EC countries would seem to be a close substitute for fiscal federalism in terms of their effect on employment. According to conventional (Keynesian) models of fiscal policy, national governments within the EC should be able to stabilize employment through (discretionary or automatic) changes in taxes and expenditures accompanied by lending and borrowing on EC-wide financial markets.

Sala-i-Martín and Sachs criticize this conventional view on two grounds. First, they argue that Ricardian Equivalence may frustrate any attempt to stabilize employment by changes in regional fiscal policies. Second, they argue that anticipated fluctuations in regional taxes may induce movements in factors of production, eroding the tax-base in regions that must raise their tax rates to retire debt.

I think both of these arguments, to some extent, contradict the basic premises behind the paper. It seems difficult to imagine a world with sticky prices in which Ricardian Equivalence still holds. It also seems difficult to combine high factor mobility in face of regional tax differentials with the basic premise of low labour mobility despite regional employment and income imbalances.

Turning to a more pragmatic point of view, in recent years, the EC seems to have avoided major regional imbalances without quantitatively significant fluctuations in most bilateral exchange rates. Thus, setting aside the possibility of unprecedented regional disturbances, the current fiscal system may be expected to function reasonably well under EMU.

Finally, although I am not convinced that the feasibility of EMU hinges on establishing a federal fiscal system, it may be worth noting that the absence of such a system has implications for policy issues that are peripherally linked to EMU. Specifically, if the path to EMU involves imposing ceilings on national budget deficits and on outstanding amounts of public debt, the flexibility of national fiscal policies may be significantly reduced. In this event, the past performance of national economies may be a poor guide to the likely effects of regional disturbances in the future.

ALBERTO GIOVANNINI

1   Introduction

The paper by Xavier Sala-i-Martín and Jeffrey Sachs takes a position on the issue of European currency integration that I find difficult to interpret. On one side the authors claim that the debate on the desirability of a currency union among European countries has in the past been largely misguided, because it has been too heavily influenced by 'Keynesian' economists. On the other side the paper adopts the most traditional 'Keynesian' views, that in a currency union region-specific shocks cannot be dealt with via the exchange rate, and therefore a system of fiscal transfers needs to be in place.

Despite what seems to me a sort of ideological contradiction, this paper is quite stimulating, and offers important empirical evidence. In my comments I will first discuss the main point of the authors, on the presence of regional automatic fiscal stabilizers in the US and Europe. Then I will relate this discussion to the debates currently being held by European governments and the EC on the appropriate fiscal rules in a European monetary union.

2   Automatic stabilizers in a currency union

Sala-i-Martín and Sachs provide evidence about automatic fiscal stabilizers in the US. Using state data aggregated with the Bureau of Census definition of regions, they estimate the extent to which transfers and taxes respond to region-specific income fluctuations, and the resulting response of disposable per-capita income to fluctuations in output. Their estimates suggest that, in a typical US region, a 1-dollar fall in output leads to a fall of disposable income of only 56 to 65 cents.

This result is explainable, as the authors suggest, by the presence of a progressive federal income tax. A fall in income produces a more-than-proportional fall in taxes, while an increase in income produces a more-than-proportional increase in taxes. In addition, transfers like unemployment compensation are triggered automatically, and automatically shut off, with fluctuations in income and employment. What is the effect of these automatic stabilizers? They redistribute resources from regions experiencing increases in income to regions experiencing income falls. They thus provide a form of insurance against income fluctuations, which might be desirable if individuals' access to financial markets is more limited, or more costly, than the government's.

The authors observe that in Europe a federal income tax is absent, and the size of the EC budget does not indicate that such a system could be put in place soon. They conclude that the conditions for a single currency might not be there. There are two possible objections to this argument. The first is that one should, strictly speaking, indicate precisely the market failures that prevent European citizens from insuring against income fluctuations on their own, in the capital markets. Yet, even in the absence of evidence to the contrary, I am willing to believe that the integration and liberalization of financial markets that is currently under way among European countries will not make automatic fiscal stabilizers irrelevant.

The second objection to Sala-i-Martín and Sachs's conclusion is more serious. The automatic stabilizers already in place in Europe might work better than those in the US. What is the situation in Europe now? Despite the absence of a federal fiscal authority, a system of automatic transfers is already in place. The difference between the system in Europe and that in the US is that, while the latter is internal to the working of a large federal government, the former relies on the market mechanism. An adverse economic shock in one country leads to a more than proportional fall in tax revenues (because the tax system is progressive) and an increase in transfers, thus limiting the fall in disposable income of the private sector. Atkeson and Bayoumi (1991) conclude that in European countries taxes and transfers from national governments insure labour income against specific regional shocks to a similar extent as in the US.

The buffer in European countries, however, is represented by fluctuations in the government budget deficit. To the extent that European governments have access to a single European capital market, countries hit by adverse shocks will be able to borrow in the capital market, and the funds will be provided by countries in surplus, that is by countries hit by favorable shocks.

Thus fiscal deficits in Europe provide as much insurance against asymmetric shocks as the federal fiscal budget in the US. Indeed, the European system might be superior to the US system in that it is subject to market discipline. While transitory deficits by individual European governments need to be financed in an ever-more-integrated capital market, and hence the resource transfers go through a market 'check', in the US such transfers across states are by no means transparent, and are left to the control and discretion of the federal government. The system currently in place in Europe forces countries that are hit be adverse shocks to *pay back* the borrowed funds, while this does not necessarily happen in the US. This in Europe countries are continuously forced to choose between adjustment and financing of adverse shocks. This does not happen to a federal fiscal system, where the decision of adjustment versus financing can be easily avoided.

3   Implications for the debate on excessive budget deficits

In the last few months the debate within the Monetary Committee has concentrated on the disparities in the level of government debt and budget deficits among EC member countries. At the Monetary Committee these disparities are a source of concern for three reasons:

(1) 'Excessive' budget deficits are regarded as a booster of aggregate demand, and high aggregate demand is regarded as a powerful fuel of inflation. Disparities in budget deficits, according to this argument, would therefore impede the convergence in inflation rates that is regarded as a necessary condition for EMU.

(2) 'Excessive' budget deficits are usually associated with high levels of government debt, and they are certainly the cause of them. High government debt raises the spectre of unsustainability, triggered by the debt-deficit spiral.

(3) 'Excessive' budget deficits are regarded as an inefficient absorber or private saving, that crowds out productive investment spending.

Buiter and Kletzer (1991) and Giovannini and Spaventa (1991) discuss the theoretical and empirical underpinnings of these concerns, and I do not want to restate their points here. The important policy question is about the likely effects of the proposed constraints on national budget deficits. In response to the concerns of the effects of deficits listed above, the Monetary Committee has recently proposed three principles designed to identify excessive deficit. These principle are:

- Stocks of public debt must not be so high as to bring a danger of unsustainability.
- Deficits must not be so high in relation to GDP as to threaten price stability.
- Deficits must not exceed expenditure on capital formation.

Reference values have been provided for the first two principles: they are, respectively, 60 percent and 3 percent of GDP. Failure to satisfy the principles above would trigger a procedure whereby the Monetary Committee, with the assistance of the Commission, will present the case to the Council with an opinion (the procedure could be started by the Commission even if these principles were not infringed). If the Council decides that an excessive deficit exists, the country concerned will be in breach of its legal obligations and respect for those obligations will have to be enforced.

Since the principles of excessive deficits and the procedures to deal with them are being discussed as permanent rules, it is important to speculate what would be their effects in the long run. Most likely, the excessive deficits principles will achieve their stated objective, to eliminate budget deficits in the EC countries. The question is whether the elimination of budget deficits will put pressure elsewhere.

In the limit, without considering the limited flexibility provided by the deficits-investments rule, residents of countries hit by adverse shocks will see their disposable income decrease 1-for-1 with the fall in output, because governments will not be able to borrow in the private capital markets in their place. Those individuals with ready access to the capital market will be able to shield part of the negative effects of the shock, via their own borrowing. Those individuals who cannot easily borrow will exercise political pressure for some other form of corrective action.

Where would the pressure go to? the two natural places will be, on one side, the European budget, and in particular structural funds; on the other side, the European central bank, which will be asked to facilitate adjustment to sectoral shocks by lowering interest rates, and by easing its stance of monetary policy, perhaps allowing the ECU to depreciate in foreign exchange markets. In conclusion, eliminating the possibility of budgetary deficits at the national level will make it more difficult for the European central bank to pursue price stability, and will put pressure for an increase in the size of the EC budget. Currently, member countries strongly object to both these outcomes.

The question is then how to establish principles of budgetary discipline – that is, to avoid excessive borrowing by member countries and the ensuing risks of instability of European financial markets – but at the same time preserve a degree of fiscal flexibility to national governments – that is, to avoid pressures on the EC budget and the European central bank. I propose two main avenues:

- The first is to adopt principles of budgetary discipline that utilize business-cycle corrections in the measure of fiscal deficits, and to allow for the occurrence of exceptional circumstances, beyond the control of governments, leading to larger-than-expected budgetary problems.
- The second is to require those countries whose debts and deficits are currently a threat to the stability of financial markets to embark on corrections (possibly including structural measures) that will drastically decrease their debt-GDP ratios over an appropriately short horizon, and to deem those corrections a condition for participation in later stages of EMU.

NOTE

This note is part of a CEPR research program on 'Financial and Monetary Integration in Europe,' supported by a grant from the Commission of the European Communities under its SPES Programme (No. E89300105/RES).

REFERENCES

Atkeson, A. and T. Bayoumi (1991), 'Do Private Capital Markets Insure Against Risk in a Common Currency Area? Evidence from the United States', mimeo, University of Chicago and International Monetary Fund, July.

Buiter, W. H. and K. M. Kletzer (1991), 'Reflections on the Fiscal Implications of a Common Currency', in A. Giovannini and C. Mayer (eds.), *European Financial Integration*, Cambridge: Cambridge University Press.

Giovannini, A. and L. Spaventa (1991), 'Fiscal Rules in the European Monetary Union: A No-Entry Clause,' CEPR Discussion Paper No. 516.

8 Market-based fiscal discipline in monetary unions: evidence from the US municipal bond market

MORRIS GOLDSTEIN and GEOFFREY WOGLOM

1 Introduction

It is widely accepted that participation in a currency union is inconsistent with independence in the conduct of monetary policy. Indeed, in the ongoing discussions about the path to economic and monetary union (EMU) in Europe, much attention is being devoted both to the establishment of a *central* monetary authority and to securing a mandate for that institution which would give primacy to the goal of price stability. In this sense, there would appear to be an emerging consensus about how to constrain or 'discipline' monetary policy.[1]

Less settled at this stage is what constraints, if any, should be placed on national fiscal policies in a currency union. The debate is influenced by two observations. First, ten years of experience with the European Monetary System (EMS) – during which exchange rate commitments became progressively 'harder' – does not suggest that the exchange rate regime itself will be sufficient to force a convergence around sound fiscal policies. In the words of the Delors Report (1989, paragraph 3):

> the EMS has not fulfilled its potential. ... the lack of sufficient convergence of fiscal policies as reflected in large and persistent budget deficits in certain countries has remained a source of tensions and has put disproportionate burden on monetary policy.

Second, if fiscal policy discipline was not forthcoming in an EMU, then the key objective of the union itself could well be threatened. Specifically, if a member of the union accumulated so much debt that it eventually became unable to service it, there would be pressure either on the central monetary institution to monetize the debt or on other members to bail out the errant borrower. In these circumstances, the central bank would find it difficult to credibly commit itself to price stability and other members would find their own incentives for implementing sound fiscal policies distorted. In time, the private sector would incorporate higher inflation

228

expectations into its wage and interest rate contracts. In the end, the social advantages associated with using one money of stable purchasing power would be forfeited.

Reflecting these concerns, there is strong support for including in any EMU treaty explicit provisions prohibiting monetary financing and bailing out of budget deficits. Still, debate continues on whether such provisions are all that is required to encourage fiscal discipline. At least three separate schools of thought have surfaced.

One view, echoed in the Delors Report (1989), is that binding *fiscal rules* represent the preferred solution to the problem. These rules would impose effective upper limits on budget deficits and on debt stocks of individual member countries, as well as limit recourse to external borrowing in non-member currencies.[2] In brief, the case against rigid fiscal rules is that they are incapable of taking adequate account of differences in the circumstances of members. For example, the same budget deficit (relative to GNP) is apt to be less cause for concern in a country with a high private saving rate, a low stock of debt, a temporarily high unemployment rate, and a good track record on inflation than in one with the opposite characteristics. There are also questions of effectiveness. In this connection, von Hagen (1991) reports a greater tendency for US states with debt limits and stringent balanced budget requirements to substitute unrestricted for restricted debt (by delegating functions and debt-raising power to off-budget entities and local governments).

A second approach, which finds expression in more recent EC Commission reports (see *Economic and Monetary Union*, August 1990, and *One Market, One Money*, October 1990), also calls for constraints on national fiscal policies, but adopts a more discretionary format. Specifically, it proposes that peer group, *multilateral surveillance* be reinforced to discourage errant fiscal policies of individual member countries; in addition, it suggests that the EMU Treaty incorporate the principle that ' ... excessive budget deficits must be avoided' (EC Commission, 1990a). Suffice to say that this tack too is open to criticism. Multilateral surveillance exercises typically employ a broad set of economic indicators. This sets up the risk that different indicators will send conflicting signals for policy adjustment, thereby allowing an errant fiscal position to continue for too long.[3] Moreover, without previously agreed upon rules available to settle disputes, there is a risk that negotiations, cum pressures for 'solidarity' within the union, could delay unduly the needed fiscal adjustment.

Yet a third – albeit very different – route to fiscal discipline is to entrust private financial markets with that role. Such *market-based fiscal discipline* would take the form of an initially rising default premium on the debt of a member country running excessive deficits. If those deficits persisted, the default premium would increase at an increasing rate, and eventually the offending country would be denied access to additional credit. This increase in the cost of borrowing, along with the threat of reduced availability of credit, would then provide the incentive to correct irresponsible fiscal behaviour. Advocates of the market approach (Bishop *et al.*, 1989) recognize that it will work only if certain conditions are satisfied, namely: (i) capital must be able to move freely, (ii) full information must be available on the sovereign borrower, (iii) the market must be convinced both that there are no implicit or explicit outside guarantees on sovereign debt and that the borrower's debt will not be monetized, and (iv) the financial system must be strong enough to withstand the failure of a 'large' borrower. They do not regard these conditions as unrealistically restrictive. Not surprisingly, those who favor the fiscal rules or surveillance options are less convinced, and point to the developing-country debt crisis of the early 1980s and to the New York City financial crisis of the mid-1970s as graphic illustrations of the limitations of the market's disciplining process.[4] Skeptics also note that high public debts often reflect political polarization or distributional conflicts over the sharing of the fiscal burden – factors that can make fiscal adjustment relatively insensitive to a rise in the cost of borrowing.[5] Presumably, these doubts lie behind the assessments that ' ... the constraints imposed by market forces might either be too slow and weak or too sudden and disruptive' (Delors Report, 1989, paragraph 30), and that ' ... the effectiveness of market discipline cannot be taken for granted' (EC Commission, 1990b, p. 100).

In choosing among these alternative mechanisms for achieving greater fiscal discipline, it is natural to seek guidance from the experience of federal states. The experience of the United States is of particular interest for ongoing EMU discussions. For one thing, the viability of the United States as a common currency area is long since firmly established; in operational terms, this implies that one can legitimately disregard expectations of an exchange rate change as contributing to differences in borrowing costs paid by different fiscal jurisdictions. Second, state governments do not have access to central bank financing; as noted above, a similar provision is expected to be included in any EMU treaty. Third, with regard to creditors, US states enjoy immunity from bankruptcy courts, much like a sovereign country does (see English, 1991, and Orth, 1987). Fourth, while many US states have voluntarily imposed their own statutory limits on their deficit-spending and/or borrowing, there are no *federally-imposed* borrowing limits; this provides enough autonomy at the state level to test the market-discipline hypothesis using a cross section of states, while also giving some scope to gauge the influence of fiscal rules on borrowing costs. Fifth, the US capital market is probably closest to the kind of integrated, deep, informationally efficient financial area that Europe seeks to become after 1992. Finally, while individual state and local governments have at times run sizable fiscal deficits, there have been *no* state or municipal defaults on general obligation bonds during the post-World War II period (Davidson, 1990, and Cohen, 1988); (state) fiscal discipline has therefore been more the rule than the exception.

To be sure, there are also significant differences between the United States and Europe that are worthy of explicit mention. As noted by Lamafalussy (1989) and others, in Europe there is a greater concentration of expenditures and, especially, borrowing needs in a few regions; for example, Italy's budget deficit alone – at some 2 percent of EC GDP – is equal to more than half of the aggregate EC deficit. This in turn may mean that a 'no bail-out' pledge will carry less credibility in Europe than in the United States. Another difference is that ratios of debt to total product are much higher – by almost an order of magnitude – in European countries than in American states. Whereas the heavily indebted European countries have (total) debt-to-GNP ratios near and in some cases above 100 percent, their state counterparts in the New England and Pacific regions have ratios on the order of 10 to 20 percent; see Eichengreen (1990).[6] Labour mobility is also much higher in the United States than in Europe[7] – a factor that should make it easier for Americans to discipline higher spending local authorities by fleeing jurisdictions where higher tax burdens are not offset by more generous provisions of public goods.[8] Yet a fourth difference is that the involvement and relative size of the central fiscal authority is much greater in the United States than in Europe. The Community budget is presently about 1 percent of EC GNP and even after creation of the single market, it is not expected to exceed 3 percent; by way of contrast, the federal budget in the United States accounts for roughly a quarter of US GNP. One implication of this difference is that American states do not have as much access (via tax collections) to their residents' incomes as do member countries of the EC; at the same time, region-specific income fluctuations are cushioned to a much greater extent (via variations in tax and transfer payments) in the United States than they are in Europe.[9]

Taken together, these differences imply that the market for EC country debt after EMU may not generate the same default premium for any given risk of default as does the municipal bond market in the United States. But the size of the default premium is not as important as the broader issue of whether changes in the default premium accurately reflect changes in the probability of default, that is, whether interest rates move in response to those aspects of fiscal policy behaviour that alter the probability of default. For if the bond markets do operate in such an informationally efficient manner, then the practical options for leaning more heavily on a 'market-based' approach to fiscal discipline are enhanced. To mention but one possibility, observed relative default premia might be employed as 'indicators' to trigger multilateral surveillance discussions; in this way, the 'incentive' to correct excessive fiscal imbalances could be large even in the face of small increases in the market's cost of borrowing.

The primary purpose of this paper is to provide new empirical evidence on market-based fiscal discipline by estimating the relationship between the cost of borrowing and measures of default risk in the US municipal bond market. Our efforts are aided by access to a set of survey data on yields of state general-obligation bonds that covers 39 states from 1973 to the present.[10] We believe that this survey data, collected by the Chubb Corporation, offers a richer medium for testing the market discipline hypothesis than has been available heretofore; not only is there a much larger sample of observations, but problems of comparability across bonds with different maturities, call provisions, and coupon yields are effectively eliminated by the survey design.[11]

In addition to testing the market discipline hypothesis, the US state data have implications for the first approach to fiscal discipline, binding fiscal rules. The state data contain a variety of self-imposed fiscal rules. Thus we can test whether financial markets perceive these rules to be effective in limiting default risk. While there may be important differences between voluntarily and involuntarily imposed fiscal rules, the state data allow us to test whether it is possible to credibly 'tie one's own hands'.

The rest of the paper is organized along the following lines. Section 2 reviews the theory of default risk in the context of the supply and demand for state borrowing. Section 3 describes in detail the (Chubb) survey data and the other data used, and reviews the specification issues raised by the theory of default risk. The econometric results are presented in Section 4. Anticipating what follows, we do find evidence that states with larger stocks of debt, larger (current) fiscal deficits, and higher trend rates of growth of debt relative to income, pay more to borrow in the municipal bond market than do states with more conservative fiscal-policy track records. Moreover, we also find that, ceteris paribus, states with more stringent, voluntary, constitutional limits on borrowing face a lower cost of borrowing. Concluding remarks are contained in Section 5.

2   The market for state borrowing

2.1   The supply of funds to state borrowers

Theories of the supply of funds to states typically assume that any state's borrowing is a small fraction of total borrowing in the capital markets.[12] Consequently, the market interest rate is assumed to be unaffected by any individual state borrowing. Put another way, states are price takers (with respect to the expected, risk-adjusted interest rate) on credit markets. This does not, however, imply that all states face the same promised interest rate (equivalently, yield to maturity). The promised interest rates on state bonds in fact show considerable variability. It is not atypical for the spread between the lowest and highest yields to be over 100 basis points. This section looks at the theoretical reasons used to explain these spreads in spite of a common, market-determined interest rate. The explanations can be separated into two factors: (i) default risk; (ii) risk premia.

2.1.1 Default risk

Modern capital theory is a theory of the determinants of expected returns. In the case of securities subject to default, the expected return is determined by the stated or promised interest rate and the probability and consequences of default. For example, in the case of a one-period bond on which there is a positive probability of complete default, $(1 - P)$, the relationship between the promised interest rate, R, and the expected interest rate, E, is given by:

$$E = (1 + R)P - 1 \qquad (1)$$
$$= R - (1 - P)(1 + R) < R$$

Because of the probability of default, the expected interest rate is less than the promised rate. Therefore, the promised interest rate on these bonds has to be higher than the interest rate on safe assets, which bear the (after-tax equivalent) risk-free rate, R_T. There are two reasons why the interest rate on loans with the possibility of default are higher than the risk-free rate: default premia and risk premia. Default premia compensate a lender for the expected losses from default. Risk premia compensate a lender for the possible increased riskiness of the total portfolio that results from the possibility of default. Unfortunately, many authors use the terms risk premia and default premia interchangeably in this framework.

Finance theory implies that default premia must be positive for assets subject to default risk, but risk premia may be zero even with default risk. The possibility of a zero risk premium on a loan with default risk occurs when the default risk can be diversified away (i.e., when the default risk is unsystematic). In this case, the lending to one risky borrower does not increase the risk of the total portfolio because of diversification. With diversification, the default risk from one loan is combined with offsetting risks on other loans. To focus initially on the determinants of default risk, we start with the case of no risk premia.

With no risk premia, the expected interest rate on a bond with default risk must equal the risk-free rate, or

$$E = (1 + R)P - 1 = R_T \qquad (2)$$

Adding one to both sides of (2) yields:

$$1 + E = (1 + R)P = 1 + R_T \qquad (2')$$

Written in this way, the equality of the expected interest rates implies that the expected repayment of principal and interest on the risky and risk-free securities must be the same. The theory of the promised interest rate on risky debt in this case becomes a theory of the determinants of the risk of default, or, in terms of equation (2), the theory of the determinants of P. The relationship between default risk and the rate on risky state debt can be written explicitly by rearranging (2) to yield:

$$R - R_T = (1 + R_T)(1 - P)/P \qquad (3)$$

This equation shows that as the default probability increases, the spread between the interest rate on risky state debt and the after-tax, equivalent risk-free rate also increases.

For our purposes, the most interesting determinants of the probability of default are debt variables and current borrowing. In many different contexts, (e.g., Stiglitz and Weiss, 1981, Eaton and Gersovitz, 1981, Metcalf, 1990, and Capeci, 1990), it has been shown that when current borrowing affects the probability of default, the supply curve can be backward bending, as in Figure 8.1 (a more technical derivation is detailed in the Appendix). At low levels of debt, an increase in borrowing, B, causes the promised rate to rise in order to compensate the lender for the increased probability of default. Notice, however, that the increase in the promised rate, R, also worsens the borrower's financial position by raising the interest expense on new borrowing. Thus, increasing the promised rate, by itself, increases the probability of default.

At some critical interest rate (R_C) and level of borrowing (B_C), the supply curve becomes vertical. At this point with $B = B_C$, any increase in the interest rate would cause the expected rate to *fall* because of the increased probability of default. The only way the promised rate could rise above R_C while fulfilling (2), would be if the level of borrowing fell below B_C; hence the backward bend to the supply curve. Promised rates

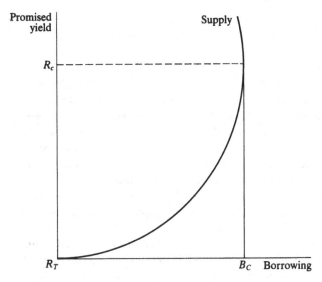

Figure 8.1 The supply curve of borrowing

above R_C, however, are unlikely to be observed in the market for reasons discussed below.

While the supply curve, at least initially, has the normal upward slope, lenders are *not* being induced by higher *expected* rates to increase their supply of credit. Recall that we began the analysis by assuming that the supply of credit to a state was infinitely elastic because any state's borrowing is a small fraction of total borrowing. That assumption is fulfilled in Figure 8.1, in spite of the shape of the supply curve. While the promised rate in Figure 8.1 varies with state borrowing, the expected rate is constant throughout. The slope of the supply curve solely reflects the change in the promised interest rate needed to keep the expected rate constant as the probability of default varies.

While the analysis so far has been very simple, the qualitative results on default risk are more general. For example, while the analysis was done for one-period bonds with the possibility of total default, it generalizes fairly easily for multiperiod bonds and partial defaults. In fact, if the probability of default is constant over time, the analysis immediately generalizes for the case of longer maturity bonds (see Yawitz *et al.*, 1985). In this case, however, one must take account of the fact that only the current deficit must be financed at the current promised rate. As is shown in the Appendix, this complication suggests that the slope of the supply curve increases at an increasing rate the larger the fraction of new borrowing in total borrowing. Thus, positively-valued current deficits may have a strong effect on the cost of state borrowing.

2.1.2 Risk premia

Risk premia complicate the relationship in equation (2) between the interest rate on risky debt, the risk-free rate, and the probability of default. Most theories of risk premia, however, suggest that premia should either be proportional to default risk, or more than proportional to default risk. Thus while equation (3) no longer holds, the interest spread in (3) provides an upward-biased measure of default probabilities, where this bias increases with the probability of default.

Specifying the risk premia associated with state debt requires a specification of planned holding periods. For example, if most lenders are planning to hold state debt to maturity, the only nominal risk is related to the probability of default. Risk premia arise when this default risk cannot be eliminated through diversification (when default risk has a systematic component). In this case, buying risky state bonds would increase the risk on the total portfolio and financial investors would seek to be compensated for their greater exposure to risk by a higher promised yield. While equation (2) no longer holds, the promised yield would still be a positive function of default probabilities.[13]

Many investors, however, either have shorter holding periods, or are concerned for other reasons with the current market value of risky bonds throughout the holding period. A good example of the latter type of investor is a municipal bond mutual fund, which must 'mark to market' each day. In either case, these financial investors are concerned with the volatility of the market value of the state bond throughout its maturity. This volatility will depend on changes in the current interest rate on the bond (i.e., the secondary market yield). Volatility of secondary market yields can result from two causes: (i) cyclical changes in the risk of default, which are independent of debt variables; and (ii) changes in credit ratings. In both cases, these risk premia are likely to be positively related to default risk.

The relationship between debt variables and promised yields is non-linear. As discussed above, as debt variables increase, the promised rate is likely to rise at an increasing rate. This suggests that an exogenous increase in default risk caused by a major recession is likely to have a larger impact on heavily indebted states. Thus, the volatility of yields and the associated risk premia are likely to be increasing functions of default risk. Davidson (1990) presents evidence showing that the spread between municipal bond rated by Moody's as Baa and Aaa is more volatile over time than the spread between the Aa and Aaa rates.[14] This evidence is consistent with the hypothesis that risk premia due to cyclical volatility increase with default risk.

Credit-rating changes are also associated with changes in yields. Rating changes are generally regarded as primarily reflecting unanticipated changes in a state's fiscal position.[15] While one can argue that an Aa state is just as likely to experience either a deterioration or improvement in its fiscal position as a Baa state, risk premia from rating changes still increase with default risk. This relationship results from an important non-linearity between ratings and yields. Many financial intermediaries are prohibited from holding securities rated below investment grade quality (below the Moody's rating Baa, or the S&P rating BBB). With the removal of these large holders, yields would have to rise dramatically to induce the remaining holders to absorb the total supply of debt. Thus, while changes either way in ratings may be equally likely, the *consequences* of a rating downgrade for a Baa state are more severe. An A state, however, faces a greater likelihood of a downgrade below Baa than does a Aaa state. Thus one would expect the risk premia associated with ratings changes to rise with the probability of default.

2.1.3 Conclusions

There are additional factors that affect the interest rates on specific issues of state debt, namely (i) maturity, (ii) callability, (iii) the coupon yield, and (iv) insurance.[16] The complication of these factors, however, can be avoided if interest rates on bonds with identical characteristics with respect to these factors are compared across states. After controlling for these factors, the expected interest rates for all state bonds, after adjusting for risk premia, should be equal to the equivalent after-tax interest rate on Treasuries. The equality of expected interest rates, however, implies that the promised rates, the rates observed directly on financial markets, will differ because of differences in default and credit risk across states. Default and credit risk should be an increasing function of state borrowing.

2.2 The demand for funds by state borrowers

The key issue in the states' demand for funds is whether the quantity demanded is sensitive to the cost of borrowing. If it is, the promised yield could never reach R_C in Figure 8.1. Metcalf (1990) estimates a model of the demand for state borrowing, where states choose between borrowing and tax finance based on demographic factors and the after-tax cost of borrowing. He finds that states do vary their borrowing based on the after-tax cost of borrowing.

This model of the demand for borrowing is important because while states must be price takers with regard to the expected risk-adjusted interest rate, it is implausible to assume that they would be price takers with regard to the *promised* interest rate. The state must recognize that by borrowing more, the promised rate on all new borrowing increases. Specifically, the marginal cost of borrowing one more dollar exceeds the promised rate on this borrowing, and is equal to the promised rate plus the change in the promised rate (which depends on the slope in Figure 8.1) times the volume of new borrowing. But as borrowing approaches B_C, the change in the promised rate is large for small changes in borrowing (i.e., the slope in Figure 8.1 goes to infinity). As a result, the marginal cost of borrowing increases without limit as B approaches B_C, and the state has a strong incentive to keep total borrowing below B_C.

While this model is plausible and receives empirical support, it is not consistent with the credit rationing part of the market approach to fiscal discipline. The credit rationing story can be resurrected, however from different models of state borrowing. For example, Eaton and Gersovitz (1981) develop a model for sovereign country borrowing where a country borrows to smooth its consumption stream. In this model, if the state of nature is adverse enough, a country might wish to borrow above B_C. In this case, the credit markets would limit borrowing to B_C at the promised interest rate R_C. The country is credit-constrained because it would be willing to pay a higher promised rate in order to borrow more, but no lender will lend more. In this model, credit constraints arise out of unforeseen, large shifts in the demand curve.

These two models need not be viewed as mutually exclusive. For example, trend borrowing may be determined by Metcalf's interest-sensitive model, with unanticipated variations around trend being explained by the Eaton and Gersovitz model. The data certainly suggest that there can be unanticipated increases in borrowing. Louisiana's experience during the 1980s provides a dramatic example. In December of 1982, Louisiana was an Aa rated state with promised yields below those of Aaa-rated New Jersey. Five years later, Louisiana was Baal-rated with yields over 100 basis points higher than New Jersey's. During this time period, deficits in excess of 18 percent of state expenditures were incurred by Louisiana. This suggests that while the trend demand for debt is interest-sensitive, unanticipated increases in demand also occur.

In this paper, we are primarily concerned about estimating the *supply curve* of funds to risky state borrowers. Market-based fiscal discipline can work even with interest-insensitive borrowers via credit rationing. In addition, the simultaneity issues, described below, make estimating the demand curve problematic. For estimating the supply curve, the determinants of the demand for state borrowing are important chiefly because of the identification problem.

3   Data and issues of econometric specification

3.1   Data on market yields

The primary data needed to test for the existence of default premia on state debt are market yields on the obligations of the various state governments. States, however, issue two basic types of bonds: revenue bonds and general obligation bonds. General obligation bonds (GOs) are 'full faith and credit' obligations of the state, whereas revenue bonds are only backed by the revenues of the specific project being financed by the bond. For example, the repayment of interest and principal on a Florida Department of Transportation Bond, a revenue bond, could come from toll revenues. Florida State Board of Education bonds, on the other hand, are financed from the general tax revenues of the state. Given our interest in the fiscal position of state governments, we need yield data on general obligation bonds.

The need for market price data on general obligation bonds, however, raises immediate problems because these bonds are not actively traded. For example, J. P. Morgan tracks the yields on over 75 actively-traded tax exempt bonds in their *Municipal Market Monitor*. Of these bonds, only 5 are state GOs. Surprising as it may seem, information is *not* widely available on the market prices of individual state debt.

As previously noted, however, financial market participants, particularly mutual funds, have a need for current market values. This need is met by brokerage firms (e.g., J. J. Kenny) that place values on bonds issues for a fee. These bond values, however, are not in general transactions prices. Instead, the relationships between the prices on particular issues are specified in what is called a 'pricing matrix'. This matrix uses a relatively small number of transactions prices to infer the values of all the other securities being evaluated. The information that goes into the specification of the pricing matrix is proprietary and not generally available. While it is difficult for an outsider to determine the validity of these matrix prices, it is noteworthy that these pricing services are widely used. In fact, one of the widely-reported municipal bond indices, the Bond Buyer 40, is based on municipal bond 'prices' from these services. Thus, the financial markets' own needs for current market values are not met solely with transactions prices.

Transaction price data and matrix prices suffer from another problem. In addition to default risk, risk premia and tax effects, municipal bond prices and yields are affected by other features that vary by issue. Unless one compares *identical* securities across states, these other features can have a significant impact on yield spreads. For example, a randomly selected issue of J. P. Morgan's *Municipal Market Monitor* (1989) lists the market yields on two Florida State Board of Education Bonds. These market yields are based on the closing bid price at Morgan. On August 24, 1989, the two market yields were 7.05 and 7.27 percent. The bonds were identical, except that the lower yielding bond matured in 2013 as opposed to 2010, was callable at 100 in 1996 as opposed to 102, and bore a coupon of 5 percent instead of 7.25 percent. During the same week, the yield spread between AA and AAA 20-year municipal bonds was reported by Delphis Hanover as 20 basis points. Thus, the yield spread caused by the special features on the two Florida State GOs was wider than the yield spread between two credit-rating categories.

Fortunately, there is a data source that allows us to avoid the problem of comparability on GO bonds, The Chubb Relative Value Study. The Chubb Corporation, an insurance company, has conducted since 1973 a semi-annual survey of 20–25 (sell-side) municipal bond traders. The traders are asked to give the yields on 5, 10 and 20 year maturity GOs for 39 states and Puerto Rico, relative to the yield on a comparable New Jersey state GO. The survey results for December 1989 are reproduced in Table 1. This survey implies that, on average, traders felt that a *comparable* California 20-year GO should have a market yield 14.04 basis points below New Jersey's market yield, while a *comparable* Louisiana 20-year GO should bear a yield 70 basis points higher than New Jersey's. Most important, for our purposes, the Relative Value Study implies that the yield spreads between comparable California and Louisiana 20-year GOs should be 84.04 basis points.[17] Since the bonds being evaluated are comparable across states, the differences in yield spreads can only reflect default risk, risk premia, and tax effects. Thus while the data are not based on transactions prices, they do solve the problem of special features such as call provisions.[18]

As one would expect, these yield spreads vary over the course of the business cycle: over time, the spread for a particular state can vary considerably. For example, during the recession year of 1982, the spread between the highest and lowest rated states of Oklahoma and Michigan was over 170 basis points: in contrast by 1989, the high-low spread fell by a factor of 2 and Michigan was a higher-rated state than Oklahoma (see Table 8.1). These yield spreads behave as one might expect if they, in fact, reflect changes over time in default risk.

Table 8.1. *Chubb relative value study, December 1989. (Basis point spread for a 20-year state GO, relative to a New Jersey 20-year GO.)*

Ranking:		Moody's Rating	Avg. Response	Std. Dev.
1	California	Aaa	− 14.04	3.84
2	North Carolina	Aaa	− 11.91	4.32
3	Virginia	Aaa	− 10.65	4.76
4	Connecticut	Aa1	− 9.96	5.09
5	Missouri	Aaa	− 8.30	5.28
6	South Carolina	Aaa	− 6.74	5.58
7	Georgia	Aaa	− 6.39	2.58
8	Maryland	Aaa	− 4.65	3.51
9	Tennessee	Aaa	− 4.09	5.80
10	New Jersey	Aaa	0.00	0.00
11	Ohio	Aa	1.39	3.41
12	Utah	Aaa	5.57	4.84
13	Maine	Aa1	7.00	4.95
14	Minnesota	Aa	8.13	3.79
15	Montana	Aa	8.39	5.25
16	Delaware	Aa	8.61	4.51
17	Kentucky	Aa	8.70	5.31
18	New Hampshire	Aa1	9.52	3.84
19	Rhode Island	Aa	10.26	3.58
20	Vermont	Aa	11.17	3.56
21	Alabama	Aa	12.09	3.83
22	Wisconsin	Aa	12.13	3.93
23	Pennsylvania	A1	12.91	4.83
24	Mississippi	Aa	13.39	4.49
25	Hawaii	Aa	13.87	3.83
26	Michigan	A1	14.04	4.84
27	New Mexico	Aa	14.48	3.59
28	Illinois	Aaa	14.48	4.67
29	Oregon	A1	16.57	3.59
30	Florida	Aa	17.26	4.11
31	Nevada	Aa	18.74	4.00
32	New York	A1	20.39	4.75
33	Oklahoma	Aa	21.61	7.29
34	Texas	Aa	22.74	5.93
35	North Dakota	Aa	22.83	10.11
36	Washington	A1	24.48	3.05
37	Alaska	Aa	27.39	7.49
38	West Virginia	A1	28.22	5.34
39	Puerto Rico	Baa1	48.09	6.99
40	Massachusetts	Baa1	62.39	11.50
41	Louisiana	Baa1	70.00	12.07

3.2   Other data

To measure state debt, we used data on net, tax-supported debt as reported by Moody's. This debt figure is calculated each time Moody's issues a Credit Report on a new issue. Net tax supported debt includes all debt serviced from state tax revenues even when the state itself was not the issuer (e.g., Massachusetts Bay Transportation Authority bonds in Massachusetts), and deducts from gross debt, obligations that are serviced from non-tax revenues (e.g., Oregon general obligation debt that is backed by mortgage lending). Moody's publishes the latest available numbers for each state annually. These data reflect the most accurate picture of state's fiscal position from the perspective of one of the two major credit rating agencies. Unfortunately, the numbers are not updated at a uniform time during the year. These data are available from 1981 through 1990. To derive measures of the relative size of debt, the nominal debt numbers were deflated by the implicit GNP deflator for the year and divided by trend Gross State Product (based on Department of Commerce, real Gross State Product data). Bond ratings are the Moody's ratings.

Finally, state 'constitutional' debt limitations were measured by an index devised by the Advisory Commission on Intergovernmental Relations (ACIR, 1987). These limitations can vary from a requirement for the governor to submit a balanced budget to a prohibition on the issuance of general obligation debt. The ACIR index tries to measure in one number the restrictiveness of the various provisions adopted by a particular state. The index varies from 0 in Vermont, a Aa-rated state with no restrictions, to the maximum of 10 in 26 states. These 26 states include 8 of the 9 states with no general obligation debt, 7 of the 11 Aaa-rated states, 10 of the 23 Aa-rated states, and West Virginia, an A1 state. For the 5 states (other than West Virginia) rated below Aa, the index ranges from 6 to 3.

The summary statistics for all of our variables are given in Table 8.2. At first glance the data in Table 8.2 seem to indicate that debt levels among the US states are orders of magnitude lower than among the European countries. This conclusion is unwarranted, however, because the Federal government is much larger in the United States than it will be in Europe, at least for the immediate future. As a result, states have less access to the incomes of their residents than do the European countries. Thus it is inappropriate to compare relative debt levels of the US states to the relative debt levels of the European countries. A better comparison of the relative importance of government debt between the US states and the European countries is provided by the fraction of total government expenditures accounted for by interest on the debt. During the 1989 fiscal

Table 8.2. *Summary statistics for major variables*

	Mean	Minimum	Maximum	Std. Dev.
Yield spread	16.5	−28.4	143.5	23.5
Debt	2.3	0.2	7.1	1.4
'Deficit'	0.2	0.0	2.3	0.3
Trend growth in debt	1.5	−11.9	20.6	6.7
ACIR index of debt limitations	7.6	0.0	10.0	2.8

Note: The yield spread is measured in basis points; debt and deficit in percentage points of trend gross state product, and trend growth in debt is percentage points per annum.

year, interest as a fraction of total expenditures ranged between 1.5 and 10 percent (US Census, 1990) for the 50 states. Bishop (1991) reports statistics that suggest the comparable numbers for the European countries range between 5 and 25 percent. Thus, while debt levels are higher in Europe than among the US states, these differences are not as large as the numbers in Table 8.2 might suggest.

3.3   Specification issues

As outlined earlier, our basic aim is to estimate the relationship between the promised interest rate and default risk, where default risk in turn is related, inter alia, to the quantity of debt – or more generally, to a state's past and prospective fiscal policy behaviour. Put in other words, we hope to be able to trace out the supply curve illustrated in Figure 8.1.

The dependent variable in all our regressions is the yield spread on a 20-year state, general obligation bond relative to the yield on a 20-year New Jersey general obligation bond. In a cross-section regression, this implies that the constant term can be thought of as capturing New Jersey's yield.

In contrast to earlier empirical studies, we see four aspects of fiscal policy behaviour as potentially impacting on the probability of default. The first of these is the existing stock of debt (relative to income), which summarizes the scale of the state's past borrowing; ceteris paribus, the higher this ratio, the higher the default probability. Our second fiscal policy indicator is the expected growth of relative debt. This is captured in our regressions by the difference for each state between the trend rate of growth in real debt and trend growth in real state product. A state for which this trend variable is positive will have, on average, a rising relative debt, and thus a larger risk of default over the life of a 20-year general obligation bond.

Recall from Section 2 that the theory of default premia suggests that the slope of the supply curve should increase more rapidly the greater the proportion of new borrowing that must be financed at the current interest rate. If new borrowing causes an increase in the promised yield, then a deficit should affect the yield independently of its effect on total debt outstanding. This provides the rationale for our third fiscal policy variable, namely the increase in debt over the preceding year. We give this variable a value of zero if debt falls and a value equal to the deficit when it is a positive number. The expectation is that the deficit will carry a positive sign in the regressions. Last but not least, we have included the stringency of the state's constitutional debt limitations as also affecting default risk. Here, the argument is that stringent constitutional limitations make it more likely that any deviation from responsible fiscal policy will be corrected before it reaches crisis proportions; as such, we expect the constitutional stringency index to appear in the regressions with a negative sign.

So much for the fiscal variables. Next, we need to consider the likelihood that there are additional factors, particular to each state, that should help to explain default risk. Bond ratings are a discrete measure of all the factors (including fiscal variables) in each state that affect default probabilities. Liu and Thakor (1984) have proposed a two-step regression procedure designed to use the information in these, otherwise omitted state-specific factors. For each year, the rating categories are replaced with the average yield spread for the states in that category. A regression is then run for each year that estimates the numerical value of each state's rating category based on the included fiscal variables (i.e., debt, deficit, trend of the debt-to-income ratio, index of constitutional debt limitations). The *residuals* from these regressions, which we will call the ratings residuals, are an estimate of the quantitative importance of the factors that have *not* been captured by the included fiscal variables. In the second stage, the yield spread is regressed on all the variables employed in stage one plus the ratings residual. This procedure allows one to capture the information that is embedded in bond ratings and that is not already accounted for by the fiscal variables.[19]

Two related specification issues are the non-linearity of the relationship between fiscal variables and promised yields and variations in the risk of default over the business cycle. With regard to the first issue, we assumed that the non-linear supply curve in Figure 8.1 can be approximated by a quadratic function in the debt variables. The problem of the variation in the risk of default with the business cycle was handled with dummy variables. Because the risk of default is higher during a recession year (even with the same debt stock), we included dummies in our regressions to allow the constant term to vary by year. In addition, the non-linearity of the supply curve suggests that the slope may also vary by year. A higher risk of default is likely to change both the location of the supply curve in Figure 8.1 as well as the slope for any value of borrowing. Thus we included slope dummies in our regressions to allow the effect of an increase in the debt variables on yields to vary by year.[20]

The final specification issue is to account for the simultaneity between the promised interest rate and the debt variables. Recall that the issue of simultaneity arises when the states' demand for borrowing is interest-sensitive. The simultaneity problem is therefore likely to be most severe for cross-sectional differences in trend levels of debt. To account for this possibility, we tested our basic pooled equation against a panel model with fixed effects. The fixed-effects model, however, uses deviations from state sample means to estimate the supply equation. As a result, the time-invariant state variables (viz., trend debt growth and debt limitations) must be dropped from this specification.

The fixed effects model has the advantage of controlling for state-specific omitted variables that we cannot measure quantitatively, but which market participants report are important. For example, Delaware is an Aa-rated state, with GO bond yields typically below the average for all Aa-rated states. Yet, Delaware is one of the 4 states with the largest relative debt. Oregon, on the other hand, is an A1-rated state with a well-below average value for its relative debt, about one-fifth the size of Delaware's relative debt. The larger relative debt in Delaware primarily reflects the fact that the municipal government system is much less well developed in Delaware because of its small size. Therefore, the Delaware relative *state* debt is closer to a measure of the relative size of the *state and local* debt for other states.

These unobserved, fixed effects may impart a downward bias to our estimates for the effects of debt on yields. For example, because financial markets know about Delaware's unique state and municipal system, Delaware is able to borrow at relatively low yields (i.e., the supply curve in Figure 8.1 is shifted to the right for Delaware). But given these relatively low yields and an interest-sensitive demand, Delaware has a incentive to borrow more. Our supply curve expects to find a *positive* relationship between cross-section differences in relative debt and yields, but the unobserved, fixed effects impart a *negative* relationship between promised yields and relative debt.

With the fixed-effects model, we avoid having to explain why Delaware has a lower yield than Oregon in spite of the higher relative debt. Instead, we must explain how deviations from the mean in debt. The disadvantage of this approach is that we can only include variables that change over time. Therefore, with this approach, we cannot test for the importance of debt limitations, or for importance of the growth in trend debt.

The fixed-effects model solves the simultaneity problem if mean debt levels are interest-sensitive, while the deviations from the means are not (Hsiao, 1986). It is, of course, possible that deviations from the mean in debt and yield variables are simultaneously determined. Therefore, we also estimated the fixed-effects model with two-stage least squares. The problem here, however, is to find appropriate instruments, variables that affect the demand for borrowing, but are unrelated to supply. Finding appropriate instruments presents a problem because virtually all of the instruments that affect demand also affect the probability of default, and thereby also affect supply. Metcalf (1990) argues that demographic factors, such as the percentage of elderly, and current economic conditions are important exogenous factors in the demand for state borrowing. These same factors, however, are also likely to affect the probability of default. Take for example Metcalf's argument that a large population of elderly in a state can lead to a reliance on debt finance. It seems to us that the same argument implies that that state will have a higher probability of default for any level of borrowing. Default places a heavy burden on a state's residents. Defaulting on a newly issued 20-year state GO, when the bond approaches maturity, however, will not adversely affect the current generation of the elderly. While it is not clear how to solve this simultaneity problem, we experimented with lagged values of debt and economic conditions as instruments.

Table 8.3 presents the basic equation of our pooled regressions along with a pirori implications from the discussion of theory and specification issues.

4   Empirical results

Our basic regression results for the yield spread are presented in Table 8.4. These regressions use the largest sample period available with both the Chubb data and the Moody's debt data (i.e., 333 observations).[21] Two versions of our theoretical model are shown. The first one, which we call the full model, includes the current deficit and its squared value, along with all the other determinants of default risk outlined earlier. The second version, which we label the abbreviated model, is identical except that it excludes the deficit variables.

The results in Table 8.4 offer broad support for our theoretical model. The coefficient on relative debt (the ratio of debt to trend state product) is

Table 8.3. *Specification of full model and definitions of variables*

Yield spread $= a_0 + a_1$ Debt $+ a_2$ Deficit $+ a_3$ Debt$^2 + a_4$ Deficit^2
$+ a_5$ Trend growth in relative debt $+ a_6$ Debt limit
$+ a_7$ Ratings residual $+ a_{8-14}$ Year dummies
$+ a_{15-22}$ (Year dummies) debt $+ a_{23-30}$ (Year dummies) deficit
Yield spread is the basis point value of the spread between the yield on a given state's 20-year GO debt and New Jersey's yield.
Debt is Moody's real net tax supported debt as a fraction of the trend value of real gross state product; $a_1 > 0$, $a_3 > 0$.
Deficit is the change in debt when positive, or zero; $a_2 > 0$, $a_4 > 0$.
Trend debt growth is the difference between trend growth in real tax-supported debt and real gross state product; $a_5 > 0$.
Debt limit is the ACIR index of the restrictiveness of a state's constitutional limitations on debt; $a_6 < 0$.
Ratings residual is the residual from a regression of the moody's rating for each state regressed against the preceding fiscal variables. The rating category is assigned the average value of the yield spreads for the states in that category; $a_7 = 1$.
Year dummies take on the value of 1 for one year between 1983–1989, and zero otherwise; a_{15-22} and a_{23-30} should be larger the greater the default risk in that year (i.e., during a recession).

---

significant with the expected positive sign, suggesting that debt stocks have a significant influence on borrowing costs. This is a robust finding for our pooled samples, and contradicts Eichengreen's (1990, p. 151) conclusion – based on yield spreads for a single year and on measures of gross state debt – that 'there is weak evidence that higher debt burdens increase the cost of borrowing.' The full model also indicates a significant effect for the current fiscal deficit in increasing a state's promised interest rate. Also, as is suggested by theory, the higher the trend rate of growth of the relative debt, the higher both the default risk and the cost of borrowing. Taken together, these estimates for the debt variables suggest that states which have implemented relatively conservative fiscal policies are perceived by the market as having a lower default probability and thereby reap a market dividend in the form of a lower borrowing cost.

Interestingly enough, the estimated coefficient on our 'constitutional fiscal rule' variable is also significant and with the expected negative sign. Indeed, and somewhat to our surprise, this constitutional debt limitation variable (measured by the ACIR index of fiscal stringency) was the most consistent performer among all the fiscal policy variables, typically emerging as significant with the expected sign not only in the pooled, time-series results but also in the single-year cross-sections. (We also estimated several pooled regressions where the constitutional

Table 8.4. *OLS estimates for the abbreviated and full models*

	Full model (1)	Abbreviated model (2)
Debt	8.26	9.98
	(3.51)	(4.92)
Deficit	23.26	
	(2.37)	
Debt^2	-0.25	-0.40
	(0.86)	(1.55)
Deficit^2	-11.40	
	(2.55)	
Trend debt growth	0.28	0.35
	(2.51)	(3.47)
Debt limits	-1.99	-2.01
	(7.31)	(8.18)
Ratings residual	0.98)	0.99)
	(24.0)	(26.7)
Std. error of est.	12.77	11.94
$\bar{R}^2$	0.70	0.74
Number of observations	333	333

Notes: Sample Period 1982–90; 't' statistics in parentheses. In addition, each regression contained a constant term, year dummies for 1983–90, and slope dummies for the debt variable for 1983–90. Thus the coefficients on debt and the deficit refer to the 1982 coefficients for these variables. The variables are as described in Table 8.3.

debt-limitation variable entered interactively with the debt and deficit variables but the results showed little pattern or reason.)[22]

The implication, for what it is worth, is that states which have voluntarily imposed limitations on their borrowing and debt accumulation are seen by the market as having lower default risk, even after controlling for their past fiscal-policy track records. Using the point estimate in column (1) of Table 8.4, a state with an 'average' set of constitutional limitations (an index value of 7.6) pays 5 basis points more than a state with the most restrictive set of limitations. Presumably, market participants view these fiscal rules as constraining future fiscal adventurism. Because the ACIR index combines a group of rather diverse restrictions (ranging from the requirement that the governor must submit a balanced budget to an absolute dollar ceiling on the amount of general obligation debt), it would be unwise to read too much into this finding. But it does suggest that the benefits of 'tying one's hands' – so emphasized in the literature on the credibility of monetary policy – may be applicable to certain aspects of fiscal policy as well.

This brings us to the ratings residual, which is highly statistically significant with the expected positive sign and with a coefficient that is not significantly different from its expected value of one. Our results do therefore support the notion that credit rating categories contain important information about default risk that is *not* captured by the fiscal variables. It also shows why trying to infer the presence of market discipline from eyeball observations of yield spreads and fiscal policy differences, without attempting to hold 'other things equal' is apt to be misleading. The first-stage regressions that attempt to explain the ratings are not presented, but are qualitatively similar to those estimated in earlier studies.

It would of course be desirable to show not just that default premia increase with looser fiscal policy, but also by how much. This can be calculated – and we in fact do so below – but the estimates, we are afraid, are subject to considerable margins of error. To reflect the theoretically appealing notion that default risk should rise at an increasing rate with higher levels of debt, we attempted to capture the non-linear nature of the supply curve with a quadratic in debt (and in the deficit). Most typically, however, the squared terms appeared in the regressions with the wrong sign and in some cases with a 't' value above 2. This is the case with the estimates for the full model shown in column (1) of Table 8.4: the estimated coefficient on the squared debt stock is negative but insignificant, while that on the squared deficit term is negative with a 't' value in excess of 2. Nevertheless, this imprecision should not overshadow the strong qualitative conclusion implied by our estimates that promised yields increase with the stock of debt.

Earlier on, we also speculated that default risk could vary over time, perhaps on account of the business cycle. Because we have included year-by-year shift and slope dummy variables, the estimated slope coefficients on debt and the deficit refer to 1982. Because 1982 was a recession year, it is not unreasonable to posit that default risk was then at a peak. In fact, the spread between Baa-Aaa municipal bonds was widest for any year in our sample during December of 1982. Thus it is reassuring that the point estimates (the results for the abbreviated model are shown in Table 8.5) for all of the slope dummies on debt are negative and 6 out of the eight are statistically significant. The constant term dummies are primarily positive, but none are statistically significant.

While there is broad support for the theoretical model, our attempt to test for the additional effect of new borrowing was not successful, as is shown by a comparison of the estimates for the full and abbreviated models in Table 8.4. In the results for the abbreviated model in column (2), the relative debt stock, the trend growth of the debt stock, the

Table 8.5. *Time dummies for the abbreviated model (Results for regression of column (2), Table 8.4)*

	1983	1984	1985	1986	1987	1988	1989	1990
Constant term	4.30	8.54	4.44	7.40	3.63	0.67	-1.40	-5.50
dummy:	(0.84)	(1.69)	(0.85)	(1.43)	(0.68)	(0.13)	(0.28)	(1.11)
Coefficient on	-2.58	-3.88	-4.53	-5.97	-4.23	-4.12	-3.97	-1.19
debt dummy:	(1.36)	(2.05)	(2.27)	(3.04)	(2.09)	(2.09)	(2.11)	(0.66)

constitutional debt limitation index, and the ratings residual all appear as statistically significant with the theoretically expected signs. The squared value of the debt stock carries the wrong (negative) sign but has a high standard error.[23] In short, all the same qualitative conclusions apply. It is worth noting that the explanatory power of the abbreviated model (as measured by both the unadjusted and adjusted R-squared) is actually superior to that of the full model.[24] From this, we conclude that our attempts to capture with our deficit variable the additional effects on default risk stemming from new borrowing were unsuccessful (despite the significance of the deficit variable in the regressions for the full model).

Using the estimated coefficients in the abbreviated model, it is possible to calculate some suggestive statistics about the quantitative effect of relative debt on borrowing costs. For example, during the recession year of 1982, relative debt had a mean value of 2.2 percent. An increase in relative debt of one percentage point would have led to an increase in borrowing costs by more than 8 basis points, and the promised yields rise with the relative debt as long as debt was less than 12.3 percent of Gross State Product. The lowest estimates of the effect of debt on yields occurs for 1986, when the slope dummy on debt takes on the largest negative value of -5.97 (from Table 8.5) with a statistically significant 't' value of 3.0. For this year, our estimates imply that an increase in the relative debt by one percentage point (from the mean value of 2.2 percent) would raise borrowing costs by over 2 basis points and promised yields rise with relative debt as long as relative debt is less than 5.0 percent of Gross State Product.

We also estimated the full and abbreviated models on a cross-section of states for single years. Not unexpectedly, estimated coefficients on the fiscal policy variables were typically much less well determined than in the pooled samples, and the sizes – and sometimes even the signs – of the coefficients often changed quite markedly from period to period. For illustrative purposes, we show in Table 8.6 estimates of the abbreviated model for the years 1982, 1987, and 1990. Note in particular how the estimated coefficient on the debt-to-income variable, as well as that on its

Table 8.6. *OLS estimates of the abbreviated model for single years*

	1982	1987	1990
Debt	17.12	3.49	−3.45
	(2.65)	(0.59)	(1.84)
Debt^2	−1.63	0.06	1.40
	(1.63)	(0.05)	(5.31)
Trend debt growth	0.88	0.32	0.16
	(1.87)	(1.22)	(1.21)
Debt limits	−3.83	−1.58	−2.23
	(3.59)	(2.39)	(6.72)
Ratings residual	0.95	1.03	0.96
	(9.98)	(10.13)	(14.95)
Standard error of estimate	16.96	10.85	5.26
$\bar{R}^2$	0.791	0.762	0.930
Number of observations	37	37	37

Note: The variables are as described in Table 8.3.

squared value, differ across the three years. For example, if one had only the estimates for 1982, it would be concluded that promised yields increased – albeit at a decreasing rate – with the stock of debt, whereas a dramatically different conclusion would emerge from the 1990 results. And if reliance had to be placed on the 1987 estimates, the conclusion would be that there was *no* significant association between promised yields and the stock of debt. In our view, these single-period, cross-section results indicate how constraining it can be to ignore time-series variation in default risk – and even more so – how hazardous it can be to draw conclusions on the market discipline hypothesis from estimates based on a small sample of observations taken at one point in time.

As discussed in Section 3, theory suggests that debt stocks and interest rates should be simultaneously determined. The results discussed so far do not, however, take account of this possible bias. Table 8.7 presents our attempts to account for this simultaneity. The pooled regression of the abbreviated model (from column (2) of Table 8.4) is reproduced in column (1) for comparison. The second column gives OLS estimates of the fixed effects version of the abbreviated model, which are unbiased in the case where mean levels of debt are interest-sensitive, but deviations from the mean are not. The third column gives a two-stage, least-squares estimate of the fixed effects model, where lagged values of debt, debt squared, and the unemployment rate are used as instruments.

The results from Table 8.7 indicate that simultaneity is important, which is what we would expect for interest-sensitive state borrowers. Notice that

Table 8.7. *Accounting for simultaneity in the abbreviated model*

	Pooled OLS (1)	Fixed effects OLS (2)	Fixed effects 2SLS (3)
Debt	9.98	8.53	19.7
	(4.92)	(2.44)	(3.68)
Debt^2	−0.40	0.11	−1.54
	(1.55)	(0.24)	(1.76)
Trend debt growth	0.35	—	—
	(3.47)		
Debt limits	−2.01	—	—
	(8.18)		
Ratings residual	0.99	0.99	1.02
	(26.7)	(24.3)	(22.5)
Std. error of est.	11.94	8.42	8.61
$\bar{R}^2$	0.74	0.68	0.67
Number of observations	333	333	333
Tests of restrictions:			
Test of Col. (2) over col. (1):			$F(34,277) = 8.11$
Test of fixed effects in col (2):			$F(36,277) = 6.88$
Test of time dummies in col (2):			$F(16,277) = 4.61$
Test of fixed effects and time dummies in col (2):			$F(52,277) = 6.30$

Notes: Sample period 1982–90; 't' statistics in parentheses. The regression in column (1) contained a constant term, and each regression also contained year dummies for 1983–90, and slope dummies for the debt variable for 1983–90. Thus the coefficients on debt and the deficit refer to the 1982 coefficients for these variables. The variables are as described in Table 8.3.

in the second column, the squared debt term is still insignificant, but the point estimate is no longer negative. Given the small size of the squared term in the first two columns of Table 8.7, however, the quantitative effects of increases in debt on yields are very similar. The first 'F' test reported at the bottom of Table 8.7 shows that the introduction of 34 extra coefficients in the fixed effects model *does* significantly lower the standard error of the regression over the pooled model of column (1).[25] This result suggests that we must interpret the coefficients on debt limitations and trend debt growth in the pooled sample with care. The significance of these variables in the first column indicates that these variables capture significant information about the cross-state variation in default risk. The rejection of the pooled model in favor of the fixed-effects model, however, indicates (not surprisingly) that there are other cross-state factors that are also relevant. To the extent that debt limitations and trend debt growth are correlated with omitted cross-state factors, the causal effect of these 2 variable on promised yields may be overstated in column (1).

In the third column of Table 8.7, we employ a two-stage, least-squares estimation to account for possible simultaneity between deviations from state mean debt levels and deviations from state mean yields; again, there are substantial changes in our estimates. In this case, the squared debt term reverts to negative, but there is a substantial increase in the size of the positive coefficient on debt. The two-stage, least-squares estimates of the fixed-effects model imply that during 1982 a 1 percentage point increase in relative debt above its mean value of 2.2 percent would lead to an increase in *over* 12 basis points in the promised yield on that state's debt (as opposed to the 8 basis points implied by the OLS estimates in column (1)). Even in 1986 when the slope dummy for debt again takes on its largest negative value, a one percentage point increase in the relative debt would increase the promised yield by almost 7 basis points. Thus, while our attempts to deal with simultaneity have not resolved the anomaly of nonpositive signs on the squared debt terms, they do point to much larger effects of increases in debt on promised yields.

5   Concluding remarks

In the ongoing debate on the need for constraints on national fiscal policies in a monetary union, it is perhaps not surprising that *both* sides have claimed the US experience as supporting their position. Proponents of binding fiscal rules are able, for example, to point to the existence of states' own voluntary constitutional limitations on borrowing as demonstrating their usefulness, as well as to allege lags, overreactions, and inconsistencies in yield spreads across states as arguing against heavy reliance on market forces. Likewise, opponents of fiscal rules can highlight the joint absence of (postwar) defaults by state governments and of federally-imposed fiscal rules; they also regard the observed differences in market yields across states with different fiscal stances as illustrating the sufficiency of 'market-based' discipline. Suffice to say that without some empirical evidence on the link between state fiscal policy and state borrowing costs – while holding other factors constant – it is difficult to choose between these competing claims.

In this paper, we have used survey data on yield spreads for general obligation municipal bonds to get a first fix on the empirical regularities involved. On the whole, we see our empirical results as lending qualified support to the 'first half' of the market-discipline hypothesis. Specifically, we do find evidence that US states which have followed 'more prudent' fiscal policies are perceived by market participants as having lower default risk and therefore are able to reap the benefit of lower borrowing costs. In this context, 'more prudent' fiscal policies encompass not only a lower stock and trend rate of growth of debt relative to income, but also relatively stringent (albeit voluntarily imposed) constitutional limitations on the state's borrowing authority. In this latter connection, however, it remains to be shown whether a fiscal policy rule imposed by a higher level of government would carry the same credibility with the market as one initiated voluntarily by the lower-level borrowing authority itself.

On the basis of our point estimates from the abbreviated model in Table 8.4, we calculate that a (hypothetical) state which has fiscal-policy characteristics that are one standard deviation 'looser' than the mean of our sample would pay roughly 15–20 basis points more on its general obligation bonds than another (hypothetical) state with fiscal policy characteristics one standard deviation 'tighter' than our sample mean.[26] This is in the same ballpark as Capeci's (1990) estimate (for local municipalities in New Jersey) that a one standard-deviation loosening of fiscal policy is associated with an increase in borrowing costs of 22 basis points. In evaluating the size of our fiscal-policy-related default premium, one should keep in mind at least four points. First, there have been *no* defaults on general obligation bonds in the postwar period – a factor that suggests a low probability of default. Second, even if a default did occur, the consequences for borrowers may be much larger than those for creditors. Third, if a state pays say, a 6 percent promised yield on its general obligation bonds, a default premium of say, 20 basis points represents an increase of 3 percent in its nominal cost of borrowing – not necessarily a trivial addition expense. And, as a fraction of its real borrowing costs, the 20 basis point increase would be substantially higher. Fourth, and as noted in the Introduction, it is possible to conceive of (non-market) mechanisms that would magnify the market signal in yield spreads to increase the incentive to discipline errant fiscal policy. But this takes us beyond the scope of this paper and toward the 'second half' of the market-discipline hypothesis, namely, the proposition that authorities faced with increased borrowing costs will rein in their errant fiscal policy behaviour.

Appendix   The supply of state loans

To illustrate the possibility of a backward bending supply curve in the simplest context, assume no risk premia and that the probability, P, of no default is:

$$P = P(Z) \tag{A.1}$$

where $Z = B(1 + R)$; $P(0) = 1$; $P'(0) = 0$; $P' \geq 0$; and P is zero for some large, but finite value of Z.

In this case, equation (2) in the text holds for all risky state borrowers, and the variation in interest rates on risky debt can be determined by totally differentiating (2) by B, and R (using (A.1)):

$$(1 + R)P'[dB(1 + R) + BdR] + dRP = 0 \qquad (A.2)$$

which upon rearranging yields:

$$dR/dB = -(1 + R)^2 P'/[P + (1 + R)P'B] \qquad (A.3)$$

While the exact, detailed relationship between borrowing and the promised rate depends on higher-order derivatives, two key result follows from (A.3): first, the denominator in (A.3) is initially positive, since $P(0) = 1$ when $B = 0$; second, since P becomes zero for some finite Z, the denominator eventually is nonpositive. The convexity of the supply curve in Figure 8.1, however, does not follow from (A.3) but depends in a complicated way on the second derivative of P.

To illustrate the qualitative nature of the complication of existing debt, consider the case where borrowers have issued some long-term bonds, B, at the rate $\bar{R}$, and only the current (positive valued) deficit, D, is issued at the current rate R. In this case, the end-of-period financial obligations of the borrower are given by:

$$Z = B(1 + \bar{R}) + D(1 + R) \qquad (A.4)$$
$$\text{for } D \geq 0.$$

In this case, the analogues to (A.3) are given by:

$$dR/dB = -(1 + R)(1 + \bar{R})P'/[P + (1 + R)P'D]$$
$$dR/dD = -(1 + R)^2 P'/[P + (1 + R)P'D] \qquad (A.5)$$

Consequently, the effect of higher debt on the yield differs from the effect of a higher positively valued deficit only to the extent that the current interest rate differs from past interest rates.

While the signs of the second derivatives still depend on P'', one interesting result does follow from (A.5):

$$d^2R/dB^2 = -\{(1 + \bar{R})P'/[P + (1 + R)P'D]\}dR/dB$$
$$\qquad + \text{other terms proportional to } dR/dB$$
$$d^2R/dD^2 = -2\{(1 + R)P'/[P + (1 + R)P'D]\}dR/dD$$
$$\qquad + \text{same other terms but proportional to } dR/dD \qquad (A.6)$$

The first-terms on the right-hand sides of (A.6) are both positive and the first term for d^2R/dD^2 is larger, as long as $2(1 + R) > (1 + \bar{R})^2$. The remaining terms will be nearly equal as long as R is nearly equal to $\bar{R}$. All this analysis suggests that $d^2R/dD^2 > d^2R/dB^2$.

NOTES

The views expressed are the authors' alone and do not represent the views of the International Monetary Fund. In addition to colleagues in the Research Department of the IMF, the authors are grateful to Tom Barone, John Capeci, R. B. Davidson III, James Dearborn, Peter Garber, Gilbert Metcalf, Michael Mussa, Carmen Reinhart, Lars Svensson, Thomas Swartz, and Irene Walsh for helpful comments on an earlier draft. Ravina Malkani provided much appreciated research assistance.

1 For a discussion of monetary policy issues in an emerging European EMU, see Frenkel and Goldstein (1991).
2 In some proposals, an additional fiscal rule would be that public borrowing would be permissible only to finance investment.
3 For a fuller discussion of this conflicting-signals problem, see Frankel (1990).
4 In the case of the developing-country debt crisis, interest rate spreads on bank loans to developing countries were slow to rise in the mid-to-late 1970s, and the transition to highly restricted access (in the early 1980s) came abruptly. One explanation for the relatively narrow loan spreads is the perception of a bail-out – either of the indebted countries themselves or of the deposit liabilities of the large international banks extending the loans; see Folkerts-Landau (1985). In the case of the New York City financial crisis, it apparently took some time for market participants to realize that New York City was diverting approved funds and pledging future receipts – both earmarked for other purposes – to meet current operating deficits; see Bishop et al. (1989).
5 EC Commission (1990b).
6 The state debt-to-GNP ratios used in this paper are much lower than the figures cited above because we employ a more restrictive measure of state debt that is more closely linked to default risk; see Section 3.
7 Eichengreen (1990). The difference between Europe and United States on the degree of labour mobility is reduced if one only considers mobility across states, since much of US mobility is apparently within states.
8 Obstfeld (1990).
9 Sala-i-Martín and Sachs (1992). It should be noted, however, that estimates of the 'cushioning effect' of the US federal tax and transfer system on region-specific shocks appears to be quite sensitive to the time dimension of the shock – and perhaps also to the level of disaggregation of regions. In this connection, von Hagen (1991) finds a much lower cushioning effect than Sala-i-Martín and Sachs, using a shorter-run definition of shocks and more disaggregated definition of regions.
10 While the municipal bond market includes obligations of cities as well as of states, we consider only the latter in this paper.
11 In a broad survey of the relevance of the US currency union for European Economic and Monetary Union, Eichengreen (1990) estimates the effects of debt variables on yields. Liu and Thakor's (1984) paper is typical of the finance literature on state default risk and fiscal variables. Capeci (1990) provides a broad survey of the municipal bond literature related to default risk.

Most of the studies reviewed, however, are of the local municipal bond market.

12 In credit markets, it is arbitrary on which side of the market the borrowers and lenders are placed. One can talk about the supply and demand for credit, in which case borrowers are on the demand side and lenders on the supply side, or alternatively the supply and demand for debt, which reverses the sides. In this paper, we use the former categories so that lenders supply funds to states and state borrowing leads to a demand for funds.

13 The question of risk premia on sovereign debt is tested empirically in Stone (1990) and Cottarelli and Mecagni (1990).

14 US bonds are given credit ratings principally by Moody's Investor Service and Standard & Poor's. The qualitative description of the Moody's Ratings categories are: Aaa – Best Quality; Aa – High quality; A – Upper medium grade; Baa – Medium grade; Ba – Possess speculative elements; B – Generally lack characteristics of desirable investment; Caa – Poor Standing; may be in default; Ca – Speculative in a high degree; often in default; C – Lowest grade; very poor prospects. In addition to each broad category, a 1, 2, or 3 can be added to the letters to indicate whether the security is in the high, middle, or low end of the ratings category. See Van Horne (1990) for a discussion of the relationship between credit ratings and default risk.

15 The rating agencies, however, try to measure default risk independently of the business cycle. Thus for example, the Baa – Aaa spread widens during a recession instead of the spread remaining constant with fewer Aaa states and more Baa.

16 In principle, the yield on state debt can vary because of taxes. To a state resident, neither federal nor one's own state's securities are subject to state and local taxation. State, general obligation debt, however, is also free of federal taxation, so that the marginal rate of federal taxation for the marginal investor who is indifferent between Treasuries and state debt with appropriate default and risk premia. Various competing theories (summarized in Poterba, 1989) have identified the relevant marginal investor as banks, insurance companies, corporations, or individuals. Poterba (1989) presents empirical evidence in support of the hypothesis that individuals were the indifferent investors during the 1960–88 period, particularly for the case of long-term municipal debt.

In fact, such differences in marginal tax rates are frequently cited for what would otherwise be anomalies in yields across states. For example, Swartz (1989) refers to 'tax related demand' to explain why the yields on Connecticut and California state bonds were consistently among the six lowest during the late 1980s in spite of credit ratings below Aaa. During the same time period, the bonds of at least 5 other Aaa states traded with higher yields. We tested for differences in yields due to differences in average, marginal rates of federal taxation across states, but found anomalous results.

17 The 10 excluded states include the 9 states who have no outstanding GO debt and Arkansas. In addition, we excluded New Jersey, Alaska and Hawaii. The latter 2 states were excluded because of their unique fiscal status.

18 The Chubb Relative Value Survey does not include explicit instructions to evaluate comparable bonds. Tom Swartz of Chubb, however, reports that these instructions are implicit, and that whenever a survey respondent asks they are instructed to evaluate comparable bonds.

19 Cranford and Stover (1988) criticize Liu and Thakor by noting that because the error from the first-stage regression is orthogonal to the fiscal variables, the

point estimates of the fiscal coefficients in the second-stage regression will be identical to an OLS regression of yield on the fiscal variables, omitting the ratings variable. In response, Liu and Thakor point out that while the point estimates will be the same, the standard errors will be lower in the second-stage regression. The question then becomes which are the appropriate standard errors. We believe that the standard errors from Liu and Thakor's procedure are more appropriate for our test. The ratings residual allows us to capture the effects of omitted factors, which if not accounted for would mask the statistical significance of the relationship between fiscal variables and yields.

20 Notice that the ratings variable is also capturing variations in the risk of default over the business cycle. For example, the spread between the numerical values assigned to Baa and Aaa ratings in the recession year of 1982 was 153.6 basis points, whereas the same spread during 1989 was less than half as much at 70.9 basis points.

21 The 333 observations derive from observations on 37 states over the 1982–90 period (9 years).

22 There may well be a problem of multicollinearity here given the preponderance of high values for the debt limitation index.

23 In addition to problems of simultaneity (discussed later in this section), there may also be a multicollinearity problem at work as between the debt and squared-debt variables. In this connection, it is worth noting that when the abbreviated model was re-estimated using *either* the level or the squared value of debt-to-income, the estimated coefficients were significant with the expected positive sign.

24 Note that the ratings residual variable is not the same between the two regressions. In the abbreviated model, whatever information there is in the deficit variable is captured by the ratings variable. This adds to our suspicion that the deficit variable is capturing the increased probability of default from new borrowing.

25 The dependent variables for the regressions in columns (1) and (2) are the yields and deviations from state mean yields, respectively. The latter variable has a smaller variance, which accounts for the lower $\bar{R}^2$ reported in column (2) in addition to the lower standard error.

26 The fiscal-policy characteristics included in this calculation are debt, debt^2, the trend of the debt to income ratio, and the constitutional debt limitation index.

REFERENCES

ACIR (Advisory Commission on Intergovernmental Relations) (1987), *Significant Features of Fiscal Federalism*, Washington, D.C.: US Government Printing Press.

Bishop, Graham, Dirk Damrau, and Michelle Miller (1989), '1992 and Beyond: Market Discipline CAN Work in the EC Monetary Union,' Salomon Brothers, London.

Bishop, Graham (1991), 'The EC Public Debt Disease: Discipline with Credit Spreads and Cure with Price Stability,' Salomon Brothers, London.

Capeci, John (1990), 'Local Fiscal Policies, Default Risk and Municipal Borrowing Costs,' Brandeis University, Department of Economics, No. 259.

Cohen, Natalie R. (1988), 'Municipal Default Patterns,' Enhance Reinsurance Co.

Cottarelli, Carlo, and Mauro Mecagni (1990), 'The Risk Premium on Italian Government Debt, 1976–88,' IMF Working Paper No. 90/38.

Cranford, Brian, and Roger Stover (1988), 'Comment on Interest Yields, Credit Ratings, and Economic Characteristics of State Bonds,' *Journal of Money, Credit, and Banking* **20**, 691–95.

Davidson, R. B. (1990), 'Municipal Market Analysis: A Framework for Analyzing Quality Spreads,' J.P. Morgan, 29 March.

Delors Report (1989), *Report on Economic and Monetary Union in the European Community*, Committee for the Study of Economic and Monetary Union, Brussels: EC Commission.

Eaton, Jonathan, and Mark Gersovitz (1981), 'Debt with Potential Repudiation: A Theoretical and Empirical Analysis,' *Review of Economic Studies* **49**, 289–309.

EC Commission (1990a), 'Economic and Monetary Union: The Economic Rationale and Design of the System', Luxembourg: EC Commission.

(1990b), 'One Market, One Money – An Evaluation of the Potential Benefits and Costs of Forming an Economic and Monetary Union', *European Economy*.

Eichengreen, Barry (1990), 'One Money for Europe? Lessons from the US Currency Union,' *Economic Policy* **5**, (10), 119–86.

English, William (1991), 'When America Defaulted: American State Debt in the 1840's,' Mimeo, University of Pennsylvania.

Folkerts-Landau, David (1985), 'The Changing Role of International Bank Lending in Development Finance,' *IMF Staff Papers* **32**, 317–63.

Frankel, Jeffery (1990), 'Obstacles to Coordination, and a Consideration of Two Proposals to Overcome Them,' in William Branson, Jacob Frenkel and Morris Goldstein (eds.), *International Policy Coordination and Exchange Rate Fluctuations*, University of Chicago Press for the National Bureau of Economic Research, Chicago, pp. 109–45.

Frenkel, Jacob and Morris Goldstein (1991), 'Monetary Policy in an Emerging European Economic and Monetary Union', *IMF Staff Papers*, forthcoming.

Hsiao, Cheng (1986), *Analysis of Panel Data*, Cambridge: Cambridge University Press.

Lamafalussy, Alexandre (1989), 'Macro-coordination of Fiscal Policies in an Economic and Monetary Union in Europe,' Supplement to Delors Report.

Liu, Pu and Anjan Thakor (1984), 'Interest Yields, Credit Ratings, and Economic Characteristics of State Bonds: An Empirical Analysis,' *Journal of Money, Credit and Banking* **16**, 345–50.

Metcalf, Gilbert (1990), 'Federal Taxation and the Supply of State Debt,' NBER Working Paper No. 3255.

Obstfeld, Maurice (1990), 'Discussion,' *Economic Policy* **5**, (10), 166–69.

Orth, John V. (1987), *The Judicial Power of the United States: The Eleventh Amendment in American History*, New York: Oxford.

Poterba, James (1989), 'Tax Reform and the Market for Tax Exempt Debt,' NBER Working Paper No. 2900.

X. Sala-i-Martín and Jeffrey Sachs (1992), 'Fiscal Federalism and Optimum Currency Areas: Evidence for Europe from the United States', in this volume.

Stiglitz, Joseph and Andrew Weiss (1981), 'Credit Rationing in Markets with Imperfect Information,' *American Economic Review* **73**, 393–410.

Stone, Mark (1990), 'Are Sovereign Debt Secondary Market Returns Sensitive to Macroeconomic Fundamentals?' IMF Research Department Seminar Paper.
Swartz, Thomas (1989), 'State General Obligation Trading Values – Back to the Future,' *Municipal Analysts Forum* 7–10.
Van Horne, James (1990), *Financial Markets Rates and Flows*, 3rd edition, Englewood Cliffs, NJ: Prentice-Hall Inc.
von Hagen, Jurgen (1991), 'Fiscal Arrangements in a Monetary Union: Evidence from the US,' mimeo, School of Business, Indiana University, March.
United States Census (1990), *State Government Finances in 1989*, Washington, D.C.: Department of Commerce.
Yawitz, Jess, Kevin Maloney, and Louis Edderington (1985), 'Texas, Default Risk, and Yield Spreads,' *Journal of Finance* **40**, 1127–40.

Discussion

MERVYN KING

Goldstein and Woglom have provided us with a very timely paper. The question of fiscal discipline is very much a live issue in the Inter-Governmental Conference on monetary union in the European Community. Moreover, whatever provisions emerge in the treaty that is finally signed, the rules on fiscal discipline and excessive deficits are likely to be controversial both in the period running up to entry into monetary union as well as during an eventual union itself. All member countries of the Community recognise that there is a problem of how to deal with excessive deficits in the monetary union. But there is, as yet, less agreement on the set of solutions that have so far been proposed.

Two issues are at the heart of the current negotiations. First, the *trigger mechanism* that brings into play action against an offending country. Second, the *sanctions* that would be taken against a country deemed to have triggered the procedure. The mechanical approach to the trigger mechanism has been discussed in some detail, and three criteria have been at the centre of these proposals. They are:

(1) A debt rule; the debt to GDP ratio in excess of a critical value, say 60%, would be the trigger.

(2) A deficit rule; the deficit to GDP ratio in excess of a critical value, say 3%, would be the trigger.

(3) The permissible deficit would be limited to the amount of public investment – sometimes, rather unfortunately, known as the 'golden rule'.

In addition to the purely arbitrary nature of the critical values that would trigger the procedure, all three criteria raise enormous conceptual and measurement problems. The difficulties of measuring, comparing, and even defining, budget deficits across countries are well known. Differences in the size of publicly owned industries, the financing of public services, the off-budget treatment of pensions and other transfers, the definition of 'government' itself, all suggest that the application of sanctions cannot easily be made the automatic consequence of violating an arbitrary trigger mechanism threshold.

There have, therefore, been suggestions that a better approach be to exploit multilateral surveillance, or peer group pressure. If the trigger mechanism were used merely to invoke a multilateral surveillance programme then the difficulties of definition would create fewer problems. But this approach too will run up against problems if the criteria for excessive deficits are such that, as may well be true in the next year or so, most countries are caught by the criteria. That outcome would devalue the entire process.

So although there is general agreement that we recognise a problem country when we see or visit one on holiday, there is a reluctance to apply automatic sanctions on the basis of arbitrary criteria. This is particularly true when sanctions might take the form of either

(a) fines, or
(b) a suspension of payments from the European Community to the offending country.

Hence it is not surprising that there has been growing interest in the use of market-based sanctions, in which there is no need for an officially agreed set of criteria to trigger a collective mechanism, nor for a collectively administered punishment that would be almost certain to arouse the worst sort of political divisions of which the Community is capable. But there must be a question mark over the effectiveness of market-based sanctions. In the absence of empirical evidence, there is genuine disagreement and uncertainty within the Community on their potential effectiveness. It is important, therefore, that we examine any empirical evidence that might shed light on the effectiveness of market-based sanctions. The Goldstein-Woglom paper is especially interesting in this context.

In order to assess the relevance of the Goldstein-Woglom evidence to the question of monetary union in Europe, it is important to distinguish between two reasons for concern over excessive fiscal deficits. The first is that it is thought that there might be pressure on the European Central Bank to monetise an excessive deficit incurred by a member country if the alternative were for that country to default. In principle, a 'no bail-out' provision would leave the responsibility for debt in the hands of member countries. Some have questioned whether such a provision is really credible in a monetary union. This is, I think, rather too pessimistic a view. The second issue is that excessive deficits – at least in large countries – affect the fiscal stance of the Community as a whole and hence the likely level of interest rates in the monetary union. Of course, these 'externalities' of excessive deficits can occur outside a monetary union as well. But the crucial difference between the two areas of concern is that the former is concerned with the debt ratios for an individual country no matter how large it is and the second is concerned with the increase in total debt issued regardless of how it affects the debt ratios of any one country. The construction of trigger mechanisms and sanctions seems more appropriate to the former than to the latter concern. Hence, even in the absence of sanctions for excessive deficits, the fiscal stance of the larger member countries is likely to be of interest to the monetary authorities even if the trigger criteria have not been violated.

The evidence presented in this paper tests the hypothesis that differences in expected returns on bonds issued by different states in the USA reflect differences in the probability of default. The basic difficulty in testing this hypothesis is obvious. The probability of default is unobservable. Moreover, we cannot use observable frequencies to measure the probability of default because it is such an infrequent event – so infrequent in fact that it has never actually occurred, at least since the Second World War and hence, a fortiori, in the sample period used for estimation post-1973. I interpret the results of the paper, therefore, as telling us about correlations between spreads in bond yields and measures of debt to income ratios, deficits and the underlying growth of real debt. And here there is indeed evidence – for thirty-nine states – that differences between spreads, which can vary by 100 basis points or more, are positively correlated with such indicators of 'fiscal indiscipline'. These spreads are small in comparison with those that exist at present within Europe. For example, the spread between Spain and Germany has varied around 500 basis points. How should the correlations found by Goldstein and Woglom be interpreted? There is one point of enormous econometric difficulty concerning *identification*. The aim is to estimate the supply curve of credit to governments, but some of the unobservable variables that affect the supply also affect the demand for such securities. The authors are clearly aware of this problem and use fixed-effects models to deal with the problem but it surely cannot wholly have been removed. Leaving this point to one side, the interpretation of the results must depend upon the model of political behaviour that we believe underlies the decisions that were made in the sample period. Consider two possible models.

The first is a model of an optimising government that attempts to implement an optimal tax schedule over time. With sufficient conditions on the separability of preferences, it can be shown that a government maximising the welfare of a representative agent will choose tax rates such that

(i) the wedge between consumption and leisure is constant over time, and

(ii) the wedge between consumption in successive periods is zero *ex ante*, but *ex post* will imply a capital levy equal to the innovation in the present discounted value of innovations in government expenditure. This means that deficits will depend on the autoregressive nature of shocks to government expenditures or to the tax base. Countries or states might well differ in this respect, and so the optimal time path of government deficits might well vary across countries. This casts further doubt on the wisdom of specifying arbitrary criteria above which point sanctions are levied.

A second model is one of stochastic shocks to the identity of the government in power, and possibly to the probability of repudiation of a previous administration's debts. These factors are unlikely to be correlated in a simple way with observable variables. Criteria for binding budgetary constraints are a blunt weapon to deal with alleged excessive deficits on the part of a small minority of countries in a population of only twelve members of the community. Market-based discipline does, as the authors point out, enable other influences on default probabilities to be reflected in market default premia.

VITO TANZI

I am happy to comment on a nice paper that deals with an important and topical question and does it clearly and competently. With the help of unpublished and up-to-now unutilized data, the paper reaches interesting conclusions. Given the topic of this conference and the implications of Goldstein and Woglom's paper for the European Monetary Union (EMU), I will focus my discussion on those implications. However, by so doing, I will not do full justice to the authors' work since that work extends well beyond those implications.

It is, by now, widely recognized that, as the authors put it; 'if fiscal discipline was not forthcoming in an EMU, then the very objective of the union itself could well be threatened.' The authors identify three possible approaches to encourage the member countries to promote the required fiscal discipline:

(a) *Binding fiscal rules* as proposed in the Delors Report. Several such rules could be devised relating to the size of the fiscal deficit a country would be allowed to have in a given year; to the level of the public debt; to the change in that level and so forth. A simple example could be a balanced budget rule, or one that requires that the ratio of public debt to gross domestic product does not change. While it is not difficult to think of several such rules, it is difficult to think of rules that are both feasible and good. The experience of countries with laws that require the balancing of the budget, for example, is not very encouraging. These laws have often resulted in a proliferation of extrabudgetary accounts. Furthermore, as the literature of the 1960s emphasized, the fiscal deficit is highly influenced by the behaviour of the economy. Given that cyclical developments influence the performance of the budget, and that these developments are not going to disappear in the future, these rules might require what many economists would consider as highly destabilizing fiscal policies.[1] Going from rules that relate to the behaviour of relevant variables (fiscal deficit, public debt, etc.) in *particular years*, to rules that relate to that behaviour over longer periods (say balancing the budget or stabilizing the ratio of public debt to GDP over the duration of the business cycle) would introduce elements of discretion that might make possible for particular countries to delay taking the needed fiscal actions or might lead to debates over the desirable actions.

(b) *Multilateral surveillance* plus the incorporation in the EMU treaty of the principle that 'excessive budget deficits must be avoided.' The extent of the impact of multilateral surveillance on the policymaking process of some countries is debatable. If the policy-making process were sensitive enough to be significantly influenced by multilateral surveillance, it would probably have avoided the country's getting into fiscal difficulties in the first place. This, of course, does not mean that multilateral surveillance is totally ineffective. It does mean, however, that one must be modest about what can be expected from this process.

(c) *To entrust private financial markets with the role of encouraging fiscal discipline.* In other words, do not impose any specific requirements on the country but put your faith in the market or in God, whichever is relevant, and hope that the market will discipline the countries.

The Goldstein and Woglom paper has an important bearing on the 'put your faith in the market' approach although its relevance may also extend to the fiscal rules approach since they show that the states that have fiscal rules generally followed more conservative fiscal policy. The market approach recognizes that a lax fiscal policy leads to higher (default and premium) risk for those who buy government bonds. This in turn raises the interest rate at which governments can borrow. Higher interest rates presumably discourage additional government borrowing, thus helping restore fiscal discipline.

For this market-related approach to be able to promote fiscal discipline, several conditions, in addition to those mentioned in the Goldstein and Woglom paper, must be satisfied.

First, the default premium in the interest rate must fully and accurately reflect the degree of fiscal discipline. There must not be conceptual or statistical problems which introduce a wedge between the actual fiscal situation and the one reflected, via the default and premium risk, in the interest rate. Given the difficulties that economists have in assessing precisely the fiscal situation of countries, this condition cannot be assumed to be easily met. A few days ago, for example, Professor Modigliani was cited in Italian newspapers to the effect that there is no fiscal problem in Italy, and Professor Eisner has repeatedly stated that the United States has no fiscal problem either. Clearly this is an area where different economists and different investors may see things differently.

Second, and closely related to the first, the relationship between the fiscal situation and the borrowing rate on government bonds must be well-behaved and continuous so that a country's borrowing rate is always a good barometer of that country's fiscal stance. This condition rules out the possibility of sudden changes. No catastrophe theory is applicable here. If the fiscal house falls, it will be smoothly and continuously. This assumption implies that the debt crisis of 1982 in developing countries could not have happened since the lenders would have increased their lending rates and the borrowers would have reduced their borrowing well before the situation reached a critical level.

Third, it requires that the political process within the relevant countries is such that, faced with a significant increase in the cost of borrowing, a well-identified group of policy-makers has the wisdom, the interest, and more importantly, the political power to react in the most desirable way possible by legislating tax increases or cuts in noninterest expenditure.

Furthermore, they will do so immediately regardless of whether the next election is just around the corner or a long time away.

Work on political cycles and on public choice would raise serious questions about this third condition. Also, the experience with fiscal policy in many countries, and the observation of the policy-making process in those countries, make this condition appear even more questionable.[2] The demand for borrowing with respect to changes in the interest rate may be inelastic either because noninterest public expenditure (tied to entitlement or to well-established government programs) is seen as beneficial or productive, or because it would be politically difficult to cut it, or to increase tax revenues, by enough to compensate for the increase in the rate of interest. The junk bond experience of the 1980s may be relevant to countries as well as to enterprises. High interest rates did not prevent excessive borrowing by many enterprises. It is unlikely that they will prevent excessive borrowing by countries. Governments that can remain in power for a while longer by borrowing more and spending more, will be tempted to do so. The additional cost of borrowing would be faced by some other government, and, of course, there is always the possibility that international developments may force down the general interest rates, thus alleviating the fiscal situation.

Goldstein and Woglom estimate the effect of fiscal deterioration on the interest rate. They show that borrowing becomes more expensive when the fiscal situation of the state deteriorates. Thus, at the margin, the cost of government services goes up. However, they do not specifically address the implication of that increase for the servicing of the existing debt in magnifying that effect. Given the existence of large stocks of debt (exceeding 100 percent of GDP in some European countries), it is important to consider the impact of an increase in interest rates not just on the cost of the marginal program but also on the servicing of the existing debt.

The increase in interest rate will have a substitution and an income effect for the government. If the increase in interest rate affected only new borrowing, as would be the case where the existing stock of debt is very low, only the substitution effect would be important. By increasing the cost of borrowing, this effect might induce some reduction in spending. However, if the existing stock of debt is large, an increase in interest rate may not just increase the cost of *net* borrowing but, given the relatively short maturity structure that characterizes the existing debt of many countries, it may quickly translate into a large increase in total interest payments. This can be interpreted as a substantial reduction in the net income of the public sector. The public sector will have less financial resources to finance its non-interest expenditures. In this situation, it will be more difficult to reduce the size of the fiscal deficit since the increase in interest rate will require more borrowing just to service the existing debt. Higher tax revenue or lower noninterest expenditure will be required to maintain the fiscal deficit unchanged. The magnitude of this income effect will depend on the size of the debt-GDP ratio and, in the short run, on the maturity structure of that debt. The obvious conclusion is that it is far easier to be fiscally virtuous in a country that does not have a large public debt to service.

One of the major problems facing the EMU is the initial, highly different, debt-GDP ratios among the member countries. Some of these countries have ratios that, as Goldstein and Woglom put it, are an order of magnitude higher than those of the American states. For this reason the experience of the American states cannot provide much guidance for the European countries. The American states have not had to face the magnitude of the income effect discussed above. It would be nice if the existing public debts would just disappear at the beginning of the European Monetary Union. But, of course, they will not.

Another basic difference touched upon but not discussed in the Goldstein and Woglom paper is the fiscal role played by the federal government in the United States. More than two-thirds of all public spending in the United States is carried out by the federal government which accounts also for about two-thirds of all tax revenue. That role provides powerful fiscal stabilizers to the states. It maintains an expenditure floor when the income of a particular state falls and it reduces the state's disposable income when the state's income rises by more than the average. In Europe there is no central fiscal authority that plays this role and none is planned for the foreseeable future. It may thus be far more difficult for a European country to scale down its public spending. In a monetary union it will also be difficult for countries with large fiscal imbalances to raise the tax level substantially because of the constraint that the harmonization of the tax systems will put on some taxes.[3] Thus, fiscal discipline will require significant expenditure reductions.

Goldstein and Woglom do not have much to say about the states' reaction to the increases in the cost of their borrowing. They limit themselves to assessing the impact of the states' fiscal policy on their cost of borrowing. But this is where the US example could, in spite of the limits mentioned above, have relevance for the European Monetary Union. It is not surprising that lenders prefer to lend to states with sounder fiscal policies. But how quickly have the states responded to the rise in the cost of borrowing? Was the speed and extent of adjustment affected by the size of the stock of debt? Was it affected by the timing of the next elections? By fiscal rules? Have interest rate differentials between fiscally sound and other states persisted over time, or have they been eliminated quickly?

While the experience of the American states can provide some insight for the European Monetary Union, one further fundamental difference between the situation that characterizes the American states and the situation that will characterize at least for some time the European countries must be kept in mind. In spite of their distinct legal identity and their important functions, the American states are integral parts of a whole from which they cannot separate themselves. It is difficult to think of the American states without thinking of the United States of America. When, in the last century, some states tried to break away from the Union, the Union went to war to prevent that. Thus the idea that the United States will remain a united state is never questioned. This idea has acquired full credibility. For the foreseeable future the European countries will retain far more independence. Even after joining the EMU, a country would still have an important separate identity and would still have the option of getting out of the union if, in the judgement of those who determine its policies, the cost of remaining in the Union became too high. It would be naive to think that a commitment to join the Union would be an irreversible action which would not be affected by the perceived economic or political cost of joining and remaining in the Union and which would thus promote the necessary fiscal adjustment.

I have a few comments on the model used by Goldstein and Woglom for the empirical estimations. First, and perhaps of lesser significance, is the fact that the model includes among the independent variables both the current ratio of (net) debt to income and the trend growth of debt relative to income. These two variables are largely the same variable measured in two different ways and I wonder whether they should both be included.

A second comment relates to the way in which the authors have tried to take into account tax effects. Unless I have misunderstood the paper, the authors implicitly assume that the bonds of a given state are largely bought by the residents of that state. They argue that ' ... the [marginal tax rates] in the different states can vary because of differences in the proportion of high-income taxpayers by state. The larger the proportion of high-income taxpayers, the higher the MTR for that state and the lower the yield.' However, in a federation with perfect capital mobility and with full information, there is no reason why the demand for the bonds of a given state should be limited to the residents of that state. As long as the local bonds are tax free, they will attract investors with high marginal tax rates from all over the United States.

A tax aspect that is ignored in the paper is the tax on capital gains. In fact, while the yield on a state or municipal bond is tax free, the capital gains incurred in the sale of that bond are fully taxable and capital losses are deductible. This fact probably influences what the authors call risk premia since it may affect the willingness of investors to buy or sell in the secondary market when capital gains or losses are present.

Finally an aspect of the data used that I found puzzling is the following. If, as they maintain, there has been no default by states since at least World War Two, why is the default premium for some states as large as shown by their Table 8.1? Is this an indication that the market is highly irrational?

In conclusion, this is a rich and interesting paper that has a lot to say about the US municipal bond market. It also has a lot to say about the European monetary system. However, caution is required in extending the US results to the European situation.

NOTES

1 For example, they might require tax increases and/or expenditure cuts in recession years. Only those who believe in an extreme version of Ricardian equivalence would dismiss the potentially destabilizing effects of these policies.
2 For an elaboration of this point see Tanzi (1992).
3 Of course, this does not rule out increases associated with reductions in tax evasion.

REFERENCE

Tanzi, V. (1992), 'The political Economy of Fiscal Deficit Reduction', forthcoming in a World Bank volume, *The Macroeconomics of the Public Sector Deficits*.

Part IV Global implications of a European Central Bank

9 European Monetary Union and international currencies in a tripolar world

GEORGE ALOGOSKOUFIS and RICHARD PORTES

The European Community countries appear to be locked into a process that may eventually lead their economies to full monetary unification. Although the road to monetary union in the EC is bound to be bumpy, all countries appear committed to the final goal, with the possible exception of Britain. According to plans under negotiation at the inter-governmental conference that started in December 1990, the currencies of twelve European economies, which include a number of leading international currencies such as the Deutschmark, sterling and the French franc, will ultimately be replaced by a new currency, likely to be called the 'ecu'.[1]

European monetary union, when and if it occurs, is bound to have important international implications. The new currency will be issued on behalf of a large economic area, by a new Central Bank which will be responsible for the joint monetary policy of the EC. Other international institutions such as the G-7, the IMF and the OECD will have to adapt (see Alogoskoufis and Portes, 1990), but, more importantly, there will be a major shock to the existing international monetary and exchange rate system. The ecu will be a serious challenger for the role of the US dollar as the dominant international means of payment, unit of account and store of value, and the monetary policies of the new European Central Bank will have far more important international spillovers than those of any of the existing central banks of the EC countries. The extent of these spillovers is likely to affect the process of international policy coordination, and even the exchange rate regime of all the main industrial economies.

The purpose of this paper is to examine the prospective implications of Economic and Monetary Union (EMU) in the EC for the international monetary system. We make a giant leap forward in confining attention to the implications after Stage III, when, according to the time-table first set in the Delors Committee Report, the existing EC currencies will have been replaced by a single currency. Thus, what we compare is the status quo (alias Stage I), in which ten of the twelve EC countries participate in the Exchange Rate Mechanism (ERM) of the European Monetary System (EMS), and two more (the Greek drachma and the Portuguese escudo) are expected to join in the not too distant future, with full monetary union, in which all currencies will be replaced by one. We shall have nothing to say on the transitional Stage II, in which the fluctuation banks for intra-EC exchange rates will be eliminated, but each country will retain its national currency.

We concentrate on two main issues: first on the prospective role of the ecu as an international vehicle and reserve currency, and second on the prospective changes that EMU will imply for the international coordination of monetary and fiscal policies between the USA, the EC and Japan, and the exchange rate regime between the dollar, the ecu and the yen.

1   The international role of the ecu

Like national currencies, international currencies have three major roles. They serve as means of international payments, as units of account and as stores of value. But, there is one major difference between national and international currencies.

Within national borders, the sole use of one currency is usually imposed by government fiat. Thus the question which characteristics make one currency more in demand than another does not usually arise, as market participants have little option but to use the currency designated by the government and supplied by an agency such as the national central bank. It is only in extreme circumstances, such as very rapid inflation, that national currencies are replaced as means of payment, units of account and stores of value by other currencies or commodities.

In the international economy demand factors play a much more important role in the determination of which currencies are being used for these purposes. Since there is no supranational authority that can impose the use of a single currency, these issues are decided in the market place, by the decisions and actions of public and private agents of all countries. Because of the economies of scale in the use of currencies, the externalities involved and the considerable degree of uncertainty and asymmetric information, there is no guarantee that the world will end up with the best monetary system, let alone a single international currency. In addition, there is the possibility of multiple equilibria and considerable instability, as the expectations and beliefs of agents are among the major factors that will determine which equilibrium will prevail.[2]

The history of the international monetary system suggests a series of efforts by the governments of the major economies to coordinate on better equilibria than the ones that would prevail in the international marketplace in the absence of coordination. Since there is no guarantee that the unregulated market will yield a satisfactory international (or indeed national) monetary system, governments have jointly intervened, either in the form of agreeing to implicit rules of the game (as in the classical gold standard), or in the form of designing explicit sets of rules and international institutions (as in Bretton Woods or the EMS) that would ensure that the international monetary equilibrium possessed a minimum of desirable characteristics. In other periods, such as the inter-war period and a large part of the 1970s and early 1980s, international coordination broke down or took a much looser form (e.g. the G-7 summits).

Yet many of the institutions and modes of behaviour from previous regimes do not completely disappear, so there has been considerable continuity to the international monetary system even after the breakdown of coordination and major changes in regime, following shocks to the fundamentals or the preferences of governments. In a world with many equilibria, history and institutions also play a key role in choosing one and may delay the switch from one to another.[3]

EMU can be seen as an important change in the fundamentals of the international monetary system. A sub-set of countries have decided to coordinate on the use of a single currency. The remainder of this section is concerned with the implications of this decision for the currencies that are used as international means of payments, units of account and stores of value.

1.1 The means of payment function

Let us first start with the means of payment function of international currencies. Many seem to think that this function is the most important. For example, according to Cohen (1971), 'An international economy with only national moneys is like a barter economy. . . . Transactions costs are high because of the practical problem of achieving the required double coincidence of wants in the foreign exchange market. However, as in a barter economy, transactions costs can be substantially diminished for an individual if he adapts his own currency mix to that of other individuals, holding for specific use, as international exchange intermediaries, inventories of the most widely demanded foreign currencies. These are of

Table 9.1. *% share of national currencies in foreign exchange reserves, all countries*

	1973	1976	1978	1980	1983	1986	1988	1989
US Dollar	84.5	86.7	82.8	68.6	71.4	67.1	64.9	60.2
Pound Sterling	5.9	2.1	1.6	2.9	2.5	2.6	2.8	2.7
Deutsche Mark	6.7	7.3	10.1	14.9	11.8	14.6	15.7	19.3
French Franc	1.2	1.0	1.0	1.7	0.8	0.8	1.0	1.3
Swiss Franc	1.4	1.6	2.1	3.2	2.4	2.0	1.9	1.7
Dutch Guilder	0.4	0.5	0.5	1.3	0.8	1.1	1.1	1.1
Japanese Yen	–	1.2	1.9	4.4	5.0	7.9	7.7	7.9
Major EC curr.	14.2	10.9	13.2	20.8	15.9	19.1	20.6	24.4

Source: IMF *Annual Report* (1990)

course the currencies of the countries that are predominant in world trade – the countries that account for the largest proportion of international transactions' (pp. 25–26). To assess the potential role of the ecu we must look to demand for means of international payments by official bodies and by the private sector.

We begin with the demand by official bodies. As Krugman (1984) among others suggests, 'Probably the most important reason for holding reserves in dollars is that the dollar is an intervention currency' (p. 273).

Table 9.1 presents data on the composition of official international reserves. It demonstrates that the share of the US dollar in official reserves, although declining, is overwhelmingly higher than the share of any other single currency. In fact it is higher than the combined share of all other currencies taken together. The share of major European currencies shows a slow increase, especially since the depreciation of the dollar in 1985–86. It is important to note, however, that these trends are not simply the outcome of revaluations following changes in exchange rates, but also the result of diversification away from the dollar (IMF *Annual Report*, 1990, p. 65).

The data in Table 9.1 probably overstate the position of the dollar, as (after 1979) they add to the SDR value of dollar holdings the SDR value of ECUs issued against dollars, while the SDR value of ECUs issued against gold is not counted as part of exchange rate reserves. If the ECUs issued against dollars are treated as EC reserves, then the share of the dollar for 1989 falls to 52% of the total, and the share of the major European currencies rises to 32.9%. This is more than four times as large as the share of the Japanese yen. But as the IMF *Annual Report* of 1990 comments, 'The overall picture of changes in the trend in the currency

Table 9.2. *% share of national currencies in foreign exchange reserves, industrial economies and LDCs treated separately*

	Indust. Economies			LDCs		
	1980	1984	1989	1980	1984	1989
US Dollar	77.2	73.5	59.4	59.5	66.6	62.1
Pound Sterling	0.8	1.4	1.4	5.1	4.4	5.7
Deutsche Mark	14.3	15.2	22.9	15.4	10.0	11.4
French Franc	0.7	0.1	1.1	2.7	1.5	1.8
Swiss Franc	1.7	1.5	1.5	4.8	2.6	2.4
Dutch Guilder	0.7	0.6	1.2	1.9	0.8	0.8
Japanese Yen	3.3	6.3	8.2	5.4	5.2	7.1
Unspecified	1.3	2.1	4.4	4.8	8.8	8.7
Major EC Curr.	16.5	17.3	26.6	25.1	16.7	19.7

Source: IMF *Annual Report* (1990)

composition of foreign exchange reserves is similar if ECUs . . . are treated separately.' (p. 67).

Table 9.2 contains a breakdown of the composition of foreign exchange reserves for industrial economies and LDCs. It suggests a much larger trend decline in the share of US dollars for the industrial economies than for LDCs. In addition, the LDCs seem to have diversified towards the Japanese yen rather than European currencies.

The trend decline in the share of dollar reserves in the portfolios of central banks of industrial economies is likely to be strongly reinforced as a result of the process of EMU. The reduced need for exchange market intervention in dollars by EC central banks that will follow establishment of EMU will entail a significant decline in the use of the dollar as an international means of payment by official bodies. However, this will not make the ecu a major reserve currency outside the EC, unless foreign exchange intervention by non-EC countries is also in ecu. The ecu will substitute for the dollar in the portfolios of non-EC central banks that decide to peg their exchange rate to the ecu. For example, as we show below, the EFTA countries appear to be pegging to the EMS already, although officially most are either floating or pegging to a basket of currencies (Gylfason, 1990, discusses the exchange rate policies of the Nordic countries). In addition, following liberalization in Eastern Europe, Poland and Czechoslovakia have introduced current-account convertibility for residents, and Hungary is not far behind. Convertibility is likely to continue to be a major feature of the economic transformation process in the formerly planned economies (Portes, 1991). That will increase their demand for reserves, in which the ecu is likely to occupy an important position.[4]

Additional demand could arise in case the European Bank for Reconstruction and Development (EBRD) were to conduct a large part of its borrowing and lending in ecu rather than dollars or yen. Such a preference towards the ecu on the part of the EBRD would of course cause an even higher increase in the demand for ecu reserves by the central banks of the Eastern European economies.[5]

In conclusion, EMU is likely to involve potentially significant substitution of ecu for dollars by central banks in the EC. Central banks in other European economies, such as the EFTA countries and the formerly planned economies, are also likely to use the ecu as their principal intervention currency, and the lending policies of the EBRD may further boost its position as an international means of payment. The position of the ecu may be strengthened even further if the worldwide increase in the demand for reserves by central banks continues. Since 1985 policy-makers in the G-7 and elsewhere have been much more positive towards exchange rate management. One expects an increase in the demand for reserves when there is a stronger commitment to defend exchange rates (see Dooley et al., 1989; Black, 1985, however, suggests that the evidence on that is mixed).

We next turn to the means of payment function of international money as it applies to the private sector. Note that whereas international transactions in goods markets are arranged between importers and exporters, eventual payment is intermediated through commercial banks. Thus, what one should look for are the 'thickness' externalities that cause dealers to prefer indirect exchanges through a vehicle currency to direct exchanges of one currency for another. These externalities have to do with transactions costs, and the solution to the problem of double coincidence of wants by the use of money. If there are many dealers prepared to exchange dollars (the dollar market is 'thick'), then a dealer wishing to exchange pesetas for drachmas may find it less costly to go through two exchanges, one of pesetas for dollars and one of dollars for drachmas, than to go through a direct exchange of drachmas for pesetas. However, even when this is not the case, a vehicle currency is still used to finance bilateral trade imbalances (Krugman, 1980).

In a recent article on turnover in the foreign exchange market, the Banca d'Italia *Economic Bulletin* reports on a survey of 21 countries in April 1989. Europe accounted for 50% of the volume of transactions, of which half was in London. The dollar still accounts for 45% of total turnover; the Deutschmark and yen together for slightly over 25%. In Italy (a useful 'representative' case), the dollar and DM account for 39% and 32% of non-lira turnover respectively, and for 54% and 24% of lira turnover. In the forward market the dollar accounts for 40% of transactions against other foreign currencies and 97% of transactions against lire.

The market for ecus will be thicker than the market for any of the current EC currencies. This will make it more likely that the ecu will emerge as a medium of exchange on a par with the dollar in interbank markets. Thus, the fundamentals point towards a potentially large change.

To see this point consider the following example, based on the model of Krugman (1980). Assume that the world consists of three countries, U (whose currency is the dollar), G (whose currency is the DM) and F (whose currency is the FF). Assume that U runs a trade surplus I with F, that F runs a surplus I with G, and that G runs a surplus I with U. Imports of F from U are equal to R, imports of U from G are equal to T, and imports of G from F are equal to S. The structure of payments flows is depicted by arrows in Figure 9.1.[6]

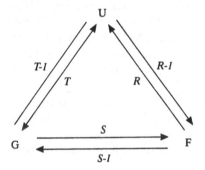

Figure 9.1   The structure of payments between U, F and G

Assuming as in Krugman (1980) that the percentage of transaction costs in the inter-bank market is a negative function of total volume in the market, and that the structure supports the dollar as a vehicle currency, we examine two potential equilibria. The one depicted in Figure 9.2(a) involves partial indirect exchange. The volume of transactions in the DM-FF market is equal to S-I, the imports of F from G, while the volume of transactions in the $-DM and $-FF markets is equal to T and R respectively. The dollar ($) is a vehicle currency, as the financing of the trade deficit between G and F is intermediated through dollar markets, but the financing of trade imbalances between G and U and F and U is not intermediated through the DM-FF market. Figure 9.2(b) depicts the second potential equilibrium. This involves total indirect exchange, as all

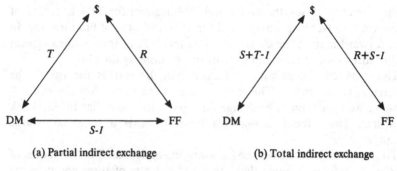

(a) Partial indirect exchange   (b) Total indirect exchange

Figure 9.2   The dollar as a vehicle currency; partial and total indirect exchange

of the financing of trade between F and G is intermediated through dollar markets. This would apply if the economies of scale were so large as to make two exchanges in the dollar markets less costly than one exchange in the DM-FF market. In each of these cases the dollar plays a special role as a vehicle currency as it enters into more transactions than the role of U in world payments justifies itself. As Krugman (1980) suggests, and Figure 9.2(a) makes clear, the $ 'will play a limited vehicle currency role even when roundabout exchange involves higher transactions costs than direct exchange. The reason is that some indirect exchange is necessary to clear the currency markets ...' (p. 519).

Now suppose the G and F merge into a monetary union and create a common currency, the ecu. There will now only be one inter-bank market for foreign exchange, that between the dollar and the ecu. The dollar will lose its special status as a vehicle currency, and it will be equally important as the ecu.

This example is oversimplified in that it ignores transactions involving countries other than the USA and the EC 12. The dollar's role is important because it also intermediates in the financing of trade between the EC 12 and third countries, as well as trade of third countries among themselves. One of the reasons is again lower transaction costs in the interbank market. Thus, there is no guarantee that the ecu will substitute for the role of the dollar in these other markets. However, the reduction of transaction costs in all markets involving the ecu, vis-à-vis the markets involving the current EC currencies, will make this far more likely than in the absence of EMU.

Table 9.3 serves to highlight the importance of the European Community for world trade. It demonstrates that the EC accounts for a higher percentage of world exports and imports than the USA, even when intra-EC trade is netted out. The average share of the EC in world exports

Table 9.3. *% shares in world exports and imports of US, Japan and EC*

	1974	1979	1984	1989
		Exports		
USA	12.7	12.0	12.2	12.5
Japan	7.2	6.8	9.5	9.4
EC				
Gross	36.1	38.5	34.4	38.9
Net	14.8	13.6	16.6	15.7
		Imports		
USA	20.0	20.3	18.5	16.4
Japan	11.5	10.2	7.4	7.0
EC				
Gross	55.5	56.9	34.5	38.8
Net	25.4	23.4	16.9	16.6

Source: IMF, *Direction of Trade Statistics*, Yearbooks, 1981, 1990.
Note: The 'net share of the EC has been calculated by excluding intra-EC trade from the total trade of the EC. However, to preserve comparability with the other shares intra-EC trade was not subtracted from world trade (the denominator).

in the 1970s was of the order of 14%, as opposed to about 12% for the USA and 7% for Japan. In the 1980s the EC share rose to about 16% and Japan's rose to 9.5%, as opposed to a stagnant share for the USA. A similar position applies with regard to world imports, although the comparison between the 1970s and the 1980s is distorted by the effects of the oil and commodity price shocks of the 1970s that served to swell the share of imports of industrialized countries.

These facts point towards a significant potential for the ecu as a means of payments in international markets. The dollar will certainly be displaced in intra-EC trade as a result of Stage III of monetary union (intra-EC trade was a massive 22% of world trade in 1989), and will also be displaced with a high probability in trade involving the EC and third countries. Thus, the trade fundamentals are very favourable to the ecu.

In all this it is worth keeping in mind a second lesson from the Krugman (1980) model. This is that 'history will matter: once an exchange structure is established, it will persist unless the structure of payments shifts enough to make it untenable, or unless the system experiences a shock large enough to shift it from one equilibrium to another' (p. 523). We feel that EMU is a large enough shock, that will make the current position of the dollar untenable. It is bound to cause an unprecedented upset in the inter-bank market. Even the experience with the replacement of sterling by the US dollar in the inter-war period may not have involved as large and as abrupt a change in the fundamentals of the international monetary system as EMU is likely to bring (see Brown, 1940, for a classic treatment of this episode). However, the exact nature of the new equilibrium is difficult to predict, especially as even the simplest triangular exchange models (as those examined in the Krugman, 1980, paper) have multiple equilibria, and beliefs may play an important role in determining which equilibrium prevails. To paraphrase Newlyn (1962), international money 'falls within that perplexing but fascinating group of phenomena ... affected by self-justifying beliefs. If the members of a community think that money will be generally acceptable, then it will be; otherwise not' (p. 2).

It is also worth noting that for both the interbank market and the non-bank private sector the ecu will not be adopted unless transaction costs are low and banking in it is as cheap as the alternatives. The extent to which this will be the case will also depend on the success of financial deregulation in bringing down the cost of banking in the EC (Giovannini and Mayer, 1991). It will also depend on central bank and regulatory policies determining the costs of using the ecu payments mechanism (Folkerts-Landau and Garber, 1992).

1.2   The unit of account function

We next turn to the unit of account role of international money. This is closely linked to the means of payments role for national economies, although less so in the international monetary system. The unit of account role for an international currency depends first on whether importers and exporters invoice in that particular currency. Black (1985) presents evidence that whereas European firms invoice a very large proportion of their exports in their own currency, the proportion of their imports that is invoiced in other currencies, and especially dollars, is quite significant. On the other hand, Japanese firms invoice mainly in dollars, while more than 70% of LDC exports, 95% of OPEC exports and 85% of Latin American exports are invoiced in dollars. In an update and re-examination of these trends, Black (1989) finds that the share of Japanese exports invoiced in dollars has been falling over time, while the share dominated in yen has been rising. He also reports some indirect evidence that the share of US trade denominated in foreign currencies is rising. At the same time the Japanese and European shares of world exports have also been rising, while the share of US exports seems to have been stagnant (Table 9.3). The consequence seems to be a trend decline in the share of dollar-denominated world trade.[7]

In all probability EMU will result in almost exclusive invoicing in ecu by

EC firms. The only likely exceptions are imports from the US and Japan, and some primary commodities, if invoicing by commodity producers were to continue to be in US dollars. It is also quite possible that the economies of scale created by the substitution of a number of European currencies by a single one will induce firms from other areas that trade mainly with the EC to start invoicing in ecu. This may include the EFTA countries, many Middle Eastern and Mediterranean economies, as well as the newly liberalizing economies of Eastern Europe. It may also induce many multinational Japanese and US firms to follow suit, as they will also benefit from such economies of scale.

To the extent that trade relations become concentrated in regional blocs (e.g. Europe–Africa, Japan–Asia, US–Latin America), we might end up with at least three vehicle cum unit-of-account currencies. But insofar as trade is more uniformly distributed geographically and multilateral, there will still be powerful forces behind the use of a single dominant currency for these roles. In the latter case the change in the fundamentals will favour the ecu, but history (inertia) will favour the dollar. For example, it seems unlikely, although not unthinkable that the OPEC countries and producers of other internationally traded commodities will switch from dollar to ecu invoicing soon after the establishment of EMU. Again any change will depend on the extent and the speed with which the ecu displaces the dollar as a means of payment in international trade. As we suggested above, the fundamentals point towards a big displacement of the dollar as a means of international payments. Displacement of the dollar as an international unit of account is bound to follow at least partially, and possibly at a later stage.

The second aspect of the unit of account role of an international currency is related to whether there are countries that peg their own currency against it. Table 9.4 reports the number of countries that peg their exchange rate to the US dollar and other currencies. This is also a reflection of the importance of a currency as an international unit of account. Of the 55 countries that either pegged their currency or maintained limited flexibility against a single other currency in March 1990 (all these are LDCs), 34 did so against the US dollar, and 14 against the French franc. However all these economies are small, and even jointly they do not amount to much in terms of the world economy. In any case, as we suggested above, pegging against the ECU is on the increase. It is now official policy in Sweden and Finland (and unofficial policy in other EFTA countries), and the ECU is proposed as the unit of account in the payments system to be established between the Soviet Union, Czechoslovakia, Poland and Hungary (see footnote 2), and the lending of the EBRD.

Table 9.4. *Exchange rate arrangements, March 31, 1990: Number of currencies that peg against a single currency*

	Fixed Peg	
US $		30
French Franc		14
Other		5
	Limited Flexibility	
US $		4

Source: IMF *Annual Report* 1990.

Thus, although the ecu has a long way to go in order to become a major international unit of account, a number of factors will favour such a development. One is the momentous changes in Eastern Europe. The East European economies will necessarily have closer trade and financial links with Western Europe than with the United States or Japan. This makes it far more likely that both their firms and their central banks will use the ecu as a unit of account.[8] The process will also depend on the stability of exchange rates between the dollar, the yen and the ecu. If the US dollar were to display high volatility against the yen and the ecu, while their exchange rate was relatively stable, it would boost the chances of the ecu (and the yen) to substitute for the dollar as an international unit of account.

Table 9.5 reports correlation coefficients of dollar exchange rates for a number of currencies, with the DM-dollar rate. It demonstrates the high correlation of the EFTA currencies with the Deutschmark rather than the US dollar, especially since 1987 when EMS realignments stopped. Since January 1987 the correlation coefficient of the EFTA currencies with the DM is much higher than the correlation coefficient of sterling and the Portuguese escudo, let alone the Greek drachma which has been following an independent crawling peg policy, fully accommodating inflation differentials with the rest of the EC. It is also instructive to compare the high EFTA correlations with the low correlation of DM and yen exchange rates, in a period in which the G-7 were supposedly cooperating closely in exchange markets. Thus, exchange rate developments since 1987 suggest that the ecu may be an important unit of account for other economies with strong links with the EC, such as the current EFTA currencies.

Traditionally, the means of payment (international reserve) and unit of account (vehicle currency) functions of money go hand in hand. This was the case with sterling during the gold standard, and with the dollar during

Table 9.5. *Correlation coefficients of exchange rates against the US dollar with the DM/$ rate*

		Mar 1979–May 1991	Jan 1987–May 1991
	Currency		
EC			
France	Franc	0.718	0.994
Italy	Lira	0.615	0.987
UK	Pound	0.581	0.808
Belgium	Franc	0.858	0.996
Denmark	Krone	0.868	0.992
Greece	Drachma	0.023	0.028
Ireland	Pound	0.727	0.998
Holland	Guilder	0.997	0.999
Portugal	Escudo	0.123	0.793
Spain	Peseta	0.556	0.904
EFTA			
Austria	Schilling	0.999	0.999
Finland	Markka	0.093	0.936
Norway	Krone	0.589	0.954
Sweden	Krona	0.570	0.968
Switzerland	Franc	0.976	0.949
Japan	Yen	0.740	0.185

Note: The correlation coefficients have been calculated from end of month spot exchange rates, from OECD *Main Economic Indicators*, various issues.

the Bretton Woods system and beyond. It is very likely that the ecu will eventually become the dominant unit of account and means of payment in Europe and its immediate vicinity like North Africa and the Middle East. But it is more uncertain whether it will replace the dollar elsewhere. Much will depend on whether the dollar displays weakness because of the persistence of global imbalances, as well as on the attitudes of traders in the inter-bank markets, the Japanese and the LDCs.

1.3   The store of value function

The final issue related to the fundamentals of whether the ecu will become an important international currency has to do with the willingness of private investors to hold ecu assets. Some of the factors that affect the international investor also affect central banks, although central banks have an additional transactions motive as they have to intervene in support of their currencies.

Table 9.6. *Currency structure of the international bond market: total stocks, end of year*

	1982		1988		1989	
	US$bn	%	US$bn	%	US$bn	%
Total	259.1		1,085.4		1,175.7	
US Dollar		56.1		43.3		45.8
Swiss Franc		16.4		12.8		11.2
Japanese Yen		6.4		12.2		10.4
Deutsche Mark		12.1		9.6		7.5
Sterling		1.8		6.7		6.1
ECU		1.2		4.3		3.9
Major EC currencies		15.1		20.6		17.5

Source: BIS *Annual Report* 1990.

As in the case of central bank reserves, US dollar bonds make up a significant proportion of the international bond market. Table 9.6 contains data for selected years. The data suggest a small decline of the role of the US dollar since the early 1980s, and a slight increase in the share of EC currencies, from 15.1% in 1982 to 17.5% in 1989. The small dollar retreat has been accompanied by a sharp rise in the share of Japanese yen-denominated bonds.

Since stocks are slow to change, we also present in Table 9.7 some data on new bond issues. The decline of the dollar in the 1980s is more apparent from these data. Note that in 1990, admittedly a year of dollar weakness, the share of new bond issues in EC currencies exceeded the share of dollar-denominated bonds.

Clearly the fundamentals are related to risk and return, and there are considerable uncertainties both about the fundamentals and about the appropriate model for thinking about international financial investment (see Hall and Miles, 1991). A number of developments may work in the ecu's favour in the longer term. First we may witness a diminution of the so-called 'safe haven' motive for dollar holdings. If the liberalization of the East European economies proves durable and not a forerunner of political instability, and if the EC is successful in 'widening' as well as 'deepening', then Europe may eventually seem a much safer 'haven' than previously. This, together with the liberalization of financial markets in the EC, could increase the attractiveness of ecu-denominated assets. The second factor at work may be the anti-inflationary reputation of the Bundesbank, if it can credibly be transferred to the European Central

Table 9.7. *International issues of bonds, breakdown by currency of issue*

	1971	1976	1981	1986	1987	1988	1989	1990
Total ($ bn)	3.8	15.4	26.5	187.7	140.5	178.9	212.9	179.6
			%					
US dollar	59.7	65.1	80.2	62.9	41.3	41.7	55.2	38.4
Japanese Yen	–	–	1.5	9.9	16.1	8.9	7.3	12.9
EC Currencies	39.9	22.5	12.2	21.1	29.3	35.0	27.1	40.9
Deutsche mark	22.9	18.4	5.2	9.1	10.7	13.2	7.7	10.2
Sterling	1.6	–	2.0	5.6	10.7	13.2	8.7	12.0
French franc	1.3	0.4	2.0	1.9	1.3	1.3	2.1	5.0
Italian lira	–	–	–	0.2	0.5	0.9	1.6	3.0
Dutch guilder	7.1	3.0	1.6	0.5	0.8	0.1	1.1	0.8
ECU*	7.0	0.7	1.4	3.8	5.3	6.3	5.9	9.9
Other Currencies	0.4	12.4	7.6	6.1	13.3	14.4	10.4	7.8

Source: OECD *Financial Statistics Monthly*, various issues.
Note: * Before 1981 European Unit of Account.

Bank. Conversely, if liberalization in Eastern Europe and detente were to stall in the run-up to EMU, or if the economic strains of unification were to raise German inflation significantly, it would be that much more difficult for ecu assets to displace dollar assets in international portfolios.

At this stage, the uncertainties involved are reflected clearly in recent issues of the OECD *Economic Outlook*. In December 1989 it stated that: 'Over a longer period, portfolio diversification considerations point to some factors that could continue to favour the dollar, but others that are unfavourable. On balance, the unfavourable factors could be the stronger' (p. 44). Among such factors the OECD suggests that 'The growing importance of the ECU in financial transactions – notably bond issuance – combined with the creation of the EC single market and progress toward some form of monetary union in Europe, could over the longer-term result in a significant erosion of the status of the dollar as "the" international currency' (pp. 44–5). In December 1990, commenting on the narrowing of the differentials between US long rates and those for Japan and Germany it suggests that: 'What is important about these movements in relative yields is that they may be fundamental rather than temporary ... There is growing evidence that Japanese life insurance companies have reduced investment in foreign securities, while significantly increasing domestic loans. At the same time they have begun to diversify away from US securities towards increased holdings of European and Canadian assets. Similarly there has been less capital outflow

from Germany, as domestic investment possibilities have risen significantly following unification.' (p. 11).

On the other hand, the 'thickness externalities' discussed above in
respect of trade are not absent from financial transactions. Here,
however, worldwide financial integration and globalization seem inex-
orable, in contrast to the possibility of regional trading blocks. Thus,
financial globalization may slightly favour the continued dominance of
the US dollar in bond markets.

2   Lessons from the experience of sterling

It is worth considering what history has to teach us about the speed with
which EMU will bring about the possible changes in the international
monetary system in favour of the ecu that we discussed in the previous
section. A shock to the international monetary system such as full monetary union between so many large economies issuing important international currencies is unprecedented. The only historical experience that
is remotely relevant is the decline of Britain in the world economy, and the
replacement of sterling by the US dollar as an international currency. In
this section we try to draw some of the parallels with that experience.

As is well known, before World War I, sterling had no serious rivals in
its role as the main international currency, and London was by far the
most important financial centre in the world. In the era of the international gold standard sterling convertibility was unquestioned. Britain
was the world's principal creditor nation, the greatest exporter of new
capital, and trade with Britain was a large part of the international trade
of virtually every country in the world. As Cohen (1971) remarks,
'Especially after 1860, sterling came to circulate almost universally as a
transactions and quotation currency' (p. 60). Due to the unique position
of London as a financial centre, sterling served as a store of value for both
private agents and governments, and this gave the Bank of England a
leading role in the management of the international gold standard (see
Eichengreen, 1987).

World War I brought about many changes in the fundamentals underlying the role of sterling in the international monetary system. The
convertibility of sterling into gold became doubtful, Britain's role in
international trade diminished and its foreign assets were depleted. New
forms of international settlements caused a diminution of the role of
London as a clearing house for international trade, and New York and
Paris emerged as important financial centres, breaking the virtual mono-
poly of London. This caused difficulties for monetary management by the
Bank of England. The dollar (and to a lesser extent the French franc)

emerged as serious competitors for the role of sterling. It is worth noting, however, that even in 1925 sterling still accounted for a larger proportion of international trade and international assets than any other currency.

A landmark in sterling's replacement by the US dollar as the main international currency was the devaluation of 1931, the inconvertibility of the pound, and the creation of the sterling bloc (Cairncross and Eichengreen, 1983, discuss this episode). This was followed by other countries and gave the coup-de-grace both to the attempted restoration of the gold standard in the inter-war period, and to the role of sterling as a major international currency.

However, sterling retained a significant international role, through the creation of the durable sterling bloc, or sterling area as it came to be known after World War II. To quote from Cohen (1971), 'Since 1931 the predominant trend seems to be towards a regionalization of sterling's international status. ... In a sense, before 1931 all of the world was a sterling region. That was the meaning of globalization. But with the suspension of convertibility, sterling's world began to shrink.' (p. 65). By 1971 its functions as an international currency also seem to have shrunk to virtually nothing, both inside and outside the sterling area.

What lessons can one draw about the impact of the creation of the ecu on the international role of the dollar? As we saw in the previous section, there is a slow but identifiable diminution of the international role of the dollar already. The reasons are not yet fully understood, but they must have to do with the reduced importance of the United States for international trade and finance, the emergence of the United States as a net international debtor, exchange rate instability, and a worse record on inflation than countries such as Germany and Japan. Unless these trends are reversed, and we see this as unlikely, EMU may not be more than the 'straw that broke the camel's back'. As the analysis suggested, EMU is likely to be a very large shock to the current international monetary system. It is a change in the fundamentals that is probably greater than the change of the underlying position of Britain in the inter-war period and the further weakening of its international economic position in the aftermath of World War II.

What is likely to emerge in the place of the current international monetary system? Shall we see a trend towards regionalization, as the experience of sterling in the 1930s seems to suggest, or shall we see a new urge for global monetary cooperation, in the spirit of Bretton Woods?

Answers to such questions would be even more speculative than answers in other parts of this paper. The experience of sterling suggests that both routes are possible. The regionalization route involves protectionism and the creation of semi-separate trading and currency blocs. This route was

290 George Alogoskoufis and Richard Portes

followed in the early 1930s, and according to Nurkse (1944) and Kindleberger (1986) it led to the international propagation and amplification of the Great Depression. The cooperation route was followed in the post-war period. It led to the establishment of the Bretton Woods system with institutions like the IMF, the World Bank, the GATT and others, which have served the interests of the world economy well. The chances are that EMU will serve as a catalyst for closer international cooperation, in the context of a tri-polar international monetary system. The danger of regionalization is serious, however, and it should not be too heavily discounted.

3   Transitional issues

It is also worth examining in somewhat more detail the process by which the ecu could become a major international currency after the establishment of EMU. For this to happen there must be a demand for ecu from the rest of the world, which we have examined, but there must also be a matching supply. Ecus will be supplied at the beginning of the third stage of EMU, by the translation of the stock of financial assets denominated in the current EC currencies into ecu. This will of course include assets held by the rest of the world. However, since one expects a reduction in the dollar holdings of EC countries, new ecu will be accumulated in the rest of the world only if the EC runs a series of balance of payments deficits. Whether the deficits are due to the current or capital account matters only insofar as current account deficits are usually seen as a sign of weakness, and may undermine the credibility of the European Central Bank. If past trends and current fiscal policies are maintained, however, only a sharp fall in private savings (a possible consequence of financial deregulation) or a rise in private investment could lead to the EC running significant current account deficits. Table 9.8 reports current accounts as a percentage of GNP/GDP for the EC, Japan and the USA. This picture may change markedly in the run-up to EMU.

A rapid buildup of ecu balances in the rest of the world would require significant private and official capital outflows. Such outflows will take place, for example, if the liberalization of Eastern Europe continues and creates investment opportunities that attract direct investment from the EC countries. If the EC becomes an important capital exporter to the rest of the world, then the ecu may eventually become a widely held international currency. It was exactly this process that led to the establishment of the international role of sterling in the 19th century and the role of the dollar after World War I. However, one should not discount the possibility of an 'ecu shortage', in the same way as there was a 'dollar shortage'

Table 9.8. *Current balances of EC, Japan and US, % of GNP/GDP*

	1971	1976	1981	1986	1987	1988	1989	1990	1991	1992
EC	0.8	−0.6	−0.7	1.4	0.8	0.3	0.2	0.0	−0.6	−0.4
Japan	2.5	0.7	0.4	4.4	3.6	2.8	2.0	1.2	1.2	1.5
US	−0.1	0.2	0.3	−3.1	−3.2	−2.6	−2.1	−1.8	−0.2	−1.0

Source: OECD *Economic Outlook* (June 1991).

in the 1950s.

Of course, the EC's balance of payments deficit need not correspond to the supply of ecu. Central banks can borrow ecu from financial markets to build up ecu reserves and private financial intermediaries can increase the supply of ecu assets.[9]

What also has to be considered in assessing the prospects of the ecu as an international currency is the willingness of the Europeans to allow it to become one. The European Central Bank may resist the widespread international use of the ecu because of a perceived burden of acting as an international lender of last resort. There are two recent historical examples; the post-war prohibition on the part of the UK of the use of sterling balances for third country credits, which may have been a stimulus to the growth of the Euromarkets; and the Bundesbank's reluctance to allow the DM to be used as an intervention currency in the EMS because this would have led to increased external influences on domestic monetary policy.

If the European Central Bank pursues the opposite route of actively promoting the international use of the ecu, one cannot discount the possibility of a tug of war between the ecu, the incumbent (the dollar) and the major other contender (the yen) for international monetary supremacy. This could be a dangerous development. One might draw this lesson from the interwar experience of the rivalry between sterling and the dollar, with the French franc on the sidelines (Eichengreen, 1987). Even without such a potential rivalry, if EMU results in large-scale substitution of ecu for dollar balances, the tendency for ecu appreciation vis-à-vis the dollar may be a cause for concern. There may well be an increased need for better monetary policy coordination at the international level to cope with such an eventuality.

4   Costs and benefits of EMU in a tripolar world

What are the likely cost and benefits for Europe and the rest of the world? Benefits lie in the generalized reduction in transactions costs for Europeans and possibly for the rest of the world. There may also be benefits if the rise in the ecu and the reduction in the number of players in the international money game cause closer international monetary policy coordination. There may be costs for Europeans in the lender of last resort function of the Central Bank issuing a leading world currency. We have covered some of the issues above; the main new points we introduce here are the possible redistribution of international seigniorage, which we find insignificant, and the possible consequences for policy coordination and the international exchange rate regime, which may be significant indeed, although difficult to assess with precision.

Lender of last resort costs are currently shared between the IMF, the Federal Reserve Board, the Bank of Japan and the Bundesbank. EMU will upset the current sharing of responsibilities, in substituting the European Central Bank for the Bundesbank in an enhanced role. However, it is unlikely that there will be additional costs on that score for the EC as a whole.

The ecu foreign exchange market will be thicker than the markets of individual EC currencies. A thick market is inherently less volatile than thin markets and it may imply lower transactions costs, but it will also be harder to control by official intervention. Even if volatility were to increase, however, costs may be very small. For example, Baxter and Stockman (1989) failed to find any real effects from the higher volatility of real exchange rates under flexible exchange rate regimes, although Kenen and Rodrik (1986) and Peree and Steinherr (1989) have done so.

EMU might redistribute international seigniorage. If the ecu were to become a major international currency, there would be possibilities of raising seigniorage from the rest of the world. What would be the quantitative significance of such seigniorage? A comparison with other international currencies may be instructive. Cohen (1971) estimated that the seigniorage extracted from the fact that sterling was still a major regional currency in the 1950s and 1960s was almost zero. On the other hand, recent estimates by the Fed put the stock of dollar notes and coins held outside the United States at about $130 bn. With treasury bill rates of the order of 8% per annum over the longer run, this amounts to around $10 bn per annum, which is equal to about 0.2% of the 1988 US GNP. Corresponding numbers for the EC would be substantially lower. If they were to rise to one-fifth of the dollar seigniorage (say $2 bn), then international seigniorage would amount to about 0.05% of EC GNP.[10]

We now turn to the implications of EMU for international macro-economic policy coordination. There are several types of uncertainty that constitute obstacles to successful coordination (see Frankel, 1988). The players may have incomplete or inaccurate knowledge of the initial position – the state of their own economies and those of other players. We may expect EMU and the associated development of intra-EC surveillance to improve this knowledge. On the other hand, it may be more difficult for the Community as a whole to agree on the weights to assign to target variables than for the individual major EC economies that now participate in G-7 coordination.[11] Without formal modelling, however, it is hard to say *a priori* whether coordination is easier with seven players having relatively well-defined objectives than with four, of whom one then speaks with somewhat less clarity. At this stage of our knowledge it is unlikely that we could obtain analytical results for such a problem. Nor is it clear whether the need for (benefit from) coordination is greater or smaller: there is no such need with only one agent, nor with an infinite number of atomistic agents. However, we know very little about how the costs of coordination failures vary between these two extremes.

An important set of issues relates to analytical aspects of the international coordination of monetary policies. Is the reduction in the number of major players in the international monetary arena likely to make coordination of monetary policies easier? Will EMU promote greater exchange rate instability worldwide, i.e., between a European currency and the dollar and yen? Some of the relevant factors can be examined with the help of three-country models. A major prior question is whether the US currently acts as a Stackelberg leader vis-à-vis the G-7. If so, the emergence of another major player (in fact two – the EC and Japan) will transform the nature of the game.

For example, Giavazzi and Giovannini (1989) suggest that more symmetry may generate instability in the international monetary system. If one economy is much larger and more closed than the others, it may be quite happy to act as a Stackelberg leader, using the money supply as its monetary policy instrument, without regard for its nominal exchange rate. One may then have an equilibrium in which the large economy sets its money supply, while the small economies intervene to affect their nominal exchange rates. However, if another major player were to emerge, in the absence of full cooperation, the greater symmetry may lead to instability. Both economies will have an incentive to try to use exchange rate policy, as their bilateral exchange rate vis-à-vis the other large country matters more, and in such a case insability will arise. Thus, in the presence of large shocks we may see both economies trying to manipulate their exchange rates, i.e. use beggar-thy-neighbour monetary policies, in which case there is a reversion to flexible exchange rates. As the authors put it, 'when the size of the Nth country is much larger than that of the other country (or countries), so that bilateral exchange-rate fluctuations do not significantly affect the Nth country's output and real income, a regime of managed rates does not display the instability that characterizes the symmetric case' (p. 208). These results suggest that the greater symmetry that EMU will imply for the international monetary system may result in a reversion to flexible exchange rates internationally.[12]

Our view is that such a conclusion is unwarranted in the circumstances. The international monetary system today is not as asymmetric as (say) the classical gold standard or Bretton Woods. The leadership of the United States has been significantly eroded, and Japan and Germany have been major players for some time now (see Group of Thirty, 1988).[13] Thus, EMU will not result in a qualitative switch from an asymmetric to a symmetric system, as the current system is already symmetric in many ways. In fact, the current arrangements, especially after the meetings at the Plaza in September 1985, can be interpreted as cooperative management of exchange rates and world monetary policy by the G-7. For example, Funabashi (1988) in his wide-ranging assessment of the process from the Plaza to the Louvre suggests that 'One of the achievements of the Plaza strategy was to force consensus despite the existence of ideological obstacles' (p. 229). To the extent that the current international monetary system is already symmetric and cooperative in the setting of monetary polices, there is little scope for EMU to destabilize it. In fact, Germany and France in the Plaza to the Louvre process clearly had the concerns of the EMS in mind. According to Funabashi 'as the EMS factor was vital to the West German Plaza strategy, so it was to that of the French. The Germans sought to avoid a painful schism within the EMS that a free fall of the dollar might cause, while the French wanted to keep the West Germans from taking over the EMS' (p. 125).

Thus, the shift to a more symmetric system as a result of EMU will not be substantial. The current system already seems to be characterized by some cooperative determination of monetary policies with exchange rate targets, although it may be second-best in that there is little use of fiscal policies for stabilization purposes (Alogoskoufis, 1989). In fact, in some ways the system resembles the blueprint of Williamson and Miller (1987), although there is the important difference that the central parities that constitute the targets of the monetary authorities of the G-7 are not publicly announced (see Miller et al., 1989, for theoretical and empirical investigations of alternative blueprints).

In conclusion, EMU is unlikely to undermine the evolution of the international monetary system towards greater nominal exchange rate stability between the dollar, the yen and European currencies. Monetary policies are already being determined in a coordinated manner, and this looks likely to continue insofar as there is no clear 'hegemon' in the system. If anything, more symmetry among the players is likely to increase the need for (benefits from) coordination. An EC currency can unilaterally peg to the Deutschmark (accepting EMU discipline), but the ecu cannot unilaterally peg to the dollar or yen – close and reciprocal monetary policy coordination will be required to maintain exchange rate stability (see Portes, 1990). The implementation of monetary (exchange rate) policy in the EC will naturally be in the domain of the European Central Bank. To the extent that it is independent and non-accommodative it will contribute to price stability both in the EC and internationally (see Alogoskoufis, 1991). However, finance ministers, both in the European Council and the G-7, will ultimately decide the Community's views on the choice of the international exchange rate regime and will also be involved in issues such as (for example) the determination of target zones.

Issues relating to the international coordination of fiscal policies and the adjustment of external imbalances should also be considered. Recent discussions of blueprints for international monetary reform and their associated assignment rules provide an appropriate context.

Nation states will remain sovereign even under EMU. Under the most probable institutional scenarios, and unless the provisions envisaged in the Delors Report are adopted in their most extreme form, it is unlikely that the nature of the fiscal coordination game will change significantly. But fiscal outcomes will condition the Community-wide monetary policy. In addition, without independent national monetary policies, there will be more pressure in individual countries to use fiscal policy for domestic stabilization, as well as incentives to consider incomes policies. On the other hand, EC-level taxation and expenditure cannot be expected to grow markedly relative to national budgets, nor to become significantly more amenable to use as tools of discretionary stabilization policy.

There are a number of ways in which EMU may promote appropriate fiscal adjustments. The first has to do with the rules envisaged in the Delors Report for limits on national budget deficits. It now seems unlikely that such precise limits will be applied, but EMU may well result in more fiscal policy coordination within Europe. On the other hand, to the extent that European fiscal policies are coordinated, the EC may have more bargaining power in international institutions like the G-7, to avoid a repetition of the outcomes of the early 1980s, when disagreements among the Europeans weakened pressure on the US administration to consider the international repercussions of its macroeconomic policy mix. For example, Putnam and Bayne (1987) suggest that since 1981 'the non-American summit participants would be unanimous in complaining about US interest rates, the budget deficit and the strength of the dollar, at least until the dollar turned down in 1985. But there was less unanimity about causes and cures. The simplest remedy, which appealed to the French Socialists, would be for the Americans to loosen their monetary policy. However, the other governments were committed to the path of monetary rectitude embarked upon after the second oil shock, and they were uneasy about recommending the opposite course to the Americans. ... Thus ... the Americans mostly temporized. "Wait a while", was their message in Ottawa; "Let's study it", the approach in Versailles; "Our boom will solve it", the line in Williamsburg; and "After our elections", the promise at London II. Serious action on the dollar and the budget deficit had to wait till 1985.' (pp. 127–8).

The question whether EMU would increase potential coordination gains for the rest of the world and therefore induce the US to be more cooperative does not admit an easy answer. The existing views and the available empirical evidence are mixed. For example, as Currie *et al.* (1989) report in their recent survey (p. 26), the US benefits from coordination in empirical studies appear to be half as large as the benefits for Europe, irrespective of whether one examines coordination between the US and Germany or between the US and the EC. However, such studies do not take into account the major changes in the international monetary system that EMU may bring about. On the other hand, Alogoskoufis and Martin (1991) and Cohen and Wyplosz (1991) suggest that the nature of the international monetary system in the early 1980s was an important constraint on the ability of Europeans to act independently and counteract the fiscal shocks emanating from the United States (Reaganomics). They suggest that EMU will relieve this external constraint on European macroeconomic policy, and would in turn make it more difficult for the US to be uncooperative, as it would not be able to get away with beggar-thy-neighbour policies.

Economic policy coordination is ultimately and essentially political. Distributional issues must be resolved by a political process, both among countries in the EC and between the Community and its partners. Even if policy coordination is expected to bring gains, it will not be implemented unless there is some *ex ante* understanding about the distribution of such gains. The bargaining necessary to reach such an understanding will be easier for the Community as a unit vis-à-vis the US and Japan than for the four major EC countries acting individually in the G-7. On the other hand, *ex post* verification of compliance with an agreement on policies and enforcement of sanctions for non-compliance may be harder for the US and Japan vis-à-vis the EC than in dealing with individual countries. And it will take some time for the EC to establish the credibility in implementing policy commitments that some of its major member countries currently possess.

NOTES

We have benefited from the comments of Paul Masson, and the remarks of participants in workshops at the European Commission and the Georgetown Conference on the European Central Bank, in particular Bill Branson, Guillermo Calvo, Jeroen Kremers and Niels Thygesen. Neither they nor the CEC are in any way responsible for errors or for any aspect of our analysis. Financial support from the Commission of the European Communities and the CEPR FIMIE Project is gratefully acknowledged.

1 Throughout this paper we use 'ecu', with lowercase letters, to refer to the future common currency of the European Community. We use ECU, with uppercase letters, to denote the initials of the European Currency Unit, the existing unit of account of the European Monetary System, which is defined as a weighted average of EC currencies.

2 There is a theoretical literature investigating the emergence of media of exchange when there are more than two traders. Excellent examples ar the models of Jones (1976) and more recently Kiyotaki and Wright (1989) and Matsuyama et al. (1991). Typically such models have a multiplicity of equilibria. For example, in the Kiyotaki and Wright model there are equilibria with one money, but also equilibria with more than one.

3 See Yeager (1976) for a comprehensive history of the international monetary system since the 19th century. Kindleberger (1984) provides a history focused on Western Europe.

4 Poland introduced convertibility of the zloty in trade transactions on 1st January 1990, with an adjustable peg for the exchange rate, but it pegged against the dollar. However, according to a recent report 'The central banks of Soviet Union, Czechoslovakia, Poland and Hungary . . . pledged support for a new banking payments system for trade among east European nations. The system would use as a common currency the Ecu, the basket of the main west European currencies.' (Financial Times, 24 April 1991). In addition, the Polish devaluation of May 1991 was accompanied by a move to a basket peg (trade-weighted).

5 Note that the capital of the EBRD is denominated in ECU. The trend towards the use of the ECU by the central banks of eastern European economies has already started, as the report quoted from the Financial Times confirms.

6 Note that although there are bilateral trade imbalances between countries, each country is assumed to be in balance of payments equilibrium, which in this simple model is defined as a zero trade balance.

7 These trends have also been examined in two recent papers by Tavlas (1990) and Tavlas and Ozeki (1991).

8 However, this tendency, which was also mentioned before, will not be unopposed, either at the micro or at the international macro level. A symbolic example is the reported resistance from the United States to the use of the ECU as unit of account for fixing the quotas of the new European Bank for Reconstruction and Development.

9 We are indebted to Paul Masson for this point.

10 The CEC (1990) study, using a different method and assuming a treasury bill rate of 7% arrives at 0.045% of GDP. Both their calculation and ours consider only high-powered ecu, netting out interest-bearing obligations.

11 In Alogoskoufis and Portes (1990) we discuss the changes that EMU will

probably imply for the institutions of macroeconomic policy coordination, such as the G-7. See also Dobson (1991).
12 The results in Kremers and Lane (1990) suggest that it may be easier for a European Central Bank to control the money supply than any of the current national central banks in the EC.
13 In any case, there is a lot of confusion about the definition of leadership in a repeated game. Stackelberg leadership is not an appropriate concept, and even the less precise notion of asymmetry may no longer be appropriate.

REFERENCES

Alogoskoufis G. S. (1989), 'Stabilization Policy, Fixed Exchange Rates and Target, Zones', in M. Miller, B. Eichengreen and R. Portes (eds), *Blueprints for Exchange Rate Management*, London, Academic Press and CEPR.
   (1991), 'Monetary Accommodation, Exchange Rate Regimes and Inflation Persistence', CEPR Discussion Paper No. 503, London (forthcoming in *The Economic Journal*).
Alogoskoufis G. S. and C. Martin (1991), 'External Constraints on European Unemployment', in G. S. Alogoskoufis, L. Papademos and R. Portes (eds), *External Constraints on Macroeconomic Policy: The European Experience*, Cambridge, Cambridge University Press and CEPR.
Alogoskoufis G. S. and R. Portes (1990), 'International Costs and Benefits from EMU', CEPR Discussion Paper No. 424, London (forthcoming in *European Economy*).
Baxter M. and A. C. Stockman (1989), 'Business Cycles and the Exchange Rate Regime: Some International Evidence', *Journal of Monetary Economics* 23: 377–400.
Black S. (1985), 'International Money and International Monetary Arrangements', in Kenen P. B. and R. W. Jones (ed), *Handbook of International Economics*, Volume 2, Amdsterdam, North-Holand.
   (1989), 'The International Use of Currencies', in Y. Suzuki, J. Miyake and M. Okabe (eds), *The Evolution of the International Monetary System: How Can Stability and Efficiency be Attained?*, Tokyo, University of Tokyo Press.
Brown, W. A. Jr (1940), *The International Gold Standard Reinterpreted, 1914–1934*, New York, AMS Press and NBER.
Cairncross A. and B. Eichengreen (1983), *Sterling in Decline*, Basil Blackwell, Oxford.
Cohen B. J. (1971), *The Future of Sterling as an International Currency*, London, Macmillan.
Cohen D. and C. Wyplosz (1991), 'France and Germany in the EMS: The Exchange Rate Constraint', in G. S. Alogoskoufis, L. Papademos and R. Portes (eds), *External Constraints on Macroeconomic Policy: The European Experience*, Cambridge, Cambridge University Press and CEPR.
Commission of the European Communities (1990), 'One Market, One Money', *European Economy* 44: 1–347.
Currie D. A., G. Holtham and A. Hughes Hallett (1989), 'The Theory and Practice of International Policy Coordination: Does Coordination Pay?', in

Bryant R. C., D. A. Currie, J. A. Frenkel, P. R. Masson and R. Portes (eds), *Macroeconomic Policies in an Inderdependent World*, Washington DC, International Monetary Fund.
Dobson W. (1991), *Economic Policy Coordination: Requiem or Prologue?*, Washington DC, Institute for International Economics.
Dooley M. P., J. S. Lizondo and D. J. Mathieson (1989), 'The Currency Composition of Foreign Exchange Reserves', *IMF Staff Papers* **36**: 385–434.
Eichengreen B. (1987), 'Conducting the International Orchestra: Bank of England Leadership under the Classical Gold Standard', *Journal of International Money and Fincance* **6**: 5–29.
Folkerts-Landau D. and P. Garber (1992), 'The ECB: A Bank or a Monetary Policy Rule?', this volume.
Frankel J. (1988), *Obstacles to International Macroeconomic Policy Coordination*, Studies in International Finance No. 64, Princeton University.
Funabashi Y. (1988), *Managing the Dollar: From the Plaza to the Louvre*, Washington DC, Institute for International Economics.
Giavazzi F. and A. Giovannini (1989), 'Monetary Policy Interactions under Managed Exchange Rates', *Economica* **56**: 199–213.
Giovannini A. and C. Mayer (eds) (1991), *European Financial Integration*, Cambridge, Cambridge University Press and CEPR.
Group of Thirty (1988), *International Macroeconomic Policy Coordination*, New York and London, Group of Thirty.
Gylfason T. (1990), 'Exchange Rate Policy, Inflation and Unemployment: The Experience of the Nordic Countries', CEPR Discussion Paper No. 377.
Hall S. and D. Miles (1991), 'An Empirical Study of Recent Trends in World Bond Markets', Discussion Paper in Financial Economics FE-3/91, Birkbeck College, London.
Jones R. A. (1976), 'The Origin and Development of Media of Exchange', *Journal of Political Economy* **84**: 757–75.
Kenen P. B. and D. Rodrik (1986), 'Measuring and Analyzing the Effects of Short Run Volatility in Real Exchange Rates', *Review of Economics and Statistics* **68**: 311–15.
Kindleberger C. (1984), *A Financial History of Western Europe*, Allen and Unwin, London.
(1986), *The World in Depression, 1929–1939*, revised edition, Berkeley, University of California Press.
Kiyotaki N. and R. Wright (1989), 'On Money as a Medium of Exchange', *Journal of Political Economy* **97**: 927–54.
Kremers J. M. and T. Lane (1990), 'Economic and Monetary Integration and the Aggregate Demand for Money in the EMS', *IMF Staff Papers* **37**: 777–805.
Krugman P. (1980), 'Vehicle Currencies and the Structure of International Exchange', *Journal of Money, Credit and Banking* **12**, 513–26.
(1984), 'The International Role of the Dollar: Theory and Prospect', in J. F. O. Bilson and R. C. Marston (ed), *Exchange Rate Theory and Practice*, Chicago, University of Chicago Press (for NBER).
Matsuyama, K., N. Kiyotaki and A. Matsui (1991), 'Toward a Theory of International Currency', Discussion Paper No. 931, Department of Economics, Northwestern University.

Miller M., B. Eichengreen and R. Portes (1989), *Blueprints for Exchange Rate Management*, London, Academic Press and CEPR.

Newlyn W. T. (1962), *Theory of Money*, Oxford, Oxford University Press.

Nurkse R. (1944), *International Currency Experience*, Geneva, League of Nations.

Perree E. and A. Steinherr (1989), 'Exchange Rate Uncertainty and Foreign Trade', *European Economic Review* 33: 1241–64.

Portes R. (1990), 'Macroeconomic Policy Coordination and the European Monetary System', in P. Ferri (ed), *Ten Years of the EMS*, London, Macmillan.

——— (1991), 'The Transition to Convertibility for Eastern Europe and the USSR', in R. Brunetta (ed), *Economics for a New Europe*, London, Macmillan.

Putnam R. D. and N. Bayne (1987), *Hanging Together: Cooperation and Conflict in the Seven Power Summits*, Revised Edition, Cambridge Mass., Harvard University Press.

Tavlas G. (1990), 'On the International Use of Currencies: The Case of the Deutsche Mark', IMF Working Paper 90/3, Washington DC.

Tavlas G. and Y. Ozeki (1991), 'The Japanese Yen as an International Currency', IMF Working Paper 91/2, Washington DC.

Williamson J. and M. Miller (1987), *Targets and Indicators: A Blueprint for the International Coordination of Economic Policy*, Washington DC, Institute for International Economics.

Yeager L. (1976), *International Monetary Relations*, New York, Harper and Row.

Discussion

JEROEN J. M. KREMERS

This paper examines important aspects of the process of European integration and the role of the ecu in that process. It was born, as indicated by Richard Portes at the Georgetown conference, out of a feeling that the current focus on 'Europe 1992' is turning into intra-European 'navel staring', and that important international monetary aspects are being overlooked. Let me summarize some of the main points, and place a few footnotes. The paper relates to the final stage of EMU, so – with the authors – I abstract from transitional issues and refer to the ecu as the single European currency managed by the European Central Bank (ECB).

The paper examines if, in addition to the expected reduction of transaction costs, an important argument favoring monetary union in Europe might be the increased role of the ecu in the international monetary system. Will a major role for the ecu be *worthwhile* for Europe? It turns out that the benefits may in fact turn out rather modest:

(1)   The ecu foreign exchange market will be thicker than any of the markets currently existing for EC currencies, so there will be less market volatility. However, this benefit has more to do with the increased efficiency of Europe's financial markets more generally (associated with the EC internal market program) than with the international role of the ecu.

(2)   The scope for raising seigniorage from the rest of the world turns out to be quantitatively rather small.

These benefits do not look too impressive. And they may be counterbalanced by significant costs. Just as the Bundesbank has long been reluctant to allow the deutsche mark to play a prominent international role since this could render domestic monetary control in Germany more difficult, the ECB may be cautious on the international role of the ecu. This may be true particularly in the first years of EMU, when the ECB will need to gauge the EC-wide demand for a single European currency. This will be difficult enough even without any promient demand for the ecu from outside the EC.

Thus, the reader is left wondering exactly why anybody in Europe would wish the ecu to enter a tug of war with the dollar and the yen for international monetary supremacy (Section 3). The paper does not indicate precisely who stands to gain.

A related but separate issue addressed in the paper concerns the *potential* international role of the ecu, quite apart from the question of who stands to gain. Several fundamental factors would seem to point to scope for a larger role for the ecu than for the total of the present European currencies:

(1)   The open EC market will lead to more extra-EC trade, hence to an enlarged role for the ecu as a means of payment and unit of account.

(2)   Financial liberalization in the context of the internal market program will enhance the efficiency of ecu markets.

(3)   The EMU will broaden the zone of monetary and price stability in Europe beyond the current 'hard core' of the ERM, which might enhance the role of the ecu as a store of value and, together with enhanced trade links, might entice non-EC countries to peg their currencies to the ecu.

(4)   The authors expect a greater emphasis on exchange rate management in the world, and hence a greater need for ecus in official reserves.

The bottom-line: scope probably exists for a larger international role for the ecu; it remains unclear, however, how soon this might materialize; and it is, moreover, unclear who in Europe stands to gain. My conclusion, therefore, would be that the potential of an increased role for the ecu can hardly be a major argument favoring monetary union in Europe.

Such a conclusion would in my view not be an unhappy one. For in order to appreciate fully the importance of EMU, one ought to step back a bit and remember that the prime rationale for EMU was, and is, to provide a stable financial environment for the free and open EC internal market (to be completed as early as by the end of this year!). Together, the internal market and the EMU are to greatly improve the functioning of market forces in the European economy and the utilization of Europe's resources. This process, which is already well under way, goes a great deal further than the reduction of transaction costs or the ecu being a contender with the dollar in the international market place. Thus I would not consider the focus on EMU and the internal market 'navel staring' – particularly so since, despite much progress so far, a lot of work still remains to be done.

Surely, nevertheless, the paper deals with important issues. Referring to the growing role of Germany, Richard Portes in his welcoming words to the conference mentioned the new slogan: 'Ein Markt, ein Geld, und eine Sprache.' That indeed it remains important to weigh – as in this paper – the pros and cons of European integration also in the international monetary field, is obvious in the light of rumours that, in a variation on Keynes, the logo of the European Central Bank will carry the motto: 'In the long run we are all German anyway'!

Index

Printed in the United States
By Bookmasters